John Philip Newman

From Dan to Beersheba

John Philip Newman

From Dan to Beersheba

ISBN/EAN: 9783743325340

Manufactured in Europe, USA, Canada, Australia, Japa

Cover: Foto ©ninafisch / pixelio.de

Manufactured and distributed by brebook publishing software (www.brebook.com)

John Philip Newman

From Dan to Beersheba

FROM

Dan to Beersheba

A DESCRIPTION OF THE

WONDERFUL LAND

WITH

MAPS AND ENGRAVINGS

AND

A PROLOGUE BY THE AUTHOR CONTAINING THE LATEST
EXPLORATIONS AND DISCOVERIES

BY

JOHN P. NEWMAN, D.D., LL.D.

Bishop of the Methodist Episcopal Church and Member of the London
Society of Biblical Archæology

REVISED EDITION

NEW YORK: HUNT & EATON
CINCINNATI: CRANSTON & CURTS

Copyright, 1892, by
JOHN P. NEWMAN,
NEW YORK.

TO

MY WIFE,

THE

JOY

OF

MY LIFE.

This edition of Bishop Newman's book on Palestine—*From Dan to Beersheba*—is demanded by its introduction into the course of study prescribed for the undergraduates in our Annual Conferences, who, during their ministry, will have frequent occasion to refer to the history, topography, and customs of the Holy Land, of which this book so fully and clearly treats.

THE PUBLISHERS.

CONTENTS.

CHAPTER I.

The two Boundaries.—The parallel Mountains.—The great Valley.—Inspired Eulogies.—Sterile Soil.—Gibbon's Comparison.—Natural and miraculous Causes of present Sterility.—Testimonies of pagan Authors on the ancient Productions of Palestine.—Land coveted by the great Nations of Antiquity.—A Land of Ruins.—Present Fertility and Fruits.—Richness of the North.—Volney on the Variety of the Climate of Palestine.—Beauties of Spring in the Promised Land.—Flowers.—Magnificent Scenery.—Standard of Landscape Beauty.—Palestine is a World in Miniature.—Illustrations.—Prophetical Descriptions of the twelve Tribeships.—Wonderful Correspondence .... Page 13

CHAPTER II.

Location of Jerusalem.—Strong defensive Position of the City.—Surrounding Hills and Valleys. — Its Situation compared to that of Athens and Rome.—True Meaning of the 125th Psalm.—Tower of Psephinus.—The two Valleys.—Height of the adjacent Mountains.—A City without Suburbs.—Modern Wall.—Goliath's Castle.—Immense Stones of Solomon's Age.—Ancient Portals.—Beautiful Corner-stone.—Pinnacle of the Temple from which Christ was tempted to throw himself.—Golden Gate.—Tower of Antonia.—Objection to Prophecy answered.—The Bevel the Sign of Jewish Masonry.—Great Cave beneath the City.—Wanderings by Torchlight. — Solomon's Quarry. — Tyropean Valley. — Five Hills of Jerusalem. — Mount Zion. — Royal Abode. — Herod's three Towers. — Splendid Church of St. James.—House of Caiaphas.—Scene of the Last Supper and of Pentecost.—Tomb of David.—Royal Plunderers.—Proof of its Antiquity.—Home of the Lepers.—Sad Sight.—Akra.—Bezetha.—Napoleon's Church.. 33

CHAPTER III.

Mount Moriah.—Site of Solomon's Temple.—Surrounding Walls.—Great Fosse.—Pasha's Palace—Council Chamber of the Jewish Sanhedrim.—Jews' Place of Wailing.—Their cruel Treatment.—Scene on Friday Afternoon.—Mournful Spectacle.—High-priest.—Prophecy fulfilled.— Solomon's Bridge.—Its Antiquity.—Temple Area.—Tower of Antonia.—Shrines within the Inclosure.—Imposing View.—Dome of the Chain.—Mosque of Omar.—Its grand Exterior.—Its History.—Its Portals.—Its magnificent Interior.—Sacred Rock within the Mosque.—Traditions.—Scene of the Offering of Isaac and of other Scriptural Events.—Mosque of

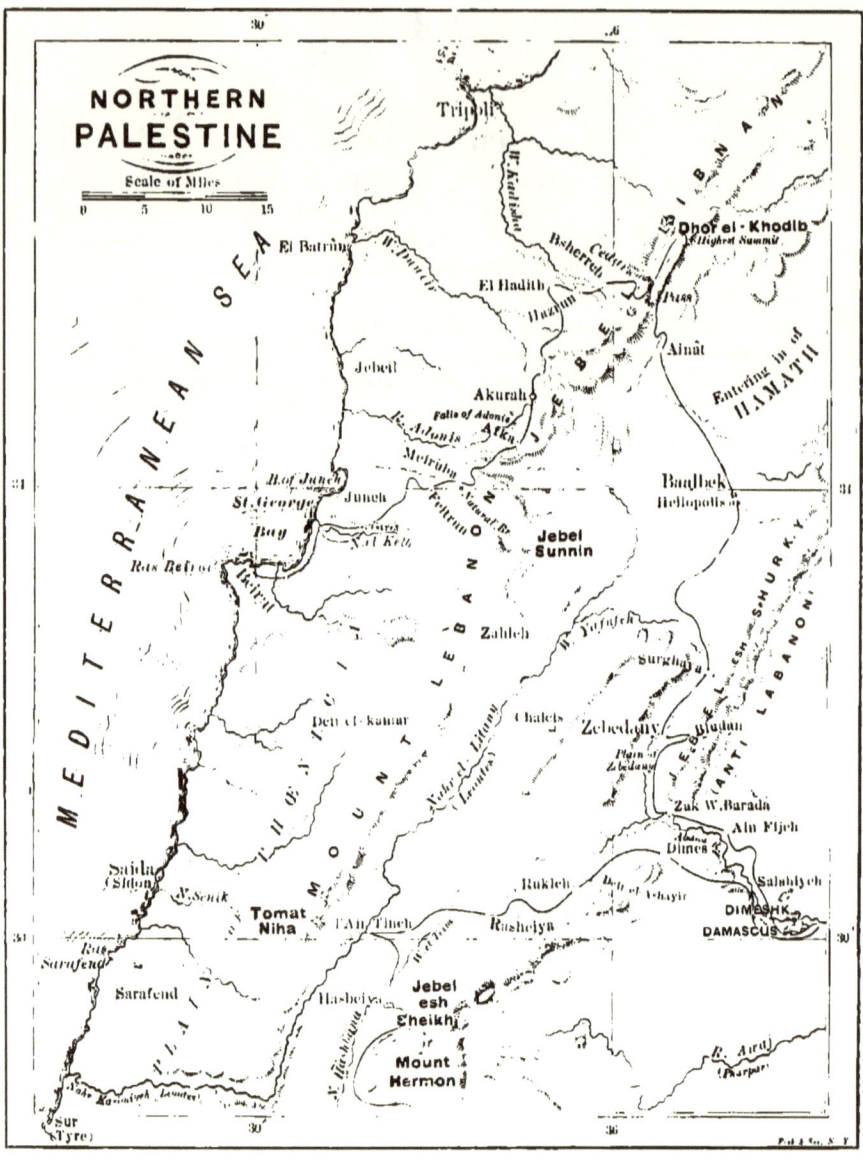

of the City.—Field of the Arrow.—Parting of David and Jonathan.—
Nob.—Massacre of the Priests.—The View.—Birthplace of Jeremiah.—
Geba.—Pottage.—Benighted.—Yusef Shang, of Beeroth.—A Night of
strange Experience.—Town of Beeroth.—Ancient Bethel.—Its Desolation.
Site of the City.—Abraham's Altar.—Parting of Abraham and Lot.—
The Fountain.—Jacob's Flight and Dream.—Idolatry.—Prophecy ful-
filled.—Route to Shiloh.—Romantic Scenery.—Robbers' Fountain.—Wild
Glen.—Robbers.—Their Dance.—Sinjil.—Shiloh.—Remains.—Site dis-
covered in 1838.—Tower.—Damsels of Shiloh carried off.—Death of
Eli.—Approach of the Robbers.—An Attack.—Resistance.—Again as-
sailed.—Again resist.—Revolvers drawn.—Escape.—Overtaken.—Third
Attack.—Revolvers in demand.—Sixteen against Four.—Serious Moment.
—One of the Party whipped.—Narrow Escape.—Lebonah.—Ride to Na-
blous.—Grand View.—Evening on the Plain of Mukhrah.—Antiquity of
Nablous.—History.—Its beautiful Situation.—Population.—Inside View
of the Town.—Character of the People.—Christian School.—Origin of
the Samaritans.—Remnant of the Nation.—Their Creed.—Their religious
Peculiarities.—Their High-priest.—Their sacred Writings.—Vale of She-
chem.—Its Length and Beauty.—Cursings and Blessings of the Law.—
The Scene.—Great Congregation.—Twin Mountains.—Jacob's Well.—
History.—Sweet Water.—Evidence of its Antiquity.—Jesus at the Well.
—Woman of Samaria.—Accuracy of its evangelical History.—Well Sold.
—Tomb of Joseph.—Symbol of his Life.—Ascent of Mount Ebal.—Twen-
ty Lepers.—Ascent of Mount Gerizim.—Almond-groves.—Ruins on the
Summit.—Holy of Holies of the Samaritans.—Traditions.—Not the Scene
of the Offering of Isaac.—Samaritan Passover.—Impressive Moment.—
Lambs slain.—The Feast..Page 289

CHAPTER XI.

A Price for Politeness.—Escort.—Picturesque Scenery.—Samaria.—Its
Founder.—Its Vicissitudes.—Residence of Elisha.—Famine.—City beautified by Herod.—Its Location.—Hill of Omri.—Grand Ruins.—Tomb of
John the Baptist.—Temple of Augustus.—Prediction fulfilled.—Departure for Cæsarea.—Night on the Plain of Sharon.—The Sick brought out.
—Plain of Sharon.—The Lost Lake.—Cæsarea uninhabited.—Dangers.—
History.—Imperial City under Herod the Great.—Grand Ruins.—St. Paul
a Prisoner.—Death of Herod Agrippa.—Athlit.—Mount Carmel.—Scene
of the Sacrifice.—Great Event.—Abode of Elisha 325

CHAPTER XII.

Plains of Palestine.—No Farm-houses.—Great Plain of Esdraelon.—Its
Fertility.—Topography.—River Kishon.—World's Battle-field.—Waters
of Megiddo.—Deborah and her Victory.—Jeneen.—Bethshean.—Encamp-
ment.—Modern Sheikhs and ancient Patriarchs.—City of Ruins.—Jabesh
Gilead.—Pella.—Gideon's Fountain.—Mount Gilboa.—Battles.—Jezreel.
—Napoleon and the Turks.—Shunem.—Nain.—Endor.—Witch's Cave.—
Saul and Samuel.—Witches.—Mount Tabor.—Its Form.—Woods.—
View.—Misnomer.—Transfiguration.—It occurred at Night.—Argument.
—Benighted Party 352

CHAPTER XIII.

Jerusalem and Capernaum the great Centres of our Lord's Ministry.—Christ a limited Traveler.—Judea and Galilee contrasted.—Provinces of Galilee.—The Herods.—Meaning of Galilee.—Sea of Galilee.—Its Characteristics.—Hallowed Associations.—Imperial City of Tiberias.—Founded by Herod Antipas.—His Crimes.—John the Baptist.—It became a Jewish City and the Metropolis of the Race.—Home of eminent Scholars.—Now an Arab Town.—Citizens.—Miraculous Draught of Fishes.—Jesus never visited it.—Warm Baths of Tiberias.—Site of Tarichea.—Naval Engagement.—Bridge of Semakh.—River Jarmuk.—City of Gadara.—Ruins.—Tombs.—Not the Scene of the Destruction of the Swine.—Argument.—Ruins of Gamala.—Near here was the Scene of the Miracle.—Mouth of the Jordan.—Bethsaida Julias.—Feeding of the Five Thousand.—Our Lord Walking on the Sea.—Home of Mary Magdalene.—Rich Plain of Gennesaret.—Parables.—Site of Capernaum.—Fountain of the Fig.—Thrilling History of the City as connected with Christ.—The Woe.—Desolation.—Bethsaida.—Birthplace of Peter, James, and John.—Not Bethsaida Julias.—Influence of natural Scenery upon the Formation of Character.—Chorazin.—Sudden Gale upon the Sea.—Extensive Remains of the City.—Without an Inhabitant.—Upper Jordan.—Waters of Merom.—Tell el-Kâdy.—City of Dan.—Its Fountain.—Cæsarea Philippi.—Town of Hasbeiya.—Fountain.—Highest perennial Source of the Jordan.—Mount Hermon.—Vast and grand Prospect from its lofty Summit.—Scriptural Allusions.—" Valley of the Pigeons."—Sublime Ravine.—Mount of Beatitudes.—Battle of Hattin.—Defeat of the Crusaders.—Triumph of Saladin.—Route to Nazareth.—Its authentic History is not older than the Christian Era.—Its Valley and Mountains.—Population.—Schools.—Legendary Sites.—Scene of the Annunciation.—House and Shop of Joseph.—Pictures.—Fountain.—Beautiful Girls of Nazareth.—Mount of Precipitation.—True Mount.—View.—Scene of our Lord's Childhood and Manhood..Page 377

CHAPTER XIV.

Phœnicia.—Its Extent and Fertility.—Origin of the Phœnicians.—Their Commerce.—Their Learning.—Departure from Nazareth.—Cana of Galilee.—First Christian Wedding.—Beautiful Vale of Abilin.—Plain of Accho.—City of 'Akka.—Names.—Metropolis of the Crusaders.—Their Destruction.—Gibbon.—The Moslem Nero.—Napoleon's Defeat.—Road to Tyre.—Summer Palace.—Excavations.—Wild and dangerous Pass.—Antiquity of Tyre.—Three Tyres.—Stupendous Water-works.—Continental Tyre.—Sins and Judgments.—Glory departed.—How Prophecy was fulfilled.—Insular Tyre.—Tyre of the Crusaders.—Cathedral.—Tomb of Hiram.—Wonderful Temple.—Sarepta.—Zidon.—Gardens.—Ancient Glory.—Wars.—Harbor.—Citadel.—Tombs.—Interesting Discoveries.—Ornaments.. 432

CHAPTER XV.

Mountains of Lebanon.—Grand Scenery.—Sublime View.—Mountain Traveling.—Scriptural Allusions.—Cedars of Lebanon.—Their Number, Appearance, and symbolic Character.—Population of the Mountains.—Districts and Peculiarities of the Druzes and Maronites.—New Road.—Crossing the Mountains.—Plain of the Bukâ'a.—Leontes.—A swollen River.—Ancient Cities —Imposing Cavalcade.—Wives of the Pasha of Damascus.—First View of Damascus.—Splendor and Enjoyments of the Interior of the City.—Great Plain of Damascus.—Abana and Pharpar.—Scene of St. Paul's Conversion.—City without Ruins.—Antiquity and thrilling History of Damascus.—House of Judas.—Home of Ananias.—"Street called Straight."—Naaman's Palace.—Tombs of the Great.—Location of Damascus.—Walls and Gates.—Old Castle.—Great Mosque.—Gardens of Damascus.—Commerce of the City.—Curiosities in the Bazars.—Population.—Christian Citizens.—Origin of the Massacre of 1860.—Its Progress.—Terrible Scenes.—American Vice-Consul.—Ruins.—Sad Results.—Defense of the Christians by Abd-el-Kader.—Visit to the Chieftain of Algiers.—Our Reception.—Testimonials.—His Appearance.—Conclusion.—Political History of Palestine.—Its Condition under the Turks.—It is now in a Transition State.—Possessions of European Nations.—Future of the Holy Land.—Christian Missions.—Decline of Mohammedanism.—Religious Liberty.—Future Glory..................................Page 460

LIST OF ILLUSTRATIONS.

	PAGE
Jerusalem	Frontispiece.
Maps of Southern and Northern Palestine	To face page 13
Immense Stones of Solomon's Age	38
Golden Gate—Interior View	39
Mount Zion and Tower of Hippicus	47
Jews' Place of Wailing	59
Solomon's Bridge	62
Mount Moriah, with a View of the Mosque of Omar	66
Solomon's subterranean Passage-way	73
Tombs of the Judges	80
Tombs of the Kings	82
Absalom's Pillar restored	85
Tombs in the Valley of Jehoshaphat	88
Fountain of the Virgin	92
Pool of Siloam	94
Lower Pool of Gihon	100
Pool of Hezekiah	104
Bethany	113
Gethsemane and the Mount of Olives	119
Via Dolorosa and the Arch of the Ecce Homo	131
Church of the Holy Sepulchre—Front View	137
View of the Holy Sepulchre	142
Ground Plan of the Church of the Holy Sepulchre	147
View of Modern Jerusalem, from the Mount of Olives	159
Raven	180
Plain of Jericho and View of the Dead Sea, from the North	185
Shooting the Rapids	191
Dead Sea	197
Masada	205
Convent of Mâr Sâba	210
View of Bethlehem	212
Cave of the Nativity	216
Interior of the Church of the Nativity	219
Tomb of Herod the Great—Herodium	224
Hebron	232
Urtâs	247
Solomon's Pools	250
Gaza	261
Ruins of Askelon	267

	PAGE
Ashdod	270
Joppa from the North	274
Ramleh, or the "Look-out"	277
Church of St. George	279
Gibeon	283
Nablous	308
Jacob's Well	316
Samaria	330
Ancient Cæsarea	342
Women grinding at a Mill	356
Arab Encampment	357
Jezreel	363
Nain	367
Mount Tabor	370
Tiberias and the Sea of Galilee	381
Ruins and Tombs of Gadara	390
Plain of Gennesaret and Home of Mary Magdalene	397
Upper Jordan	412
"Valley of the Pigeons"	417
Nazareth	425
Acre from the East	437
Ladder of Tyre	441
Tyre	444
Ras el-'Aln	447
Tomb of Hiram	452
Sidon	455
Cedars of Lebanon	465

PROLOGUE.

The Land and the Book are inseparable. Like prophecy and history they complement each other. They are the reciprocal witnesses of the same great truth. They stand or fall together. Our chief interest in Palestine is the confirmation of scriptural allusions to its topography, the scene of personal and national history. The sacred writers make incidental references to towns and cities, to valleys and mountains, to lakes and rivers, to battlefields and other scenes of important events, around which will forever cluster the most hallowed associations of our religious faith. They make these allusions with an accuracy of statement which to-day is in proof of the sincerity of their purpose and the truthfulness of their record. There is a sublime naturalness in their narration which is monumental evidence of the facts which they have transmitted to mankind. These frequent off-hand references clearly indicate that the sacred writers resided in Bible Lands, that they witnessed the events they recorded, and were familiar with the times, places, and persons of which they wrote.

Unbelievers realize the force of this argument and have sought, but in vain, to charge the inspired penmen with inaccuracy, and thus throw distrust upon their history; but they have found to their consternation, both by personal observation and the testimony of travelers, that the Bible is the most reliable handbook of Palestine extant.

During one of my visits to Jerusalem I chanced to meet a venerable English barrister who had made a pilgrimage to the Holy Land to write a book against the Bible founded on the supposed discrepancies between the Land and the Book;

and I subsequently met him at Beyroot, after his *fruitless* journey from "Dan to Beersheba." While at Mosul, opposite ancient Nineveh, I met George Smith, sent forth by a London journalist to explore the Assyrian ruins, and who, as archæologist and philologist, ranks with Layard and Rassam. He went out an unbeliever, but such is the agreement between the record of the ruins and the record of the Book, that Mr. Smith returned to London a believer, and lectured before the Society of Biblical Archæology on the marvelous synchronisms of the Assyrian tablets and the sacred historians.

From Dan to Beersheba was written to verify these references. It has the advantage of having been written on the scene of the recorded event, in notes taken for future elaboration of all that had transpired thereon, whether in sacred or profane history. It was my custom, from which I seldom deviated, to read on the spot every reference in the Bible to each locality I visited, and to record my observations and impressions while my mind was aglow with the recollections of the hallowed associations of the place and impressed with the extraordinary agreement between the inspired narration and the present aspect of the scene where the grand events had transpired; so that the traveler of to-day, with this book in hand, will have his memory refreshed and his mind inspired by a picture of what once occurred on the accredited historic site.

Through all the turbulent centuries since Christ ascended, Palestine has been a "changeless land," whose social customs, mechanic arts, commercial and manufactural methods have suffered little from contact with Western civilization, and it should be the ambition of Christendom to preserve it *intact* to the last generation of mankind. Providence calls us to preserve this monumental land. The changeful influence of the mighty West is seen to-day on lower Egypt, on Asia Minor, on Grecia and Rome in Europe, but Palestine abides the same forever; as Christ and his apostles left it we now see it, and so should it be seen by all future ages. Impelled by sectarian zeal or for political purposes, the nations of Europe have sought supremacy there, and the Promised Land is the larger factor in the Eastern Question, but neither France, nor Russia, nor England should take possession, but rather a syndicate, representing all nations and all creeds, should hold it in fee simple by purchase from the Sultan subject to such rights of property as may vest in the present inhabitants.

It is a land of buried cities which await the coming of the spade. Names are to be verified, places are to be identified, dates are to be reconciled. The whole land should be open to research. Modern Jerusalem should be removed. The Jerusalem of Solomon and of Christ is from two to three hundred feet buried beneath the present city. That religious metropolis of the world has suffered twenty-seven sieges, and eleven cities have been built upon the ancient site. Each conqueror leveled the *débris* and thereon reared his new capital. Vital questions await the spade of the explorer. Much has been accomplished within the last twenty years, and more awaits the efforts of the future.

The whole of western Palestine has been surveyed, and the biblical gains have been immense. Not less than six hundred and twenty-two names west of the Jordan are given by the sacred writers. Of these we had knowledge of two hundred and sixty-two, and by the survey one hundred and seventy-two were discovered and added to our list, leaving one hundred and eighty-eight to be uncovered by the archæologist. Some of these are insignificant, but others are of intense interest, such as Mamre, Gethsemane, and Arimathea, around which cluster most hallowed memories. The surveyors have determined the boundaries of the tribes, the march of armies, the routes of pilgrims, merchants, and kings. Beautiful Tirzah, royal residence of Jeroboam, has been identified, with its enchanting landscape—" Beautiful as Tirzah, comely as Jerusalem "—and in the rocks are to be seen the tombs of the kings of Israel. The famous battlefield of Sisera and Deborah has been traced, the relative positions of the contending hosts by the waters of Megiddo, the path of the flight of Sisera, when " the river Kishon swept them away, that river of battles, the river Kishon," the site of the black tent of Heber the Kenite, where the generous Jael gave the royal fugitive Leban a delicious preparation of curdled milk, and then, when he infringed upon oriental etiquette and insulted her womanhood by forcing himself into the women's apartments, the avengeful Jael drove the iron tent-peg into the offender's brain.

The " Brook Cherith," from which Elijah drank, and the " Valley of Achor," where Achan was stoned, have been identified, and the site of Bethabara, dear to all Christians, has been recovered. The native name Abárah, a passage or ferry, now marks one of the fords of the Jordan, just above where the Jalúd debouches into the sacred river, and means the same as Bethabara—a "ferry." This disarms the critics of the fourth gospel, inasmuch as Cana of Galilee is but twenty-two miles from Abárah, a day's journey, while from the traditional site of our Lord's baptism the distance is eighty miles. Forty fords of the Jordan have been identified; hundreds of ancient names have been recovered; the site of Gilgal has been determined; the tombs of Joshua and of Nun, and the tombs of Eleazar and Phinehas, successors of Aaron in the priesthood, have been rescued from oblivion, and are to be seen in Mount Ephraim, south of Shechem, all of which appear of great antiquity.

In the first chapter of this book I gave what seemed to me at the time the wonderful correspondence between the prophetical descriptions of the twelve tribeships and the present aspects and conditions of those twelve sections, as to climate, physical features, soil, cultivation, and natural products, and the recent surveys more than confirm this correspondence. It is now apparent that the boundaries of the tribal possessions were rivers, ravines, ridges, and the watershed lines of the country, and, above all, the fertility of the soil was in accordance with the density of population, and this density is now indicated by the larger number of ancient ruins.

While excavations have been made with more or less success in all the notable sections of the land, those of chief interest to the biblical scholar are in and about the holy city. There shafts have been sunk through the *débris* one hundred and twenty-five feet below the present surface of the ground. In those researches the foundation stones of the walls of the temple area were laid bare; Phœnician jars were found, on which are Phœnician characters; a subterranean passage was uncovered, a secret passage for troops from the citadel to the temple in times of danger; old aqueducts were brought to light; the ancient wall on Mount Ophel was traced hundreds of feet; the first wall on Mount Zion, and the probable site of the second wall, on which so much depends touching both the Temple and the Church of the Holy Sepulcher, were discovered. The explorer has confirmed the historical statement of the glories of the temple of God, one thousand feet long and two hundred feet high, the grandest structure ever dedicated to divinity.

In their explorations they found fragments of earthenware at a depth of ninety feet, belonging to the city of the Jebusites, B. C. 1500; they uncovered pavements, one of mezzah stone, and between the pavements rubbish twenty feet deep, and under a second pavement was found Haggai's seal, bearing the Hebrew inscription, "Haggai, son of Shebaniah," B. C. 500 And in those depths of the ages were found lamps, dishes, stone weights, and a Phœnician jar, standing upright where the workmen of King Hiram of Tyre left it 3,000 years ago, and beautiful vases of black ware covered with crimson glaze. They were rewarded for their patient toil by uncovering immense columns, broken arches, vast vaults, the bases of great towers, and large water tanks, four hundred feet long, subterranean passageways, with their steps *in situ*, and strong triple gates; they exhumed the lower courses of Solomon's city wall, seven hundred feet long and whereon are painted Phœnician characters in red paint, still bright, and they brought to light a stone cross inscribed, "The light of Christ shines forth for all." For these magnificent results we are indebted to two Americans, Robinson and Barclay, and to two Englishmen, Warren and Conder.

In my visits to the holy city I experienced a keen regret that I was not treading the streets trodden by Christ and his apostles. They are hidden beneath the accumulated rubbish of ages. As I walked the crooked, neglected lanes of modern Jerusalem I felt I was treading upon the buried temples and palaces and avenues of Solomon's glorious reign which await a resurrection by the spade, when the crescent goes down and the cross goes up. The regret I had experienced was relieved when I stood upon Mount Moriah, whose summit remains in its form and aspect as when Jesus "walked in Solomon's Porch;" or when I crossed the little stone bridge which spans the Kedron, so often pressed by his weary feet; or when I sat on the slopes of Olivet and "beheld the city" which in its former majesty and glory rose before his divine vision.

Until the uncivilized and uncivilizing Turk is driven from the holy city, and until Christendom owns that religious metropolis of the world, and until the archæologist can pursue his noble work unmolested, two questions will remain in dispute—the site of Calvary and the site of the tomb of Joseph of Arimathea. Greeks and Latins claim that both are within the Church of the Holy Sepulcher, a claim which rests upon the traditions of centuries, but which can never be substantiated beyond a doubt until the second wall of the Jerusalem of Christ can be definitely traced. Both English and American explorers of to-day place Calvary on the ridge over the Grotto of Jeremiah, north of the city and near the Damascus Gate. From immemorial time this has been called the "Hill of Execution;" it resembles the human skull, and the Jews esteem it accursed, and exclaim as they pass it, "Cursed be he who destroyed our nation by aspiring to be king thereof." And to the west of the hill, two hundred yards north of the Damascus Gate, on one side is a lane leading to St. Stephen's Church, and opposite is an arched gateway of stone, with wooden door, which opens into a garden, and in the garden is the tomb. The tomb has never been finished, yet it has been occupied; its construction is Herodian, about the time of Christ; it has been occupied for only one burial; it is a Jewish tomb and designed for one of wealth and influence; it has been used for Christian worship, and upon its walls can now be traced faintly a frescoed cross with the sacred monograms.

Interesting and remarkable as are the recoveries thus far made, a larger future awaits the archæologist. There are venerable traditions which point to hidden vaults and subterranean passageways beneath ancient Jerusalem wherein were secreted during the last and fatal siege of the city the Ark of the Covenant, the autograph copy of the Pentateuch, and the sacred vessels of the temple which were brought back from Babylon, and these traditions have been confirmed by the excavations of the present day. And there is good reason to believe that St. Matthew's gospel in Hebrew, together with some of the apostolic letters, were deposited in a place of security when the storm of persecution burst upon the Church in Jerusalem. A few inscriptions have been found and translated, illustrative of the Scripture record. A tablet has been recovered on which is an inscription in Greek—the characters are monumental in size—which is a notice to strangers not to pass through the sacred inclosure of the temple: "No stranger is to enter within the balustrade round the temple inclosure; whoever is caught will be responsible to himself for his death, which will ensue." This recalls the episode recorded in Acts xxi, 28, when St. Paul, after his purification, was accused of introducing into the temple the Gentile Trophimus of Ephesus, which caused a riot, that was quelled by the intervention of the Tribune, who rescued Paul. In the Pool of Siloam there was discovered an inscription, the letters of which closely resemble those on the Moabite stone. On this tablet, twenty-seven inches square, is recorded in six lines a commemoration of the completion of the tunnel, which is a third of a mile long and connects the Virgin's Fount with the Pool of Siloam, and dates back to the reign of Solomon. And at Bethphage a stone was uncovered on which are frescoes representing the raising of Lazarus and the triumphal procession in honor of our Lord, and strong arguments are adduced that on this stone the Saviour rested when he sent his disciples to the city. These are but intimations of the future, when biblical research can be carried forward unhindered by the greed of the Turk or the fanaticism of the Jew.

While we wait patiently for the incoming of that better day, Jerusalem is attracting the attention of all peoples. Palestine is still the "high bridge" of the nations, over which the commerce of the world must pass from west to east. The old saying of Scripture is still true : "I have set Jerusalem in the midst of the nations," and for some wise purpose it is destined to be the religious metropolis of the world. Sixty thousand people dwell within her walls; eight thousand Turks hold the city and rule it with an iron hand. They have neither patriotism nor honor ; they are robbers in the disguise of government officials. Forty-two thousand Jews have come from Spain, Poland, and the ends of the earth, who are paupers, and who divide their time between wailing over their departed glory and living on the charity of others. Ten thousand Christians are denizens of the once proud city, who stand guard over the "sacred places" and are the thrift and hope of the place. Four thousand orthodox Greeks and four thousand orthodox Latins watch each other with a jealous eye, and are ready for the fray whenever the "Silver Star of Bethlehem is stolen." The Arminian Christians are merchant princes ; the Syrians live on the venerable past ; the Copts and Abyssinians are few and poor; and the four hundred Protestants represent the brain, the heart, the enterprise, the piety, and the charity of modern Jerusalem. They are American and Scotch Presbyterians, German Lutherans, and Anglican Episcopalians. They have founded hospitals, organized schools, built churches, created a healthful literature, and are the energy of public opinion. While many are waiting for the restoration of the Jews these noble Protestant Christians are preparing the way for the coming of the Lord, when Jerusalem shall be rebuilt and made holy and once again be the joy of the whole earth.

John P. Newman

FROM DAN TO BEERSHEBA.

CHAPTER I.

The two Boundaries.—The parallel Mountains.—The great Valley.—Inspired Eulogies.—Sterile Soil.—Gibbon's Comparison.—Natural and miraculous Causes of present Sterility.—Testimonies of pagan Authors on the ancient Productions of Palestine.—Land coveted by the great Nations of Antiquity.—A Land of Ruins.—Present Fertility and Fruits —Richness of the North.—Volney on the Variety of the Climate of Palestine.—Beauties of Spring in the Promised Land.—Flowers.—Magnificent Scenery.—Standard of Landscape Beauty.—Palestine is a World in Miniature..—Illustrations.—Prophetical Descriptions of the twelve Tribeships.—Wonderful Correspondence.

The boundaries of Palestine are defined by the sacred writers according to the Land of Possession and the Land of Promise. The extreme length of the former is 180 miles from north to south, the average breadth 50 miles from east to west, and it has a superficial area of 14,000 square miles. The latter is 360 miles long, 100 broad, and contains 28,000 square miles, being three and a half times larger than New Jersey, twice as large as Maryland, of equal extent with South Carolina, and of exact proportion to New Hampshire, Massachusetts, and Vermont combined. The limits of the lesser area are from "Dan to Beersheba" north and south, and from the Jordan to the Mediterranean east and west. The boundaries of the greater area are from the "Waters of Strife, in Kadesh," on the south, to the "entrance of Hamath" on the north, and from the eastern shore of the Mediterranean to the western border of the Arabian Desert.[1] Moses describes the Land of Promise;[2] Samuel, the Land of Possession;[3] the former, what was included in the original grant; the latter, what was actu-

---

[1] Num., xxxiv., 2-12; Ezek., xlvii., 15-20.   [2] Num., xxxiv.
[3] 2 Sam., iii., 10.

ally possessed by the "chosen people." And although the twelve tribeships remained substantially the same as surveyed by Joshua, yet both David and Solomon held dominion from the Nile to the Euphrates, and in them was fulfilled God's promise to Abraham.¹

It is the remark of an eminent writer that "there is no district on the face of the globe containing so many and such sudden transitions as Palestine, being at once a land of mountains, plains, and valleys."² Far to the north, at the "entering of Hamath," commence two parallel ranges of limestone mountains, extending southward to the Desert of Tih and Arabia Petraea, which are branches of the ancient Taurus chain, and a continuation of that mountain tract stretching from the Bay of Issus to the Desert of Arabia, called Lebanon. The western ridge attains its greatest altitude, opposite Ba'albek, in Jebel Mukhmel, whose summit rises 13,000 feet above the level of the sea. Continuing southward to the point opposite Tyre, the chain is broken by the River Leontes flowing through a sublime gorge into the Mediterranean. Decreasing in height, but expanding in breadth, the ridge continues south of the ravine to the hills of Nazareth and the wooded cone of Tabor, where it is broken again by the great plain of Esdraelon, through which the Kishon flows to the sea, separating the hills of Galilee from the mountains of Samaria. Coming up from the Bay of 'Akka in a southeasterly direction is Mount Carmel, immediately to the south of which are the hills of Samaria. Rising from the southern border of Esdraelon, and stretching southward thirty-three miles, they terminate in Ebal and Gerizim, where the chain is broken for the third time by the Plain of Mukhnah. Beyond this vale are the mountains of Ephraim, extending to Bethel, where the Heights of Benjamin begin, which extend to the valley of the Kedron. Here the ridge takes the name of the "Hill Country of Judea," running in a wide, low, irregular mountain tract to the southern limit of Palestine. Excepting the promontory of Carmel, the southern section of the Lebanon range is farther removed from the sea, leaving at its base a maritime plain more than 150 miles long, embracing the beautiful Sharon on the north, and the Land of Philistia on the south.

Twenty miles to the east of the Lebanon, and at the "enter-

¹ Gen., xv., 18; 2 Sam., viii., 3; 1 Kings, iv., 21-25. ² Volney's Travels.

ing of Hamath," the anti-Lebanon chain begins, running parallel to the former in a southwestern direction. Though of less general altitude than its companion ridge, it includes Mount Hermon, 10,000 feet high, and rivaling in the grandeur of its form and the sublimity of its scenery the loftiest peaks of Syria. Thirty-three miles south of Hermon the eastern range sweeps round the Sea of Galilee, taking the name of the Mountains of Gilead along the east bank of the Jordan, and the names of Ammon and Moab along the shore of the Dead Sea, and finally terminating with the hills of Arabia Petra at the head of the Bay of Akabah.

Next to these mountain chains, the most remarkable feature in the physical geography of Palestine is the great valley, which, commencing amid the ruins of ancient Antioch, runs southward between the two parallel ridges of Lebanon and anti-Lebanon. Measuring more than 300 miles in length, and being from seven to ten miles broad, it serves as the bed of the Orontes, the Litâny, and the Jordan. Bearing the name of Cœlesyria, its southern section has an elevation of 2300 feet above the sea; but from its westerly branch, through which the Leontes flows to the village of Hasbeiya, it rapidly descends, and at its intersection with the Plain of el-Hûleh, a distance of less than twenty miles, *it is on a level with the sea*. At the Lake of Tiberias it has a depression of 653 feet, and reaches its greatest depth in the chasm of the Dead Sea, the surface of whose waters is 1312 feet below the level of the Mediterranean.

To the cursory observer there is an air of extravagance in the inspired descriptions of the Promised Land. Dwelling with delight upon the fruits of the soil, the pleasures of the climate, and the grandeur of the scenery, the poets and historians of the Bible ascribe to it a marvelous fertility, and in their glowing encomiums other lands sink into insignificance when compared to the favored inheritance of Jacob, and even the rich valley of the Nile is to be cheerfully exchanged for the rich hills and valleys of Palestine.[1] Such was to be its richness, that from the "cattle on a thousand hills," and from the thymy shrubs and the numberless bees inhabiting its venerable forests, it was to be "a land flowing with milk and honey."[2] Such was to be its fruitfulness, that the "threshing

[1] Ex., iii., 17.   [2] Ib.

was to reach unto the vintage, and the vintage reach unto the sowing-time."[1]

Such was to be its metallic wealth, that it was to be "a land whose stones are iron, and out of whose hills thou mayest dig copper."[2] Unlike Egypt, which is dependent upon the Nile for a supply of water, it was to be a country superior in its mountain springs and in its "early and latter rains."[3] Repeating the eulogistic utterances of Moses, and realizing the promises he had made, five centuries later David sings, "The pastures are clothed with flocks; the valleys are covered with corn; they shout for joy; they also sing. The Lord causeth the grass to grow for cattle, and herb for the service of man, that he may bring forth food out of the earth, and wine that maketh glad the heart of man, and oil to make his face to shine."[4]

But, whatever may have been the appearance of Southern Palestine in those distant ages, it appears at present, especially its mountain regions, to be little better than a vast limestone quarry, covered with small gray stones, offensive to the eye, painful to the foot of man and beast, and seemingly incapable of a harvest. An aspect so sterile and forbidding induced the author of "The Decline and Fall of the Roman Empire" to institute the comparison that "Palestine is a territory scarcely superior to Wales either in fertility or extent."[5] Conceding this apparent barrenness, the causes of the change which has taken place in the lapse of so many centuries are at once natural and miraculous. The frequent changes of government, the rapacity of officials, the insecurity of property, the religious animosity of rival sects, the barbarian ignorance of the peasantry as to the enlightened principles of agriculture, together with a moral degradation universally prevalent, are adequate causes, when operating during a long series of years, to change the face of any country, and doom it to almost irreclaimable barrenness. It is also true that the destruction of the woods of any section on the earth's surface, and particularly the trees on the mountain-tops, which invite and arrest the passing clouds, tends to the diminution of rain and to the consequent evils of the drought. The condition of Germany since the disappearance of its great forests, and of Greece since the

---

[1] Levit., xxvi., 5.   [2] Deut., viii., 9.   [3] Ib., xi., 10-12.
[4] Ps. lxv., 13; civ., 14, 15.   [5] Gibbon's Rome, vol. i., p. 27.

fall of the large plane-trees which once shaded the bare landscape of Attica,[1] illustrates the fact that where the land is denuded of its herbage and foliage, which casts a cooling shade upon the ground, the scorching rays of the sun penetrate more certainly and intensely, promoting evaporation, causing the springs and fountains to fail, and at the same time increasing the absorbent capacity of the soil;[2] but where the valleys are clothed with verdure, and the mountains with forests, a larger quantity of moisture is retained in the ground, a lower temperature exists in the atmosphere, and the clouds are drawn to the spot in obedience to meteorological laws.[3] To Titus belongs the shame of having stripped the hills about Jerusalem of their magnificent olive-groves, and, from the destruction of the Holy City to the present century, Southern Palestine has been a vast common for the marauding and predatory bands of Saracens and Persians, of Mamelukes and Turks, whose innumerable herds and flocks have wandered at liberty over gardens and fields, through groves and forests, consuming and destroying both plants and trees, and thereby diminishing the usual quantity of rain in the proper seasons.

While to every candid mind such are sufficient causes for this apparent sterility, yet to the Christian a miraculous interference with the ordinary course of nature for the attainment of a moral end is an additional consideration why Palestine is not now what it was in the days of Moses and David. Assuming to exercise a special care over the land, Jehovah represents himself as sending and withholding rain according to the obedience or disobedience of his chosen people : "Thou hast polluted the land with thy wickedness, therefore the showers have been withholden, and there has been no latter rain."[4] "I have withholden the rain from you when there were yet three months to the harvest; and I caused it to rain upon one city, and caused it not to rain upon another city."[5] Hazardous as it would seem, in human estimation, to suspend the continuance of rain and national prosperity upon the continued faithfulness of human beings, yet it most evidently appears that, so long as the Jews remained faithful and obedient as a nation, just so long, and no longer, was their land blessed with prosperity ; and, whenever they became guilty of defection,

[1] Stanley's Palestine, p. 121. [2] Olin's Travels, ii., p. 429.
[3] Barclay's C. G. K., p. 416. [4] Jer., iii., 3, 4. [5] Amos, iv., 7.

the rains of heaven were withheld, and their land became desolate. The evil, however, experienced by the present tiller of the soil is not the want of rain, but rather its proper distribution. Whatever effect the denudation of the country of its foliage may have had to diminish the vernal and summer showers, it is a remarkable fact that it rains more copiously in Syria than in the United States; but, commencing in November, the rainy season continues only till February, while during the eight or nine succeeding months there is scarcely a shower falls. Such an unequal distribution of rain could not fail to injure the most fertile portions of the globe.[1]

Though unquestionably true that the structure and composition of the soil for miles around Jerusalem must always have been essentially what it is now, of a rough limestone nature, and as such it must have appeared in the palmiest age of the Jewish commonwealth, yet in those happier days, under a mild and an enlightened government, no part was waste; the more fertile hills were cultivated in artificial terraces, others were covered with orchards of fruit-trees, while the more rocky and barren districts were converted into vineyards. But in the process of time the terraces which supported the soil upon the steep declivities have been destroyed, and the accumulated earth has been swept away by the rains, leaving naked hills " where once grew the corn and crept the vine."

Those who quote Gibbon against Moses and David with so much triumph, should also cite pagan authors of higher antiquity and of equal authority in their favor. In his description of Jericho, Strabo speaks of " a grove of palms, and a country of a hundred stadia full of springs and well-peopled." According to Tacitus, " the inhabitants of Palestine are healthy and robust, the rains moderate, and the soil fertile." Ammianus Marcellinus is even more explicit than his predecessors: " The last of the Syrias is Palestine, a country of considerable extent, abounding in clean and well-cultivated land, and containing some fine cities, none of which yield to the other, but, as it were, being on a parallel, are rivals."[2]

Regarding it as a valuable accession to their dominions, Palestine was a prize for which the Assyrians and Egyptians, the Greeks and Romans, the Persians and Saracens, fought to conquer and retain. To each it was the "diamond of the desert;"

[1] Barclay, p. 53.   [2] See Milman's note in Gibbon's Rome, i., p 27, 28.

and coveting the fruits of the soil, and sighing for the delights of the climate, they each in turn also contended for the advantages its central position afforded as a military station between the east and west, the north and south. Charmed with its gardens, the fascinating Cleopatra induced Antony to take from Herod the Great the noble plain of Jericho and annex it to her dominions, that she might possess the celebrated balm and the other valuable drugs and fruits it then produced.[1] Delighted with its fertility, its opulence, and populousness, Chosroes of Persia aspired to its permanent conquest; and, a quarter of a century later, the Saracens feared to have Omar see Jerusalem, lest the richness of the surrounding country and the purity of the air might tempt him never to return to the holy city of Medina. As significant of its fruitfulness, both Vespasian and Titus caused medals to be struck on which Palestine is represented by a female under a palm-tree; and there are medals still extant on which Herod is represented as holding a bunch of grapes, and the young Agrippa as displaying fruit.[2]

Confirming alike the testimony of both sacred and profane writers, there are still two traces of the ancient productiveness of the soil. On the plains, in the valleys, upon the hills, everywhere, from the river to the sea, from "Dan to Beersheba," are ruins—broken cisterns, prostrate walls, crumbling terraces, and old foundations, indicating the greatness of an earlier population, and the abundant harvests which supported the millions once dwelling within these narrow limits. These silent but unmistakable indications of the populousness of a former age are more significant than the testimony of Tacitus and Josephus. Though wanting the air of grandeur of the ruins of Thebes and Palmyra, yet there is the vineyard tower, the peasant's cottage, the streets, the walls, the dwellings of the once large and thriving village; and on the hillside and in the field is seen the ruined sheepfold, the wine-press, the ancient oil and flour mill; while along all the highways, and in many a retired valley, are water-tanks and reservoirs now dry and broken. Neither in Egypt nor in Greece is the aspect of desolation more complete. In the one and in the other are the remains of mighty cities, with their stupendous temples and magnificent palaces; but here, in close proximity, as one might expect to

---

[1] Josephus, anti B., c. iv.
[2] Milman's note on Gibbon, i., p. 27, 28.

find in a country of shepherds and husbandmen, is the mound of ruins, the forsaken village, the desolate city.

Like the remains of those ancient habitations, there are still evidences, in the present capacity and products of the soil, sustaining the claim that the Holy Land was once a land of "wheat and barley," of "wine and oil." As of old, the Plain of Jericho repays the toil of husbandry, and only requires proper tillage to make it "even as the garden of the Lord." For many miles around Joppa the Plain of Sharon is a vast and beautiful garden, yielding the most delicious oranges, lemons, plums, quinces, apricots, and bananas. In the Vale of Eshcol and on the Heights of Urtás are produced the finest grapes in the world; while around all the larger towns of Philistia, and in the environs of Hebron, Bethlehem, Jerusalem, and Gibeon, are the largest and richest olive-groves, fig and almond orchards in the East.

Though forbidding in aspect and apparently hopelessly sterile, yet, considering the nature of the soil, the kind of crops it is best adapted to produce, and the crude husbandry here practiced, the flinty region of Southern Palestine is equal in productiveness to many of the best portions of Europe and America. All that can be reasonably demanded of a country is to yield in fair proportion, with ordinary appliances, the indigenous fruits of the climate. The mountain tract from Shiloh to Hebron is the proper region for the olive and the vine, and one acre of the stony surface of Olivet, planted with olive-trees and carefully tended, would yield more through the exchanges of commerce toward human subsistence than a larger tract of the richest land in New York planted to corn. While corn is simply an article of food, the olive berry subserves a variety of purposes. Besides being used by the natives for food, and, as such, in large quantities exported to other countries, it contains a delicious oil, which, in domestic life, is the substitute for butter and lard, and in manufacture is employed in making soap and candles, and for lubricating machinery.[1] While, as in the days of the Psalmist, the olive and the grape, together with wheat, barley, and corn, are the staples of life, yet there are here annually raised in great abundance cauliflowers, cabbages, radishes, lettuce, beans, peas, onions, garlic, carrots, beets, leeks, lentiles, celery, parsley, cucumbers, tomatoes, potatoes, pumpkins, together with the egg-plant and sug-

[1] Olin's Travels.

ar-cane. There are also cultivated, in all their deliciousness, figs, apricots, peaches, plums, oranges, lemons, citrons, limes, mandrakes, pomegranates, apples, pears, dates, bananas, quinces, cherries, watermelons, muskmelons, with almonds, pistachios, and walnuts. In many northern districts cotton and tobacco are extensively cultivated, while in all sections herds of cattle and flocks of sheep and goats are raised for food and raiment. Possessing a climate marked with the peculiarities of the three zones, and yielding annually such harvests of grains and fruits for the sustenance of more than a million and a half of people, the Promised Land, under an enlightened Christian government, might be restored to its original fertility and pristine beauty.

Whatever apology is necessary for the vindication of the sacred writers as to the southern portion of their native land, none, however, is needed to sustain them in their loftiest praises of all their ancient territory north of the ruins of Bethel. While in the south "Judah washed his garments in wine and his cloths in the blood of grapes," in the north the powerful house of Joseph had the "precious things of heaven and the precious things of the lasting hills." Beyond the tribal possessions of Benjamin the soil is no less rich than the scenery is grand; within the inheritance of Ephraim, the Plain of Mukhnah and the Vale of Shechem resemble vast gardens, while the mountains and valleys of Samaria, the plains of Sharon and Esdraelon, and the fields and hills of Galilee, stretching from the lakes to the sea, pronounce their own eulogy.

An elegant writer has justly observed that "Syria unites different climates under the same sky, and collects within a small compass pleasures and productions which nature has elsewhere dispersed at great distances of time and place. To the advantage which perpetuates enjoyments it adds another, that of multiplying them by the variety of its productions."[1]

Though lying within the same parallels of latitude with Washington and New Orleans, yet, owing to its peculiar geological structure and configuration, the climate is essentially different. On the higher slopes of Lebanon the summer months are cool and pleasant as on our native Catskills, but in the deep valley of the Jordan, and on the shores of the Dead Sea, the heat is as intense and debilitating as on the plains of

[1] Volney's Travels.

Southern India. Along the sea-board the same variety prevails. Where the high mountains crowd down upon the coast, reflecting the light and heat of a Syrian sun, the region is sultry and unhealthy, but where the mountains retire and the soil is dry the air is pure and delightful.

Properly speaking, there are but two seasons in Palestine, appropriately described in that sublime repetition—"winter and summer, cold and heat, seed-time and harvest;" but on the mountain range the four seasons are distinctly perceptible. Though the loftier summits of Lebanon are covered with snow the year round, yet frost and ice are only occasionally seen in the vicinity of Jerusalem. While in summer a gentle breeze from the Mediterranean plays over the central ridge from morning till night, at other seasons of the year the winds blow a tornado. Sand-storms arise, blinding to the eyes, and rendering near objects indistinct; hail-storms are frequent and violent, and, as of old, the "south wind" blows, lasting for many days at a time, and frequently assuming all the dreadful characteristics of the sirocco.

Commencing with the beginning of November, the winter rains continue with short intervals until March, when spring wears her floral mantle, and, casting its ample folds over the Land of Promise, hides its otherwise rougher features; then follows the long rainless summer, with transparent atmosphere and hazy skies alternating, and with intense heat, parched soil, and streams few and scanty, which is succeeded by autumn, with its red and golden vintage, and atmosphere of unsurpassed balminess.

But spring is the most delightful season of the year in the Holy Land, whether to enjoy the pleasures of the climate or behold the magnificence of the scenery. Then the skies are bright, the air balmy, and the vernal sun lights up the landscape with a thousand forms of beauty. Then sparkling fountains are unsealed, silver brooks go murmuring by, and wild cascades, leaping from their rocky heights, come dashing down the mountain side, scattering in their descent wreaths of rainbow spray. Then the valleys and the hills are clothed with verdure, the fields are green with grains and grasses, the fig and palm-tree are in blossom, the almond, apricot, olive, and pomegranate are ripening, and the cypress, tamarisk, oak, walnut, sycamore, and poplar are decked with the clean fresh foliage of a new year. Then herds of camels and buffaloes are browsing on the meadows, and flocks of sheep and goats go gamboling up the mountain sides. Then, in all the glens, on all the vast prairie plains, and over all the highest mountains are flowers blooming—anemones, oleanders, amaranths, arbutuses, poppies, hollyhocks, daisies, hyacinths, tulips, pinks, lilies, and roses, growing in unbounded profusion, delighting the senses, and transforming the land into a garden of flowers.

But whatever is beautiful in the scenery of Palestine is peculiar to the north. In the south there is a sameness of outline and of color that wearies the eye and makes one sigh for variety; but north of the mountains of Ephraim the beholder is charmed with green plains and fertile valleys, with wooded dells and graceful hills, with rippling brooks and sylvan lakes, with leaping cascades and rushing rivers, with sublime chasms and profound ravines; and with lofty mountains, broken into beetling cliffs and craggy peaks, whose higher summits are capped with perpetual snow, and down whose furrowed sides rush a thousand torrents. There the most fastidious taste would be delighted with the wild mountain gorge encircling Tirzah, and the wilder chasm of el-Hamâm—with the beautiful glen of el-Haramîyeh, and the more lovely Vale of Abilîn—with the woodland parks of Carmel and Tabor—with the crystal lakes of Merom and Gennesaret—with the foaming, rapid waters of the Jordan, the Leontes, and the Adonis—with Mount Hermon, with summer at his feet, spring in his lap, and winter on his head—and with the magnificent scenery of Kadisha, where the Syrian Alps lift their awful forms 13,000 feet high, covered with snow 100 feet deep—where the melting snows feed cascades, which in their descent are beaten into spray by the rocks, and which, reflecting the sunlight, seem like the infinite fragments of some gorgeous rainbow—and where rills from the hills and torrents from the mountains unite to swell the river below, which, after winding through the noblest and wildest of nature's chasms, whose sides are lined with shrubbery, adorned with hamlets, and dotted with convents high up in the everlasting rocks, and whose solemn bells awaken the echoes of Lebanon, pours its accumulated waters into the Western Sea.

If the standard of landscape beauty be the regular alternation of plain and mountain, as in Greece and Italy; the clean meadows, the well-made farms and green hills, as in France and England; or the continent-like prairies, the miniature seas, and multiform mountains of America, then the Land of Promise must yield the palm to those more highly-favored countries. But if the combination of all these characteristics on a smaller scale constitute the beautiful and grand in natural scenery, Palestine is not unworthily praised by the sacred writers for the variety and magnificence of its landscape.

Viewed from such a stand-point, the Holy Land is a world in miniature, possessing the three great terrene features of the globe—sea-board, plain, and mountain. Yielding the fruits of every climate, and containing a population corresponding in their physique to that of the inhabitants of every zone, there is displayed in this variety of scenery and climate the wisdom of God. Selected by Providence to be the medium of divine truth to men of all lands, it was necessary that the national home of the Bible writers should open to their imaginations the most wonderful and varied of the works of the Creator. Naturally inclined to express our adoration of the Deity in allusions to his wisdom and goodness displayed in nature, we experience a unison of devotion with those who were the oracles of inspired truth to us in their sublime illustrations, drawn from the sea and land, the valleys and hills, the climate and fruits, and the beasts and birds of the country that gave them birth. Had they dwelt at the poles, or on the equator, or in the heart of Arabia, or on the banks of the Nile, they could not have given the same universality of expression to the message they were sent to announce. It is evidence of the presence of that All-wise Spirit that the prophets and psalmists, the Savior and the apostles, drew their simplest, noblest figures from nature, such as can not fail to arrest the attention of the untutored mind in every land, and inspire intellects of the highest culture with admiration.

Who of all the great maritime nations of earth can fail to appreciate the Psalmist's description of his native sea, as from its shore, or from some mountain-top, he beheld its wonders: "O Lord, how manifold are thy works! in wisdom hast thou made them all; the earth is full of thy riches; so is this great sea, wherein are things creeping innumerable, both small and great beasts."[1] And who that has ever crossed the ocean, or

[1] Ps. civ., 24, 25.

witnessed a storm at sea, does not realize the perfection of his description: "They that go down to the sea in ships, that do business in great waters, these see the works of the Lord, and his wonders in the deep; for he commandeth and raiseth the stormy wind, which lifteth up the waves thereof: they mount up to heaven, they go down again to the depths; their soul is melted because of trouble."[1] The mountaineer feels that the Psalmist sings of

"What oft was thought, but ne'er so well expressed,"

when he describes, "The high hills are a refuge for the wild goats, and the rocks for the conies."[2] The dweller at the poles is conscious of a fellow-feeling when he reads those sublime words: "He giveth snow like wool; he scattereth the hoar-frost like ashes: he casteth forth ice like morsels: who can stand before his cold?"[3]

The nomad of the desert finds his own country portrayed in the graphic allusions to a "dry and thirsty land where no water is;"[4] to the "shadow of a great rock in a weary land;"[5] and feels himself kindred to the patriarchs in his predatory life.[6] They that dwell upon the equator comprehend that grand but terrific passage descriptive of the earthquake and volcano, "He looketh on the earth, and it trembleth; he toucheth the hills, and they smoke."[7] And to the denizens of all lands are familiar those impressive references to the sun, moon, and stars; to the "thunder of his power;" to the "lightnings that lighten the world;" to the storm of hail and rain; to the shepherd on the mountain, to the husbandman in the field, and to the merchant in the marts of commerce.

But the correspondence between the prophetic descriptions of the several tribeships, as given by Jacob and Moses, and the land as it now appears, is even more exact; and in recalling the former and in surveying the latter, one knows not which to admire most, the adaptation of the soil for various products, or the unanswerable argument afforded for the inspiration of those who wrote. In the final and permanent division of the territory the portion fell to each tribe by lot, just as Jacob had foretold in the last moments of his life, 250 years before, and just as Moses had predicted immediately prior to his demise.

[1] Ps. cvii., 23-26.   [2] Ib., civ., 18.   [3] Ib., cxlvii., 16, 17.   [4] Ib., lxiii., 1.
[5] Isa., xxxii., 2.   [6] Gen., xx., 1.   [7] Ps. civ., 32.

Though it was not possible for the former, with his extraordinary powers of observation and penetration, to have passed and repassed through the whole length of the land without observing the peculiarities of each section, and though equally impossible for the latter, with his capacious mind, and with the means of information at his command, to have remained ignorant of the chorography of the several parts, yet the knowledge of those eminent men had no influence upon the ultimate settlement of the tribes. Human foresight is never equal to the uncertainties of the lot; only superhuman knowledge can foretell to whom the lot will fall. In their prophetic visions they saw the Land of Promise mapped out into tribal possessions, and on each they read the name of the future inheritor. Years after, when the lots were drawn by Joshua and Eleazer at Shiloh, each tribe received its portion exactly on the spot which had been foretold.

Pre-eminently pastoral, Reuben, Gad, and the half tribe of Manasseh received the vast pasture-fields of Ammon, Gilead, and Bashan, extending from the River Arnon on the south to the base of Hermon on the north, and from the Jordan on the west to the desert of Arabia and the Haurân on the east. Called by the Arabs Belka, they can pronounce no higher praise upon its rich plains and green sloping hills than in their pastoral proverb to declare, "Thou canst not find a country like the Belka." Deprived of the "excellency of dignity"— the priesthood; of the "excellency of power"—the kingdom; and of the "double portion" of wealth and temporal blessings which, by the rights of primogeniture, belonged to the first-born son of Jacob, here, between the Arnon and the Jabbok, Reuben was "unstable as water" in the rapid diminution of his numbers, and in being the first of the tribes to be carried into captivity by Tiglath Pileser of Assyria;[1] and never producing a great man to honor his name, and never rising to dignity and influence in the councils of the nation, here also a father's curse was fulfilled, "Thou shalt not excel."[2] His tribeship extending from the Jabbok to the Sea of Galilee, and from the Jordan to the desert, and harassed by the Arabian plunderers on his eastern border, but in turn driving them from his dominion, it was said of Gad, "A troop shall overcome him, and he shall overcome at last."[3]

[1] 1 Chron., v., 26.   [2] Gen., xlix., 3, 4.   [3] Ib., xlix., 19.

Occupying the Hills of Bashan, together with the rich and picturesque regions along the eastern shore of Gennesaret as far north as Mount Hermon, and rising to distinction in rank and numbers, and in giving to the nation three eminent characters—"the pious Gideon, the opulent Jair, and the valiant Jephtha"[1]—the prophetical benediction on Manasseh was here accomplished: "He also shall become a people, and he also shall be great."[2]

Omitted by Moses from the list of the blessed, and sentenced by his father to be "divided in Jacob and scattered in Israel," Simeon occupied with Judah the extreme south; and in one generation after the exodus from Egypt to Canaan his posterity had decreased more than 37,000 souls.[3] Destined to rule rather than to serve, to be cunning rather than brave, "Dan shall judge his people; and he shall be a serpent by the way, an adder in the path, that biteth the horse-heels, so that his rider shall fall backward."[4] Unable to subdue the Philistines, whose lands were allotted to them from the Hills of Judah to the Mediterranean, the Danites were compelled to conquer new territory for their rapidly increasing numbers. Described by Moses to be "a lion's whelp," and foretold by him that "Dan shall leap from Bashan," a colony of the tribe passed northward to the sources of the Jordan, and, taking the city of Laish by surprise, 600 armed men, like a young lion pouncing upon its prey, "leaped from Bashan," captured and burnt the town, and upon its ruins founded another city, calling it "after the name of Dan, their father." Thus, while at a later period the southern branch of the tribe gave to the nation Samson, who "judged Israel twenty years," the new colony stamped its tribal name upon the utmost limit of Palestine, which has since passed into the proverbial saying, "From Dan to Beersheba."[5] Foretold that "his eyes shall be red with wine, and his teeth white with milk," to Judah fell that mountain region from Jerusalem southward to Arabia, and from the Dead Sea to the hills which overhang the Mediterranean, and which for vineyards and pasturage is unsurpassed in all the Holy Land. Here, in the days of his prosperity, he was seen "binding his foal unto the vine, and his ass's colt unto the choice vine; and

---

[1] Hibbard's Palestine.   [2] Gen., xlviii., 19.
[3] Gen., xlix., 7; Deut., xxxiii.; Num., i., 23, and xxvi., 14.
[4] Gen., xlix., 16, 17.   [5] Deut., xxxiii., 22; Judges, xviii., and xvi., 31.

here he washed his garments in wine, and his cloths in the blood of grapes." Selected to be the tribe whence the Messiah should come, "Judah, thou art he whom thy brethren shall praise." Ordained to retain his tribeship, his ensigns, his government "until Shiloh come," his home was amid the fastnesses of the Judean Hills, from which, till the appointed time, when God abandoned him to his enemies, he could not be dislodged. Ascending to his mountain lair from the swellings of Jordan, "Judah is a lion's whelp: from the prey, my son, thou art gone up;" and after the Ten Tribes had been scattered, and the identity of Benjamin lost, and when the foe approached, the "Lion of the tribe of Judah," confident of his security, "stooped down, he couched as a lion, and as an old lion; who shall rouse him up?"[1]

By nature a martial people, cruel in war, and ambitious to be free, the children of Benjamin received that wild highland tract from the Jordan to Bethhoron, and from Jerusalem to Bethel. Here, on his impregnable heights, with a courage, an independence, a ferocity, at one time successfully resisting the combined attack of all the tribes, " Benjamin shall raven as a wolf; in the morning he shall devour the prey, and at night he shall divide the spoil."[2] The Vale of Hinnom being his southern frontier, Jerusalem originally belonged to Benjamin, but, failing to dispossess the Jebusites, it was reserved for David, with the warriors of Judah, to capture the strong-hold of Jebus, and elevate it to the dignity of an imperial city.[3] It was to this proximity to the Holy City that Moses refers in those remarkable words, "The beloved of the Lord shall dwell in safety by him." The Temple being Jehovah's dwelling-place, "The Lord shall cover or protect Benjamin all the day long;" and as Zion represents the throne and Moses the church — God's two shoulders — "he shall dwell between his shoulders."[4] There is an air of freedom and an aspect of defiance about the bold, rugged summits of Benjamin; and moulded among the crags of Gibeon and Gibeah, of Ramah and Ophrah, of Geba and Michmash, and the mind partaking of the features of the place of birth, it is no marvel that this tribe gave to the nation Ehud, the judge;[5] Saul, the king;[6] Jona-

---

[1] Gen., xlix., 8–12.
[2] Ib., xlix., 27.
[3] Josh., xviii., 16, 17; 2 Sam., v., 6–9.
[4] Deut., xxxiii., 12.
[5] Judges, iii., 15.
[6] 1 Sam., ix., 21.

than, the warrior;[1] the inflexible Mordecai,[2] the resolute Esther,[3] and the heroic Paul.[4]

Rewarded for the most exalted virtues, and possessing the privileges of the birthright which had been transferred from Reuben, the powerful house of Joseph, represented by the tribe of Ephraim and the half tribe of Manasseh, received the heart of Palestine—the garden of the Holy Land. Stretching its verdant lines from the waters of the Jordan along the northern boundary of Benjamin to the Mediterranean, and with the river on the east and the sea on the west, it extended northward to the Plain of Esdraelon, including the Hills of Samaria. Eminently deserving the benedictions of two worlds, Joseph was blessed with unbounded goodness by his dying father and by the Prophet of Abarim. Promised a numerous posterity, in two and a half centuries from the time Jacob placed his hands upon the heads of Ephraim and Manasseh, his descendants had increased to nearly half a million of souls.[5] "Joseph is a fruitful bough—even a fruitful bough by a well, whose branches run over the wall;"[6] and in anticipation of the fact, Moses breaks forth in that sublime strain, "They are the ten thousands of Ephraim, and they are the thousands of Manasseh."[7] Occupying a section of land on both sides of the Jordan, the present richness of which is beyond dispute, Joseph had "the precious things of heaven from above"—gentle showers, a serene sky, a sublime atmosphere; "the blessings of the deep that lieth under"—the springs and wells,[8] "the precious fruits brought forth by the sun," which come to perfection once a year; "the precious things put forth by the moon," such as mature in a month; "the chief things of the ancient mountains"—the forests that cover their summits; "the precious things of the lasting hills"—the metals and minerals which abound within them; and his glory is like the firstling of his bullocks, and his horns are like the horns of unicorns" —the inspired symbols of his strength, sovereignty, and renown.[9]

Agricultural in his taste and habits, to Issachar fell the immense and rich Plain of Esdraelon, including the mountains of Carmel, Gilboa, and Tabor. Patient in labor and invinci-

---
[1] 1 Sam., xiv., 1.   [2] Esther, ii., 5.   [3] Ib., ii., 7.   [4] Phil., iii., 5.
[5] Hibbard's Palestine, p. 76, and Clark on Num., xxvi.   [6] Gen., xlix., 22.
[7] Deut., xxxiii., 17.   [8] Gen., xlix., 25.   [9] Deut., xxxiii., 13–17.

ble in war, but weary in bearing such burdens, like the overloaded ass lying down with the two panniers on his back, "Issachar is a strong ass couching down between two burdens." Charmed with his possession, and unable to expel the powerful Canaanites from all his plains and mountains, but convinced that peace with taxation was better than war, "He saw that rest was good, and the land that it was pleasant, and he bowed his shoulder to bear, and became a servant unto tribute."[1] Valiant in arms when the tyranny of Sisera became intolerable, "The princes of Issachar were with Deborah;"[2] and having broken the power of a flaunting foe, "Issachar shall rejoice in his tents."[3]

Chosen to be the maritime tribe of the nation, the portion of Zebulun extended from the Lake of Gennesaret on the east to the Mediterranean on the west, and trafficking on both waters, "Zebulun shall dwell at the haven of the sea, and he shall be for an haven of ships."[4] As Issachar was to rejoice in his "tents"—in the abundance of his harvests, "so Zebulun was to rejoice in his going out"—in his successful voyages. By a mutual interest in agriculture and commerce, both were to "suck of the abundance of the seas;" and manufacturing glass from the vitreous sand found on the Mediterranean coast, or exporting it in large quantities to other countries, both were to grow rich from the "treasures hid in the sand." Dealing largely with the Gentiles, who were attracted to their shore and inland cities by commercial interests, these favored tribes "shall call the people unto the mountain; there they shall offer sacrifices of righteousness."[5]

Though doomed to obscurity in the annals of national greatness, yet, as if by way of compensation, Asher obtained the fruitful plain of Accho, "the key of Palestine,"[6] extending from Mount Carmel to Zidon on the coast. By the richness of the soil, "His bread shall be fat, and he shall yield royal dainties;"[7] and possessing luxuriant olive-groves, "He dipped his foot in oil."[8] Promised to be "blessed with children," the descendants of Asher numbered, on entering Canaan, 267,000 souls;[9] and on the accession of David to the throne, the tribe sent an

[1] Gen., xlix., 14, 15.   [2] Judges, v., 15.   [3] Deut., xxxiii., 18.
[4] Gen., xlix., 13.   [5] Deut., xxxiii., 19.   [6] Napoleon.
[7] Gen., xlix., 20.   [8] Deut., xxxiii., 24.
[9] Hibbard's Palestine, p. 97.

army of 40,000 troops to acknowledge the new sovereign.[1] Subject to the sudden attacks of the plundering Phœnicians, whose territory they occupied, and compelled at all times to be upon their guard, armed with their metallic greaves and sandals, "Thy shoes shall be iron and brass; and as thy days, so shall thy strength be."[2] Though the Asherites gave Israel neither king, judge, nor warrior, yet the names of two illustrious widows shine out from the general obscurity—"Anna, a prophetess, the daughter of Phanuel, of the tribe of Aser, which departed not from the temple, but served God with fastings and prayers night and day;"[3] and the "widow of Sarepta, a city of Sidon, unto whom Elijah was sent."[4]

Celebrated for their activity, bravery, and independence, and represented in the prophetic symbols by a tree planted in a rich soil, and growing to a prodigious size, Naphtali received "Galilee of the Gentiles," whose fruitfulness of soil is only excelled by the beauty of the scenery: "Naphtali is a spreading oak, producing beautiful branches."[5] Foreseeing the prosperity awaiting him, in an eloquent apostrophe Moses addressed the tribe: "Oh Naphtali, satisfied with favor, and full with the blessing of the Lord, possess thou the west and the south."[6] Embracing within his possession the green hills and valleys of "Upper Galilee," together with the Sea of Tiberias, his posterity grew rich from the fruits of the one and the products of the other. But, reserved for a higher glory and assigned a more exalted destiny, the inheritance of Naphtali remained undistinguished for any great event till the dawn of our own era. Driven from his native city, our Lord chose Capernaum as his chief residence, situated within this tribeship.[7] Here was his home during the three most eventful years of his life; here the Galileans received him gladly; here is the scene of his greatest miracles and of his most touching parables; here, on the shore of its inland sea, were born most of his apostles; here he founded his infant church; and thus enlightened in the persons of the first Christians and earliest teachers of Christianity, Naphtali possessed the "west and the south" by the spread of the Gospel among the southern tribes, and by its more general diffusion over the "Great Sea" through Europe

---

[1] 1 Chron., xii., 36.   [2] Deut., xxxiii., 25.   [3] Luke, ii., 36.
[4] Luke, iv., 26.   [5] Bochart's translation.   [6] Deut., xxxiii., 23.
[7] Matt., iv., 13.

and America. And now, after more than three thousand years, each tribal possession retains its ancient physical characteristics, yields its former agricultural products, while prophecy has become history in the fortunes and destiny of the whole nation.

CHAPTER II.

Location of Jerusalem.—Strong defensive Position of the City.—Surrounding Hills and Valleys. — Its Situation compared to that of Athens and Rome.—True Meaning of the 125th Psalm.—Tower of Psephinus.—The two Valleys.—Height of the adjacent Mountains.—A City without Suburbs.—Modern Wall.—Goliath's Castle.—Immense Stones of Solomon's Age.—Ancient Portals.—Beautiful Corner-stone.—Pinnacle of the Temple from which Christ was tempted to throw himself.—Golden Gate.—Tower of Antonia.—Objection to Prophecy answered.—The Bevel the Sign of Jewish Masonry.—Great Cave beneath the City.—Wanderings by Torchlight. — Solomon's Quarry. — Tyropean Valley. — Five Hills of Jerusalem. — Mount Zion. — Royal Abode. — Herod's three Towers. — Splendid Church of St. James.—House of Caiaphas.—Scene of the Last Supper and of Pentecost.—Tomb of David.—Royal Plunderers.—Proof of its Antiquity.—Home of the Lepers.—Sad Sight.—Akra.—Bezetha.—Napoleon's Church.

On the southern section of the Lebanon range, in N. lat. 31° 46' 45", and in E. long. 35° 13' from Greenwich, stands the memorable city of Jerusalem. Elevated 2610 feet above the level of the Mediterranean, and 3922 above the River Jordan, it is thirty-three miles from the former and sixteen from the latter. Situated on a mountain summit, the crown of which is broken into a wilderness of bleak limestone peaks, divided by numberless ravines, it is by nature one of the most strongly fortified cities in the world. Occupying the summits of five hills, it is encompassed, except on the north, by deep valleys, which in the earlier stages of military science must have been formidable obstructions to an assailing foe. That well-known passage in the Psalms, "As the mountains are round about Jerusalem, so is the Lord round about his people,"[1] most evidently includes the valleys that circumvallate the platform on which the city is built, as well as the surrounding mountains. Indeed, there is but little difference in the altitude of Olivet and Moriah, of the Hill of Corruption and Mount Zion. In the olden times, when an invading foe approached the walls of

[1] Ps. cxxv., 2.

a town with towers, battering-rams, ballistas, and catapults, an intervening valley was a more serious obstacle to encounter than a mountain to be scaled, especially as it served as a fosse, in crossing which the besiegers were exposed to the arrows of the besieged, who crowded the ramparts above. Approach Jerusalem from the north, west, or south, and the city rises above the hills that environ it, its embattled towers, graceful minarets, and swelling domes standing out against the sky as against a background. In this regard it is not unlike the Acropolis of Athens, which, rising like a thing of life from the Attic plain, has Lycabettus, the Pnyx, the Museum, and the Areopagus near, and Hymettus, Pentelicus, Mount Parnes, and Ægaleos in the distance; but it resembles more truly Rome, sitting on a cluster of hills, with an ample plain for future expansion, with hills near and mountains distant, the Janiculum answering to Olivet, and the Apennines to the Heights of Moab.[1]

To reconcile this passage with the topographical facts as they appear to every observer, some have pointed to the white mountains of Tih on the south, to the wall-like ridge of Moab on the east, and to the rugged summits of Lebanon on the north; but it is simpler and more natural to suppose that the Psalmist had in his mind Olivet, the Mount of Corruption, and the Hill of Evil Council, rising from the two valleys which, like some deep moat, circumvallate the city on the east, south, and west; referring not so much to the height of the hills above the level of the city, as to their height from their valley beds, in which their everlasting bases rest. But on the north there is no such natural obstruction to impede the advance of an enemy. The ground rises gently to the summit of Scopus, which is a western projection of the Olivet ridge, a mile distant from the town, and which gradually disappears toward the west. To strengthen by art what nature had left defenseless, the celebrated tower of Psephinus was erected at the northwest corner of the ancient wall, which, being 70 cubits high, was not only a "tower of strength," but also afforded from its top at sunrise a view of Arabia and of the sea.

Less than two miles to the northwest from Jerusalem are two slight depressions, separated by a rocky swell three quarters of a mile in width. The one on the north is the head of

[1] Stanley's Palestine, p. 174.

the Valley of the Kidron. At first a gentle depression, it runs eastward a mile and a half; then turning suddenly southward, it contracts and deepens, and becoming precipitous in its course, sweeps round the bases of Bezetha, Moriah, and Ophel, joining the Vale of Hinnom at the beautiful Gardens of Siloam. Varying in depth and breadth, it is seventy-five feet deep at the northeast corner of the city, twenty-five deeper opposite St.Stephen's Gate, and reaches its greatest depth of 150 feet at the southeast angle of the Temple area. Varying in breadth from a hundred to a thousand feet, it is narrowest opposite the southeast corner of the town, and has its greatest breadth between Moriah and Olivet, on a line drawn from the Golden Gate.

The depression south of the rocky swell is the commencement of the Valley of Hinnom, which at first is almost imperceptible; but, deepening and contracting as it winds round the western side of the city, it runs for three quarters of a mile east by south to the Yâffa Gate, where it turns at right angles round the base of Mount Zion, having broken cliffs on the right, and shelving banks on the left. Running nearly due east for half a mile, it joins the Valley of the Kidron at the Pool of En-Rogel, where these two famous valleys become one, pursuing its sinuous course to the Dead Sea. Though but 44 feet deep near the Yâffa Gate, and 500 wide, it descends to the depth of more than 500 feet below the southern brow of Zion, and is broadest at the point of conjunction with the Kidron. From the beds of these valleys rise the defensive mountains around the Holy City. Though the lowest is less than 50 feet above the average level of the town, and the highest not more than 200, yet the triple summit of the Mount of Olives is more than 400 feet above the site of "Absalom's Pillar" in the Valley of Jehoshaphat, the Mount of Corruption is 422 feet above En-Rogel, and the Hill of Evil Council rises 500 feet above the scorched rocks that line its base in the Vale of Gehenna.

Occupying the southern portion of its ancient site, and surrounded, as in former days, with a massive wall, Jerusalem is a city without suburbs. Unlike the approach to Zidon on the coast, which is in the midst of groves of fig, orange, and mulberry-trees, covering many miles in extent; unlike the approach to Damascus, which is inclosed with gardens of exquisite beauty, through which the Abana flows in " pearly brightness and perennial music the livelong day," the approach to Jerusalem is arrested by high walls and guarded gates, beyond which are no habitations excepting the wretched huts of Silwân on the south, clinging to the rocky fastnesses of the Mount of Scandal. Being a capital city, and situated in the most turbulent district of the country, such a defense is necessary as a protection against the sudden attacks of the wild Bedouins of the Desert and of the Ghôr. Strongly fortified in the time of Jebus, when captured by David, its enlarged area was afterward protected by massive walls and towers, on which the sacred poets dwell with so much religious pride and delight.[1] In the days of our Lord there were two walls—one inclosing Mount Zion, the northern section of which extended a distance of 1890 feet east and west; the other, inclosing Mount Akra, extended from the Garden Gate in the first wall to near the present Damascus Gate, and, curving to the southeast, intersected the Tower of Antonia on Mount Moriah. Mount Bezetha, with the table-land beyond, then formed the suburbs of the town; but after the crucifixion the space was inclosed by a third wall, by order of Herod Agrippa. During the bloody wars occurring between the death of Solomon and the Egyptian conquerors, the walls were alternately demolished and rebuilt by the respective captors of the city; but it was not till the year 1542 A.D. that, by order of the Sultan Suleiman I., the present single wall was built. Having been constructed out of the old materials, it contains blocks of stones representing every age of the city, from the magnificent reign of Solomon to the fluctuating rule of the Crusaders.

The modern wall is of the common gray limestone of Palestine, formed of blocks of different dimensions, and ranging in thickness from ten to fifteen feet, and from twenty-five to forty in height, according to the nature of the ground. Being two and a half miles in circumference, it is less by two miles than the circuit of the ancient wall. Having many indentations and projections, with salient angles, square towers, loopholes, and battlements, it is surmounted with a parapet, protecting a pathway which is frequently thronged with people enjoying the fine promenade and beholding the commanding prospect.

At the northwest corner of the city, which is 251 feet higher

[1] Ps. xlviii., 12, 13.

than the southeast corner of the Temple area, the native rock has been cut away to the depth of many feet on the outside of the wall, while within are massive foundations of beveled stones bearing marks of high antiquity, and now called "Goliath's Castle." At this point the western wall begins, running southeast as far as the Yâffa Gate; then, turning southward, and crossing Mount Zion along the brow of Hinnom to a point nearly opposite to the Protestant Cemetery, it joins the south wall, which, by a series of zigzags, is carried eastward over the level summit of Zion, down its eastern declivities, across the Tyropean Valley, and up the Hill of Ophel, where it joins the Haram wall 550 feet from its southeast corner. Here are huge stones as old as the days of Christ, if not as old as the reign of Solomon. At the place of junction where the city wall joins that of the Haram, there is a section of an ancient arch, beneath which is a small grated window opening into that long subterranean avenue leading up an inclined plane and a flight of steps to the Temple area. Here also are three circular arches, now walled up, twenty-five feet high and fourteen wide, marking the ancient portals leading to those stupendous vaults constructed by Solomon to elevate the side of Mount Moriah to a common level. At the southeast corner of the Haram wall there are sixteen courses of large stones, some of them measuring nineteen feet long, four high, and eight thick, and bearing on their edge the unmistakable Jewish bevel. From the natural topography of the hill, this corner of the wall must occupy the same spot on which stood the earliest wall, as it stands on the very brow of the Valley of Jehoshaphat, and there can be no doubt but that these are the identical stones laid down by Solomon himself. Here is to be seen a beautiful specimen of a "precious corner-stone,"[1] the inspired symbol of a virtuous and lovely woman,[2] and a significant type of the Messiah.[3] The material employed is a finer limestone and otherwise of a superior quality to that used in the common wall; the joints are more closely formed; and the finishing of the facing and of the beveling is so clean and fine, that, when fresh from the hands of the builder, it must have resembled gigantic relievo paneling. Surmounting this corner of the wall, no doubt, stood that pinnacle of the Temple from which Satan tempted Christ to cast himself down, assur

[1] 1 Pet., ii., 6.   [3] Isa., xxviii., 16.   [2] Ps. cxliv., 12.

ring him of the charge of angels over him.[1] According to Josephus, "a broad portico ran along the wall, supported by four rows of columns, which divided it into three parts, forming a triple colonnade." The central portico was 100 feet high, which, with the height of the wall and the depth of the valley below its base, gave an elevation of 310 feet. "And if from the top of the portico the beholder attempted to look down into the gulf below, his eyes became dark and dizzy before they could penetrate to the immense depth."[2]

IMMENSE STONES OF SOLOMON'S AGE.

From this corner to the Golden Gate, a distance of more than 1000 feet, is one unbroken line of wall, composed mostly of large rough stones, interspersed with which are fragments of antique columns. Near the top of the wall, and projecting several feet, is a round porphyry column, on which, according to a Moslem legend, Mohammed is to sit astride and judge the world, the people having been assembled for judgment in the vale below. Overlooking the Kidron, and facing the Mount of Olives beyond, is the Golden Gate, now walled up, but

[1] Matt., iv., 5, 6.   [2] Anti B., xv., c. xi. ; Robinson's B. R., i., p. 290.

which attracts the traveler's attention by its conspicuous location and its uncommon beauty. Being the centre of a projec-

GOLDEN GATE INTERIOR VIEW.

tion fifty-five feet long, and standing out six feet, it consists of a double portal, spanned by two semicircular arches richly ornamented. From what resemble corbels spring two Corinthian capitals, sustaining an entablature bending round the entire arch. Within the gate is a noble chamber fifty-five feet square. The ceiling is divided into flattened domes, supported by arches springing from side pilasters, and from two Corinthian columns of polished marble, adorned with elegant capitals; and beneath the arches a pretty entablature is carried from pilaster to pilaster, giving an air of exquisite beauty to the entire structure.

The origin of this imposing gate is unknown. It may be as old as the time of Herod the Great; it may not be older than the reign of Constantine. Impressed with its beauty, some have regarded it as occupying the site of the "Beautiful Gate" at which Peter and John healed the cripple. That, however, was a gate of the Temple; this is a gate of the city; and the two can be identical only by supposing that "gate to the Temple" is synonymous with "entrance to the Temple," which is neither supported by fact nor analogy.

Near St. Stephen's Gate, a distance of less than 500 feet to the north, is the northeast angle of the Haram wall, and unquestionably is the original angle of the wall which inclosed the Temple area. Five courses of antique stones distinctly beveled, beautifully hewn, and of great dimensions, remain *in situ*, and are as entire as when laid there by the hand of the Jewish mason. The largest of the blocks is twenty-four feet long, three high, and over five wide, at once reflecting the wealth and mechanical art of that early age. This section of the wall projects eight feet, forming a corner tower eighty-four feet long; and the five courses of stone, measuring nearly twenty feet from the base to the top of the quoins, suggest that this was one of the bastions of the famous Tower of Antonia in which Pilot held his "Judgment Hall." But to suppose the antiquity of these stones, and that they occupy their original places, is regarded by some as a confutation of our Lord's prediction, "There shall not be left one stone upon another that shall not be thrown down."[1] Reference, however, to the prophecy in all its scope, will disclose the fact that Christ spoke of the stones of the Temple, and not of the stones composing the wall of the city; and both history and research now prove how terribly have been fulfilled his fearful and exact words. The manner in which these lower layers have been preserved intact is simple and natural. In the demolition of the walls of the city by Titus and also by subsequent conquerors, the lower courses escaped notice, having been buried up in the débris of the upper layers; and in the reconstruction of the wall by Suleiman I., he permitted them to remain

[1] Mark, xiii., 2.

undisturbed in their primeval beds. The modern portions of the wall are too heterogeneous in their character and of too mean a masonry to have any claim either to antiquity or to Jewish workmanship, and the upper and lower layers no less mark two distinct periods of national history than two eras in mural architecture. The former indicate an age of weakness and poverty, the latter of power and wealth; the one discloses haste and confusion, the other deliberation and artistic accuracy; the modern is in keeping with the art and taste of the sensual Moslem, the ancient is in harmony with the pride and genius of the Jew. Nor is there any reason for supposing the lower layers to have been the work either of the Romans or of the Saracens, as the bevel is the masonic sign of the Jewish builders, and, having originated with them, it was a peculiarity of their architecture.[1] Consisting of a narrow strip along the edge of the stone, cut down half an inch lower than the rest of the surface, which had been hewn and squared, the bevel was a simple and beautiful mural ornament; and when these beveled stones were laid up in a wall, such as encompassed the city in the days of Solomon, the depressed edges must have resembled grooves or lengthened lines, producing the appearance of immense panels.

But of all the objects of interest which met my eye during my tour of the walls, none was more thrilling than the "Great Cave" beneath Jerusalem, the entrance to which is just east of the Damascus Gate. In constructing the north wall of the city, the Hill Bezetha has been cut through the solid rock to the depth of forty feet, the excavation having been extended 600 feet east and west, and 450 north and south. Lower down, and near the base of the rock on which the wall stands, is what might have been designed for a fosse, but which is now the receptacle of carrion. The existence of a "Great Cave" beneath the city, and in some way connected with the Temple of Solomon, has been the subject of a legend familiar to the aged, but the entrance to which, if known to the living at all, remained a secret with the few till accidentally discovered through a missionary's dog.[2] Attracted to the spot by the scent of the bones of animals destroyed by jackals, the dog pushed away the dirt in pawing to reach his prey, and revealed to his master one of the greatest wonders connected with a city whose

[1] Robinson's B. R., i., p. 287. [2] Barclay's C. G. K., p. 459.

history and topography have engaged the attention of the learned in all ages.

Accompanied by the American consul and a single servant, we entered the cave without difficulty, and, lighting our wax tapers, proceeded along carefully for a hundred feet, when we began rapidly to descend. To our surprise, on our right sat an Arab maiden who had become the sibyl of the cavern, surrounded by several natives, to whom she was delivering her sibylline oracles. Rapidly descending toward the southeast, we soon found ourselves in a cave three thousand feet in circumference, more than a thousand feet in length, and more than half that distance in breadth. The air was damp; the darkness that of a rayless night; the ground on which we walked was strewn with the chippings of the quarrier; the walls around us were marred with marks of the chisel, and the ceiling above us adorned with stalactites of a rose-color hue, from which trickled the percolating waters of the city; while, disturbed by our approach, bats screamed their grief and flapped their long black wings against their solid nests. Moving southward, we came to the verge of a precipice a hundred feet across and fifteen feet deep, on the bottom of which the skeleton of some lost explorer had been found. Threading a long gallery on the left, we saw a fountain as deep as it was wide, partially filled with water strongly impregnated with lime. Turning eastward, we entered a second gallery of greater depth, in the sides of which are immense blocks of limestone, in part detached from their native bed, just as they were left by the unknown quarrier thousands of years ago. Here, as elsewhere, were the unmistakable marks of a broad chisel-shaped instrument, evidently used to detach the blocks on either side and at top and bottom, and then by the pressure of a lever the mass was broken off from the rock behind. Occasionally we passed huge pillars supporting the ceiling above, and in several instances saw blocks hewn and squared ready to be hoisted to their destination. On the right and left winding passage-ways led us to noble halls, white as snow, and supported by native piers, on which are engraven the cross of some Christian pilgrim or knight of the Crusades; and on the sides of the chambers are Hebrew and Arabic inscriptions, the memorial of some wandering Jew and some conquering son of the Prophet.

Seeking in vain for an entrance other than that on the north, we returned to daylight full of curious thoughts. What tales of woe are written on these walls! and, could we hear their voices, too low for mortal ear, what secrets would they reveal! In the time of sieges this has been the retreat of Jew and Christian, of Saracen and knight; the last refuge of helpless womanhood, of tender children, of infirm old age, and the death-bed of dying heroes wounded in the fight.

Being unquestionably a quarry, many facts lead to the conclusion that here were hewn the stones for the construction of Solomon's magnificent temple. The material, both as to grain and color, is the same as that found in the antique walls and buildings of the city; the extent of the quarry, together with the vast amount of stone removed, and in such large blocks, suggest the erection of some grand temple; the ancient tradition coming down from the days of Jeremiah and pointing to this quarry; the remarkable absence of another adjacent to the city; and the important fact that the mouth of the quarry is many feet higher than the surface of the Temple area, which must have facilitated the transportation of those immense blocks of limestone, which were no doubt conveyed on rollers down the inclined plane of the quarry to the site of the Temple, where, hewn and finished, they were silently elevated to their destined place—the magnificent fane of Solomon, with all its courts and porticoes, rising noiselessly into being, as of old the world rose from naught, at once explaining and fulfilling the words of sacred history: "The house, when it was in building, was built of stone made ready before it was brought thither, so that there was neither hammer nor axe, nor any tool of iron heard in the house while it was building."[1]

Nothing more impressively indicates the complete destruction of ancient Jerusalem than the impossibility of identifying with exactitude the location of its former gates, the scene of so many thrilling events. Fire and sword, plunder and time, have removed those landmarks of great historic deeds. These gone, we are left to conjecture as to the location of the "Valley Gate," through which Nehemiah passed on his nocturnal exploration to ascertain the condition of the city;[2] of the "East Gate," from which Jeremiah went forth with the ancients of the people to the Valley of the Son of Hinnom, to illustrate

[1] 1 Kings, vi., 7. [2] Neh., ii., 13.

the destruction of the Jews by breaking in their presence a potter's vessel;[1] of the "Horse Gate," out of which the ambitious Queen Athaliah was led to execution;[2] of the "Gate betwixt the two walls," "whence Zedekiah and all his men of war fled before the King of Babylon;[3] and of the "Gate of Benjamin," where the king sat when the kind Ebed-Melech, the Ethiopian, interceded in behalf of Jeremiah, then in a loathsome dungeon beneath the royal palace.[4]

Of the seven gates which penetrate the walls of modern Jerusalem, the noblest and most ancient of the number is the one standing in the mouth of the broad depression sweeping southward through the city, called the Damascus Gate. Surmounted with turrets and battlements, it not only presents an imposing appearance, but its ornamental architecture indicates its Saracenic origin and style. Judging from the formation of the ground it occupies, it probably marks the site of an older gateway. As of old, so now, from its portal runs the great northern road to Nablous; and from it, no doubt, Saul of Tarsus went forth, leading his band of persecutors to crush the infant church of Jesus in Damascus. Constructed in the form of an elliptical arch, flanked with massive towers of great antiquity, and inclosed with huge doors incased with iron, it wears the appearance of a prison. Within is a large chamber, grim and gloomy, formed by the arch and towers, and from which a square-shaped and winding staircase leads to the top of the parapet. Guarded by four Turkish soldiers, the traveler has illustrated before him St. Luke's description of the Roman guard on the night of our Lord's trial: "And when they had kindled a fire in the midst of the hall, and were set down together, Peter sat down among them."[5] In the northeast corner of the hall, within the gateway, the soldiers build a fire of juniper coals when the weather is cold, the smoke of which deepens the gloom of the already blackened walls.

Midway between this gate and the northeast corner of the city is the "Gate of Flowers," consisting of a small portal penetrating a tower, but which is now inaccessible, having been walled up since 1834. In the eastern wall of the city is St. Stephen's Gate, a simple structure, and without ornaments, except the carved figures of two lions over the entrance. From

---

[1] Jer., xix., 2.   [2] 2 Kings, xi., 16–19.   [3] Ib., xxv., 4.
[4] Jer., xxxviii., 7–13.   [5] Luke, xxii., 55.

it a path descends the steep sides of Moriah, and, crossing the small stone bridge that spans the Valley of the Kidron, leads up to the Garden of Gethsemane and to the Mount of Olives. Compelled to fly before the rebellious Absalom, it was out of the gate that stood on the site of the present one that David fled, and, a thousand years later, a greater than David went forth out of the same portal on the night of his betrayal. As it is the chief entrance to the city on the east, streams of pilgrims from the Heights of Benjamin on the north, and from the Valley of the Jordan on the east, incessantly flow in and out of this well-known gate.

Situated in the southern wall, nearly in the centre of the Tyropean Valley, is the "Gate of the Western Africans," which is of inferior construction, and is opened and shut according to the caprice of the governor. Fortunately, it was opened when I passed, an event which may not occur again for many years. From it a path descends to the charming gardens of Silwân. On the summit of a ridge beyond is the Gate of Zion, the cleanest and most quiet of the seven. But the great and most usually thronged portal of the town is the Yâffa Gate, located in the western wall of the city, between Mount Zion and Mount Akra. Consisting of a massive square tower, it has a quadrangular hall within. Probably standing on the site of Nehemiah's "Valley Gate," it is the point to which all the great thoroughfares converge, from Bethlehem and Hebron on the south, and from Yâffa on the west. Carefully guarded during the day by a band of soldiers, all the gates are closed at night when the evening gun is fired. From a superstition as suggestive of fear as it is precautionary against surprise, the gates are closed on Friday between the hours of twelve and one, because of an old and prevalent tradition that on that day and at that hour the Christians will attempt to retake Jerusalem.

Running north and south through the very heart of the city is a broad depression, and coming up from Siloam, on the south, is the Tyropean Valley, joining the former at the northeast corner of Mount Zion, where the latter abruptly diverges to the westward, intersecting the Valley of Gihon. Upon its divergence hangs the long and fierce controversy touching the topography of the ancient city. Though its upper section is filled with rubbish from twenty to fifty feet deep, yet there is a perceptible ascent from Christian Street to the Hippic Tower, as there is a descent from the Yáffa Gate into the valley beyond. If the intervening ridge is not accumulated earth, it is difficult to conceive how Mount Zion could ever have been the "strong-hold" represented by sacred and profane writers. The construction of the three famous towers on the northwest portion of the hill by Herod the Great was not to supply a natural defect, but to honor the king's favorites, and to be the depositories of his royal treasures. As recent excavations in the vicinity confirm the correctness of the supposition, so future excavations will remove the last doubt that this is the "Valley of the Cheesemongers" described by Josephus, separating the "upper city from the lower."[1]

As of old, Jerusalem stands upon five hills, formed in part by valleys without the city, and by depressions within. Though, when viewed from within the town, their altitude is not great, yet in their general outlines all are distinctly defined. Of these hills, covering an area of four and a half miles in circumference and half a mile in diameter, Zion, Moriah, and Ophel are mentioned by the inspired historians, while, together with the former, Akra and Bezetha are described by Josephus. Rising in the form of a parallelogram, Mount Zion is the largest of the five sacred hills. Attaining an average height of more than 500 feet above the surrounding valleys, its southern and western sides are as rugged as they are steep. Though lower than the northwest corner of Akra, yet, when viewed either from the Tyropean or the Hinnom valleys, the bold brow of Zion is seen to best advantage, justifying the confidence reposed in it as a strong defensive position. Sloping down toward the King's Gardens, where three valleys meet, its southeastern sides are terraced from base to summit, and planted with corn and olives, fulfilling the words of the prophet, "Zion shall be plowed like a field."[2] Directly opposite the Haram, the naked rocks rise from the "Vale of the Cheesemongers" more than thirty feet high, and on the verge of the precipice once stood the "House of the Mighty." Less than half the hill is included within the present walls, occupied by the Citadel, the English Church, the American Consulate, the Post-office, the Prussian Hospital, the Church of St. James, the Jewish Synagogue, private residences, and the Lepers' Quarters; while beyond the walls are the Diocesan school-house, the Ar-

[1] Book v., chap. iv., p. 528.   [2] Jer., xxvi, 18.

menian Convent, the Tomb of David, and the Protestant Cemetery.

Emotions of joy and sadness are awakened as one stands upon the site of those great historic events which have filled the world with their renown, and impressed their inevitable results, for "weal or woe," upon the opinions and actions of mankind. As the religious sensibilities of our nature are most susceptible of excitement, so no spot on earth excites the mind to the same degree as where the events of sacred history occurred. Around Mount Zion cluster memories of human shame and glory. Here the defiant words of the Jebusites

MOUNT ZION AND TOWER OF HIPPICUS.

kindled the martial soul of David, who, summoning all his military skill and courage for the attack, captured the "stronghold of Jebus." Here he reigned for thirty-three years in unrivaled wealth and glory, and here he penned many of his sublime psalms. Here the ruder palace of the father gave way to the grander palace of the son. Here, in regal magnificence, unequaled in the annals of kings, Solomon held his court, displaying a wisdom as vast as his wealth was exhaustless, and achieving for himself a name that was borne to the uttermost parts of the earth in accents of praise and gladness. Here, for a thousand years, their descendants reigned in power and glory; and here, on the very summit of their pleasures and greatness, they, with fourteen of their successors to the throne, were entombed. Here stood the palace of Caiaphas, in whose judgment-hall Jesus was tried and Peter swore. To gratify personal ambition, and perpetuate the memory of his royal favorites, here Herod the Great reared those three massive towers which were the pride and admiration of the triumphant Titus. Calling one Mariamne, in honor of his queen, whom he afterward slew in a passion of jealousy, he named the second Phasaëlus, after his friend, and the third Hippicus, in memory of his brother, both of whom were slain in battle, fighting in his behalf.[1]

Of these towers but one remains, that of Hippicus, which is the citadel of the modern town. Spanning the moat is an old bridge leading to the castle. Several flights of stone steps lead to the parapet, on which a number of guns are mounted, fit only for firing occasional salutes, and from the top an extraordinary view is gained of Jerusalem and its environs. Aside from its dingy appearance, Hippicus is invested with thrilling associations. With an antiquity unquestioned, the most reliable authorities agree that it occupies its ancient site. As it now stands, it represents two great eras in the world's history—that of Herod and that of the Crusaders; the foundations belonging to the former, the superstructure to the latter. Composed of a group of square towers, it resembles a quadrangle, though not a perfect square, its sides varying from sixty to seventy feet in length. The tower next to the Yäffa Gate is the most interesting, as it is the most ancient. The height of the antique portion, from the bottom of the broad fosse, is forty feet, and, being entirely solid, it has for nineteen centuries resisted the battering-rams of the Romans, the cannon of the Egyptians, and the prying curiosity of the modern explorer. Recent excavations have shown that for several feet upward from its base the foundation is formed of the natural rock, hewn

[1] Josephus, B. J., b. v., c. iv., p. 3.

into shape, and faced with immense stones, distinctly beveled, indicating their Jewish origin, and evidently remaining where they were originally placed. In addition to its antiquity, this tower is of great importance, as it marks the starting-point of the first and second walls of the ancient city, and unmistakably points out their general direction.

Leading from the Hippic Tower to the south wall of the city is a spacious and grand avenue. On its western side are the *Caserne di Sion* and the residence of the Armenian patriarch; opposite are the English Church and the Armenian Convent. The entrance to the convent is through a large but simple portal, opening into a court around which rise the dormitories, capable of accommodating 8000 pilgrims. Adjoining the monastery is the Church of St. James, the most sumptuous building of the kind in the East, and, next to the Church of the Holy Sepulchre, the largest religious edifice in Jerusalem. Belonging formerly to the Georgians, who failed to pay the enormous tax levied upon it, it was sold to the Armenians in the fifteenth century. The interior is gorgeous to a fault. The floor is inlaid with rich mosaics; the pillars supporting the roof are incased with tiles of blue and green porcelain, and ornamented with gilded crosses, and the walls are decorated with pictures of the Byzantine school. The high altar is indescribably grand, adorned with silver vases filled with flowers, with pictures representing scriptural scenes, and with golden lamps suspended from the ceiling.

But the chief attraction of the church is the chapel of St. James, marking at once the scene of his martyrdom and the place of his burial. All that affection could suggest, art produce, and wealth procure, adorns this splendid mausoleum. The doors are enameled with a mosaic-work of coral and mother-of-pearl, dazzling with their brilliancy the eye of the beholder, and charming him with their extraordinary beauty. The interior is faced with polished marble; from the ceiling hang golden lamps, ever burning; while from a costly censer incense ascends in perpetual memory of the sainted dead.

Around this sepulchral church are lovely gardens, dressed and beautified by the monks of Armenia, whose love for flowers and trees is only excelled by the taste displayed in training them. From these gardens an iron portal opens toward the Zion Gate, 100 yards beyond which is the traditional House of Caiaphas, dating back in its authentic history to the fourth century, and now a dependency on the large establishment within the walls. Within this house is a small cell, richly decorated with pearl and porcelain, in which Christ is said to have been kept in durance the night previous to his crucifixion. Near the prison is a marble statue of Jesus tied to the pillar of flagellation, which devout women were approaching on their knees and kissing; and just beyond is the legendary stone which closed the mouth of our Lord's sepulchre.

Not far to the south is the Tomb of David, now a mosque, whose graceful minaret never fails to attract the traveler's attention as he approaches the Holy City from the south. The edifice was once a Christian church, and, besides covering the tomb of the renowned King of Israel, contains the "upper room" where Christ ate the Passover with his disciples,[1] and where he washed their feet;[2] where, after his resurrection, the disciples were assembled with closed doors, and, Jesus appearing in their midst, said, "Peace be unto you;"[3] where the doubting Thomas was permitted to thrust his hand into the Redeemer's side;[4] and where, on the day of Pentecost, the apostles received the Holy Ghost.[5] The "upper room" is a large chamber, fifty feet long and thirty wide, with ribbed ceiling and pendents. Its appearance indicates great age, and though, through neglect, it wears a dreary aspect, it is so firmly built that, without violence, it will stand for a thousand years to come. In the middle of the fourth century it was regarded by Cyril, then Bishop of Jerusalem, as the scene of the Pentecost, and a few years thereafter it was seen by Epiphanius, who declared it one of the few buildings which had escaped destruction when Titus captured the city. Whether this is the "guest-chamber" where so many great events occurred or not, Zion is the designated place whence were to go forth the conquering forces of the Messiah: "Out of Zion shall go forth the law, and the word of the Lord from Jerusalem." Zion was always the place of convocation, and the only one in the Holy City, excepting Mount Moriah, where great assemblies could gather; and somewhere on its broad summit the representative Jews out of all nations were in solemn convocation when, "hearing a sound from heaven as of

---

[1] Luke, xxii., 12   [2] John, xiii., 12.   [3] Ib., xx, 19.
[4] John, xx., 25.   [5] Acts, ii., 1.

a rushing mighty wind," the vast multitude came together, unto whom the promise of the Spirit had been made.[1] In the east end of the room is a small niche where it is said Christ sat at the "Last Supper," and where the Latin monk now sits when, at stated periods, he is permitted to celebrate mass within its consecrated precincts; and here, in imitation of our Lord, the Franciscan monks wash the worn feet of the pious pilgrim, who, from the uttermost parts of the earth, has come to worship at these holiest of earthly shrines.

Beneath this mosque is the reputed Tomb of David. Of its antiquity there can be no doubt, as no historic fact is better attested; of its identity there is no dispute, as Jews, Christians, and Moslem revere it as only second in holiness to the site of the Temple. At all hours of the day venerable Jews and beautiful Jewesses may be seen there, silently standing at its closed portal, as if half expectant that their Great King will again awake to power, and vindicate their rights. With undying affection the Jews have ever regarded the sepulchres of their fathers, and Nehemiah assigned as a reason for his sad countenance in the presence of Artaxerxes "that the place of my fathers' sepulchres lieth waste, and the gates thereof are consumed with fire."[2] And when that noble prophet returned to his beloved Jerusalem, he completed the wall which Shallum had commenced, extending it "unto the place over against the sepulchres of David, and to the pool that was made, and unto the house of the mighty."[3]

According to Josephus, Solomon interred his father here "with great magnificence, and with all the funeral pomp which kings used to be buried with;"[4] and deposited immense wealth within the tomb, which remained undisturbed through all the revolutions of the kingdom, down to within 150 years of the Christian era. Driven by the stern necessities of war, Hyrcanus, the son of Simon Maccabeus, and successor of his father to the high-priesthood, plundered the royal vault, extracting therefrom the enormous sum of 3000 talents of silver, which he gave to Antiochus Pius to raise the siege of Jerusalem and grant him terms of peace.[5]

Finding the treasure in an adjoining vault, Hyrcanus did not approach the dust of David; but years later, hearing of the

---

[1] Acts, ii., 2-39. [2] Neh., ii., 3. [3] Ib., iii., 16.
[4] Anti B., vii., c. xv., s. 3. [5] Ib.

success of the son of Simon, and wanting means to complete his magnificent works in the city, Herod the Great made a similar attempt; but failing to discover the treasure, he essayed to enter the very chamber which contains the bodies of David and Solomon, and was only deterred in the consummation of his purpose by the accidental death of two of the guard, who were killed by a flame suddenly bursting upon them.[1]

In his interpretation of the Messianic prophecies, on the day of Pentecost St. Peter refers to this venerable monument, declaring that "his sepulchre is with us unto this day."[2] At the close of the twelfth century, one of the walls of the building covering the tomb gave way, and, in order to repair it, the patriarch of the city commanded his workmen to take stones from the original wall of Zion; in gathering them, they uncovered the mouth of a cave; on exploring it, they reached a large hall supported by marble pillars incased with gold, and in it were two tablets, and on each lay a crown and sceptre of gold. Near the sarcophagi were iron chests carefully sealed, and, when they were on the point of opening them, a blast of wind issuing from the cavern drove them back, throwing them senseless to the ground. Recovering, they heard a voice commanding them to depart. On reporting their adventure to the patriarch, he concluded that what they had mistaken for tables were the tombs of David and Solomon, and immediately ordered the vault to be closed. In 1839, Sir Moses and Lady Montefiore were permitted, by paying an immense sum, to look through the "lattice of a trellised door," and behold the tombs of their renowned ancestors.[3] Of the size and appearance of the sepulchre it is impossible to speak with accuracy, as the fanatical Moslems, who guard it with religious superstition, only suffer the traveler to approach the outer entrance. Like most of the tombs of that age, it is probably hewn in the solid rock, and decorated in a manner becoming royalty; but of its proportions and grandeur the world must remain in ignorance till the Holy City shall have passed into the hands of Christians, when those of every faith shall be permitted to linger around the dust of Israel's great kings, who sleep in death amid the scenes of their greatest glory.

A few paces within the wall, and to the east of the Zion

---

[1] Josephus, anti B., xvi., c. vii., s. 1.   [2] Acts, ii., 29.
[3] Barclay's City of the Great King, p. 214, 215.

Gate, are the "quarters of the lepers." Though formerly excluded from the city, they are now suffered to build their wretched huts along the wall. In obedience to a law prevalent throughout the East, all lepers are compelled to live together in three colonies, and it is a coincidence no less singular than true that the cities in which these colonies are located were the residences of three historic lepers — Naaman of Damascus,[1] Gehazi of Nablous,[2] and King Azariah of Jerusalem.[3] Numbering in all 200, those on Mount Zion are supported by charity. Their homes are miserable huts, low, dark, and loathsome. Allowed to marry only with each other, their offspring, when born, are usually fair, and apparently healthy. Retaining their health and beauty up to the period of puberty, the fatal disease, like a scrofulous spot, then makes its appearance on a finger, on the nose, or on the cheek, and, spreading over the system, it ultimately reaches some vital organ, and the unhappy victim dies.

Preparing their evening meal, men and women moved with feeble step from hut to hut, exchanging articles of food, and also their rude cooking utensils. Their garments were old and torn, their voices were dry and husky, their faces were red like a coal of fire half extinguished, their eyes swollen and restless, their hair was gone, their lips and cheeks, nose and ears were corroded with ulcers, and the flesh of their hands and arms had been eaten away, leaving the bone red and bare.

Standing afar off, as in the days of Christ, they stretched out their hands, and begged in tones so piteously that none could resist their entreaties. In the plaintive accents of their native Arabic, they hailed me, "Pilgrim, give me; for the Lord's sake, give me." Dropping a few piastres in the folds of their infected robes, I hastened away, hearing their tones of pity, and seeing their horrid forms in memory days after the spectacle had been withdrawn. Alas for them to whom this world is one great hospital, and life the vestibule of the grave!

In a country where sanitary regulations are ignored, it is not strange that such persons are allowed to marry and propagate their unfortunate progeny. Their marriage, like that of idiots and lunatics, should be treated by the government as a crime against humanity. Were marriages among them prohibited, this leprous race would soon become extinct, and society would

[1] 2 Kings, v., 12.   [2] Ib., v., 27.   [3] Ib., xv., 5.

he relieved of one of its worst maladies. In cases of spontaneous leprosy the victim is banished from his home, and, becoming a denizen of the infected quarter, he contracts matrimonial alliances, and perpetuates the evil. Though the continuance of the disease is mostly hereditary, yet occasionally it is contracted. While only the proximate cause of leprosy has been determined, the Scriptures assume it to be an evil inflicted upon the guilty for the commission of heinous offenses against the divine law; and, if modesty permitted, it could be easily shown that the unmentionable crimes too prevalent in the East justly merit such a condemnation. Retaining all its ancient characteristics, leprosy still infects the garments worn by leprous persons, and also the stones and mortar of the buildings they occupy. Two centuries ago, Calmet made the suggestion that the former was caused by vermin infecting clothes and skins, and the latter was caused by animalculæ which, like mites in cheese, erode the stones and mortar.

Connected with Mount Zion on the north by a small isthmus is the Hill Akra. Though not mentioned in the Bible by a name at present known, it holds a conspicuous place in Jewish history as the scene of some of the most fearful struggles between the defenders and the assailants of the city. Called by Josephus the "Lower City," to distinguish it from the "Upper City," situated on Mount Zion, it is described by him as being separated from the latter by the Tyropean Valley, the buildings on the two hills facing each other, and terminating at the intervening ravine. At present Akra is a long, stony ridge of a gibbous shape. Extending from the Yáffa Gate to the northwest corner of the town, and including the site of the Church of the Holy Sepulchre, it extends eastward to the western wall of the Haram. It is now the Christian quarter of the city, and the site of several fine convents. Though covered with buildings, its gibbous form is perceptible, both in ascending from St. Stephen's Street, and also from the Yáffa Gate. Originally it was crowned with a lofty rock, which proved such a strong position that the Syrians under Antiochus Epiphanes successfully resisted the attacks of the Jews for twenty years, and, after the enemy had been dislodged, it "required the constant labor of all Jerusalem during three years to level it" to its present height.

Separated from Akra by a valley which the Asmoneans partially filled up is the Hill Bezetha, a long, irregular ridge running north by west from the Temple area. On the east it rises abruptly from the Valley of Jehoshaphat, on the south it is separated from Mount Moriah by a deep fosse, while on the north it has been cut into two parts by a broad and deep excavation. When carefully compared, the two parts exactly correspond. The north wall of the city crosses the southern half of this ridge, and in the face of the opposite section is the famous Grotto of Jeremiah. It was to inclose this entire hill, then extending 1000 yards north and south, and from 500 to 1000 east and west, that Herod Agrippa built the third wall of ancient Jerusalem. Up to that time it was the suburb of the city, and, though the last of the five hills to become inhabited, it ultimately became the most populous, receiving as its name Bezetha — "The New City." It is now the Moslem quarter of the town. On the traditional site of Herod's palace stands the Mosque of the Dervishes. True to their low conceptions of architecture, the Mohammedan dwellings are destitute of taste and design. On the northeast corner of this ridge there is a large area devoted to pasturage, where the pasha's elegant horses are kept. Not far from St. Stephen's Gate is the Gothic Church of St. Anne, recently presented to the Emperor of the French by the Sultan for services rendered during the Crimean War. It has been repaired by order of its new proprietor, and around it the Latins are erecting a nunnery for the "Sisters of the Sacred Heart."

CHAPTER III.

Mount Moriah.—Site of Solomon's Temple.—Surrounding Walls.—Great Fosse.—Pasha's Palace—Council Chamber of the Jewish Sanhedrim.—Jews' Place of Wailing.—Their cruel Treatment.—Scene on Friday Afternoon.—Mournful Spectacle.—High-priest.—Prophecy fulfilled.—Solomon's Bridge.—Its Antiquity.—Temple Area.—Tower of Antonia.—Shrines within the Inclosure.—Imposing View.—Dome of the Chain.—Mosque of Omar.—Its grand Exterior.—Its History.—Its Portals.—Its magnificent Interior.—Sacred Rock within the Mosque.—Traditions.—Scene of the Offering of Isaac and of other Scriptural Events.—Mosque of El-Aksa.—Its Interior and History.—Solomon's subterranean Passageway.—Extraordinary Workmanship.—Mosque of Jesus.—Solomon's great Vaults.—They reflect his Genius.—Evidence of their Antiquity.—Solomon's great Lake beneath his Temple.—His Work.—Vicissitudes of Mount Moriah.

GREAT events monopolize great names. Originally the term "Land of Moriah" was applied to Jerusalem and its environs, but in the lapse of ages the name "Moriah" became more restricted, and is now employed to designate the smallest of the five hills on which the Holy City stands. Mount Moriah was formerly a continuation of the Bezetha ridge, from which it is now separated by a deep fosse, traditionally called Bethesda. Bounded on the west by the Tyropean Valley and the broad depression coming down from the Damascus Gate, it has the Fosse of Antonia on the north, the Valley of Jehoshaphat on the east, and Mount Ophel on the south. Ophel is also a part of the Bezetha ridge. Its summit is 100 feet lower than the top of Moriah, and is separated from the latter by the Haram wall. Having a length of 1560 feet, it is 300 wide from brow to brow. It is the fifth hill of the city, and is at present terraced like Mount Zion, and planted with fruit-trees. In the reign of Solomon it was included within the city walls, and after the return of the Jews from captivity under Nehemiah it was occupied by the Nethinims, or Temple servants.

What is now known as the Temple area is a beautiful inclosure of thirty-six acres, surrounded by a wall nine feet thick at the base and three at the parapet, and ranging from fifty to eighty feet high on the exterior, and from ten to fifteen on the interior, according to the surface of the ground. It is composed of large blocks of limestone, many of which are of great antiquity. The area being inclosed on the east and south by the city walls, which have already been described, it only remains to consider those on the north and south.

A hundred feet south of St. Stephen's Gate the north wall of the Haram commences, running westward 1060 feet, nearly the whole of which is encumbered with buildings clinging to the side and top. Judging from the description of the extent and form of the Temple area as given by Josephus,[1] this wall has been carried some 600 feet north of the line of its original location. It is now penetrated by three portals—the largest and most beautiful one is reached by a path from St. Stephen's Gate. Extending from this portal east and west is one of the most remarkable excavations in Jerusalem, supposed to be the fosse mentioned by Josephus for the defense of the Tower of Antonia.[2] In length 460 feet, 130 broad, and seventy-five deep, its sides are constructed of small stones covered with cement, suggesting that in times of peace it served as a reservoir, and in war as a moat. In the southwest corner are two high-arched vaults, extending side by side under the modern buildings. Whether the water which supplied this reservoir came from the clouds, or was conveyed by a subterranean conduit from the Pool of Hezekiah, or from the aqueduct of Pontius Pilate, is an undecided question. The fosse itself is one of the greatest monuments of antiquity, pointing back to the days of national grandeur, and to those sanguinary sieges when Antonia, rising from the "abyss," stood a tower of strength against the assaulting foe.

Surmounting this wall on its western end, and extending a distance of 370 feet, is the Pasha's Palace, a pile of irregular and ill-shaped buildings externally, but containing within all the magnificence and luxuries of an Oriental abode. From the Governor's House the western wall of the Haram runs southward 1528 feet, and is nearly hidden from view by the structures built against it. Seven streets approach the sacred inclosure from the west, having at their *termini* as many gates, most of which correspond in their location to the sites of the

[1] Anti B., xv., c. xi., s. 3. [2] B. J., b. v., c. v., s. 8.

ancient portals of the Temple. Attached to this wall, near the Gate es-Silsilah, is the Hall of the "Turkish Divan," which is identical with the council-chamber of the Jewish Sanhedrim. It is a square stone building, with arched ceiling and flattened domes, wearing the aspect of great age, and without violence will endure for ages to come. Here, in all probability, the apostles were arraigned for trial,[1] and here "stood up Gamaliel, a doctor of the law, had in reputation among all the people, and advised the council touching these men."[2]

Adjoining the building on the south is the "Jews' Place of Wailing," a spot no less remarkable for its antiquity than for the touching scenes which there transpire. It is reached by a narrow lane running out of the Jewish Quarter, and consists of a small quadrangular area 112 feet long, thirty wide, and is inclosed by common dwellings on the west and the Haram wall on the east. Well paved and cleanly kept, it is so secluded as to allow the worshipers to lament their departed national greatness undisturbed. The chief attraction of the spot is the five courses of large stones, bearing the well-known bevel, and remaining *in situ* where they were placed thousands of years ago. Time has dealt gently with them, and, though slightly displaced by the shock of earthquakes, and worn smooth by the kisses of pilgrims, they are well preserved.

Here, as before an altar, on each returning Friday the descendants of Abraham assemble to bewail their once mighty but now fallen nation. Proscribed by their Moslem masters, this is the nearest point of approach to which they are allowed to come, and even for a boon so humble Mohammedan cupidity demands an exorbitant sum. Unparalleled in their history, seldom have a people been treated with such unmitigated cruelty as the Jews. From the time of Adrian to the age of Constantine they were expelled from Jerusalem, and it was only by the clemency of the latter emperor that they were permitted to behold their native city from the neighboring hills; and it was by bribing the Roman guard that they at length gained admission to Jerusalem once a year, on the anniversary of its capture by Titus, to weep over the ruins of their fallen Temple. Though now suffered to dwell within the walls of the city, it is instant death to a Jew to cross the threshold of the sacred inclosure. From the beginning of the twelfth century

[1] Acts, iv., 6. [2] Ib., v., 34.

it has been their custom to linger around these ancient stones and make their complaint to Jehovah.

JEWS' PLACE OF WAILING.

It was two o'clock on a lovely Friday afternoon when, for the first time, I threaded the narrow streets leading to this mournful spot. About seventy men and women of all ages were engaged in their devotions. In their midst stood the high-priest, whose tall and majestic form distinguished him from those around him, and whose open and intelligent face was pale and sorrowful as he mingled his prayers and tears with a people whose ruined fortunes he was powerless to retrieve. Accustomed to see him, attended by his two sons, walking thoughtfully the streets of what was once the imperial city of his fathers, I had become familiar with his noble bearing and with the calm expression of his Jewish countenance; but, moved by the reflections of his own powerful mind, and touched with sympathy by the scene before him, he lifted up his voice and wept.

Around him were groups of his people, some of whom were standing, some sitting, some kneeling, while others were lying prostrate upon the stone pavement. Here sat a group of Jewish matrons, whose black tresses time had whitened, weeping as if broken-hearted; there stood an old man, leaning, like the patriarch Jacob, upon his staff, reciting, with faltering voice, his complaint before the Lord. Nearer the wall were men in the prime of life, absorbed in their recitations from the Prophets; while along the whole length of the wall, with their sacred books resting against it, were men and women of all ages, reading, weeping, and ever and anon smiting their troubled breasts.

In the northeast corner of the inclosure, half hidden by the pavement, is one stone more sacred than the rest. Around it were gathered the rich and elegantly attired mothers and daughters of Israel, waiting to bow low and affectionately kiss the relic as a thing of love.

Some, with a copy of Isaiah before them, audibly read, "Be not wroth very sore, O Lord, neither remember iniquity forever; behold, see, we beseech thee, we are all thy people. Thy holy cities are a wilderness, Zion is a wilderness, Jerusalem a desolation. Our holy and beautiful house, where our fathers praised thee, is burnt up with fire, and all our pleasant things are laid waste. Wilt thou refrain thyself for these things, O Lord? wilt thou hold thy peace and afflict us very sore?"[1] Others, reading from the Psalms, would passionately break forth, "O God, the heathen have come into thine inheritance; thy holy temple have they defiled; they have laid Jerusalem on heaps. We are become a reproach to our neighbors, a scorn and derision to them that are round about. How long, Lord? wilt thou be angry forever? shall thy jealousy burn like fire?"[2]

[1] Isa., lxvi., 9-12.   [2] Ps. lxxix., 1-5.

It is the opinion of the Jews that this portion of the wall belonged to the court of the Temple, and not to the Temple itself; but, in conceding with them the great antiquity of these stones, and that they remain intact, we do not thereby affect our Lord's prediction touching the destruction of Jerusalem. Josephus informs us that such was the unevenness of Mount Moriah, that in laying the foundation of the wall for the western court of the Temple it was necessary to lay it far below the general surface of the ground, which is evident from the fact that while the inside of the wall is only twelve feet high, the outside is seventy feet high.[1] To this circumstance is due the preservation of this wall as it was originally laid, and also to the fact that the Romans, beginning their work of destruction within the area, first removed the upper layers, throwing the broken fragments over the outside, which, accumulating at its base, inhumed the lower courses, and literally fulfilled the Savior's words, "And shall lay thee even with the ground."[2] In every particular that fearful prediction was fulfilled. The Romans cast a trench about the devoted city, keeping the inhabitants in on every side; and such was the utter destruction which followed their capture of the city, that, in the words of the historian, "there was nothing left to make those that came thither believe it had ever been inhabited."[3]

Owing to the rapid descent of the ground in the direction of the southwest corner of the Haram wall, lower courses of stones are there exposed to view. Measuring thirty-one feet in length, seven in width, and five in height, the chief cornerstone is no doubt identical with the one placed there by order of Solomon, and now marks the southwest angle of the area which inclosed his Temple. Thirty-nine feet to the north is the foot of the ancient bridge which once spanned the Tyropean Valley. Viewed casually, these stones appear to have been pushed out from their places by some violent concussion within, but, when examined with care, they indicate the design of an architect, and the occupancy of their original position. Consisting of three courses of huge stones, projecting one over the other as they rise, they form the segment of an arch. With their external surface hewn to a regular curve, they each measure from twenty to twenty-four feet long, and from five to

---

[1] Anti B., xv., c. xv., s. 3.   [2] Luke, xix., 44.
[3] Wars of the Jews, b. vii., c. i.

six high; and extending along the wall about forty feet, they spring therefrom nearly the same distance. From the apparent width of the valley from this arch to the precipitous rocks

SOLOMON'S BRIDGE.

on the eastern brow of Mount Zion, this bridge was 350 feet long, and consisted of five arches, supported by four intervening piers.

Without giving us the date of its construction, Josephus speaks of this bridge as existing in his day,[1] and the colossal proportion of the remaining blocks, together with the manner in which they are dressed, evince their great age, and also their Jewish origin. It is older than Herod, as it is mentioned in connection with Pompey's siege of the Holy City, which occurred twenty years prior to the accession of the Idumean.[2] It is not, therefore, unreasonable to suppose it as old as Solomon, whose wonderful works have ever been the admiration of mankind. Attended by a gorgeous retinue of princes and

[1] Wars of the Jews, b. vi., c. vi. [2] Antiquities of the Jews, b. xiv., c. iv.

soldiers, he often passed over it from his palace on Zion to the Temple of the Highest on Mount Moriah; and to this magnificent structure the sacred historian probably alludes, who, in describing the effect of Solomon's works upon the mind of the Queen of the South, declares that when she beheld " the ascent by which he went up unto the house of the Lord, there was no more spirit in her."[1] Centuries later, it was no doubt the way by which the Redeemer frequently passed from the Temple to the "Upper City;" and when the day of retribution came, and the hour of the destruction of Jerusalem drew nigh, the triumphant Titus stood upon one of its remaining sections and addressed the infatuated Jews, appealing to the remnant to spare themselves from farther carnage by submitting to Rome.

These mural examinations awakened a desire to stand, if possible, upon the very site of Solomon's Temple. This, however, was both difficult and expensive. For many centuries the inclosure, together with the Mosque of Omar, had been closed against all Christians, but, thanks to the civilization of the West, the fanaticism of the East has yielded to a superior power, and many places hitherto inaccessible are now open to the Christian traveler.

The Temple area is an oblong quadrangle, extending north and south 1600 feet, and more than 1000 east and west. Since the reign of Herod the Great it has been enlarged, and now includes the space formerly occupied by the Tower of Antonia. It is only on this supposition that its present dimensions can be made to correspond with the measurements of Josephus, who describes it to have been a square,[2] and such it is if the above-mentioned space is excluded. If a line be drawn from the south side of the Golden Gate, and at right angles to it, to a point 150 feet north of the modern gate, called Bal el-Katanên, an area is left for the Temple and its courts 1018 feet long and 926 wide, which, in popular language, would be called a square, and to the eye presents such a figure.

On the space north of this imaginary line stood the famous Tower of Antonia, constructed by Judas Maccabeus, or by some other member of the Asmonean family, and which, at a subsequent period, was enlarged and rendered exceedingly grand by Herod the Great, who called it Antonia, in honor of Anthony, his benefactor. Quadrangular in form, it had a tower

[1] 1 Kings, x., 5.   [2] Antiquities, b. xv., c. xi.

at each angle, three of which had an elevation of 87½ feet each, while the one at the southeast corner rose to the height of 122½ feet, uniting in this structure the strength of a fortress with the splendor of a palace. The interior was adorned with baths, courts, and porticoes. In the very centre of the inclosure was an open space for encampments, from which extended elegant passage-ways, connecting the tower with the colonnades of the Temple. From a rock eighty feet high, situated in the northwest corner, rose the Acropolis, seventy feet higher, which was incased with polished stones. As this was the fortress of the Temple, here was stationed the military guard; and, during the jurisdiction of the Romans, it was the seat of public justice. On the exterior of the present wall are two arches, now walled up, where the *Scala Santa*, or Pilate's Staircase, which led to his judgment-hall, formerly stood. Regarding it with religious reverence, Constantine removed it to Rome, where it was placed in the Basilica of St. John Lateran; and, believing that it was once pressed by the Savior's feet, the pious Catholic now ascends it upon his knees. A few paces to the west of these arches, and spanning the Via Dolorosa, is the *Ecce Homo* arch, traditionally marking the spot where Pilate, having brought forth our Lord, exclaimed, "Behold the man!"[1]

Yielding to the conquering arms of Titus, the Tower of Antonia was taken by the Romans, who, razing it to its foundation, left it a mass of ruins. Cutting away the Acropolis rock, they left but a projecting fragment, now the site of the Pasha's Palace. Removing the elegant courts and porticoes to plant their engines of war against the Temple, they cleared an area 500 feet long and 1000 wide, which is now in part a scarped rock, and the rest is dotted with patches of grass. Inhumed beneath the ruins lay the deep fosse, the foundation of the northeast tower, and the base of the loftier tower at the southeast angle, all of which remain to our own day, pointing to Antonia as one of the grandest of human structures.

Equally superstitious with the Latins and Greeks, the Moslems have many shrines within the Temple area consecrated either to the memory of their great Prophet, or to that of some eminent saint. Near a graceful minaret, which rises from the scarped rock, is a small dome, marking the spot where Solo-

[1] John, xix., 5.

MOUNT MORIAH, WITH A VIEW OF THE MOSQUE OF OMAR.

mon, after the completion of the Temple, stood and prayed. Along the western side of the Haram are cloisters, with square pillars and pointed arches, devoted to meditation and prayer, and to the accommodation of dervishes, eunuchs, and serpent-charmers. In a small room beneath one of the cloisters is the legendary iron ring to which Mohammed tied his Alborak on the night of his ascension.

In the centre of the oblong area within the walls is a raised platform fifteen feet high, 550 long north and south, and 450 wide east and west. It is paved with Palestine marble, and reached by eight flights of stone steps, spanned by light Saracenic arches. Ascending the platform by the northern steps, we lingered for a moment to enjoy a scene of extraordinary beauty. On either side rose massive walls, with parapet and tower; beneath the platform, and extending to the farthest verge of the inclosure, were fields of grass adorned with flowers; decked in all their vernal beauty were sombre olives, lofty palms, and graceful acacias, and near them were marble fountains sparkling in the morning light; beneath the trees white-veiled women reclined, and turbaned Turks moved softly through the foliage; around the platform rose airy arches; on it stood elegant pulpits, carved niches for prayer, and miniature cupolas of faultless symmetry; while from the very centre rose the Mosque of Omar, enameled with tiles of intricate patterns and of variant hues, reflecting the colors of the rainbow, and surmounted with that dome of domes, resplendent with the early light. Secluded from the outer world, peace reigned within, and no sound was heard save the solitary call of the muezzin from the balcony of a neighboring minaret. Among the minor objects of interest within the Haram is the Kubbet es-Silsilah—"the Dome of the Chain." Situated twenty feet east from the great mosque, it is a small fane of rare beauty. From seventeen slender marble columns spring semicircular arches, supporting a dome of great elegance, which is adorned with porcelain of different colors and curious devices. According to the legend, here Mohammed obtained his first view of the enchanting damsels of Paradise, and hither the faithful now resort to meditate on love.

But the great attraction within the Temple area is the "Mosque of Omar"—the pride of the Mohammedan, the contempt of the Jew, and the grief of the Christian. Though bearing the name of the celebrated Khalif Omar, who captured Jerusalem in 636 A.D., yet some Arabian writers suggest the name of Khalif Abd-el-Melek Ibn Marwan as the more probable founder of the present mosque. But so confused are the accounts of historians, and so contradictory are the prevailing traditions touching its origin, that it is difficult to reach a correct conclusion on the subject. It is stated, however, by the best authorities, that when Jerusalem capitulated to the arms of Omar, the khalif, on entering the city, refused to pray in the Church of the Holy Sepulchre, but inquired for the site of Solomon's Temple. Led by the venerable patriarch Sophronius to the sacred rock which forms the summit ridge of Moriah, Omar, with his own hands, removed the filth which Moslem contempt for the Jew had heaped upon it, and over it he ordered the erection of a mosque at once worthy the wisdom of Solomon and the conquests of Mohammed.

In the estimation of devout Moslems, this mosque is next in sacredness to the mosques of Mecca and Medina, and, with the exception of a brief interval, it has remained in their possession since its construction. In 1099 A.D. the Holy City yielded to the triumphant arms of the Crusaders, whose heroic faith was only excelled by their unwavering courage. Overpowered by their Christian conquerors, the followers of the Prophet retreated within their sacred edifice, from which they were at length driven with terrible slaughter. Some, creeping to the summit of the dome, and clinging to its gilded spire, were pierced with arrows; others, leaping into the deep cisterns beneath the mosque, were drowned or sabred in their attempt to escape; while so great was the number slain, that the whole area flowed with blood ankle deep.[1] Having removed the dead, and cleansed the mosque from the stench and stains of the slaughtered, the Crusaders consecrated it to Christ. Within they erected a choir and an altar, and on the spire which surmounts the dome they substituted the Cross for the Crescent. Receiving authority from the sovereign pontiff, they established a regular chapter of canons, endowed with all the immunities belonging to the Catholics of the West, and calling the holy house, by way of excellence, *Templum Domini*, they organized a special guard for its protection, to whom they gave the name of Knights Templars.

[1] 71,000 were slain.

But in less than a century thereafter the Mosque of Omar reverted to its former masters, and, true to his religious faith, the proud Saladin, having driven the Crusaders from the city, transferred the mosque from Christ to Mohammed. The golden cross gave place to the gilded crescent; the altar and choir were removed; the edifice was cleansed with rose-water brought for the purpose from Damascus; and from its lofty dome the muezzin announced the hour for prayer, while on his royal mat, spread beneath that dome, Saladin performed his devotions.[1] As the Egyptian conqueror left it we now behold it.

Consisting of three sections—the walls, the drum, and the dome—the lower story is a true octagon, forty-six feet high and 170 in diameter. Penetrated by fifty-six pointed windows of the Tudor style, the light passes through stained glass, rivaling in the beauty and brilliancy of its colors that of the famous cathedral windows of Central Italy. From this section rises the drum, thirty-four feet high, pierced by sixteen windows, and on which rests the dome, rising seventy feet higher, and having a diameter of sixty feet. A graceful spire surmounts the dome, supporting a gilded crescent. The exterior of the first and second sections is incased with marbles of different hues and with porcelain tiles of intricate patterns, while that of the dome is covered with lead.

Corresponding in position to the four cardinal points are as many doorways, three of which have inclosed marble porches, and the fourth has a portico formed of slender columns, with a roof of the same material. Two corridors encircle the interior of this noble edifice. One, thirteen feet wide, is formed of eight massive piers and sixteen Corinthian columns, connected at the top by a horizontal architrave; the other, thirty feet wide, is formed of twelve columns and four inner piers, from which spring the arches that support the dome. These columns are polished porphyry of a purple hue, and are crowned with richly gilded capitals. The walls and ceiling are covered with gilt stucco, on which are traced, in the graceful curves and lines of the Arabic characters, quotations from the Koran. Rising 150 feet from the marble pavement, the interior of the dome is no less impressive than the exterior is imposing; and though less in altitude than St. Peter's at Rome, it is more

[1] Robinson's B. R., vol. i., p. 298-300.

symmetrical, and from the dimness of the light the eye wearies in searching for its loftier portions.

But the great attraction within the mosque is the celebrated rock called by the Arabs es-Sukhrah. Situated directly beneath the dome, it is unquestionably the summit ridge of Mount Moriah, and consists of a naked limestone rock of a grayish color, sixty feet long, fifty-five wide, and rises five feet above the surrounding floor. Over it, suspended from the piers, is the war-banner of Omar, made of the richest crimson silk; around it is an iron railing, with arrow-headed points tipped with gilt, and on it stand metallic candlesticks resembling Syrian lilies.

The fertile imagination of the Asiatic has invested this rock with peculiar sanctity. According to a Mohammedan legend, it descended from heaven when the spirit of prophecy was withdrawn from earth, and attempted to return to its native quarry when the Prophet ascended to glory, but was only restrained by the powerful arm of Gabriel. Refusing to touch the earth again, *it remains suspended in the air seven feet above the top of Mount Moriah!* Arrogant in their spirit as they are legendary in their taste, the Moslems believe that all the water on the earth flows from beneath this rock; and that in one of its unvisited caves are still preserved the armor of Mohammed, the saddle of his favorite beast, the scales for weighing the souls of men at the last judgment, the birds of Solomon, the pomegranates of David, and a silver urn which was thrown from its pedestal by Gabriel's wing on the ever-memorable night of the Prophet's ascension.

Reached by a flight of stone steps is the "Noble Cave," excavated in the heart of the rock, which is of irregular shape, eight feet high and sixty in circumference. To deceive the unwary, and sustain the story that the rock is suspended in the air, a plastered wall incloses the sides of the vault, which, on being struck, emits a hollow sound, indicating a vacant space beyond. In the centre of the floor is a marble star, said to cover the mouth of *Hades*. It is more probably the entrance to that great cavern beneath the city, which, according to tradition, extends to this point.

Rejecting the idle tales of a false faith, the es-Sukhrah has a history replete with interest to every Christian. Forming the ridge of Mount Moriah, here Abraham offered his son;[1]

[1] Gen., xxii., 9.

here stood the destroying angel when about to smite Jerusalem for the offense of an ambitious king;[1] here was the threshing-floor of Ornan, which David purchased to offer thereon a sacrifice to stay the hand of the avenging messenger;[2] and on it rested the altar of burnt-offerings in the first and second temples.[3] Viewed in this light, the "Noble Cave" was no doubt the cess-pool of the altar of burnt-offerings, into which the immense quantity of sacrificial blood was conveyed by the drain that encompassed the altar.

From the southern portal of the Mosque of Omar a paved pathway leads to the Mosque of El-Aksa, lined on either side with olives, palms, and acacias. Near this avenue is the elegant Pulpit of David, from which prayers are offered for the health of the Sultan and the triumph of his arms. Extending a distance of 350 feet, the path terminates at the porch of El-Aksa. Standing near the southwest corner of the Temple area, and close to the southern wall, this mosque covers an area of 50,000 square feet. Measuring 280 feet long and 180 wide, its aisles and nave are forty-eight feet high, and its dome 130. Though in its general appearance the architecture is a compound of the Gothic and the Saracenic, yet, owing to the frequent alterations and numerous additions of the mosque, it is difficult to assign it a classification. Facing the north, the imposing porch extends the entire breadth of the building, and is divided into seven sections by arches supported by slender columns. It is paved with marble, and is reached by eight steps worn smooth by the feet of twelve centuries. The façade is penetrated by seven portals opening into the interior, which consists of a grand nave, three aisles on either side, and a transept surmounted with a noble dome. The aisles and nave are formed by forty-five marble columns, resembling the imposing colonnades in the magnificent basilicas of Santa Maria Maggiore and San Paolo fuori le Mura in Rome. Springing from these columns are arches connecting aisle with aisle, and supporting the roof and dome. The pavement, now of stone, was once adorned with beautiful mosaics, the remaining fragments attesting the pristine grandeur of this ancient temple of Christian worship. Beneath the dome is the elaborately-carved Pulpit of Saladin, and near it is the gallery for the singers. Deriving their name from the daughter of the Prophet, the

[1] 1 Chron., xxi., 15-20.   [2] Ib., xxi., 21-27.   [3] 2 Chron., iv., 1.

Fatimites ordered a large section of the mosque to be partitioned off and appropriated for the devotions of women. In the western end of the transept are two polished marble columns standing ten inches apart, and designedly arranged to discover the faith of him who essayed to pass between them; no one, according to the legend, but a true believer in the Koran could hope for success. Once regarded as an infallible test, the charm, however, is now broken, as many a Christian has succeeded in the attempt. Within this mosque is a fountain called the "Well of the Leaf," receiving its name from the circumstance that centuries ago, one of the faithful, having descended to the bottom to recover a lost bucket, unexpectedly found a door opening into the delightful gardens of Paradise, into which he walked, and, plucking a leaf from one of its fair trees, returned, bearing with him the celestial memento, which proved its heavenly origin and nature by retaining its freshness.

With the ever-changing fortunes of the Holy City, the Mosque of El-Aksa has passed from master to master. Originally a Christian basilica, built by order of the Emperor Justinian in the sixth century, and by him dedicated to "My Lady," the Virgin Mary, a hundred years thereafter it was converted into a temple of Moslem worship. Four and a half centuries later, Tancred and his brave knights drove out the Arabians, and reconsecrated the Church of Justinian to the Blessed Virgin. In 1119 A.D. Baldwin II. gave it to his followers, whom he was pleased to call "the poor fellow-soldiers of Jesus Christ," and for whose accommodation he erected on its eastern side a dormitory, refectory, and infirmary. A gift so humble was the beginning of the wealth, power, and glory of the Knights Templars, whose mystic kingdom afterward extended to the farthest limits of Christendom, and who received the benedictions of pontiffs, the homage of kings, and the donations of the pious. Beneath the green sod in front of the venerable basilica were interred, in the year of our Lord 1170, the four knights who, at the instigation of Henry II., assassinated Thomas à Becket in the ancient cathedral of Canterbury. Remaining in the possession of the Crusaders for eighty-eight years, in 1187 A.D. Saladin marched against Jerusalem, captured the city, put the Templars to the sword, and reopened the portals of the mosque to the children of the Prophet.[1]

[1] Robinson's B. R., vol. i., p. 299.

Whatever pleasure is experienced in recalling the ever-shifting fortunes of Moslem and Christian, and in reciting the legends of the one and the traditions of the other, the traveler turns away from scenes and memories so romantic to explore with deeper interest the works of Solomon.

Thirty feet to the east from the Mosque of El-Aksa is the en-

SOLOMON'S SUBTERRANEAN PASSAGE-WAY.

trance to a subterranean passage-way. A flight of stone steps leads down to a broad and well-made avenue 259 feet long, forty-two wide, thirty high, and having a gentle descent of 200 feet. Extending through the centre are two rows of monolithic columns, connected by arches supporting the ceiling, which is composed of flattened domes. These domes are formed of large blocks of limestone, and each one has a circular keystone six feet in diameter—a style of architecture nowhere else to be found, except in some of the ancient tombs beyond the city, indicating a contemporaneous age. Guided by the light of our wax tapers, we advanced a distance of 259 feet to a flight of nine steps leading down into an entrance-hall fifty feet long and forty-two wide. In the very centre stands a massive column twenty-one feet high and six in diameter, consisting of a single block of limestone, including a foliated capital, on which is carved a palm-branch. From this central pier, and from pilasters on the sides of the hall, spring arches on which rests a vaulted ceiling of extraordinary workmanship. And corresponding, both in its size and grandeur, is the original gateway in the south wall of the city, the exterior of which is seen in part where the city wall joins that of the Haram. Having a breadth of forty-two feet, it is divided in the centre by a rectangular pier eight feet broad, and, extending inward twelve feet, has a pillar-shaped termination. Both the pier and jambs of the gateway are constructed of bevel stones of great size and well finished. This is evidently one of the approaches to the ancient city, and no doubt up through this colonnaded avenue Christ and his disciples often passed to the House of the Lord. In some lateral vault leading from this covered way, the Jews believe the treasures and furniture of their Temple are now concealed; and so prevalent is this opinion, that a breach has already been made in the wall to discover the place of concealment.

Standing in the southeast corner of the Temple area is the Mosque of Issa (Jesus). It is a small, dome-like building, containing a large marble basin, not unlike in form a sarcophagus, called by some the "Cradle of Jesus," by others the font in which the infant Savior was washed previous to his presentation in the Temple. Through this chamber is the true and easy entrance to the great substructions of Solomon's day; but, hoping to deter us from exploring them, the guide led us to an opening in the area, down which we were compelled to leap more than ten feet. Nothing daunted, each in turn made the leap, and turning to the right, we stood beneath those grand vaults, unequaled in strength and grandeur by any thing of the kind either in Greece or Rome.

Originally the summit of Mount Moriah naturally and rapidly declined from the great rock which forms the ridge toward the southeast, leaving a narrow and uneven surface. To elevate the surface of the hill to a common level, Solomon constructed vaults supported by piers.[1] Standing ten feet apart, and extending east and west 319 feet, and north and south 250 feet, are fifteen rows of massive columns, composed of beveled stones five feet square, and connected by semicircular arches, on which rest the vaulted ceiling, five feet thick, supporting the pavement above. These piers are from ten to thirty feet high, according to the elevation and depression of the ground, and on

[1] Josephus, anti B., xv., c. xv., s. 3.

some of them has been chiseled a mason's compasses, opened at an angle of forty-five degrees, but whether ancient or modern the silent sign of the honorable craft gives no response. The eastern wall of these substructions is the eastern wall of the Haram inclosure, the blocks of which are of the same material and of similar finish with those seen from without. Through openings in an arched gateway, now closed, the Valley of Jehoshaphat is distinctly seen. Through the thick vaults above some olive-trees have forced their powerful roots, which have taken hold on the soil below, uniting, by ligaments of life, the upper and lower surfaces, while the more slender roots hang like graceful pendents from the ceiling. Running along the wall in the western aisle is a large pipe, of similar material to Solomon's aqueduct, which no doubt formerly served as a wastepipe to carry off the refuse water from the Temple; and near it is an oval well, twenty feet in diameter. In the south corner of this aisle is a triple gate of curious workmanship, consisting of an arched central doorway and two lateral ones, so arranged as to form an obtuse angle. In the centre is an octagonal column two and a half feet in diameter, from which spring the arches of the side gateways. Though well preserved, this beautiful gate is now walled up. In the palmy days of Jerusalem it opened to the villages on the south of the city, and there is still a gradual ascent to the open area above, up which the victims were driven to the Temple for sacrifice.

Whether we consider the grandeur of these works or the wealth expended in their construction, they reflect alike the wisdom and glory of Solomon. The original declination of the hill—the measurements of the Temple area as given by Josephus—the size of the stones of which they are constructed, and the manner in which they are dressed, together with the absence of any information that either Herod or any of his successors ever touched the foundations of the sacred inclosure, suggest that these substructions are coeval with the Holy House.

Returning to the surface of the area, we turned to the northwest to explore the great lake beneath the Mosque of Omar. Any one who for a moment has reflected upon the quantity of water requisite for the frequent ablutions of the priests, and for the other demands of the Temple service, must have concluded that artificial means were employed to meet the demand. Ever fruitful in inventions, the genius of Solomon was equal to the emergency, and to the aid of nature he brought the mechanical art of his day. Near the mosque there is an aperture resembling the mouth of a well, down which an inclined plane leads to a flight of forty-four stone steps cut in the living rock. Descending, we found an excavation in the solid limestone rock forty-two feet deep, 736 in circumference, and capable of holding 2,000,000 gallons. The form of the cavern is irregular, and the rudely-arched roof is supported by large piers, which were designedly left at the time of the excavation. These columns are arranged to afford the greatest support, without regard to regularity or beauty, and an attempt had been made to arch the intervening rock, but the work is so crudely done as to give it a craggy appearance. Both the arches and upper portions of the pillars were formerly incased with brass, but the metallic covering has been removed by the Vandal captors of the city. Formerly there were eight apertures in the pavement above through which the water was drawn up; but only one remains open, admitting the light to the shades below. More than three feet of water now covers the entire bottom, which is perfectly clear and of a sweetish taste. Though at present the lake is partially supplied with rain-water, which flows through a small tank, from the Mosque of El-Aksa, yet originally the water was brought from Solomon's Pools at Etham, seven miles to the south of Jerusalem, and the ancient aqueduct through which it flowed can now be traced to the western side of the reservoir.

Standing in such a cavern, where the light and darkness alternately chase each other, where no sound is heard save the measured tramp of pilgrim feet on the marble floor above, and where History silently but triumphantly points to her works in confirmation of her story, the mind is filled with admiration for the past. Of all the works of Solomon, there is nothing remaining which so impressively reflects his wonderful intellect, and so truly conveys to the mind an idea of his unbounded resources as this lake. Of its antiquity there can be no doubt; as to its design there can be no dispute; and of the glory it reflects upon the memory of its founder there can be no diversity of opinion. It was seen and described by Aristeas in the century preceding Christ, and it is subsequently mentioned by the Mishna, by Tacitus, and the Jerusalem Itinerary, and it now invites the modern traveler to its cavernous depths to drink of its crystal water, and thereby confirm those traditions which the lapse of time had transformed into fables.[1]

Though permitted to explore the Temple area the second time, yet I reluctantly left a spot where of old God had appeared to his people, and where the Redeemer often taught as one having authority. And where, on earth, have occurred events of greater grandeur and of more powerful influence? Within an area of less than forty acres the history of our religion may be said to have occurred, and there all that is now real in our faith was once foreshadowed by the most costly and imposing symbols; and to-day Moriah bears testimony no less to the fulfillment of the prophetic judgments demanded against her than to the veracity of her historians. In less than forty years after the Savior's prediction of the destruction of the Temple, his words were fulfilled by Titus, who left the holy fane a mass of scorched and smoking ruins; and now spanning the Appian Way in ancient Rome, the Arch of Titus remains the monument of his terrible work. After a period of desolation lasting seventy years, the Emperor Adrian rebuilt Jerusalem, calling it *Ælia Capitolina*—the former after the family name of the emperor, and the latter in honor of Jupiter Capitolinus. Plowing up the surface of the area, he erected on the site of the Jewish Temple one to Jupiter, which he adorned with the colossal statue of himself, placing the equestrian one on the very site of the "Holy of Holies." Nearly two and a half centuries later the Jews were permitted, by Julian the Apostate, to rebuild their Holy House, but they were deterred in the attempt by flames of fire bursting suddenly out from the earth upon them, and by other manifestations of the divine displeasure. For more than 150 years subsequently nothing is recorded of the Temple area till the middle of the sixth century, when the Emperor Justinian ordered the erection thereon of his magnificent church to the Virgin Mary, which, in 636 A.D., Omar converted into the Mosque of El-Aksa, and upon the site of Solomon's Temple and of the Fane of Jupiter he reared the famous mosque which now bears his name. Subject to the sway of the False Prophet for 463 years, it was rescued from the grasp of the Moslems by the brave Crusaders, who converted the mosques into

[1] Barclay's City of the Great King, p. 525.

Christian churches, and who for eighty years worshiped Christ where Jupiter and Mohammed had been adored. Yielding to the victorious arms of its earlier captors, Saladin retook Jerusalem in 1189 A.D., and the Crescent was again in the ascendant on Mount Moriah, where it remains the symbol of Mohammedan power and glory, to give place at no distant day to the Cross of a world's Redeemer.[1]

[1] Josephus, W. J., b. vi., c. iii., s. 4; Robinson's B. R., vol. i., p. 364-405.

CHAPTER IV.

Valley of the Dead.—Tombs of the Judges.—Of El-Messahney.—Of the Kings.—Valley of the Kidron.—Pillar of Absalom.—Traditional Tombs.—Jews' Cemetery.—Funeral Procession.—Mount of Offense.—Virgin's Fountain.—Gardens of Siloam.—Bridal Party.—Pool of Siloam.—Of En-Rogel.—Vale of Hinnom.—Burning of Children.—Valley of Slaughter.—Potters' Field.—Solomon's Coronation.—Pools of Gihon.—Pool of Hezekiah.—Supply of Water.

From time immemorial, nations have interred their dead with extraordinary care. Along the dividing line separating the Libyan Desert from the fertile plains of the Nile, the Egyptians constructed tombs of marble and porphyry, and reared the stupendous pyramids of Ghizeh, Abooseer, and Sakkara, for mausoleums for their renowned kings. Beside their noblest highways the Greeks and Romans placed the sepulchres and funeral pillars of their distinguished citizens. And the Christian cemeteries of our own day are as remarkable for the grandeur of their cenotaphs as for the beauty of their situation. Not less sensibly affected by a passion so tender, the Jews prepared the final resting-place of their beloved dead with sincere affection. With them it became a religious pride to beautify the sepulchres of their ancestors, and carefully preserve them from age to age. Though like other nations in these particulars, it is a fact no less singular than true that not a line has ever been found on or in any of the ancient tombs in Palestine;[1] hence their identification is now, as it ever has been, by tradition rather than by inscription and epitaph. It is not therefore strange that, with few exceptions, the sepulchres of kings and prophets are either entirely unknown, or are identified by mere conjecture. Like other works of art, Jewish tombs advanced from a crude beginning to a state of artistic elegance. Originally they were natural excavations in the rocks, as is the Cave of Machpelah;[2] but in the advancement of national refinement they were adorned with all that

[1] Stanley.   [2] Gen., xxiii., 4

art could invent and wealth procure,[1] as are the Sepulchres of the Kings. With slight variation in the details, there is a similarity of construction in those of the latter class.

Usually a chamber was excavated in the living rock below the surface, in the sides of which receptacles were prepared large enough to receive a human form, and arranged in tiers with much regularity; when these were occupied, a door was cut in the perpendicular rock, and other chambers were adjoined either on the sides, in the rear, or below.

Selected alike for its seclusion and its rocky sides, the Valley of Jehoshaphat is a vast cemetery. At its head are located

TOMBS OF THE JUDGES.

the "Tombs of the Judges." Though their origin is involved in mystery, they are generally supposed to have contained the remains of the members of the Jewish Sanhedrim, and the supposition is confirmed by the seventy niches within them, coinciding with the number of members composing that venerable tribunal.

[1] Matt., xxiii., 27.

Excavated in the side of a low rock, the entrance is reached by a descending path. The exterior is tastefully ornamented with a pediment resting on plain but handsome mouldings, adorned with tracery of leaves and flowers, and with a blazing torch in the centre and one at either end. Over the façade a few olives bend down their branches droopingly, and before it are the accumulated mounds of many centuries. Descending into the vestibule, which is thirteen feet long and nine wide, we passed through a richly moulded doorway into an antechamber eight feet high, twenty long, and nineteen wide. On the sides of the vault are thirteen loculi, or receptacles for the dead. In the southern wall a door opens to another chamber eight feet square, having in its sides nine arched recesses. In the east wall a second door leads to a similar vault, from which a flight of steps descends to chambers below. Silence and darkness now reign supreme in these mansions of the dead, and of all that was once human not a bone remains.

Less than two miles to the northeast are the "Tombs of el-Messahney," discovered by our distinguished countryman of Joppa.[1] Around them are the remains of what was once a large town, such as hewn stones and broken columns. The rock in front of the tomb has been beveled in imitation of Jewish masonry. Formerly an imposing entablature surmounted an open porch, but only a portion of it remains. The entrance is through a large doorway spanned by a round arch, and the spacious chamber within differs from all others in Palestine by having a window. Of the seventeen recesses which enter the wall endwise, there is one nobler than the rest and twice as large. Here, no doubt, the lifeless form of some distinguished person lay in state, under the light of the window, till his successor in office became his successor to the tomb.

Half a mile to the north from the Damascus Gate, and sixty yards to the right of the Nablous road, are the "Tombs of the Kings." In the western side of a sunken court hewn in the rock, twenty feet deep and ninety square, is a grand portico fifteen feet high, thirty-nine wide, and seventeen deep. Formerly this portal was decorated with two columns and as many pilasters, which, however, are now gone, except a fragment of one of the capitals depending from the architrave. Over the entrance was a heavy cornice and frieze, adorned with clusters

[1] Dr. Barclay.

of grapes and wreaths of flowers, alternating over a continuous garland of fruit and foliage, extending down the sides to the ground. But time and plunderers have defaced this elegant

TOMBS OF THE KINGS.

façade, leaving it a wreck of former grandeur. A solitary palm now rears its graceful form near the spot, and ferns grow out of the cracked face and sides of the portal, covering the broken entablature.

Entering the portico and turning to the right, we found the entrance to the sepulchre to be at once peculiar and complicated. Judging from what remains, the doorway was excavated below the floor of the vestibule, and was approached by a covered passage-way tunneled through the solid rock. At the commencement of this subterranean way there was a trap-door which was secretly covered with a slab. To secure greater safety against those who would sacrilegiously disturb the repose of the dead, there was beneath this trap-door a deep pit so located that none save the initiated, and they only with the greatest caution, could land upon its brink as they stepped upon it. The door of the tomb in turn was guarded with the utmost secrecy. It consisted of a heavy circular slab which was made to run in a groove. The groove inclined upward, and the slab could only be turned by means of a lever. To add to the difficulty of turning the door, both the groove and the slab were nearly concealed by the side of the passage-way, and to the left of the end of the passage-way there was a smaller slab sliding in another groove, which, running at right angles with the former, served as a bolt, and, when pushed in, was received into an aperture cut in the stone door, not only rendering the door immovable, but defying all effort to open it except by the initiated. Though to all appearance these precautions were sufficient to protect this mansion of the dead from the hand of the despoiler, yet, to render the repose of the departed doubly sure, there was an inner door of great weight, so arranged as to fit exactly in the deeply-recessed doorway, and so hung on pivots that it yielded to the slightest pressure from without, while it immediately fell back to its place as soon as the pressure was withdrawn, sealing the doom of the unfortunate one who had entered, as it fitted so exactly in its place that it was impossible to open it again from the inside. The peculiar construction of the door and its rolling in a groove explains the anxious inquiry of the Marys, "Who shall roll us away the stone from the door of the sepulchre?"

Creeping through the low entrance, we lit our candles, and found the interior to consist of five chambers, connected by narrow aisles, and in the sides of the chambers are arched recesses for the dead. The largest of these chambers is nineteen feet square. Its walls are of solid rock, hewn smooth. On its south side are two low doorways which lead to as many chambers, and on the north side a third doorway opens to another vault, which is strewn with fragments of elegantly sculptured marble. Here was found that magnificent lid of a sarcophagus which is at present in the Louvre in Paris, where it bears the name of "David's Tomb." Beneath these vaults are two others, reached by an inclined plane and a flight of stone steps. Being more concealed than the rest, and containing the most elegant sarcophagi, they were designed, no doubt, for the final repose of the most distinguished persons. But, despite such extraordinary precautions, these tombs have been plundered, the dust of the dead scattered, the sarcophagi broken, and the treasures they contained extracted.

Though by common consent they are called the "Tombs of the Kings," yet there are no sepulchres beyond the walls of Jerusalem as to the origin and founder of which there is such a variety of opinions. On these points the tombs themselves are dumb, as they contain neither device nor inscription; and, with one or two ambiguous exceptions, history is likewise silent. M. de Saulcy declares them to be the "Tombs of the Kings of Judah;" Mr. Ferguson pronounces their "architecture to be later than the reign of Constantine;" Mr. Williams asserts them to be the "sepulchral monument of Herod the Great:" Dr. Schultz identifies them as the "Royal Caverns," mentioned by Josephus as being on a line with the Agrippian Wall; Dr. Robinson ascribes them to Helena, the widow of King Monobazus, of Adiabene, who, with her son Izates, having espoused the Jewish faith, settled in Jerusalem in the reign of Claudius Cæsar, and her son, dying in the Holy City, was here interred;[1] while Dr. Thompson and Dr. Barclay regard them as having been constructed by the Asmonean kings. The latter conclusion is most in harmony with the facts of sacred and profane history. The kings of Judah were interred on Mount Zion; Herod the Great was entombed at Herodium, where there are other vaults for his descendants; other caverns along the Agrippian Wall correspond in location with the words of Josephus better than these; and the thirty loculi within this mausoleum are twenty-eight too many for Helena and her son Izates.

Passing down the Valley of Jehoshaphat to the northeast corner of the city wall, we entered the large olive-groves which cover the bed of the valley and the sides of the adjacent hills. Attended by their Nubian slaves, the women and children of Jerusalem spent the hours of the day here, reclining beneath these trees. Opposite St. Stephen's Gate is the traditional rock where Stephen was stoned to death. Above it, to the north, is the supposed site of Calvary. Below it, to the east, is the stone bridge which spans the Kidron. It is 140 feet long, and seventeen high from the bottom of the vale to the top of the arch. It is firmly built, and as it has stood for thou-

[1] Porter.

sands of years, it will endure for ages to come, if not destroyed by violence. The Brook Kidron is a winter torrent, or the accumulation of streamlets from the hill-sides, formed by the rains of winter. Though not seen in the dry season, the stream continues to flow several feet below the surface of small loose stones, sending up distinctly a low murmuring sound.

A thousand feet below the bridge is "Absalom's Pillar."

ABSALOM'S PILLAR (RESTORED).

It is of limestone, cut out of the rock, and detached from the base of Olivet by a path excavated in three of its sides. It consists of a square platform, reached by a flight of steps; a basement of solid rock twenty-four feet square, a square attic seven feet high, and a circular attic, surmounted with an inverted funnel-shaped dome, the point spreading out like an opening flower. Though its apparent altitude is less than fifty feet, yet, owing to the accumulation of stones around its base, its actual height is not ascertainable. The exterior of the basement is ornamented with columns and pilasters, on the Ionic capitals of which rests a Doric architrave. Above the first entablature are two courses of large, well-dressed stones, on which is traced a small cornice, and on the dome above is a cornice resembling rope-work. Within are two chambers, reached by the original doorway on the east, and by a breach on the west, which has been made by the inhabitants of the city, who hold the memory of Absalom in profound contempt. Within and around it are heaps of stones, thrown there by Christian, Jew, and Moslem, in condemnation of a son's rebellion against his father, and, as a more expressive mark of their disapprobation, they spit upon it as they pass. This is probably the pillar which Absalom in his lifetime reared up for himself in the "King's Dale."[1] Being a mixture of Grecian, Roman, and Egyptian architecture, the style is against the supposition; but as it was customary in the days of Herod to "garnish the sepulchres of the righteous," so the admirers of the rebel may have reconstructed his "Pillar" conformably with the architectural taste of the Herodian age.

A little to the north is the reputed tomb of King Jehoshaphat, from whom the valley takes its name. It is a subterranean sepulchre, extending several feet into the mountain. The entrance is through an ornamental portal, consisting of four columns and a pediment, adorned with foliage, cut in the face of the perpendicular rock. Believing it contains a copy of their Law, and other valuable manuscripts, the Jews guard this mansion of the dead with ceaseless vigils. But this can not be the tomb of the king whose memory it bears, as it is distinctly recorded that Jehoshaphat was buried with his fathers in the city of David.[2] The false location of his tomb has given a false name to the valley itself. Both Josephus and the sacred writers call it the "Valley of the Kidron," which signifies "Vale of Filth," from the refuse matter that flowed into it from the cess-pool in the rock beneath the Temple.

[1] 2 Sam., xviii., 18.   [2] 2 Chron., xxi., 1.

TOMBS IN THE VALLEY OF JEHOSHAPHAT.

Nor can this be the place to which the prophet alludes when he declares that God will gather all nations into the Valley of Jehoshaphat for judgment.[1] Its limits are not equal to such an assemblage. The name Jehoshaphat meaning "Jehovah judgeth," the allusion is metaphorical, the royal name being applied to some unknown valley—the rendezvous of the arraigned nations.

A few paces to the south of "Absalom's Pillar" is the traditional tomb of James the Just, where he concealed himself during the interval between the crucifixion and resurrection of our Lord, and where he was finally interred after his martyrdom. It is a cavern fifty feet long, fifteen deep, and ten broad, with an entrance high up in the face of the rock consisting of four Doric columns.

Just south of this apostolic tomb is the monument of Zachariah, who was stoned to death in the reign of Joash,[2] and who is alluded to by the Savior as having perished between the Temple and the altar.[3] Unlike the others, it is solid, designed merely as a sepulchral monument to the memory of the martyr. It is a monolithic, four-sided pyramid, whose height is equal to its base, each side measuring twenty feet. Separated from the parent rock by passage-ways on three sides, it is ornamented with columns and pilasters, each crowned with a plain Ionic capital, and above which is an entablature of acanthus leaves.

From the bed of the Kidron Valley to the Bethany Road on the crest of the hill, and from the "Pillar of Absalom" to the village of Siloam, is the cemetery of the Jews. Each grave is marked with a plain slab imbedded in the earth, and bears a Hebrew inscription. National love and religious superstition induce the descendants of Abraham to seek a place of sepulture within this vale. Expecting the restoration of their kingdom, they desire to sleep in death beneath the sceptre of their posterity. Believing that the final judgment will take place here, and that to have a part in the resurrection of the just they must here be interred, in their old age many come from distant lands to be entombed beside their countrymen. If so unfortunate as to expire in a strange land, they die in the faith that their bodies will burrow their way through the earth to this consecrated spot. Here, morning and evening, venerable

[1] Joel, iii., 2.   [2] 2 Chron., xxiv., 21.   [3] Matt., xxiii., 35.

men prostrate themselves upon the ground in anticipation of death, and hither Jewish women come to weep over buried affection.

On the opposite side of the valley, covering all that portion of Mount Moriah not included within the Haram wall, is a Moslem cemetery of great age. The graves are covered with two layers of hewn stone, with an open space between them in the centre, and ornamented with two upright shafts, one at either end. The material is limestone, and, according to a custom prevalent in Eastern countries, the tombs are whitewashed, illustrating the appropriateness of the Savior's comparison when he likened the Scribes and Pharisees unto "whited sepulchres."[1]

While standing here a funeral procession came out of St. Stephen's Gate. The bier was borne upon the shoulders of men, and, in marching to the grave, the procession rushed on tumultuously, chanting, in a low monotone, "God is God, and Mohammed is his prophet." Believing there is virtue in bearing the dead to the tomb, each man in rapid succession became a pall-bearer. Being persons of different height, the corpse rose and fell according to the altitude of the bearer. On reaching the grave a confused circle was formed, a funeral hymn was chanted, and, after the interment of the dead, an almoner, who had been appointed by the deceased, distributed paras to the throng of beggars who always attend funerals.

Near the grave stood a group of women, swinging their arms, striking their breasts, and howling in the most frantic manner. They were the hired mourners so frequently alluded to in the Bible. When a Moslem dies these mourning women are sent for, who recount, in an extempore chant, the virtues of the dead. They are persons past the pride and beauty of womanhood, and are held in high esteem by the community. Weeping being their profession, tears are at their command at the shortest notice. Their wail is the harshest sound that ever fell on mortal ear, and the habitual contortions of the face render them the impersonation of ugliness. As in all other vocations, the woman who weeps the freest, howls the loudest, and contorts the ugliest, is the chief mourner, and has the most extensive and lucrative practice. To these persons Solomon alludes in his description of death—"and the mourners go about

[1] Matt., xxiii., 27.

the streets;"[1] and St. Matthew refers to them in his account of our Lord's visit to the ruler's house, "Who, when he saw the minstrels and the people making a noise, he said unto them, Give place, for the maid is not dead, but sleepeth."[2]

This cemetery is a place of frequent resort, where, at all hours of the day, groups of females may be seen lamenting some departed friend. As of old, they carry a tear bottle, consisting of two small vials incased in a cushion, and so adjusted that the necks of the vials touch the eyes to catch the falling tear. Though as extensively used by the Mohammedans as they were by the Greeks, yet they are not so graceful as the tapering lachrymaries of the latter. The material is coarser, and the manufacture cruder, indicating a lower civilization. To these lachrymaries David alludes in those tender words of his, "Thou tellest my wanderings; put thou my tears into thy bottle."[3]

Descending the dry and stony bed of the Kidron, the path soon diverged, leading to the wretched town of Siloam, clinging to the rocky sides of the Mount of Offense. In the hill are natural and artificial caves, used in former times for sepulchres, but now inhabited by 200 Troglodytes, who dwell in poverty, filth, and crime. As a befitting background to such homes of woe, the Hill of Scandal rises up behind them. It is long and high, rocky and barren. On its summit Solomon reared altars to Chemosh and Moloch, and burnt incense and offered sacrifices to strange gods.[4] From an offense so abominable the hill takes its name. Unable to express their detestation for the idolatrous acts here performed, topographers call it "Mount of Corruption," "Mount of Offense," and "Hill of Scandal;" and, as if to typify the moral desolation of that great man's heart, Nature has planted neither shrub, nor flower, nor grass thereon, but on all its sides, and over all its summit, her sterile hand has scattered fragments of flint.

Directly opposite the village of Siloam is the famous Fountain of the Virgin, situated at the base of Mount Ophel. It derives its name from the monkish legend that here the mother of Jesus was accustomed to wash her linen. The Turks, however, call it the "Fountain of the Dragon," from the superstition that, as it is a remitting fountain, a dragon lives within it, who stops the water when awake, but when he sleeps the wa-

[1] Ecc., xii., 5.   [2] Matt., ix., 23.   [3] Ps. lvi., 8.   [4] 1 Kings, xi., 4-8.

ter flows. The reservoir is a tunnel-like cavern, twenty-five feet deep, excavated in the southern side of Ophel. Sixteen

FOUNTAIN OF THE VIRGIN.

steps lead down to a platform twelve feet wide, over which a chamber has been built of old stones ten feet high and eighteen long. From this platform there is a flight of fourteen steps, from beneath the lowest of which the water issues, which, after rising to the height of three feet, flows over a pebbled bed, and, passing through a channel, mingles with the waters of Siloam. Penetrating the mountain, this winding channel is two feet wide, from four to twenty high, and more than 1750 long.

The source of this fountain is unknown. Though subterranean water-courses, which penetrate Zion, Ophel, and Moriah, have been explored, yet it has never been ascertained whether the water flows from a fountain beneath the Temple area, or from some great central reservoir in the heart of one of the hills, from which are supplied, by lateral conduits, the numerous wells, cisterns, and fountains that here abound. For ages it has been a remitting fountain, flowing at intervals two or three times a day, and suggesting to the mind of some that this is the Pool of Bethesda. Its location, however, is more in harmony with Nehemiah's description of the King's Pool.[1] For centuries the taste of the water varied at different seasons

[1] Neh., ii., 14.

of the year, being at intervals sweet, bitter, brackish, and tasteless, which arises from the mineral and vegetable substances through which it flows, or from the waters of the bath, coming down from above and mingling with that of the fountain.

Winding round the foot of Ophel, we entered the delightful gardens of Siloam, called in Scripture the "King's Dale."[1] They extend from Kefr Silwân to the Pool of En-Rogel, and cover an area a mile in length and 150 yards in breadth. Unequaled in fertility, these gardens surpass in beauty any other spot in the environs of Jerusalem. Irrigated by rills from the neighboring fountains, they yield abundantly the most delicious figs, almonds, and olives, together with many varieties of Syrian vegetables. Rented by many tenants, the land is divided into small plots; and when viewed from an adjacent hill-side, where is seen to best advantage the deep green of the herbs, the maroon color of the soil, and the bright hues of the flowers, it has the appearance of an elegant carpet.

As in happier days, so it is still the scene of festivity and delight. Here children frolic in all the freedom of Arab life, and here the veiled beauties of the city recline in sweet repose beneath the shade of fruit-trees. On the green slopes of Ophel a group of Jewish maidens were dancing to the sound of the timbrel and song. It was a bridal party celebrating the nuptials of a happy couple on their ancient hills, and in the golden light of their ancestral sun. The scene recalled the triumphal song and dance of Miriam and her women on the shores of the Red Sea.[2] One charming creature, more beauteous than the rest, led the song and dance, while her fair and joyous maidens responded in chorus with voice and instrument, and followed in the merry dance. Unlike the veiled and seclusive Moslem women, these fair daughters of Abraham were exceedingly affable, and with open, happy faces bade us welcome to the festive scene.

Less than 500 yards from the Fountain of the Virgin, the Tyropean Valley descends, dividing Mount Zion from Mount Ophel, and intersecting the Vale of the Kidron. Its mouth is fifty feet higher than the bed of the latter, and is reached by verdant terraces. Two hundred and fifty feet up the valley, and situated in a nook in the mountain, is the Pool of Siloam. The water flows from Mary's Fountain, through an ir-

[1] 2 Sam., xviii., 18.   [2] Ex., xv., 20, 21.

regular and semicircular stone conduit, conducting it into a rectangular reservoir fifty feet long, fifteen broad, and nineteen deep. The pool is constructed of masonry, now green with the moss of ages. In the southwest corner a flight of

POOL OF SILOAM.

stone steps leads to the edge of the water. Though the western side is much broken, yet time has dealt more gently with the opposite portion, in which are six marble columns half imbedded in the wall, apparently designed to support an arch or roof over the fountain. In the centre of the pool is "a nameless column, with a buried base." In the northeast end a flight of steps leads down to a vaulted chamber excavated in the rock, where the water is gathered, flowing in from the Virgin's Fountain. From this reservoir it flows beneath the steps into the pool, where, having accumulated to the depth of three feet, it falls through an aperture into a subterranean aqueduct, conducting it to the gardens of Siloam below.

With unusual accuracy the inspired writers refer to this celebrated pool, leaving us without doubt as to its location and identity. By a bold metonymy, Isaiah substitutes the "waters of Shiloah that go softly" for Jehovah, and the waters of the Euphrates for Rezin and Remaliah's son, reminding the Jews, as they had rejected the former, that those of the latter should overflow their land.[1] Referring to repairs made by Shallun, the son of Col-hozeh, Nehemiah speaks of the rebuilding of the "wall of the pool of Siloah by the king's gardens;"[2] and hither Jesus sent the blind man to "wash in the pool of Siloam."[3]

Some suppose this to be the Bethesda of the New Testament, and there are many circumstances favoring the supposition.[4] Owing to the difficulty of the descent, the impotent man could have justly said, "Sir, I have no man, when the water is troubled, to put me into the pool." It is certainly the fountain to which the Savior sent the blind man, intimating thereby that here the infirm were gathered; and, in view of its natural scenery, it is a beautiful place for an angel to come.

A few feet to the south are the remains of a larger reservoir, separated from Siloam by an embankment, and bounded on the south by a causeway extending across the mouth of the Tyropean Valley. It is now dry, and used as a garden. On the causeway stands an aged mulberry-tree, marking the traditional spot where Isaiah was sawn asunder by order of King Manasseh. Its trunk is gnarled, bent, and hollow, and supported by a circular wall of loose stones. As if tenacious to perpetuate the memory of the greatest of prophets, new limbs have grown from those which are nearly decayed. Here, on a mound of unhewn stones, the villagers of Kefr Silwân hold their court, which in derision the Franks call "Congress Hall." The court was not in session when we were there, but the judges, old, ragged, and filthy, were wrapped in their coarse garments, sleeping beneath the prophetic tree. In plucking a leaf from this ancient shade, I unfortunately stumbled over one of them, extorting a most uncourtly grunt. Asking his pardon as my

[1] Isa., viii., 6, 7.
[2] Neh., iii., 15.
[3] John, ix., 1–7.
[4] Ib., v., 7.

only reparation, I hastily retreated, leaving him and his companions to their slumbers.

From this artificial mound the path winds round the base of Mount Zion, and, after rapidly descending into the valley, terminates at the Fountain of En-Rogel. This fountain is situated at the junction of the Kidron Valley and the Vale of Hinnom, and is the oldest and largest one in the environs of Jerusalem. Quadrilateral in form, and constructed of large hewn stones, it is 125 feet deep, and is inclosed with a small rude well-house, around which are several watering-troughs. Though the usual depth of the water is fifty feet, yet in the rainy season the fountain overflows. Its source is unknown. It is the favorite well with the inhabitants of Jerusalem, and thousands of gallons of its sweet waters are daily carried into the city in goatskins on the backs of donkeys.

By the Arabs it is called the "Well of Job;" by the Franks, the "Well of Nehemiah;" but in Scripture it is known as the "Waters of En-Rogel."[1] Neither history nor tradition gives a reason for calling it after the illustrious sufferer of Uz. Job may be a corruption of Joab, the famous warrior, who, with others, here conspired against the king, and the well may have been so named from this circumstance. According to the apocryphal book of the Maccabees it is called after Nehemiah, as here he found the holy fire, which the priests had secreted prior to their captivity in Persia.[2] In partitioning the land into tribal possessions, Joshua fixed the boundary-line between Judah and Benjamin at this fountain, and called it En-Rogel, or the "Fullers' Well"—the place where fullers were accustomed to tread their clothes.[3]

During Absalom's rebellion it was around this fountain that Jonathan and Ahimaaz secreted themselves, waiting instruction from Hushai, which was brought to them by a "wench;"[4] and years after, when the venerable David was sinking into the grave, his ungrateful son Adonijah conspired against the youthful Solomon, and was proclaimed king "by the stone Zoheleth, which is by En-Rogel."[5]

At this well the Valley of the Kidron and the Vale of Hinnom form a conjunction, after which the valley passes between the Hill of Evil Council on the west and the Mount of Offense on

---

[1] Josh., xv., 7.   [2] Maccabees, i., 19, 22.   [3] Josh., xv., 7.
[4] 2 Sam., xvii., 17.   [5] 1 Kings, i., 9.

the east, pursuing its course through the wilderness of Judea to Mâr Sâba, where it takes the name of Wady en-Nâr, and thence continues southeastward to the Dead Sea. From En-Rogel the Valley of Hinnom runs due west for half a mile, when, turning abruptly northward, it extends as far as the Yâfla Gate, from which point it gently inclines westward to the Upper Pool of Gihon.

The generic name of this deep winding gorge is "The Valley of the Son of Hinnom," so designated by Joshua as bounding Jerusalem on the south.[1] Who Hinnom was, or why this valley bears his name, are facts on which sacred and profane historians are silent. He is, however, one of those men who have left to posterity a name without a biography.

Historically this vale is divided into two sections. From En-Rogel to the southwestern spur of Mount Zion it is known in Scripture as Tophet—meaning "tabret-drum"—from the custom of beating drums to drown the cries of those children which were here burnt in sacrifice to Moloch. Here, in this deep retired glen, stood the brazen image of the idol of Ammon, with the body of a man and the head of an ox. Within the statue was a large furnace, into which, at the appointed time, and amid the wild shouts of the multitude and the beating of drums, the tender victims were thrown. First placed on the burning arms and legs of the idol, they were then caused to fall into the devouring fires within. Significantly does the name of this monster imply "Horrid King," as here, at his shrine, were practiced the most revolting rites ever witnessed under the sun. It is to such scenes Jeremiah refers in his denunciation of the children of Judah: "They have built the high places of Tophet, which are in the Valley of the Son of Hinnom, to burn their sons and daughters in the fire, which I commanded them not, neither came it into my heart."[2] Revolting at such a sight, Jehovah sends the same prophet to curse the ground for man's sake: "Therefore, behold, the days come, saith the Lord, that it shall no more be called Tophet, nor the Valley of the Son of Hinnom, but the Valley of Slaughter; for they shall bury in Tophet till there be no place."[3] In less than fourteen years from the announcement of these fearful words the valley was defiled by King Josiah, who filled it with the bones of the dead, and thereby rendered it ceremonially un-

[1] Josh., xv., 8.   [2] Jer., vii., 31.   [3] Ib., vii., 32.

clean, so that no Jew could enter it.¹ But a more terrible doom awaited it, and a more literal fulfillment of prophecy was to take place. Here, where the shrine of Moloch had stood, the last struggle between the Jews and the Romans occurred,² and from the carnage of that bloody scene the vale received the name of "The Valley of Slaughter." The dead were here interred till there was no room to bury others, and the historian verifies prophecy by this ghastly picture: "Manneus, the son of Lazarus, came running to Titus at this very time, and told him that there had been carried out through that one gate no fewer than 115,880 dead bodies, in the interval between the fourteenth day of the month Xanthicus, when the Romans pitched their camp by the city, and the first day of the month Panemus. This was itself a prodigious multitude; and though this man was not himself set as a governor at that gate, yet was he appointed to pay the public stipend for carrying these bodies out, and so was obliged of necessity to number them, while the rest were buried by their relatives; though all their burial was this, to bring them away and cast them out of the city. After this man there ran away to Titus many of the eminent citizens, and told him the entire number of the poor that were dead, and that no fewer than 600,000 were thrown out of the gates, though still the number of the rest could not be discovered."³

It was in view of the detestable custom of burning human beings to Moloch in this valley, together with the perpetual fire kept burning to consume the filth from the city thrown here, that the latter Jews regarded it a fit emblem of hell, and applied the Greek name of the valley—Gehenna—to the place of future torments. The receptacle of the dead carcasses of beasts and of refuse matter, both animal and vegetable, here the worm sought its food, which, together with the perpetual fires of the vale, suggested to the Savior's mind those solemn words, "Where the worm dieth not, and the fire is not quenched."⁴ And now, as if by appointment, a deep gloom hangs near this doomed spot, and the physical features of the valley reflect its horrid history. The gorge is deep and narrow, the cliffs are broken and barren, the hill on the north throws its shadow to meet below the deeper shades of the

¹ 2 Kings, xxiii., 10.   ¹ Josephus, W. J., b. vi., c. viii., s. 5.
³ Josephus, W. J., b. v., c. xiii., s. 7.   ⁴ Mark, ix., 44.

LOWER POOL OF GIHON.

hill on the south, while the rocks are red as if scorched by eternal fires. The sides of the Hill of Evil Council, which rises from its southern side, are perforated with tombs, now the abode of shepherds and homeless wanderers. Midway up this hill is Aceldama, the "Potter's Field," the price of "thirty pieces of silver."[1] Unmarked by boundaries, the field contains a gloomy vault, sixty feet square and thirty deep; over it is a long massive building of stone, with an arched roof, but open at each end, and on the bottom lay the bones of some poor stranger. Strangely inclined to invest all things connected with New Testament history with the supernatural, the monks assert that the soil of this field possesses the rare power of reducing dead bodies to a perfect mould in the brief space of twenty-four hours; and, according to early writers, the Empress Helena caused 270 ship-loads of it to be removed to Rome, where it was deposited in the Campo Santo, and where it preserved the bodies of the Romans, but consumed those of strangers dying in the Eternal City. On the summit of the hill is a small Latin chapel, standing on the legendary site of the "country house of Annas," in which the Jews conspired against Jesus, and from their "evil council" the hill takes its name. Within the court of the chapel is the traditional olive-tree on which "Judas hanged himself."[2] It is gnarled, pealed, and split, and is the most villainous-looking tree that ever offended human sight.

The second section of the ravine is called "The Valley of Gihon." Running north and south, its sides and bottom are tilled, covered with patches of wheat, barley, and lentils, and dotted with olive and other fruit-trees. Situated in the broadest part of the vale, and directly opposite the Tomb of David on Mount Zion, is the Lower Pool of Gihon. It is a reservoir 600 feet long, 260 broad, and forty deep, and, when full, contains a sheet of water of more than three and a half acres in extent. Its sides are formed by the opposite hills, which have been excavated for the purpose, and the ends are inclosed with walls forty feet high. It is now dry, and the flat ledge of rocks on its eastern side is used by the peasants for a threshing-floor. Seventy-three yards to the west is Solomon's Aqueduct, which, first running parallel with the western side of this pool, crosses the valley at its northern end, and, after winding round the

[1] Matt., xxvii., 4-10. [2] Ib., xxvii., 5.

base of Zion, gradually ascends the mount, and enters the Temple inclosure at the southwest corner. It was from this aqueduct that the Lower Pool was formerly supplied with water. At the southern end of the pool there is an embankment sufficiently broad for a road, leading from the Gate of Zion to Bethlehem and Hebron. In the centre of the path is an artificial fountain, into which water was conducted from the aqueduct by means of a branch pipe, and thence distributed into troughs for the accommodation of man and beast.

It was at this pool the youthful Solomon was anointed king in the room of his father David, and up the slopes of Zion he ascended, "and all the people came out after him, and the people piped with pipes, and rejoiced with great joy, so that the earth rent with the sound of them."[1]

From this point the Valley of the Gihon gradually ascends. Opposite the Yäffa Gate it is forty feet deep and 500 wide. Here in its ancient bed three roads meet, one leading to Bethlehem, a second to the home of Samson, a third to the "hill country of Judea." From here the hills recede on either side, and the valley becomes broad and shallow, covered with grain and planted with olives. Seven hundred yards above the gate is the Upper Pool of Gihon. It is situated at what may be properly called the head of the valley, which spreads out into an almost level plain. Around it is the oldest Moslem cemetery in the environs of Jerusalem. Like its companion, it is a large tank, 300 feet long, 200 wide, and twenty deep, formed of hewn stones laid in cement, and coated with the same. The bottom is reached by two flights of stone steps. Near the top a stone spout projects from the northern wall, through which the waters that come down the inclined plains around it flow into the pool. As there are neither springs nor the remains of ancient conduits adjoining the reservoir, the original source of its supply is a matter of conjecture. It probably had some connection with the Fountain of Gihon, located on the same side of the city, and which was sealed by King Hezekiah when the Assyrians threatened an invasion.[2]

Ahaz was standing here when the intelligence reached him that Rezin, king of Syria, and Pekah, king of Israel, were approaching Jerusalem to war against him; and in that critical moment the Lord said unto Isaiah, "Go forth now to Ahaz,

[1] 1 Kings, i., 40.   [2] 2 Chron., xxxii., 30.

POOL OF HEZEKIAH.

thou and Shear-jashub, thy son, at the end of the conduit of the upper pool in the highway of the fuller's field;"[1] and, thirty years later, here Rabshakeh, with a great army, stood and delivered the haughty message of Sennacherib to the ministers of Hezekiah.[2]

From the bottom of the southern wall of this pool there is now a stone conduit of rude workmanship, which conducts the water to the Pool of Hezekiah within the city. It is formed of large stones carelessly laid together, and for some distance it is subterranean, but rises to the surface on approaching the town.

The Pool of Hezekiah is just within the Yáffa Gate, surrounded with dwellings, and is the oldest fountain in the Holy City. Adjoining it are the Greek Convent, the residence of the Protestant Bishop of Jerusalem, the Monastery of the Copts, and the Mediterranean Hotel. Measuring 250 feet long, 150 wide, and eighteen deep, it is capable of holding water enough to supply half of the city. The bottom is formed of the native rock, leveled and coated with cement, and its sides are walled with solid masonry similarly covered. Though designed to supply the citizens with drinking-water, it is now a Moslem bath, called Berket el-Hammân, and usually contains six feet of water. In laying the foundation for the Coptic Convent, the builder discovered an ancient wall, two feet thick, constructed of large hewn stones, located fifty-seven feet from the north wall of the reservoir, and running parallel to it, proving that the pool is less in dimensions than when first made, and also attesting its great antiquity. This pool is among the unquestionable landmarks of the city, and the allusions to it in the Bible are numerous and explicit. Of Hezekiah it is said, "He made a pool and a conduit, and brought water into the city;"[3] and that "he stopped the upper water-course of Gihon, and brought it straight down to the west side of the city of David."[4] Threatened by the fierce Sennacherib, whose powerful army was marching against his capital, "Hezekiah took counsel with his princes and his mighty men to stop the water of the fountains which were without the city, and they did help him. So there was gathered much people together, who stopped all the fountains, and the brook that ran through the midst

---

[1] Isa., vii., 3. [2] Ib., xxxvi., 2-10.
[3] 2 Kings, xx., 20. [4] 2 Chron., xxxii., 30.

of the land, saying, Why should the kings of Assyria come and find much water?"[1] To deprive his enemies of water, and, at the same time, provide a supply for his own subjects, he sealed the fountains outside of the city, and, by constructing subterranean channels, conducted the water into large tanks within the walls, among which is the pool that bears his name. So secretly was the work accomplished, that the fountain of the Gihon remains a secret with the dead to this day, awaiting the skill and patience of the explorer to uncover its hidden waters, and trace its buried channels to their fountain-head.

In digging to lay the foundation of the English Church on Mount Zion, the architect came to a vaulted chamber, resting on the living rock, twenty feet below the surface of the ground, constructed of fine masonry, and remaining in perfect repair. Entering it, he descended a flight of stone steps, and at the bottom found an immense conduit, partly hewn out of the solid rock, and partly built of even courses of masonry, lined with cement an inch thick. He traced it east and west for 200 feet, finding, at intervals of several feet, openings in the upper side, through which buckets could be lowered to dip the water up. Had permission been granted, he might have traced it to one of the numerous sealed fountains of the ancient city.

One thing strikes the student of Jewish history as no less marvelous than true, that, in all the sieges to which Jerusalem has been subjected, the citizens never suffered from a destitution of water, while the besieging armies suffered severely, and were frequently compelled to bring it from afar. For the want of it, Antiochus Pius, and after him the Crusaders, were delayed in their attacks upon the city, while, through all the long and horrid siege by Titus, no citizen was known to have died of thirst, though thousands perished of hunger. Lying in a limestone region, Jerusalem contains but few wells and living fountains, and in its immediate vicinity but little if any living water is found. To obviate the difficulty, it was necessary to resort to artificial water-works to supply the demand of the Temple service, and also of the vast population which thronged the ancient town.

Among the public works of Solomon which he himself enumerates are "pools of water,"[2] constructed not so much to gratify royal ambition and adorn an already glorious reign as to meet a real necessity, and confer a genuine benefaction upon

[1] 2 Chron., xxxii., 3-4.   [2] Eccl., ii.

his subjects. Seven miles south of Jerusalem, and two miles south of Bethlehem, are the " Pools of Solomon." Collecting the water from one of the largest springs in Palestine into reservoirs, he conveyed it to his capital by means of an aqueduct, which still remains, a distance, including the windings, of more than twelve miles. Following his example, his successors either completed the works which he had projected, or originated new ones as occasion demanded. With a climate unchanged, and a soil as hard as ever, the people of the modern city depend upon living fountains and the clouds of heaven for their supply of water. As of old, the most delicious water is brought from a distance, principally from the fountains in the Valley of Jehoshaphat, which is brought into the city in goat-skins carried on the back of camels and asses. But attached to each dwelling are one or more cisterns, excavated in the limestone rock, and measuring from fifteen to thirty feet long, from eight to thirty broad, and from twelve to twenty deep. The rain-water is conducted, by means of small pipes from the flat-roofed buildings, during the rainy season, into these reservoirs, where it remains pure and sweet for consumption during the dry months of summer and autumn.

How beautifully this scarcity of water illustrates many passages of the Bible, imparting to them a freshness and a reality inconceivable by one who is a stranger to life in the East. In the nomadic life of the patriarchs, many were the sharp quarrels and fierce fights over a well of water. " Abraham reproved Abimelech" because the servants of the latter had violently driven the herdmen of the former from the well of Beersheba;[1] the King of Edom refused to allow Moses to lead the Israelites through his dominions lest his fountains might be exhausted;[2] the churlish Nabal enumerates water with the articles he withheld from David;[3] anticipating the feuds that might arise from drinking of another's fountain, Solomon advises, " Drink water out of thy own cistern, and running waters out of thine own well;"[4] and, ever drawing his figures from nature and the customs of society, and recalling the value and deliciousness of water, the Savior compares salvation to a " well of water springing up unto everlasting life," and the perennial joy of piety to the happiness of one who " shall never thirst."[5] An Oriental can appreciate such an ineffable delight!

[1] Gen., xxi., 25.   [2] Num., xx., 19.   [3] 1 Sam., xxv., 11.
[4] Prov., v., 15.   [5] John, iv., 14.

CHAPTER V.

Laws of the Credibility of Tradition.—Dean Trench on Words.—Scenes of the historical Events of Christianity not well defined.—Palm Sunday in Jerusalem.—Crossing the Mount of Olives.—Journey to Bethany.—Site of the City.—Home of Mary and Martha.—Tomb of Lazarus.—Christ frequented Bethany.—To his Visits is due its Significance.—Touching Legends.—Resurrection of Lazarus.—Scene of Christ's triumphal March to Jerusalem.—Garden of Gethsemane.—Old Gardener.—Walls and Iron Gate.—Place of Sweet Repose.—Flowers.—Pictures.—Aged Olive-trees.—Overwhelming Emotions.—Ascent of the Mount of Olives.—Three Paths.—David's Ascent.—Connection of the Mount with the two Dispensations.—Scene of the Ascension.—True Place.—Commanding View from the Summit of Olivet.—Passion Week in Jerusalem.—Footsteps of our Lord.—Good Friday in the Holy City.—Visit to the Garden.—Lord's Supper.—Sleepless Night.—Calvary.—True Location.—Its Appearance.—Appropriate Place.—Via Dolorosa.—Pilate's Judgment-hall.—Ecce Homo Arch.—Legendary Stations.—Crucifixion of Christ dramatized by the Latin Monks.—The Procession.—Ascent to Calvary.—Tumult.—Spectators.—Sermons.—The Cross.—Church of the Holy Sepulchre.—Architecture.—Scene in the Court.—The Façade.—Imposing Interior.—Chapel of the Greeks.—Rotunda.—Dome.—Holy Sepulchre.—Magnificent Decorations.—Its Interior.—The Tomb.—Holy Shrines.—Not the Tomb of Christ.—Difficulties of the Question.—Evidence for its Identity.—Objections.—Argument against the Site.

SOME general laws are yet to be deduced touching the credibility of tradition as to biblical topography. At present, the traditional sites of many important events in sacred history are accepted or rejected according to the taste, creed, or judgment of the traveler. There is a lack of harmony among chorographers upon the localities where occurred the great facts of our religion, and not unfrequently eminent scholars are found maintaining opposite theories. The inspired writers were too much absorbed in recording the stupendous facts of their history to define, at all times, with accuracy the boundaries of those places where such events transpired. Facts, not places, are the burden of their record. They tell us of the deed, and fearing lest, by adoring the spot, we might fail to reap the full advantage of the transaction, they leave the localities subject to inference. Yet they never ignore the sacredness of places consecrated by memorable deeds, nor could they have been unconscious of the important relation which frequently exists between the natural features of the scene and the fact they commend to our belief. Indeed, the proof of many of their statements depends upon the exact position of mountain and plain, of valley and river, of desert and sea, which we are left to gather from close investigation and comparative induction. Tradition, therefore, has its claims upon our faith no less than written history.

The traveler is guided, in his search for sacred places, by the information derived from three general sources: prevailing tradition, the language of the common people, and the Bible. The first is reliable in proportion to its approximation to the event the memory of which it perpetuates, and to the unity of the rival sects in the land upon the subject. But, owing to the fact that the prevailing traditions were first collated and recorded by Eusebius and Jerome in the fourth century, the absence of any authentic record of such legends during the three preceding centuries requires us to receive the testimony of those eminent fathers with due precaution. It is of little moment how long these traditions have since been received; the question of greater importance is, How nearly can they be traced to the events the memory of which they transmit? While with pleasure we accord to those early fathers varied learning and superior advantages to acquire information, yet it is due to an intelligent faith to accept what they record only so far as it is supported by contemporary history and by the harmony existing between the physical features of the locality and the inspired account.

Dean Trench has said that "language is fossil history."[1] With slight alterations, the familiar names of the Bible have been preserved in the Arabic language, which derived them from the Aramean, the vernacular language of the country when invaded by the Arabs.[2] In some instances the proper names of large cities have been changed, but the ancient appellations of rural places are retained, and this not unfrequently is the only hint to identify some renowned site. But the marvelous minuteness and accuracy of the Bible constitute it the great guide-book in the Holy Land, and, when read with care and reflection upon the spot, in connection with the light

[1] Study of Words, p. 13. [2] Robinson.

derived from other sources, never fail to lead to right conclusions, and at the same time they afford the reader the satisfaction of treading in the footsteps of those illustrious men whose words and deeds are the enduring glory of our race.

There is less difficulty in identifying those places connected with Jewish history than in determining those sites forever sanctified by the acts and teachings of our Lord. For more than fifteen centuries the Jews were permanent residents in the land, and during that long and prosperous period they reared monuments commemorative of historic events, which the spoliations of war have not been sufficient to efface, nor the attritions of time able to destroy; hence, without a doubt, the traveler of to-day stands with delight within their ancient cities, or lingers with melancholy interest amid their ruined towns.

It is otherwise, however, with Christian antiquities. The Founder of our faith was but a sojourner in the land, and his followers failed to become a distinct and ruling people till the early part of the fourth century. Always oppressed, and never respected, till the son of Helena bore the Cross in triumph to the gates of Jerusalem, they were without the rights and destitute of the means to perpetuate by enduring monuments the memory of those places hallowed by the presence of the Great Teacher of mankind. Driven from the city in the year 69 A.D., they were compelled to seek an asylum at Pella, on the eastern bank of the Jordan, near Jabesh Gilead, and for seventy years thereafter, from its capture by Titus to its rebuilding by Adrian, Jerusalem ceased to be the home of the Christians. It is not, therefore, surprising, that during the exile of so many years hallowed sites should have passed to the shades of oblivion, and that any attempt to recall them now should be attended with some uncertainty.

Though unable at all times to stand with confidence where Jesus stood, and walk where he walked, it is nevertheless a source of unspeakable delight to know that Jerusalem is the city in which he taught; that there are the skies he sat beneath; there the hills and vales he traversed; there the garden of his agony; and that rising above is Olivet, whose flowers were moistened with his tears, whose echoes were awakened by his prayers, and whose summit was the last spot of earth pressed by his adorable feet.

Palm Sunday dawned upon the Holy City in all the beauty of a Syrian spring. A sweet repose pervaded earth and sky; the very air was at rest, and a vernal sun shone softly from skies of a purple tint. It was the anniversary of our Lord's triumphal entry into the city of David, and I was in the spirit to join the imaginary throng on the same highway, and shout, "Blessed is he who cometh in the name of the Lord; Hosanna in the highest." From early dawn, through all the lanes and streets of the city, pilgrims were hastening to the Church of the Holy Sepulchre, thronging the spacious aisles, rotundas, and lateral chapels of that venerable edifice. Differing from the Greeks a moon or a month as to the time of the festival, the Latins were assembled in their Franciscan chapel adjoining the rotunda. The altar was decorated with vases of flowers, and over it were suspended palm-branches, the symbol of the day. The bishop and officiating priests were attired in their elegant robes; a noble organ pealed forth the responses to the intoned service, and in the vast audience were monks and nuns, officers of the state and of the army, and pilgrims and strangers from all lands.

The scene of our Lord's triumphal march from Bethany to Jerusalem is no less distinctly marked by a universally received tradition than by the everlasting hills and valleys whose awakening echoes responded to the anthems of the rejoicing multitude. The distance from the Holy City to Bethany is correctly stated by the Evangelist as fifteen furlongs, or a little less than two miles, counting eight furlongs to the Roman mile. The ancient path leads from St. Stephen's Gate down the steep sides of Moriah, and, after crossing the stone bridge that spans the Kidron, ascends to the walls of Gethsemane. From the garden three roads lead to the village home of Lazarus. One, winding up a slight depression in the western side of Olivet, sweeps round the hamlet of Jebel et-Tûr, which crowns the summit, and descends the green slopes on the eastern side. The second branches from the first just above the garden, and, winding upward, skirts the valley on the south, intersecting the former a short distance above Bethany. The third, which is the most ancient and frequented of the three, turns to the right below the garden wall, and, following the devious base of Olivet on the south, leads to Bethany, to Jericho, and to the heights of Moab beyond the Jordan. In the

East, the land itself is not older than the great highways of the nation. Chosen alike for ease and directness, the valleys and mountain slopes are the principal thoroughfares, which, to succeeding generations, remain the landmarks of the past.

Crossing the Mount of Olives, in less than half an hour I reached the native town of Lazarus. From the numerous datepalms that once flourished in its environs the village was called Bethany, or the " House of Dates;" but, in honor of him who was raised from the dead, it bears the name of El-Lazirêyeh.[1] It is situated in a semicircular vale, with an opening toward the east to admit the morning's earliest light. Amid groves of olive, fig, and almond trees are twenty Arab huts, containing 100 inhabitants. The villagers are quiet and happy, and the half-nude children leap for joy on the reception of a few piastres for the milk and fruit they sell to strangers. All the Bible memories of the place are cherished by the people, and an old man is in waiting to point out the traditional sites.

In the absence of positive proof either for or against these legendary places, the traveler is left to his own conclusions, drawn from history and from the probabilities of location. Of the house of Simon but little remains, and only a fragment of the residence of Lazarus has survived the waste of ages. The latter occupies a commanding position on a scarped rock, and in its day was a building of some elegance. Formed of large beveled stones, it was twenty-one feet square. From the top of a remaining arch a prospect of singular beauty opens to view through the ravine on the east, and, no doubt, often was enjoyed by the master and his three friends.

Archaeologists have called in question the identity of this ruin, and have claimed it as the remains of the Convent of the Black Nuns, founded in 1132 A.D. by Mesilinda, Queen of Fulco of Jerusalem, over which she placed her sister Ireta as abbess, a matron of approved piety. Yet it is highly probable that, as Bethany has always been inhabited, and as the recollection of the raising of a man from the dead would be among those longest and most tenaciously cherished by a people, either this arch is a part of the stone house which tradition asserts to have been occupied by Lazarus and his sisters, or, if the remains of the convent of Mesilinda, it marks the spot where he resided.

[1] Lazarus.

BETHANY.

Under the brow of a hill in the northeast part of the town is the supposed tomb of Lazarus. Twenty-six stone steps lead to a vaulted chamber twenty-two feet below the surface of the ground, which is excavated in the rock, and measures eleven feet long, nine wide, and seventeen high. On the left a small door opens to a narrow vault where the dead once rested. Bearing marks of great antiquity, there is no reason to doubt the identity of this tomb. The saying of those Jews who came to comfort Mary, that " she goeth unto the grave to weep,"[1] would indicate, at first, that her brother had been interred some distance from the town; this, however, does not necessarily follow, as the same remark would be appropriate if the sepulchre was in the village, whatever may have been the distance from her dwelling.

Like many other Syrian towns, Bethany has risen to importance, and inherits an imperishable name from the presence and miracles of Jesus. It was to Judea what Capernaum was to Galilee—the scene of his greatest works, and the place where he delivered his most sublime lessons of wisdom and love. When the ingratitude of Jerusalem forced him from her gates, he sought repose in Bethany, as, when driven by the Nazarenes from his native city, he selected Capernaum as the place of his adoption. Bethany was his temporary abode in his frequent journeys from Moab to Judea. Coming from the land of Moab, " a certain woman named Martha received him into her house;[2] and from the same region he came to raise Lazarus from the dead.[3] At a later period, here he dined in the house of Simon the leper;[4] here the grateful Mary washed his feet with tears, and wiped them with the hairs of her head,[5] and from an alabaster box, which " she had kept against the day of his burial," she poured the precious ointment on his head as he sat at meat. From this humble village he made his triumphant entry into Jerusalem, and here, in the house of pious orphanage, he spent the last night but one prior to his crucifixion.

There is a touching legend in the East that the father of Lazarus was a pious Levite, and his mother a Jewish matron, after the model of Hannah and Elizabeth; that Lazarus himself was a scribe, who gained a living by copying the Law and

---

[1] John, xi., 31. [2] Luke, x., 38. [3] John, xi., 7.
[4] Matt., xxvi., 6 [5] John, xii., 3.

the Prophets for the various synagogues in Palestine, and that Mary and Martha devoted their time to needle-work—embroidering veils for the Temple and garments for the priests; that previous to the visits of Jesus to Bethany the parents had ascended to their reward, leaving on earth their three orphan children; that the native sweetness of their spirit, the purity of their devotion, and their constant attention to his recurring wants, engaged his affection and secured his benediction; that here, in their midst, he laid aside the awful grandeur of Teacher and Judge of mankind, and in all the refined amenities of social life he displayed the finer traits of his character, which were hidden from the common eye. And how intimate must have been that friendship for the care-burdened Martha to come to him with her little domestic troubles;[1] and how tender the attachment for those stricken sisters to think only of him when their brother died. A greater benefactor than beneficiary, he rewarded those pious sisters with a gift worthy of a God. The brief but sad message they sent him—"Lord, behold, he whom thou lovedst is sick"—awakened all the deeper emotions of his friendship. Though even a melancholy relief to be with those we love in the hour of death, yet, that the Son of Man might be glorified, Jesus delayed his coming till after the demise and burial of his friend. Many a time had those sorrowing sisters passionately exclaimed, "Oh that the Master were here!" Coming from the fountains of Bethabara, he sought the sepulchre of Lazarus. Omnipotence stirred within him: a groan for life escaped his lips, a prayer entered heaven that knew no denial, a voice was heard in the spirit world calling back a departed soul to earth and to a new probation. That voice was obeyed. Lazarus came forth, and joy filled the hearts of those orphan sisters.[2] And now, after the lapse of so many centuries, the inspired story, read upon the spot, has all the freshness of reality; and though time has marred the beauty of that mountain home, and borne to the grave the friends of Jesus, yet Mary's alabaster box of costly ointment and spikenard, very precious, is still fragrant with the odor of undying love, and " wheresoever this gospel is preached throughout the whole world, this also that she hath done shall be spoken of for a memorial of her."[3]

In the month of March of the succeeding spring Jesus was

[1] Luke, x., 38-42.   [2] John, xi.   [3] Mark, xiv., 9.

again in Bethany. The moment of his triumph had come. The shouts of the people awaited the presence of their King. On the previous day he had descended from the Mountains of Moab, crossed the Jordan, traversed the Plain of Jericho, restored eyesight to the importunate Bartimeus, and dined with Zaccheus.[1] Resuming his journey, he passed round the base of Quarrantania, the scene of his temptation, crossed the Brook Cherith, where Elijah was fed by the ravens, ascended the Vale of Achor, where Achan was stoned to death, entered the wilderness of Judea, the scene of the parable of the good Samaritan, and, continuing his upward march, reached Bethany as the sun descended behind the heights of Gibeon. That night he was entertained in the house of Simon the leper. Attracted to Bethany to attend the feast of Simon and behold Lazarus, who had been raised from the dead, a vast multitude were the next morning on their way to Jerusalem.[2]

Solemnly intending to assert his regal rights and fulfill an ancient prophecy,[3] Jesus dispatched two of his disciples to secure an ass for the triumphal occasion. A knowledge of his coming had reached the countless strangers who had assembled in the Holy City to celebrate the Passover, and who, seized by a sudden inspiration that bore every heart upon its resistless wave, hastened to greet their coming King. Passing through the palm-groves that formerly lined the path, they cut down the lengthened branches, and descended toward Bethany with shouts of triumph.

Spreading their loose garments upon the unsaddled ass, the disciples had set their Master thereon, who was slowly approaching the city of David. At length the descending and ascending processions met, and in the rapture of the moment vied with each other in expressions of gladness and in tokens of respect. Those who had escorted him from Bethany threw from their shoulders their loose robes, and, spreading them on the highway, formed a temporary carpet for his triumphal march; and those who had come from Jerusalem spread their palm-branches before him, while from that vast multitude arose that more than regal shout, "Hosanna to the Son of David! Blessed is he who cometh in the name of the Lord! Hosannah in the highest!"[4] It was the hour of the exaltation

[1] Luke, xviii. and xix.
[2] John, xii., 1-11.
[3] Zech., ix., 9.
[4] Matt., xxi., 9.

of the Son of God. The people had gathered unto Shiloh; the visions of the past were realized, and prophecy was fulfilled.

The interruption over, the great procession re-formed. Those who had come from Jerusalem, turning round, led the advance; those who had come from Bethany brought up the rear; while in the centre Jesus rode in triumph.

Midway the two cities, the ancient path burrows the side of Olivet, and, after sweeping round a deep ravine, ascends a shoulder of the sacred mount, where the whole city, as by enchantment, bursts upon the view. Where now appears the Tomb of David then were seen the palaces of Herod, and where now stands the Mosque of Omar then stood the Jewish Temple. Charmed by a vision so grand, the people again shouted, but, unelated by the praise or view, "Jesus beheld the city, and wept over it." While the scenic grandeur of the prospect thrilled the multitude with joy, the view of a doomed city caused him to shed more than human tears. Once more the procession advanced. Descending a shelving path, with the groves of Gethsemane on the right and the Tomb of Absalom on the left, the Savior crossed the Kidron, and, mounting the sides of Moriah, he entered his Temple amid the astonishment of enemies and the acclamation of friends.

At the junction of the three roads which lead to Bethany is the Garden of Gethsemane. It is a quiet spot, and wears the air of sweet repose. Formerly it was open and accessible to all, but now it is surrounded by a stone wall twenty feet high. It is an area of 120 feet east and west, and 150 north and south. The entrance is through a low iron gate on the eastern side, and the keeper is an old Franciscan monk. With a skillful hand he has transformed the inclosure into a pretty but not gorgeous garden. On the east are three terraces, adorned with flowers. On the first is a well of delicious water, covered with trellis-work, on which are vines, and in the northeast corner is the monk's cell. A graveled walk follows the circuit of the walls, and on the interior of the walls are pictures representing memorable scenes in the last night of our Lord's life. The centre of the area is inclosed with a high picket fence, and the ground within is laid out in flower-beds. As memorials of the past, he has cultivated the graceful but bitter wormwood, and also the beautiful passion-flower—the symbol of

GETHSEMANE AND THE MOUNT OF OLIVES.

agony. Near them are a few palms and cypresses. With parental care he has nourished the eight remaining olive-trees, beneath which he thinks the fearful struggle occurred. They bear marks of great age, and are now the oldest on the face of the earth. Their trunks are gnarled and hollow, their foliage scanty, and, true to their species in old age, their roots are far above the ground, but at present covered with an artificial soil. One, more venerable than the rest, is seven feet in circumference, and has separated into four parts from the roots upward to the branches; a second is twisted with age; and a third is hollow. But the branches are strong, the leaf green, and from the aged roots young trees are sprouting—successors to these patriarchal shades.

Gethsemane is the only place in all my travels I hesitated for a moment to visit. I had passed it many times before, but always felt unwilling to disturb its solemn repose. But, unattended by companion or guide, I determined to enter. Rapping on the low gate, the venerable Franciscan bade me welcome. His countenance was pale with watchings, and a pensive smile played over his dry and wrinkled face. Entering his solitary cell, he left me alone. Not a sound disturbed the quiet of the hour. Kneeling beneath an aged olive, I gave myself up to the undisturbed reflections and hallowed memories of the place. The story of our Lord's agony had a reality I had never before experienced. This lonely vale, these ancient hills, these serene skies, heard the Sufferer's cry. Here the compassionate Redeemer lay prostrate upon the ground, and, yielding to his Father's will, accepted the cup of death. Here descended that kind angel who strengthened the fainting Savior. Here resounded the horrid tramp of that ruffian band, whose huge staves smote the earth, and whose swords glittered in the starlight. Here the betrayer's signal-kiss polluted the cheek of innocence, and the Master's words of surprise startled the dull ear of night. Here the impetuous spirit of Peter, gaining the mastery of his discretion, moved him to smite off the ear of Malchus; and, losing sight of the dangers that threatened him, and unmindful of the hatred of his foes, the benevolent Savior asked as an unselfish favor, "Suffer ye thus far, and he touched his ear and healed him." Here the Shepherd was smitten and the flock scattered. Here John fled, leaving the linen cloth in the hands of the ruffians, and Jesus was led to judgment. It was passing strange to be in such a place.

At every station where Israel had encamped *en route* for the Mount of the Law; on the awful summit of Sinai; beside the cave of Machpelah and the tomb of Rachel; in the stable of the Nativity at Bethlehem; along the Jordan; on Zion, Moriah, and Olivet; and on Gibeon, where Solomon received a wise and understanding heart, I had offered my devotions to God; but Gethsemane seemed the nearest to heaven in the hour of prayer.

Gathering a few flowers and olive leaves for loved ones at home, I left the garden with impressions as blessed as they are imperishable, and began the ascent of Olivet. The Mount of Olives is no less memorable in the annals of Jewish and Christian history than its aspect is impressive to the eye of the beholder. Rising 2800 feet above the Mediterranean, its base is 1000 feet from the city, and its summit half a mile from St. Stephen's Gate. Having an elevation of more than 400 feet above the bed of the Kidron Valley at "Absalom's Pillar," it is 104 feet higher than the crown of Zion, and rises 127 feet above the summit-level of Mount Moriah. Owing to its irregular outline, both its form and cardinal points are difficult to define. Its general direction is north and south, with spurs shooting out toward every point of the compass, and its location agrees with the description by the prophet, who places it before Jerusalem on the east.[1] Including the Hill of Scandal, it may be said to have three peaks, though with equal propriety Scopus might be enumerated among them. Topographically this may be correct, but historically the Hill of Scandal is too far southwest to be included as a part of Olivet, as Mount Scopus is too far north. The two adjacent peaks are distinct, the northern one bearing the name of Galilee, from the supposition that there the angels addressed the Galileans, and the southern one, called by the Arabs Jebel et-Tûr, but by the Christians the Mount of Ascension.

The sides of the mountain gently descend east and west, and are streaked horizontally with stripes of green and gray. From base to summit it is terraced and planted with olives, from which the mount derives its name. Though rough and stony, yet in spring-time and summer flowers bloom upon it luxuri-

[1] Zech., xiv., 4.

antly. On its broad and level summit is the small village of Jebel et-Tûr, clustering around the Church of the Ascension, and, in turn, is surrounded by fields of grain. From Gethsemane three paths lead to this Arab town; one strikes up boldly along a projecting cliff, a second winds up more gradually to the south, while the third follows a gentle ravine, and is the most ancient of the three. It was up the latter path David fled from the rebellion of Absalom, " weeping as he went up, with his head uncovered, and his feet bare." On the summit, where he lingered to worship, he was met by the faithful Hushai, who, by the king's command, returned to the city to defeat the counsels of Ahithophel. Just over the hill-top the kind Ziba met the royal fugitive with refreshments. And not far down the eastern declivities is Bahurim, where the cowardly Shimei cursed the king, and where the heroic Abishai was impatient to vindicate his insulted master.[1]

This is, no doubt, the path Jesus frequented when returning to Bethany after the thankless labors of the day in the Holy City. And how significantly do these two reverent names recall the history of Olivet, as associated with the two great dispensations of our religion. On its summit was the Luna Station, from which the first appearance of the new moon was announced by torch-light signals to the priests of the Temple, which had been previously seen and communicated in the same manner by those stationed on the loftier peaks of Moab. Somewhere on its upland slopes stood two cedar-trees, beneath which pigeons were sold as offerings for purification. In one of its depressions was the lavatory, where unclean persons washed preparatory to presenting themselves before the Lord. At its base the red heifer was burnt, the ashes of which were preserved for the purification of the people,[2] and crowning the summit the Shekinah rested, like a cloud of glory, when forced from the Holy of Holies by the ingratitude of a fallen people.[3]

But, contemplated in its connection with the private life and public ministry of our Lord, Olivet has a higher significance to the Christian, and awakens within him profounder emotions. It was his house of prayer, where he ofttimes resorted with his disciples.[4] From some of its shaded slopes, with the city

---

[1] 2 Sam., xv. and xvi.   [2] Num., xix., 2–10.   [3] Ezek., xi., 23.
[4] John, xviii., 2.

full in view, he predicted the final overthrow of Jerusalem.[1] With a matchless purity of thought and diction, he delivered to his disciples the parables of the "Ten Virgins," of the "Five Talents," and concluded his marvelous discourse by a description of the "Last Judgment."[2] At its base he was betrayed,[3] and from its summit he ascended to glory.

Charmed with the purity of his life, convinced of the divinity of his person, and conscious of a debt of gratitude for his vicarious death, the Christian seeks the exact spot where for the last time he touched our earth. But, wisely neglecting to designate any particular portion of the Mount, the Evangelists point us to Olivet as the place of ascension. According to Eusebius, the traditional site is directly opposite St. Stephen's Gate, and, prior to the visit of St. Helena, was visited by pilgrims from all lands. To honor the spot and commemorate the event, the mother of Constantine ordered the erection of a church upon the site, which, in the waste of time, has given place to a humbler structure. By a singular amalgamation, it stands connected with a Mohammedan mosque, whose solitary minaret is seen from afar.

The tradition, however, does too much violence to the text to claim for a moment the intelligent faith of the present age. He led them out as far as to Bethany,[4] and they returned unto Jerusalem from the Mount called Olivet, which is from Jerusalem a Sabbath-day's journey,[5] are the only authentic intimations we have of the place, and the only data from which we can draw our conclusions. Though "as far as to Bethany" is indefinite, it is sufficiently explicit to throw doubt upon the traditional site, and to lead us to search for another more in harmony with the spirit and letter of the text. To the southeast of the village there is a narrow isthmus, connecting the peak on which it stands with one of less altitude and more retired. It is one mile, or a "Sabbath-day's journey," from St. Stephen's Gate, and overlooks the little town of Bethany, lying 500 yards below the cliff. From the ruins which lay scattered on the rocks beneath the isthmus, it is evident that Bethany once extended farther to the northwest than at present, which more completely corresponds with the distance as stated by St. Luke. But it is enough that Olivet extends to-

[1] Matt., xxiv., 3-41.   [2] Ib., xxv.   [3] John, xviii.
[4] Luke, xxiv., 50.   [5] Acts, i., 12.

ward the home of Lazarus a "Sabbath-day's journey" from Jerusalem, and that from its summit Jesus ascended to glory, leading captivity captive, and giving gifts to men. It is enough that these hills saw the Prince of life and glory rise, and leaped for joy; that these valleys beheld him ascend, and swelled with delight; and these skies reached down their ethereal arms to bear him on high. It is enough that earth is linked to heaven, humanity is the abode of divinity, and a descendant of Adam is on the throne of the universe. Let us adore!

In all the Holy Land there is not a nobler panoramic view to be enjoyed than the one which greets the eye from the Mount of Olives. Owing to the extreme transparency of the atmosphere, and to the absence of that peculiar haze which lends such an enchanting perspective to the Italian landscape, distance at times seems annihilated, and remote objects appear to view with extraordinary distinctness of form and outline. Sweeping over an area of more than twenty miles, the prospect is as varied as it is grand. Turning to the north, the eye rests on Mizpeh, where Samuel held his court and Israel gathered for judgment; hard by are Gibeon and Ajalon, where the sun and moon paused in their brilliant course; while far to the northward is Michmash, the scene of Jonathan's exploits; and nearer are Gibeah of Saul and "poor little Anathoth," where the weeping eyes of Jeremiah first saw the light. Looking eastward, desolation and beauty compose the landscape. From Bethany to Jericho, and for many miles north and south, is the wilderness of Judea, sinking down to the verdureless shore of the Dead Sea, whose shining waters are seen through the opening cliffs. Far down in the deep chasm through which the Jordan flows appear the green banks of the sacred river, and beyond rise the Mountains of Moab, vast and craggy, and colored with "chatozant tents of azure-red." On the south is the rich Plain of Rephaim, where Daniel heard the "sound of a going in the tops of the mulberry-trees,"[1] and farther on are seen the Convent of Elias, the domes of Bethlehem, and the Frank Mountain—the "Tomb of Herod the Great," while to the west and at your feet is the "City of the Great King;" and to no other city does distance lend such "enchantment to the view." In walking its streets and in

---
[1] 2 Samuel, v., 24.

mingling in the careless throng who share not in the grateful memories of the place, the charm of its hallowed associations is broken; but when viewed from the summit of Olivet, the spell of history entrances the soul, the attention becomes serious and fixed, the eyes dreamy and motionless.

The interest experienced in standing on any historic site is increased by being present on the anniversary of the event which has given significance to the place. There is in such a coincidence somewhat of reality at no other time realized, and the emotions excited on such an occasion are no less tender than real; and to read a description of the great transaction as written by an eyewitness amid the scenes of its occurrence invests the present with the actuality of the past, and one fondly imagines he beholds what transpired centuries ago. It is in view of such apparent facts that "Passion Week" in Jerusalem has an interest to the Christian traveler not common to any other period of the year, and, conscious of such an advantage, pilgrims from all lands assemble in the Holy City at that time to recall in imagination the memorable events which occurred during the last week of our Lord's earthly career. Indebted to the Evangelists for our knowledge of what Jesus said and did on the six days preceding his death, we could wish the narrative more consecutive and the description more complete.

On Sunday he made his triumphal entry into Jerusalem as King of the Jews.[1] On Monday he cursed the barren fig-tree,[2] drove the money-changers from the court of the Temple for the second time,[3] and asserted his authority in the presence of his enemies.[4] On Tuesday he entered the Temple for the last time, was questioned again as to his authority, delivered in reply several impressive parables, warned the people against the corruptions of the age, pronounced the most fearful woes on Scribe and Pharisee, and foretold the last judgment and his second coming.[5] On Wednesday Judas contracted with the chief priests for the betrayal of his Master, while our Lord himself spent the day, either at Bethany or on the Mount of Olives, in preparation for the solemn events that were crowding upon the heel of time.[6] On Thursday he kept the Pass-

---

[1] John, xii., 1-12.
[2] Mark, xi., 12-14.
[3] Mark, xi., 15-17; John, ii., 13-17.
[4] Matt., xxi., 15, 16.
[5] Matt., xxi.-xxvi.
[6] Mark, xiv., 10, 11.

over,[1] instituted the sacramental supper in commemoration of his death,[2] laid aside his vestments and washed his disciples' feet; foretold his own death, his betrayal by Judas, and Peter's denial of his Lord; comforted his apostles, and exhorted them to mutual love; promised them the Holy Ghost, offered the customary sacerdotal prayer, and, having sung a hymn, in the darkness and stillness of that night, attended by a few chosen friends, he passed over the "Brook Kidron," entered the Garden of Gethsemane to endure the agony for the world's redemption; was there betrayed, arrested, forsaken by his disciples, led into the city for trial before Annas and Caiaphas, denied by Peter, and imprisoned till morning.[3] In the gray of the dawn on Friday he was accused before Pilate, "set at naught by Herod and his men of war," and at midday, bearing his own cross, he was led out to Calvary, where, at the ninth hour, he expiated by his death the sins of the world.[4]

Following in the footsteps of the Master, on Good Friday eve I descended the acclivities of Moriah, crossed the same stone bridge over which he had passed,[5] and, entering the Garden of Gethsemane, I sat down beneath the aged olive-trees, and read the touching story of his passion. Returning to the city, in an "upper room," in company with a few friends, I partook of the Lord's Supper. That night I could not sleep. Walking out upon the house-top, I looked down upon Gethsemane. Unbroken silence reigned. The city slumbered. The lights around the balcony of the minaret burned dimly. The night wind blew softly from over the deep sea. The paschal moon was descending in the west. A silvery haze, like a gauze of purity, overspread the serene heavens. It was four o'clock in the morning. From an adjacent court-yard a cock announced the dawn of day. The distant east began to glow with the morning's earliest light. It was Good Friday in Jerusalem—the hour and the event of all time. Well may Christian affection ask, "Where is Calvary?" Who would not approach such a place in silent prayer? Wisely its identity is unknown to earth. Though its location is the first object of research by the Christian traveler when he enters the Holy City, yet it is

---

[1] Matt., xxvi., 20.   [2] Mark, xiv., 22–25.
[3] See John, xiii.-xvii.; Matt., xxvi., 30.   [4] Luke, xxiii., 1–38.
[5] This bridge will probably last for 1000 years to come.

the last to be determined with satisfaction. Tradition designates a rock, inclosed within the Church of the Holy Sepulchre, as the Mount of Crucifixion; but the site involves a controversy so complicated, that the mind prefers the recollection of the event to the examination of the argument. Rejecting this legendary Calvary of the monks, I sought for one more in harmony with the topography of the city and with the casual allusions of the Evangelists. Though it is now impossible to identify Golgotha with certainty, yet topographical facts and sacred history are so concurrent that the mind is left almost without a doubt as to the direction of the place.

As the final scene in our Lord's trial occurred in the Tower of Antonia, which was near St. Stephen's Gate, it is more than probable that the executioners, instead of leading Jesus through the crowded and excited city, led him out of this, the nearest gate. And as at that time there was no place suitable for capital executions either on the south, west, or north side of Jerusalem, we must search for one on the east side of the city. According to St. John, "The place where Jesus was crucified was nigh unto the city,"[1] and St. Paul assures us that Christ suffered without the gate.[2] As the priests of old were accustomed to drive the red heifer to sacrifice, and the scapegoat to the wilderness, out of the eastern gate of the Temple inclosure, so it would be only another instance of the remarkable correspondence between the types of the Old Testament and the life of Jesus if the Jews, though unwittingly, led the Savior to execution out of St. Stephen's Gate. Where, then, should Calvary be sought for but in the environs of Jerusalem on the east?

Toward the northeast corner of the city wall the sides of Bezetha are steep, rocky, and broken. There desolation is complete, and the seclusion profound. The Kidron Valley winds around those rugged declivities, and the opposite sides of Olivet are barren and cheerless. Midway the hill there is a projecting rock, not unlike in form a human skull; on the north of it, a small ravine descends into the vale below, and just beneath it, on the east, the highway passes to the Heights of Benjamin. The sides are steep and covered with black moss. The term Calvary neither implies, nor is it used to designate a mount, but, coming from the Latin *calvaria* or *calva*, means

[1] John, xix., 20.   [2] Heb., xii., 12.

a skull. If Golgotha is descriptive of a place where skulls lay uninterred, then this location agrees well with the sense of the word, as the dead that were here interred were so slightly covered with earth that the bones of such now lay scattered upon the ground; or if, as is more probable, it is the designation of a place where violent deaths occurred—the place for the capital punishment of criminals, whose bones, after the flesh had been devoured by wild beasts, lay bleaching in the sun, then this, of all other portions of the environs of the city, is singularly adapted for such a melancholy purpose.

Reason and Scripture alike point to this spot as the scene of that great death, which has no parallel in suffering as it has no equal in results. Reading the four Evangelists from the brow of this desolate rock, all the details of the inspired account appeared fulfilled with an exactitude not unworthy an intelligent faith. Coming out of St. Stephen's Gate, the mournful procession proceeded along that ancient road on which Simon of Cyrene was returning from the country, to whom fell the honorable part to bear the cross of the fainting Son of God.[1] Reaching this desolate scene, the horrid tragedy was enacted. The place was no less appropriate to the mind of the Divine Sufferer than to those who were the instruments of his death. It is nigh unto the city that had rejected him.[2] Before him rose Olivet, his bower of prayer; beneath his eye lay Gethsemane, the scene of his agony; while, as if to mitigate the sorrow of the final struggle and light up the darkest hour of his life, the Mount of Ascension rose in grandeur before him, crowned with the glory of his exaltation. Around the cross, both on the summit of Bezetha and on the slopes of Olivet beyond, is room for the multitude who had assembled to witness the melancholy spectacle, and for those women who, "beholding afar off,"[3] "bewailed and lamented him."[4] From the adjacent walls of the city the chief priests, scribes, and elders beheld him, and mockingly said, "He saved others, himself he can not save."[5] On the road which passed beneath the cross came those Jewish travelers who, on reading Pilate's superscription, wagged their heads in disdain, and tauntingly greeted him, saying, "Thou that destroyest the Temple and buildest it in three days, save thyself."[6] Here the rocks are

[1] Luke, xxiii., 26.   [2] John, xix., 20.   [3] Matt., xxvii., 55.
[4] Luke, xxiii., 27.   [5] Matt., xxvii., 41-42.   [6] Ib., xxvii., 39-40.

torn and riven; for when he gave up the ghost, "the earth did quake and the rocks were rent."[1] In the hill-side are tombs, which probably are "the graves that were opened, and from which the saints who slept arose."[2] Down in the sequestered vale of the Kidron are gardens, where some old sepulchres still remain, any one of which answers well the description of the Savior's tomb—"Now in the place where he was crucified there was a garden, and in the garden a new sepulchre."[3] Where else in the environs of the Holy City should Joseph, a rich man of Arimathea, have his own new tomb but in the renowned Valley of Jehoshaphat, where sleep in death his ancestors, whose sepulchral monuments continue to this day? And where within the circuit of the city of his rejection should Jesus rise triumphant from the grave but in sight of the garden of his sorrow, the rock of his crucifixion, and the mount of his ascension?

The Via Dolorosa is a lane-like street, narrow and crooked, leading from St. Stephen's Gate to the Church of the Holy Sepulchre, and its dolorous name is no less significant of the tragical events which, according to tradition, occurred along its course, than of its forbidding and gloomy aspect. Like the "street which is called straight" in Damascus, and the Via Sacra in ancient Rome, the Via Dolorosa has a world-wide renown. Its windings, its rough pavement, its prison-like walls —penetrated with low doorways and grated windows—its rude arcade, excluding the sunlight and casting a deeper gloom within, sadden the mind, and are in keeping with the monkish legends that have given to it universal notoriety. Along this dreary walk, amid its shadows and solemn memories, a wounded spirit finds companionship. As the industrious shrine-makers of this and of other ages, the monks have consecrated eight stations in this narrow street, commemorative of as many events in our Lord's journey from the dungeons of Antonia to the site of Calvary. In the northern wall of the Temple area are the two arches, now walled up, where stood Pilate's staircase, down which our Lord descended after his sentence was pronounced, and directly opposite is the Church of Flagellation, marking the place where he was scourged. Not many paces to the west is the *Ecce Homo* arch, where Pilate exclaimed to the infuriated mob, "Behold the man!" At the

[1] Matt., xxvii., 51.   [2] Ib., xxvii., 52.   [3] John, xix., 41.

VIA DOLOROSA AND THE ARCH OF THE ECCE HOMO.

bottom of a gentle descent the lane turns to the left, and then to the right. Beyond this angle is shown a deep impression in the solid stone wall, made by the shoulder of Jesus when he leaned against it at the time he fainted. Near it is the house of St. Veronica, the illustrious woman who presented the Savior with a handkerchief to wipe his bleeding brow. From her residence to the terminus of the street the gloom and silence are painful; and at well-apportioned intervals are indicated, by broken columns, the places where Simon was compelled to bear the Redeemer's cross, where Jesus addressed the weeping daughters of Jerusalem, and where his tragical death occurred.

Throughout Good Friday groups of pious pilgrims were threading the Via Dolorosa and offering their prayers at its legendary shrines. That night the Latin monks dramatized the crucifixion of Christ in the Church of the Holy Sepulchre. At an early hour the venerable Church of St. Helena was thronged with natives and strangers, consisting of Greeks, Latins, Copts, Armenians, Turks, and Franks. To prevent a disturbance, the military governor of the city had ordered a detachment of Turkish soldiers to be present. Among the dignitaries in attendance to witness the fictitious tragedy were foreign consuls attended by liveried cawasses, a hundred French officers, with their orderlies, who had that day arrived from Beirut, and prominent among the distinguished persons was Lessep, the famous canal-digger, who had ascended from Egypt in an improvised chariot drawn by a pair of the noblest camels, and was the first who had crossed that ancient road since the day of Roman chariots.

It was past eight o'clock when the solemn drama was opened with the recitation of prayers in the sacristy of the Latin chapel. The light of a hundred gold and silver lamps, fed by olive-oil, scarcely dispelled the darkness of the hour. At 9 P.M. the pageant was fully commenced, and the long procession began its march, each person bearing a wax taper that shone dimly on the air of night. First came Augustine friars, attired in brown cowls and cassocks; then followed a stalwart monk, bearing an immense cross of light-colored wood, curiously figured. On the cross was nailed the carved figure of a man, covered with thorns, from whose side the life-blood was flowing, and around whose loins was drawn a white linen cloth. Behind the crucifix came two choirs of monks and catechumens robed in white, chanting a funeral dirge, with responsive chorus; following the singers was Rome's eminent prelate, the patriarchal Bishop of Jerusalem, crowned with a gold mitre, wearing a black velvet cloak richly trimmed with gold lace, and bearing in his right hand a gold crucifix adorned with jewels; following in his train were priests of lesser rank in dark robes, and barefooted friars with shaven heads, to imitate the crown of thorns, and nuns in blue and black garments and white linen bonnets; and next came the French consul, the military officers, the common soldiers, poor pilgrims, and strangers from all nations, whose devotion or curiosity prompted them to join the imposing procession.

Within the church are lateral chapels, regarded as shrines by the pious, such as the prison of Christ, the chapel where he was bound, where he was mocked, and where his vestments were divided by the Roman soldiers. At the chapels the procession halted to listen to sermons preached in the Italian, French, German, Arabic, and English languages. It was near midnight when the procession reached the foot of Calvary. Slowly ascending the rude steps cut in the solid rock, the heavy cross was set in its original resting-place on the summit. In imitation of the supernatural darkness, every light was extinguished. At that moment a tumult occurred. The rough voice of derision rose above the universal clamor, and echoed through the aisles and arches of that ancient building, as the Turkish soldiers charged upon the people. Enraged at the insult offered to his religion, the French consul drew his sword, threatening death to Turk or Christian who should crowd upon him. In a moment quiet was restored and the scene went on. Accident gave the charm of reality to the occasion. There stood the captain of the guard, with the smile of scorn upon his attractive though stern features; around him were his troops, and near them were fanatical Moslems reviling the spectacle; standing afar off were Christian women, robed in white sheets, concealing their person except their soft dark eyes, which peered out above their veils; and surging to and fro, like mighty waves, was a motley throng eager to behold the drama. Amid the solemnities human nature was revealed. A magnificent French priest, who had been appointed to preach at the cross of the unrepentant thief, so far forgot his duty as to pronounce a glowing eulogium upon France, and the part she had taken in supporting the Catholic faith in the East. His commanding eloquence touched alike the pride and vanity of the French, and the otherwise decorous officers, forgetting the time and place, applauded the time-serving priest.

The three sermons at the several crosses ended, the lights burn dimly again. And now began the descent from the cross, after the style of Rubens's great picture. Three venerable monks, impersonating Joseph of Arimathea, Nicodemus, and St. John the Evangelist, approached the cross to take the body down. One, climbing up behind the cross, and throwing a sheet around the body and under the arms of the image, held it fast, while another tenderly drew out the nails, kissing each one in turn as he laid them upon a silver plate; then receiving the body into his arms, with the head resting on his shoulder, wrapped it in fine linen, placed it upon a bier, and to the chant of another dirge the procession descended to the pavement of the church, where the image was placed upon the stone of unction for anointing, and hence borne to the tomb of Joseph, to await the joyous notes of Easter Sunday.

Such is a brief description of a scene which annually occurs in Jerusalem; and though producing a transient impression on the common mind, darkened by error and deluded by superstition, the sublime farce is as irreverent as it is offensive to the enlightened Christian. Debased must be the intellect and vitiated the moral sensibilities of a people who delight in such mournful tragedies, and corrupt must be the church which sanctions ceremonies so degrading to earth and repugnant to heaven. With equal propriety, the murder scene of a beloved friend might be yearly re-enacted, harrowing the soul with the bloody memories of the past, and imitating in fiction the ghastly deeds of veritable murderers. Who could be induced to witness a sight so mournful? The last request of the Redeemer to his people was to remember his death, and not to re-enact it; to cherish his memory, and not perpetuate the triumph of his foes. Devotion attains its greatest purity, and piety its highest form of spirituality, as pompous ceremonials are displaced by the simple aspirations of the heart for God, and by the practical embodiment of faith, hope, and charity.

For fifteen hundred years the Church of the Holy Sepulchre

has been the shrine of devout worshipers from all lands, and the antiquity of its traditions, together with the profound reverence in which it is held by the Christian world, render it an object worthy of consideration. Whether considered as a work of art, or as a historic site around which cluster the most sacred legends of the Eastern churches, it awakens a thrilling interest in the thoughtful and intelligent mind. Such are the number and complications of the added apartments, a delineation of the structure is as tedious as it is difficult. Though, as a whole, the architecture is of the Romanesque order, yet in its different parts it combines a greater variety of styles than any other edifice of equal notoriety extant. Standing on the eastern slope of Mount Akra, in the most populous part of the Holy City, its approaches are from the east and west through low, narrow doorways leading into a spacious court ninety feet long and seventy wide, formed laterally by the two projecting wings of the church, by the façade of the basilica on the north, and by a stone wall on the south, inclosing the green plateau once adorned by the palace of the Knights of St. John. A more novel sight is not to be seen on earth than is daily presented in this stone court-yard during Passion Week. Lining three of its sides, with now and then one in the centre, sit the hucksters of pious wares, recalling the money-changers in the court of Solomon's Temple. It is the great religious mart for holy trinkets in Jerusalem, and the most auspicious place for the ethnologist to study human varieties, for the costumer to examine diversities of dress, for the traveler to witness the manners of many nations, and for the artist to sketch the most picturesque of living scenes. There are Turks, with lofty turbans and flowing robes; wild Bedouins of the Desert, clad in capotes of camel's hair, and girt about the loins with leathern girdles, or attired in their gay, fantastic riding costume, brandishing the polished spear; Franciscan friars in coarse brown cowls, and ivory crucifix dangling at their side; Greek monks in long black flowing garments, high square hats, with magnificent beards, and hair long as a woman's, twirling a rosary of mother-of-pearl or of beautiful agate; French and Italian nuns in black, with white linen bonnets, and rosary and crucifix falling from their waist; beggars in rags, the lame with crutches, the blind protected by a dog, invoking the charities of the rich; and pilgrims from every na-

CHURCH OF THE HOLY SEPULCHRE.—FRONT VIEW.

tion—Syrians, Turks, Arabs, Nubians, Egyptians, Algerines, Armenians, Copts, Greeks, Jews, Italians, French, Russians, Germans, English, and the ubiquitous American. Passing through this motley throng, beggars implore your charities and the venders of pious wares solicit your patronage. Here are for sale sandal-wood beads from Mecca, bowls of bitumen from the shores of the Dead Sea, glass rings and bracelets from Hebron, olive-wood rosaries from Olivet, crosses of mother-of-pearl from Bethlehem, and shells on which are rudely carved representations of the birth and resurrection of Jesus, small tin cans in which water from the Jordan is carried to the ends of the earth, wax tapers to be lit at the sacred tomb, and shrouds of cotton cloth or fine linen to be laid in consecration on the Holy Sepulchre, and then borne to the uttermost parts of the earth by the faithful, to be wrapped in in death as a pledge of their resurrection.

Around the court are the ruins of antique and nobler edifices. Along the southern side are the broken bases of a colonnade once supporting a cloister or arcade. Running along the western side is an immense stone structure, from the northern end of which rises the grand unfinished tower of the Basilica of St. Helen; and on the opposite end stands a solitary column, crowned with a beautiful Corinthian capital, supporting the foot of a broken arch. Within this projecting structure are two Greek chapels, older than the days of the Crusaders; one dedicated to St. James, the other to the blessed Trinity. On the opposite side of the court is a plain stone building, the Greek Monastery of Abraham, through which entrance is had to the Armenian Church of St. John, to the Coptic Convent, and to the Chapel of St. Michael. Along the base of the building is a stone bench, where monks and priests spend their idle hours playing with their rosaries.

The best view of the face of the Church of the Holy Sepulchre is to be had from this court. It is the chief entrance to the interior, and consists of the southern end of the transept, presenting to the eye a grand old façade of Romanesque composition, now dingy with the dust of ages and the wear of time. It is divided into two stories. In the upper one are two corresponding windows, arched and slightly pointed, massive in mouldings and rich in sculpture. In the lower story is a double portal, surmounted by noble arches, supported by clustered columns, formed of layers of stone resting on heavy bases, and over the doorway are richly-sculptured architraves, representing our Lord's triumphant entry into Jerusalem. Only the western section of the portal is now open, the other having been walled up since the reign of the Crusaders. On the right of the façade are the remains of that grand tower, once consisting of five stories, only three of which remain. In each of the three sides of the second story is a massive pointed window, and in the third, rising proudly above the domes of the church, are plain and arched windows. Though conjointly owned by the Greeks and Latins, the Armenians and Copts, the church is now subject to the control of the Turkish governor of the city, who holds the keys, and levies a heavy tax upon the rival sects worshiping at its sacred shrines. On the left in entering this ancient edifice, the traveler's attention is attracted by the lordly Turkish guard and his friends, lounging on softly-cushioned divans, where the hours are idly spent drinking Mocha coffee and whiffing the best Stamboul from chibouks of elegant construction.

Except St. Peter's in Rome, there is no religious edifice now standing more imposing than the Church of the Holy Sepulchre. Owing to the addition of chapels and the numerous partitions within for the accommodation of the several sects, it is not easy to give the dimensions and form of the interior. It may be said, however, to consist of a nave 300 feet in length east and west, and of a transept extending north and south 180 feet. The ceiling is eighty feet high. Excepting the rotunda, the nave contains the magnificent chapel of the Greeks, measuring ninety-eight feet in length and forty in width, which is a church within a church. The walls are of wood, carved and gilded, reaching to the lofty ceiling above. The entrance is in the western end, beneath a pointed arch, now filled with a heavy screen, serving as a massive door. From four large piers within, fifty-two feet high, spring noble arches, supporting the central dome. In the eastern end is the gorgeous high altar, the throne of the Greek patriarchs, and on either side are stalls for the choral singers. Behind the throne, formed by a wooden screen, is the robing-room for the priests, those ecclesiastical actors of a corrupted Christianity. Nothing can excel the gorgeous decorations of the interior, which is adorned according to the barbaric taste of the Greeks. The sides of

VIEW OF THE HOLY SEPULCHRE.

their chapel are elaborately carved and gilded; from column and ceiling depend lamps and chandeliers of gold, and ostrich eggs curiously ornamented; while on pier and screen are rude pictures of the Byzantine style. Rising from the marble floor, in the very centre of the chapel, is a marble column, inclosed with an iron railing, marking the centre of the earth, and the identical spot from which was taken the red clay for the formation of Adam's body.

At the western end of this chapel is the great rotunda of the church, measuring ninety-nine feet in diameter, encircled by eighteen colossal piers, supporting a clere-story pierced with windows, above which is the majestic dome, a hundred feet from the pavement below, with a circular opening in the top for light and ventilation, similar to the aperture in the dome of the Pantheon in Rome. In the very centre of this rotunda, and directly beneath the dome, is the reputed sepulchre of our Lord. In form it is not unlike a miniature temple, ten feet in breadth, twenty in length, and of equal height. The exterior is ornamented with semi-columns and pilasters, with rich cornices and mouldings; with a dome resembling an imperial crown, and with a thousand lamps of gold and silver, interspersed with wax tapers and vases of flowers. The entrance is on the east, through a small inclosed area, along which are rows of candles perpetually burning. Over the portal floats the banner of the Cross, and beneath its silken folds is a magnificent picture of Christ's resurrection. It is the most spirited representation of that grandest of all events ever thrown upon the canvas. The Redeemer's form is drawn with all the harmony of parts and the grace of action of an Apollo Belvidere. With one foot resting on the tomb, he is leaving the sepulchre with an air of triumph as majestic as it is natural.

The interior is divided into two small chapels; the first is where the angel was seen, and contains the throne on which he sat, and in the second is the Holy Sepulchre. The vault is seven feet long and six wide, surmounted with a small dome. The tomb occupies the whole length of the north side of the chamber, incased with marble, and is three feet above the floor; the upper slab is cracked through the centre, and its edges are worn smooth by the kisses of pilgrim lips. Forty-two gold lamps burn continually before the tomb, and from a golden censer clouds of incense ascend as a memorial offering. Whether accepting or rejecting its traditional identity with the sepulchre of Joseph of Arimathea, no one can approach this revered shrine without profound emotions. For fifteen centuries Christians have guarded it with a solicitude no less tender than constant. To rescue it from the hands of infidel Moslems, Peter the Hermit and the Pontiff Urban roused all Europe to war against the Turk; to restore it to the Church, kings and princes, bishops and nobles, gave their treasure, and the millions of Christendom flew to arms to perish in the daring crusade; to it longing eyes in all lands turn, and he whose lips have pressed its cold marble in devotion is esteemed a saint with a charmed life. Such is the religious reverence with which it is held, that none are allowed to approach it till hat and shoes have been removed, while the more devout drag themselves along the marble floor and fondly kiss the unconscious stone. Impelled by a superstitious faith and a tender affection for their offspring, mothers come from afar to lay their children on the tomb, and many an invalid is only too happy if he may be laid beside his Master's sepulchre.

On leaving the tomb I fortunately met a young Irish monk whose acquaintance I had previously formed, and who on this occasion kindly offered to be my guide in the more thorough exploration of this renowned church. With singular infatuation for holy places, the shrine-makers both of the Greek and Latin Churches have identified within this venerable building the sites of nearly all those solemn events attending the death and resurrection of our Lord. In the northern end of the transept is the Latin chapel, which has been in the possession of the Franciscans since 1257 A.D.; though unpretending both in its proportions and ornaments, it traditionally marks the spot where Christ appeared to Mary, and bears the name of the Chapel of the Apparition. Passing down the dark northern aisle, we lingered for a moment in the legendary prison of Jesus, at the altar of Longinus, the repentant soldier who had pierced the Savior's side, and in the Chapel of the Division of the Vestments. A few feet beyond, we descended a flight of twenty-nine steps leading into the crypt or Chapel of St. Helena, containing the marble chair she occupied while superintending the search for the Holy Cross. A descent of twelve steps more leads to the cavern where the mother of Constantine found the three crosses, with the title Pilate wrote detached. From the sides of the rock drops of water were dripping down which had percolated the surface above, but which the young monk assured me were holy tears, the rocks still weeping for the dead. Ascending to the floor of the church, and threading the southern aisle, we came to the foot of the traditional Calvary — a natural rock thirty feet long, fifteen high, and as many wide, reached by eighteen steps cut in the living rock. The summit is reached by two flights of steps, one used exclusively by the Greeks and the other by the Latins, for, like the Jews and Samaritans, the former have no dealings with the latter. On the summit is the Chapel of the Elevation of the Cross, measuring forty-five feet in length, the floor of which is paved with marble, the walls draped with silken velvet, and from the ceiling gold lamps depend, dimly burning. At the eastern end is a raised platform ten feet long, two high, and six wide, supporting an altar; and directly before it is a hole in the rock, two feet deep by one and a half square, in which once rested the foot of the Redeemer's cross. On either side is a similar hole for the crosses of the two thieves, and near them is the rent in the rock caused by the earthquake at the moment the Lord expired. Reverently regarding it as real, the Christians of the East approach this shrine upon their knees, fondly kissing what they believe to be the summit of Golgotha. Covered as it is with a marble floor, it is impossible to determine whether the elevation is masonry or living rock; if the latter, it is remarkable that such a rocky eminence should be left in this portion of the city; and if a natural rock, its sides and top should be exposed to view. Descending the Greek staircase and turning to the right, we came to a gloomy vault called the Tomb of Adam, near where once stood the tombs of the chivalrous Godfrey and the heroic Baldwin. Returning to the transept, we passed a yellow marble slab, inclosed with a low railing which pilgrims fondly kiss, and over which lamps burn continually. It is the legendary Stone of Unction, on which the body of Jesus was anointed for his burial. Passing through the rotunda, we descended into the tombs of Nicodemus and Joseph of Arimathea, together with two others, excavated in the living rock, and which, if ancient, are the most remarkable antiquities within the Church of the Holy Sepulchre. Returning again to the rotunda, my good Franciscan gave me his benediction, and, parting from me, left me to the reflections of the hour.

Whether this church covers the Golgotha of the crucifixion and the place of our Lord's sepulture remains an open question. No subject within the range of sacred archæology presents greater difficulties, and none has been contested with a more brilliant display of acute argumentation and varied learning. Pre-eminently it is a question of two sides, and the contest is sometimes so evenly balanced that an assumed victory by the advocates of either theory is one of doubtful certainty. To argue against the supposition, one is forced to reason against his inclination to stand on the site of the Redeemer's death and sit within the shadow of his tomb; to reject it is to leave the world without a substitute, and consign the remembrance of those grand events which it commemorates to the memory of man, without a knowledge of the scene of their occurrence; to deny the identity of the spot is to call in question the traditions of fifteen centuries, to which the Christians of Europe and of the East have fondly clung, and for which the brave have died; to accept it is to argue against the unbroken silence of three hundred years—against equivocal history—against topography—against analogy—against eminent scholarship—against the Bible. The argument for it is tradition and history; the proof against it is the Bible and topography.

Traditionally considered, the argument in its favor runs thus: Such was the popularity of Jesus, and such the publicity of his death, burial, and resurrection, as to stamp the place of their occurrence with imperishable memory; that the descent of the Holy Ghost, the conversion of three thousand, the early founding of his Church in the city of his rejection, and the maintenance of its unity for thirty-seven years, combined to cherish in the public mind the recollection of the place; that though, just previous to the siege of the Holy City by Titus, his followers fled to Pella, beyond the Jordan, it was but a temporary departure, and that, after the storm of war had spent its fury, they returned to the city of their choice; that the desolation of seventy years which followed the conquest of the Romans was partial, and that, while the more wealthy of the population were sold into captivity, many of the common people retained their humbler homes; that, from the year 130 A.D.

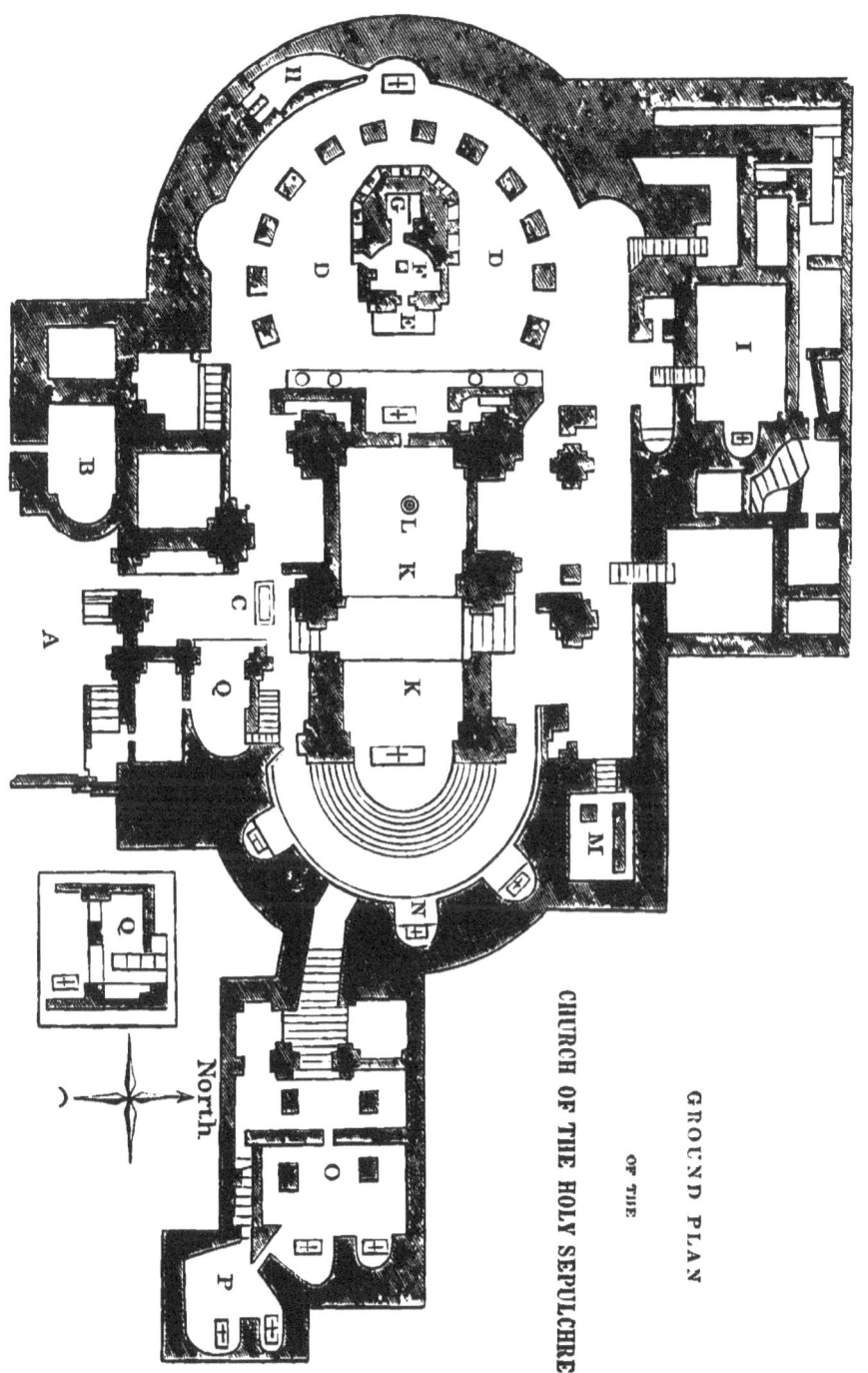

GROUND PLAN
OF THE
CHURCH OF THE HOLY SEPULCHRE

to the present time, Jerusalem has been an inhabited city, and that the Emperor Hadrian rebuilt the city, and, to dishonor alike the Jew and Christian, he reared a fane in honor of Jupiter on the site of Solomon's Temple, and covered the tomb of Jesus with a temple to Venus; and that this temple to Venus remained standing for two hundred years after its erection, and was seen by Eusebius in the year 326 A.D.

Such is the evidence for the identity of the Holy Sepulchre as the tomb of Jesus, from his resurrection down to the commencement of authentic history. It is unwritten tradition, and, at best, presumptive proof. Extending through a period of three hundred years of wars, revolutions, and desolations, it is the most unreliable period of all the centuries subsequent to the Christian era. Whatever may have been the temporary interest attached to Golgotha and to the tomb of Joseph to the idle and curious, to the friend and foe of Jesus, it is evident, from their inspired narrative, that the sacred writers neither shared the excitement, nor considered it incumbent on them to describe with minuteness the scene of their Master's death and burial. They were too much absorbed in recording the stupendous facts of our Lord's expiatory sufferings, and the glory of his resurrection, to entertain their readers with an accurate account of the rock on which he expired, and of the sepulchre from which he arose triumphant. The place is forgotten in the significance of the event; the actor, and not the stage, is the burden of their history. Their simple story is, They led him away to crucify him;[1] When they came to the place which is called Calvary, there they crucified him;[2] The place where Jesus was crucified was nigh to the city;[3] Now in the place where he was crucified there was a garden, and in the garden a new sepulchre, wherein was never man yet laid.[4] This is the sum of their record. They must have been familiar both with the place of execution and of interment, but, from Matthew to Revelation, the apostles are silent to indifference as to the one and the other. Had they deemed it important, they might have intimated out of which gate the mournful procession passed, and on which side of the city the Son of God was slain; but, regarding such information as unworthy their sublime narrative, or fearing our idolatry, they leave us to the uncertainty of conjecture. The invitation of the angels to the devoted

[1] Matt., xxvii., 31.   [2] Luke, xxiii., 33.   [3] John, xix., 20.   [4] Ib., xix., 41.

Marys, Come, see the place where the Lord lay, was not to enshrine the tomb, but to unshrine it, by convincing them by their own sight that he is not here, for he is risen, as he said; and, dear as the spot might be, they were not to linger, but to go quickly, and tell his disciples that he is risen from the dead.[1] We never read of their return to that tomb. Convinced of his resurrection, they sought him among the living and not among the dead. From the summit of Olivet they watched his ascending form, till a cloud received him out of their sight, and then returned with great joy, not to the tomb, but to an "upper room," waiting the "promise of the Father."[2] In his wondrous sermon on the day of Pentecost, St. Peter declared the resurrection of Christ, but made no allusion to his tomb, while he reminded his hearers that David's sepulchre is with us unto this day.[3] In all the subsequent apostolic letters, neither the zealous Peter, nor the beloved John, nor St. Paul, that devoted worshiper of our Lord, ever alluded to those memorable places.

History is comparatively silent as to the return of the Christians from Pella. Many of the first followers of Christ were strangers in Jerusalem, who had come to the Holy City from distant countries to celebrate the annual festivals of their nation. Such must have been most of the three thousand converted on the day of Pentecost, who, returning to their far-off homes, spread the glad tidings of a risen Savior as they went.[4] And although all who "believed were together and had all things common, and sold their possessions and goods, and parted them to all men as every man had need, and continued daily with one accord in the Temple, and breaking bread from house to house,"[5] yet in a brief time thereafter St. Stephen was martyred, "and at that time there was a great persecution against the church which was in Jerusalem, and they were all scattered abroad throughout the regions of Judea and Samaria, except the apostles."[6] The number who fled to Pella, which was but a small town on the eastern bank of the Jordan, must have been exceedingly small. Those who found refuge there remained for seventy years, during which time Jerusalem was a desolation; and, excepting the military towers on Mount Zion, "the rest of the wall was so entirely thrown down even

[1] Matt., xxviii., 6-7.   [2] Acts, i., 9-13.   [3] Ib., ii., 22.
[4] Ib., ii., 8-11.   [5] Ib., ii., 41-46.   [6] Ib., viii., 1.

with the ground by those who digged it up to the very foundation, that there was left nothing to make those who came thither believe it had ever been inhabited."[1] By some this account is regarded as exaggerated, and at most it can only refer to the walls of the city. Granting the correctness of such a supposition, and that some of the poorer inhabitants clung to the ruins of the capital, yet historians agree that the Christians did not return to Jerusalem till about the year 130 A.D., which was after the town had been rebuilt by the Emperor Adrian, and by him called *Ælia Capitolina*. And, at best, only the descendants of those who had fled returned, as during the lapse of seventy years most of the fugitives had ascended to their reward. It is also difficult to conceive how those who had never visited Jerusalem before, and especially after it had been rebuilt by the Romans, could have identified an obscure tomb which had remained unmarked by any enduring monument.

The historic accounts which have come down to us that Adrian desecrated the tomb of Jesus by erecting over it an idol monument, are as contradictory as they are inconsistent. As the emperor was the enemy of the Jew rather than of the Christian, it is impossible to conceive what motive impelled him to dishonor an humble shrine held sacred by a handful of harmless religionists. The erection of a proud fane on the site of Solomon's Temple is in keeping with the character of the man and his hatred for the Jews, but the desecration of Golgotha and of the Holy Sepulchre is inconsistent with his reign in the East, and with the admission of the Christians to his new colony and city. But the early Church historians are not agreed as to the name and character of this idol monument. Writing after the death of Constantine, Eusebius speaks of a temple to Venus covering the Holy Sepulchre, ascribing its erection to impious men; writing sixty years later than Eusebius, Jerome ascribes it to the Emperor Adrian. Eusebius declares it was a temple, Jerome affirms it was a statue; Eusebius asserts it was in honor of Venus, Jerome informs us it was dedicated to Jupiter.

There are similar discrepancies in the writings of these fathers as to the discovery of the Holy Sepulchre, and as to the founder of the first Christian church reared in honor of our Lord's resurrection. According to Eusebius, "impious men, or

[1] Josephus, B. J., b. vii., c. i.

rather the whole race of demons through the agency of impious men, had labored to deliver over that illustrious monument of immortality to darkness and oblivion. They had covered the cave (or tomb) with earth brought from other quarters, and then erected over it a sanctuary to Venus, in which to celebrate the impure rites and worship of that goddess. Moved by a divine intimation made by the Spirit of the Savior himself, the Emperor Constantine ordered the obstructions removed, the holy tomb purified, and a magnificent church to be erected in commemoration of the event." In this miraculous interposition to discover the veritable tomb of Christ, Eusebius concedes that there was no existing tradition identifying its locality. Either the place of our Lord's burial was known to Eusebius, or it was not. If it was certainly known to him by a pagan temple standing on the spot, no miracle was necessary for its recognition; if it was not known to him, then there was no unbroken tradition extending through a period of three centuries, and the question turns upon the credibility of the pretended miracle. The "Father of History" can only be saved from palpable contradiction by supposing that after the tomb had been supernaturally discovered he found over it a pagan temple. But what proof have we that such a miracle was wrought? What good to mankind has resulted from such an interposition? In all Bible miracles, the great moral purposes to be attained justified the departure from the established course of nature. The history of this church, from Constantine to our own times, has been a series of religious rivalries, of bitter contentions between opposing sects, of wars between Christians and Turks, of weary and inefficacious pilgrimages from the snows of Russia and the sands of Africa, of useless expenditures of treasure, of relic worship, and of the utter absence of moral influence on Moslem and Jew.

Such a miraculous intimation given to the apostles would have been more appropriate than to a warrior whose piety is as questionable as the results of his conversion have proved disastrous to mankind. To an enlightened Christian mind it would afford a melancholy pleasure to stand on Calvary and sit in the Savior's tomb, but the temptation to idolatry would be too strong for the common mind to brook. Duped by a mercenary priesthood for fifteen centuries, millions of Greek and Latin pilgrims have bowed in idolatrous veneration before the reputed tomb of Jesus; and for a boon so humble, immense donations have been demanded for the support of ecclesiastical establishments. The genuineness of this divine intimation is affected by the character of the age of Constantine. It was the age of pious frauds. Monkery had existed for two centuries; heresies had taken deep root; saints were worshiped, martyrs canonized, relics adored; and, sanctioned by imperial example, the people were ripe for any deception. Either the theory of an unbroken tradition coming down from the apostolic age to the time of Eusebius, and the existence of a pagan temple upon the well-known tomb must be abandoned, or the pretended miracle for its recognition must be relinquished, as the one supersedes the necessity of the other. Both can not co-exist; one or the other is without foundation in truth.

Jerome and his contemporaries, together with his successors, give a different version of the identification of the Holy Sepulchre and of the founder of the first church over the consecrated spot; and, what must appear as a little remarkable to every intelligent mind, these later historians, who wrote in succeeding centuries, are far more full and minute in their details than Eusebius, who was an eyewitness of what he wrote. According to them, the Empress Helena, the mother of Constantine, moved by a pious desire to worship at those shrines sacred to the memory of our Lord, visited Palestine in the year 326 A.D., at the advanced age of eighty. Having identified the sites of the principal events connected with our Lord's history, she determined to rescue them from oblivion by the erection of enduring monuments, no less expressive of her own gratitude than for the guidance of those devout pilgrims whose devotions might lead them in future years to the Holy Land. Discovering to her satisfaction the stable and manger of the nativity at Bethlehem, and the exact spot of the ascension on Olivet, she ordered the erection of monumental structures on the site of such extraordinary events, at once worthy the Redeemer's glory and the magnificent reign of her imperial son. Naturally desiring to supply the intermediate link, and perpetuate the memory of the Savior's death and resurrection, she earnestly sought for Calvary and the reputed tomb of Joseph. Whether the recollection of these most sacred places had been lost, or whether to confirm her faith in the traditional sites, she diligently inquired of the oldest Jewish and Christian inhabitants of the city as to their location, who pointed her to the area at present inclosed within the Church of the Holy Sepulchre. But the accumulation of rubbish during the lapse of so many years rendered the search difficult and uncertain. Intent, however, on the consummation of an object so laudable, and guided by a divine intimation, she at length came to the sepulchre of Jesus, and near it discovered the three crosses, with Pilate's tablet, still bearing his superscription. The joy experienced by the unexpected discovery of the crosses was lessened by the tablet being detached from its original cross, precluding the possibility of determining to which of the three it had belonged. Ever fruitful in expedients, Macarius, then Bishop of Jerusalem, suggested the happy thought that the three crosses should be presented in succession to the person of a noble lady at that moment afflicted with an incurable disease, and the one which should impart healing virtue should be regarded as the cross on which the Lord of life and glory suffered. Singly each cross was presented, the first and second, however, without effect, but on the touch of the third she immediately recovered. Content with the accomplishment of a work so grand, and sincerely grateful for the honor Heaven had conferred upon her, she ordered the erection of a magnificent basilica over the Redeemer's tomb, and, full of holy joy, the venerable Helena returned to Constantinople, where she expired in her eighty-second year. Nine years subsequent to her visit, and seven years after her demise, the Church of the Holy Sepulchre was completed, and with unrivaled pomp dedicated to Jesus in the year 335 A.D. With these additional facts and palpable discrepancies, it is impossible to determine to which belongs the honor of the work—to the Emperor of the West or to his imperial mother. In both accounts there is the incompatible mingling of tradition and miracle, mutually destroying the force of each other. An intelligent Christian, visiting Jerusalem for the first time, and remembering his Lord expired and was interred "nigh unto the city," would not be a little surprised to find Golgotha and the tomb of Joseph in the heart of the modern town. At the time of those great events the city was encompassed on the north with two walls. The first, beginning at the Tower of Hippicus on Mount Zion, ran along its northern brow, and, crossing the Tyropean Valley, terminated at the western wall of the Temple inclosure, a distance of 630 yards. As the third wall was not built till after the Crucifixion, a description of it is not material to the argument; but on the direction of the second wall hangs the decision of this long-contested question. According to Josephus, the second wall commenced at the Gennath Gate, which signifies "garden," and was used as a means of ingress either to a royal garden on Mount Zion, or of egress to the gardens in the Valley of Hinnom. In either case the gate would have been located near the western wall of the city, at which point the second wall commenced, and, running northward over the level portion of Mount Akra to the Damascus Gate, and thence coming down over Mount Bezetha, terminated at the northwest corner of the Tower of Antonia, including in its course the traditional Golgotha. To the most unpracticed eye such a line of wall would be in harmony with good sense, with correct civil engineering, and with the approved principles of military defensive works. To locate the Gennath Gate at the north base of Mount Zion, and run the second wall along Bazar Street up to the Damascus Gate and thence back to the Tower of Antonia, would certainly exclude the present site of the Holy Sepulchre, but would also exclude the large Pool of Hezekiah, give but a narrow space to the "Lower City" of ancient Jerusalem, and leave the whole of Mount Akra uninclosed. Such a line of wall would have left a large part, and the weakest portion, of the northern wall of Zion unprotected, and skirting, as it must have done, the steep sides of Akra, been entirely unavailing as a defensive structure. No sane engineer would have constructed a wall so as to expose to the use of an attacking enemy the large fountain of Hezekiah; and, if the second wall did not run north and south, it is impossible to understand Josephus, who informs us that, in his assault upon this part of the city, Titus stationed troops in towers along the southern part, and dispatched others to throw down the northern portion.

* The remains at the Damascus Gate of an ancient gateway with towers, the masonry of which is of equal antiquity with that in the northeast corner of the Temple area, are no doubt the ruins of the northern gate of the second wall; and the traces of an ancient wall between the old gateway and the Latin convent clearly indicate that the second wall inclosed

Mount Akra on the west, and therefore included the Calvary and Holy Sepulchre of the monks.

Though the legendary claims of this renowned church are rejected, and its pretended rights to the affections of mankind denied, yet the antiquity of its origin and the romance of its history can not fail to awaken a momentary veneration in the most indifferent spectator. Dedicated to Jesus in the year 335 A.D., it remained standing in all its primal grandeur for two hundred and seventy-nine years, when, in 614 A.D., it was ruthlessly destroyed by the Persian, Chosroes II., who, after the capture of the city, massacred thousands of the citizens, including many monks and nuns, and, as the crowning act of his vengeance, carried the Patriarch of Jerusalem, together with the "true cross," into captivity. Sixteen years later the church was rebuilt, under the superintendence of Modestus, superior of the convent of Theodosius, and the exiled patriarch returned, entering the city in triumph with the "cross" on his shoulder. Destined to the most remarkable vicissitudes, it was again destroyed in 969 A.D. by the Fatimites, who, in the madness of their retaliation, committed the aged patriarch to the flames of the burning building. Remaining a heap of ruins for more than forty years, the revengeful Khalif el-Hákim, the spiritual and fanatical Prince of the Druses, caused it to be entirely demolished, plowing up its very foundations, and attempting the utter destruction of the tomb itself. With an energy as untiring as their gifts were munificent, the Christians rebuilt their favorite sanctuary within thirty-eight years after their cruel persecution by El-Hákim, and it remained standing till 1099 A.D., when the Crusaders captured Jerusalem; the church was enlarged and beautified by them; and during the lapse of more than seven centuries it continued unimpaired till the year 1808 A.D., when, on the night of the 12th of October, a fire, originating in the Armenian chapel, consumed the noble pile. So intense was the heat that the massive walls suffered immensely; the cupola was rent in two; the roof of the nave and of the triforium gallery, together with all the altars, images, and pictures, were consumed; the marble piers in the rotunda were calcined, and the lofty dome above fell in with a tremendous crash upon the Holy Sepulchre. Inheriting the zeal and benevolence of an earlier age, the Christians of our own century determined to reconstruct their holiest of shrines, and selecting Commones, a Greek of the island of Mitylene, for the architect, the Church of the Holy Sepulchre was rebuilt in the year 1810 A.D., and remains standing to this day, the pride of the East and the most imposing of Christian monuments.[1]

[1] Robinson's Biblical Researches, vol. i., p. 407–418. Barclay's City of the Great King, p. 219-238.

CHAPTER VI.

Forty Days and forty Nights in the Holy City.—Inside View of Jerusalem.—Streets.—Buildings.—Commerce.—A Cosmopolitan City.—Government Officials.—Taxation.—Population.—Turks.—Dervishes.—Fast of Ramadan.—Feast of Beiram.—Moslem Sects.—Their Creeds.—Quarter of the Jews.—Their wretched Condition.—Their Nationalities.—Pensioners.—Jewish Passover.—Ceremonies witnessed.—Jewish Sabbath in Jerusalem.—Synagogue.—Education.—Mr. Touro and Sir Moses Montefiore.—Religious and Industrial Institutions.—Christian Sects in the Holy City.—Armenians.—Their Wealth.—Greeks.—Their Influence.—Latins.—Their Edifices.—Monastic Quarrels.—Curious Scene.—Rivalry between France and Russia.—Russian Gold.—Protestant Christianity in Jerusalem.—English Church.—House of Charity.—The two Slave Girls.

FORTY days and forty nights in the Holy City gave me ample time to thread its streets, examine its architecture, study its politics, consider its religion, and form an opinion of the social customs of its citizens. The attritions of time and the physical changes incident to war have marred the beauty of this once imperial city, and the Jerusalem of to-day holds no comparison in wealth and elegance with the Jerusalem of Solomon or of Herod the Great. Less than twelve feet wide, the streets are paved with small flag-stones, and, being without side-walks, are the thoroughfares for man and beast. Excepting the mosques and churches, the buildings are constructed in accordance with cheapness and convenience rather than in harmony with a costly and elegant architecture. They range in size from a one-story bazar-shop to a three-story dwelling. Wood being scarce and expensive, they are built of the common gray limestone of Palestine; the windows are small and barred with iron; in the centre of the edifice is an open court; and the flat roof of each is adorned with a small dome, adding not a little to the general appearance of the structure and to the comfort of the inmates. The arrangement of the interior depends upon the nationality, taste, and wealth of the occupant. Usually the furniture is of the simplest kind, consisting of low stools for tables, on which the food is placed, and a

VIEW OF MODERN JERUSALEM FROM THE MOUNT OF OLIVES.

series of divans encircling the room, which are used for seats in the daytime and for beds at night. The floor, walls, and ceiling are of stone, and are whitewashed as a substitute for carpets, paint, and paper. The bazars are in the most frequented streets, and are in either a small building or on the ground floor of a dwelling. The articles for sale are displayed on a shelf in front of the shop, or around the casement of the door. In addition to the more common necessaries of life, the principal commodities of traffic are the several kinds of Persian and Turkish tobacco, the fruits of the country, some rude silk and cotton fabrics manufactured in the city, together with beads, trinkets, and jewelry, of which the ladies are very fond. The commerce of the modern town is not equal to that of the ancient capital, when the merchants were princes, and when the caravans of the East brought to her gates the fine linen of Egypt, the steeds of Arabia, the carpets of Persia, the shawls of Cashmere, and the marvels of Bagdad.

Jerusalem is a cosmopolitan city, where the representatives from all nations congregate and live. Amounting to 20,000 souls, the present population is divided into classes according to their religious opinions, and each sect occupies a separate portion of the town called "Quarters." The Turk is now in power, swaying his iron sceptre, which he has held for more than six hundred years. The city having been elevated to the dignity of a distinct pashalic, the Pasha is appointed by the Sultan, and comes from Constantinople. The municipal government is civil and military. The civil governor is assisted by a delegated council of Moslems, of which one Jew and one Christian are members by sufferance, to represent the interests of their respective churches. Criminal and civil justice is administered by a city judge, called the "Cadi," who is judge and jury, and whose decisions are law, whether the dictates of an impartial judgment or the sentence of a bribed magistrate. The military department is under Bim-Pasha, the most dreaded of all the government officials. His troops perform the double duty of garrison and police, guarding the gates during the day and patroling the streets at night. Destitute of courtesy and the finer feelings of our humanity, they are the most brutal class of men on the globe, who are respected because they are dreaded, and feared because they are vindictive. The palaces of the civil and military governors of the city are in the northwest corner of the Haram; the common council holds its sessions in what was once the hall of the Jewish Sanhedrim, and the soldiers have their barracks in the Hippic Tower and in the Tower of Antonia, where is still the city prison.

The government is supported by taxation, which is as heavy as the military collectors are exacting. Every expedient is resorted to to avoid the payment of a tax which is imposed with rapacity and gathered with rigor. Under the pretense of poverty, rich Jews live in filth and go through the streets in rags; and to escape the system of espionage which the grasping Turk has established, both Arabs and Christians secrete their treasures in fields and cellars.

The Moslem population is estimated at 7556 souls, and their "Quarter" extends from the southwest corner of the Haram to the central bazar, thence up to the Damascus Gate, including a portion of Mount Akra, the whole of Mount Bezetha, as far down as the northern wall of the Temple inclosure. Mount Moriah is exclusively their own; and, besides the famous mosques of Omar and El-Aksa, they have several others within the limits of their districts. Five times a day from their graceful minarets the muezzins call the faithful to prayers.

Many of the Turks, especially those of foreign birth, are men of noble bearing, and in their way are polite; but the Arab Moslems are the most despicable of beings, guilty of all the crimes forbidden in the Five Books of Moses. Among the most idle, reveling, and villainous class of men in the city are the Dervishes, the embodiment of fanaticism and the cause of nearly all the religious troubles which occur within the town. In their devotions they are the Pharisees of modern times. Whether at the corner of the streets, or in the crowded bazar, or on the house-top, wherever the hour of prayer overtakes them, they count their rosaries, perform their genuflexions, and recite their Koran prayers. During our stay in Jerusalem the Mohammedan fast called "Ramadan" occurred, lasting from moon till moon. At four o'clock P.M. on the eleventh of March the commencement of the fast was announced by a cannon from the Tower of Hippicus. All that night long the balconies of the several minarets were brilliantly illuminated, and amid the glory of a thousand lamps the sonorous voice of the muezzin was heard chanting, "God is great; Mohammed is his prophet; rise up and offer prayer; prayer is better than sleep." Throughout that month no faithful follower of the Prophet ate from sunrise till sunset, but the booming of the evening gun was the signal for a night of rioting and feasting. On the evening of the 7th of April seven guns from Hippicus announced the joyful intelligence that the "Fast of Ramadan" had ended, which was received with shouts that awakened the solemn echoes of Olivet, and was immediately succeeded by the "Feast of Beiram," at which gluttony is the prevailing sin.

Like other religious bodies, the Mohammedans are divided into sects, which have originated in the different interpretations of the Koran by certain doctors whose names they bear. Deriving their faith from four principal sources—the Koran, the traditions of the Prophet, the Concordance of his primitive disciples, and from analogy, they hold to two cardinal truths: "There is no God but God, and Mohammed is his prophet." Believing their religious system, like the Mosaic dispensation, to be a part of the scheme of the Gospel, and not an antagonism to it, they regard their sacred writings to be the restoration of the Pentateuch, the Psalms of David, and the Four Gospels to their original purity. Revering Adam, Noah, Abraham, Moses, and Jesus as great prophets, to each of whom was delivered a portion of a grand system of laws and morals, they believe each succeeding revelation superseded the preceding one, and that the honor of receiving the last and grandest of all the Divine communications of God to man was reserved for Mohammed, whose name the pious Moslem always associates with that of Jehovah. They also hold to the existence of good and bad angels, to the immortality of the soul, the resurrection of the dead, a general judgment, and to heaven and hell. They believe in the miraculous birth of Christ; that he was the Messiah and the Word of God; that, after he had accomplished his mission on earth, he was received up into heaven without suffering the pain of death—another person on whom God had stamped the likeness of Jesus was crucified in his stead; and, finally, that Christ is to come again to establish the *Mohammedan religion* in the earth, and his advent will be the pre-intimation of the world's destruction and the consummation of time.[1]

[1] See Lane's Egypt.

Oppressed by their haughty masters, the Jews of Jerusalem reside in the empire city of their ancestors in the most abject poverty, despised by the Turk and lamented by the Christian. Numbering more than 7700 souls, their wretched homes cling to the eastern declivities of Zion, extending down into the Tyropean Valley. Here, where in happier days each man was a prince and each home a palace, they dwell as pensioners upon the charities of their brethren abroad. As in London and Paris, Rotterdam and Rome, Constantinople and Cairo, the Jewish Quarter is remarkable only for squalidity, and the redolence of old clothes and second-handed wares in general. Induced by patriotism, by devotion, by charity, most of the Jewish population are foreign born, and have sought a home and a tomb in the city of their fathers.

As in the days of Christ, the Jews are divided into rival sects—the Sephardim and the Askenazim. The former are of Spanish origin, and are the descendants of those whom Ferdinand and Isabella banished in 1497 A.D., presenting the rare instance of persons having been exiled to their native land. Their language is a mixture of Spanish and Arabic; and, though subjects of the Sultan, they are suffered to maintain a distinct community, governed by their Rabbinical laws. Numbering about four thousand, they have four synagogues, and are subject to a council of seven rabbis, and a high-priest called "the Head in Zion." Their poverty is the most abject, their filth the most indescribable, their wretchedness the most complete imaginable. Their brethren of the Askenazim order are principally of German and Polish extraction, and number in all less than four thousand souls. Having been readmitted to Palestine in the beginning of the present century, they remain subject to the consuls of their respective countries. Being mostly paupers, they are allowed six dollars per annum for support, which is the amount *per capita* drawn from the contributions remitted to them from the rich Jews in other lands. Hoping to enlighten their minds and preserve a knowledge of their religion, thirty-six reading-rooms have been opened for their instruction, in which teachers are employed to instruct them in the Talmud and other religious works. With becoming regularity they keep the feast of the Passover, observe their Sabbath, and assemble on Friday in their "place of reading" to recite the lamentations of their prophets.

On the Monday night succeeding Palm Sunday was celebrated the Jewish Passover, which I was invited to witness by a Christian merchant of Jerusalem, whose reputation among the Jews made him a welcome guest. The paschal moon shone softly as we threaded the narrow streets winding up the steep acclivities of Zion. Calling first on a family of moderate circumstances, we found them already seated around the table, engaged in the preliminary devotions of the feast. Since the loss of their nationality the Jews celebrate this festival at their homes, and in an unpretending manner observe as far as possible the requisitions of their law. In obedience to the command, all the members of the household were present, including parents, sons and daughters, and daughters-in-law. The dwelling had been carefully cleansed of old leaven by the father of the family; and, that his search into every nook and cranny might not seem fruitless, the busy housewife had purposely placed bits of old bread in such parts of the building where they would certainly meet his eye, and which he destroyed with much ado. The apartment in which the family were enjoying their annual feast was a large square room with vaulted ceiling. The table had been prepared with great neatness and care. On each plate was a bit of lamb, a piece of unleavened bread, a few bitter herbs, and for each person there was a glass of wine. Three lamps were burning on the table, and as many were suspended from the ceiling directly above—symbols of the Trinity. Observing a vacant chair and a well-filled plate, with a goblet of wine before it, I was informed the vacant place was for the Prophet Elias, whom they expected would come, and for whom they wished to be prepared at any moment. To represent the hasty departure of their fathers from Egypt, and in obedience to the paschal law, each person was attired as for a journey: "With your loins girded, your shoes on your feet, and your staff in your hand; ye shall eat it in haste: it is the Lord's passover." To illustrate how their ancestors had spoiled the Egyptians in borrowing "jewels of silver and jewels of gold, and raiment," they had attired themselves in their best apparel, adorned their persons with their most costly ornaments, and decorated the table with whatever silver and gold ware they possessed. The father, who was a man in the prime of life, sat at the head of the table, the mother, a neat-looking woman, sat at the opposite end, the three daughters were arranged on one side, and the two sons on the other. In a chanting tone the eldest son read from the book of Exodus the story and deliverance of the Israelites, while the whole family recited portions of their history in concert. Alternately they were jubilant and indignant: when Moses triumphed they shouted; when Pharaoh was cruel they cursed him, and in their rage they dipped their finger in the wine, and, allowing it to drop upon the floor, they enumerated therewith the plagues of Egypt, declaring Pharaoh should not have a drop of wine to cool his parched tongue. The Scripture recitation over, they began to eat, exclaiming, as they tasted the herb, "Bitter, bitter!"[1]

Ascending a pair of winding stairs, we entered another apartment, where, beside a Jewess and a little girl, three venerable Jews were partaking of their annual feast with much good cheer. The story of the ancestral sufferings had been recited, and they were engaged in common table-talk. The lady of the house was affable, and her little daughter so clean and pretty as to excite affection and merit a present. Contrary to expectation as well as to the law, they offered us a piece of unleavened bread—which was made of flour and water, and baked in the form of a thin cake—and a bit of herb, not unlike American lettuce, and exceedingly bitter to the taste. The three old Jews were advanced in years beyond the allotted time of human life, and their white hair, with their long flowing beards, gave them a patriarchal appearance. They conversed freely as to their national and religious condition, regarding themselves under the Turks as degraded and oppressed as their fathers were under the oppressive domination of Pharaoh. Yet they were not without hope; "Elias would soon come; the proud Moslem would be overthrown, their land delivered, and their ancient capital restored to all its primal glory."

Again winding through the lane-like streets, into which the pale moonlight came struggling through the broken arcade that spanned the thoroughfare, we reached the residence of a rich Jewish banker, and rapped at the court-yard gate, but received the scriptural reply, "I know you not." From the street we could see the brilliantly-lighted room where the paschal feast was held — the elegantly-robed Jewesses, as they

[1] Ex., xii., 1-20.

passed by the window—and heard the voices of joy and devotion within. The lateness of the hour, and the banker's fear lest the display of his plate and jewels might expose him to the rapacity of the Turk, were the probable causes of his refusal to admit us. Standing without in the chilly air of night, the time and scene recalled the Savior's parable of the Strait Gate: "When once the master of the house is risen up, and hath shut-to the door, and ye begin to stand without, and to knock at the door, saying, Lord, Lord, open unto us; and he shall answer and say unto you, I know you not whence ye are."[1]

Retracing our steps, we followed a narrow alley, on whose rough pavement our lantern threw a flickering light, and came to a dwelling occupied by two families. In a small room there lived a poor but industrious Jew and his wife, whose inability to keep the Passover alone induced him to invite to his abode a widow and her two daughters. Expressing surprise at her absence from home on that important festival night, the kind-hearted Jew reminded me of the provision of the paschal law that, "if the houshould be too little for the lamb, let him and his neighbor next unto his house take it according to the number of the souls."[2] In the adjoining room lived the banker's clerk, who explained why his master did not receive us. Unwilling to allow a stranger to see the immense amount of gold and silver in his possession, his cautiousness was the reason assigned for the seeming discourtesy, as his external poverty must be the safeguard of his valuable possessions. Restrained by no such fears, the clerk received us with great cordiality. His sons and daughters, and all his grandchildren, had gathered beneath the parental roof, and, forgetting Israel's ancient sorrows and present misfortunes, they gave themselves up to the freedom and unbounded joy of home. They laughed and talked, sang and shouted, ate and drank, as their emotions rose or appetite demanded.

The day succeeding Good Friday was the Jewish Sabbath, and was a "high day" with the Hebrews. Hastening to their large plain synagogue, I found them already thronging their altars. *En route* I met the high-priest, accompanied by his two sons, successors to his priestly office. His bearing was noble, his face calm and intelligent; and his lofty checkered turban and flowing robes of yellow Syrian cloth imparted to him

[1] Luke, xiii., 25.   [2] Ex., xii., 4.

an air of dignity and rendered him an object of attraction. Whatever may be their reputed poverty, those who crowded the synagogue were well attired. Behind a lattice-work the Jewesses were engaged in their devotions, while the men occupied the centre of the edifice. Most of the latter were aged, and wore an intelligent countenance; but there was one whose fiendish aspect and quarrelsome manner recalled the rabble whose cry against the Innocent was, "Crucify him! crucify him!" Nature had qualified him for an executioner, and his depravity had fitted him for the worst of deeds. He was a short, thick-set, powerful man, his face round and compact, his nose broad and flat, his mouth large and compressed, his eyes black, and burning with rage. Displeased at every person in his presence, he cursed each who passed him, and was the terror of the old men, who dreaded his fury. His ugly face haunts my memory still. He was possessed. He represents the murderers of our Lord. At the door stood two venerable Jews, one holding a lemon and the other a herb, and, as the people came out, they kissed the one and smelled the other.

With a view to dispel the ignorance which, like the pall of death, enshrouds the Jewish mind, generous efforts have been made within the last quarter of a century to ameliorate the condition of those whose temporary or permanent abode is in Jerusalem. By a munificent donation from Mr. Touro, of New Orleans, a new Jewish hospital has been erected just beyond the Yâffa Gate, on the right of the road leading to Bethlehem. Constructed of stone, with a handsome exterior, and containing forty beds, it is governed by a manager, a steward and stewardess. Attached to it is a farm and a fruit nursery, which in coming years will be of great value to the institution. It is the most home-like looking building either in the city or in its environs, and the inmates who lounge beneath its spacious portico are immeasurably happier than those who reside in stone hovels within the town. Though it is the gift of an American citizen, Sir Moses Montefiore bears the honor of being the founder of the hospital. Acting simply as disbursing agent or trustee for the fund, Sir Moses should have had the magnanimity to disabuse the public mind, and render honor to the distinguished benefactor.

Within Jerusalem there are several institutions for the religious benefit of this fallen people. The School of Industry for Jewesses, under Miss Cooper, of England, is not far from the Church of the Holy Sepulchre, on the street leading to the Damascus Gate. Nearly forty Jewesses, between the ages of ten and fifty, are there employed. Their chief work is embroidery and needle-work, some of which is so excellent as to adorn the garments of the Pasha. The inmates labor four days in the week; in summer from seven o'clock till twelve, and in winter from eight till one. The building is divided into three departments—the work-room, bazar, and school-room. Twelve Jewesses attend the day-school, eleven the boarding-school; and seven, who are proselytes, between the ages of five and fifteen, are permanent boarders. Strong in their traditional faith, and because of the influence of the morning and evening service in the institution, the parents of these children give the governess no little trouble in attempting to regain them to the faith of their national church.

To the west of the female school is the House of Industry for Converts and Inquirers, under the auspices of the "London Society for promoting Religion among the Jews." The inquirers are maintained gratuitously for two years, though required to labor at some mechanical trade. Most of the inmates are cabinet-makers, manufacturing useful and curious articles out of olive-wood and other kinds indigenous to the country. All the beneficiaries are males, ranging from sixteen to forty-five years of age. A portion of each day is devoted to such religious instruction and devotion as may lead these sons of Israel to Christ. Since the establishment of the institution in 1848, forty-two converts have been baptized in the name of the adorable Trinity, and a proselyte-meeting is daily held and well attended. With a clearness worthy of maturer Christians, some of the converts answered our questions touching their religious experience, and, if faithful to their high calling, will be lights to their brethren in the Holy City.

Among the Christian sects in Jerusalem, the Armenians are the most wealthy, aristocratic, and influential. Their chief establishment is on Mount Zion, consisting of the gorgeous Church of St. James, and a spacious convent capable of accommodating eight thousand pilgrims. Here, in a new and magnificent apartment, their patriarch resides, whose episcopal jurisdiction includes all Palestine and the beautiful island of Cyprus. Their communicants number about five hundred, who are mostly foreign born, and are among the chief merchants in the metropolis. Their hundred priests are fine-looking men, attired in neat black robes, and high hats of the same color without brims. They employ their time in conducting two theological schools for the education of neophyte priests, in running a printing-press, and in clerical duties. In doctrine the Armenians are Monophysites; in ritual, pompous; in practice, "good livers."

Priding themselves on the power of their royal patrons, the Greek and Latin Christians are contesting their respective claims to superiority. Together with their patriarch, who is head of the Church, the Greeks have three hundred bishops, priests, nuns, and theological students. The patriarch resides in elegant style in a convent attached to the Church of the Holy Sepulchre, in which there is a fine library of two thousand volumes. Extending his episcopal sceptre over fourteen sees, he also controls with absolute authority the twelve convents for monks and nuns within the city, to which are connected as many churches. In addition to a theological seminary and three common schools, they have a college of a high grade in the Convent of the Cross, a mile and a half west of the city, where one hundred young men have entered a collegiate course of seven years, maintained and educated gratuitously by Russian gold. Not less than four thousand people are under their pastoral care, most of whom are native born. Their ancient rivals, the Latins, are rising rapidly to affluence and power in the Holy City. Occupying conjointly with the Greeks and Armenians the Church of the Holy Sepulchre, they hold exclusive possession of the Chapel of the Apparition, their principal place of worship in Jerusalem. Numbering not less than fifteen hundred communicants, who are mostly Syrian born, they have a patriarch, a hundred monks, and ten nuns. Subject to their control are a number of churches, schools, and convents. Among the latter is their famous *Terra Santa* Convent on Mount Akra. It is celebrated for its immense treasures, the gifts of European royalty, and no traveler should leave Jerusalem without seeing those munificent donations. A hundred Franciscan friars here abide, living in luxury, and, though moderately temperate themselves, are only too happy to offer their guests a glass of the choicest arrakee. Here is the residence of the superior of the convent, who is always an

Italian, appointed by the Pope every three years. For the maintenance of this monastic establishment a sum not less than $45,000 is annually expended. Connected with it is the Casa Nuovo, for the entertainment of pilgrims gratuitously for two weeks, though a gift is never refused; and here is the grand bazar of pious wares, where the curious traveler may purchase rosaries, crosses, and crucifixes to any amount.

A monastic life leads to indolence and contention, and the Greek and Latin monks of Jerusalem are ignorant and idle, domineering and quarrelsome, and unworthy representatives of the Christian name. No one familiar with their character and devotion can regard them as the true successors of the apostles, or that the faithful missionary spirit underlies their zeal for temporal and spiritual conquest. It is the ancient love of power, and the perpetuation of the controversy which rent the Church of God in the ninth century. Watching the movements of each other with a jealousy as persistent as it is revengeful, their rivalries engender bitter contentions, which, culminating in a quarrel and a riot, the infidel Turk is compelled to suppress by force of arms. By a conventional arrangement, they visit in procession the sacred shrines in the Church of the Holy Sepulchre at stated hours on ordinary days, and also on festival occasions. The Greeks have the precedence, and the Latins follow. Occasionally their festivals occur on the same day and at the same hour, when their sectarian virulence gaining the mastery of their piety and reason, they aim to silence each other by louder vocal and instrumental sounds. Such was the case on Easter Sunday. Though not their Easter, it was a high day with the Greeks. As in all basilicas, a broad aisle encircles the interior of the church, serving as a path for the march of the procession. The chapel of the Latins opens into this aisle on the west, and at that time they were intoning the Easter service. Attired in their most gorgeous robes, and followed by an immense concourse of people, the Greeks had made the circuit of the church, and, turning their faces toward the open chapel of the Latins, chanted a barbaric hymn with such force that for a moment the Catholics were unable to proceed. Fortunately, the organist came to the rescue of his bishop, and, opening the stops of his magnificent organ, so thundered with his instrument as to compel the Greeks to beat a retreat.

With all their admiration for the Church of St. Helena, their mutual jealousies are allowing the building to fall to ruin for the want of timely repairs. The rain, beating in through the circular aperture in the dome, has so far detached the plastering as to leave the lathing exposed. After every storm large quantities of the plaster fall, and, while present on one occasion, a piece fell to the injury of a personal friend. Supposing it would be a concession of the right of possession to allow either sect to repair the dome and save the church from ruin, both parties refuse to do it conjointly, and neither will allow the other to do it separately.

France and Russia would confer an unspeakable benediction upon the world, and remove a scandal from the Christian name, by stopping such petty feuds, and demanding a reconciliation no less humane than Christian. But it is to be feared the emperors of those great nations have political designs in the East to be consummated which are promoted rather than retarded by such ecclesiastical broils. Both aspire to empire in the Holy Land. More fortunate than the Emperor of the North, Napoleon III., as the imperial patron of the Latin Church, has received, as a consideration for the services rendered the Turkish government in the Crimean war, the venerable Church of St. Anne, near St. Stephen's Gate, and the beautiful green square opposite the Church of the Holy Sepulchre, which was once the possession of the Knights of St. John. Russian gold, however, has purchased what Turkish liberality had withheld. In the East, "money answereth all things." A Turk will sell his soul for gold. Under the auspices of the Russian government, a piece of ground beyond the city walls on the northwest side has been purchased, and sixteen thousand square yards have been inclosed by a stone wall, not unlike, in strength and appearance, the wall of a fort. Within the inclosure four water-tanks have been constructed, several buildings erected, the Cathedral of the Holy Trinity, a large house for the ecclesiastical mission, a hospital containing sixty beds, and an asylum capable of receiving three hundred pilgrims. For the completion of this extraordinary work on the Meidan the Russian pilgrims to the shrines of the Holy City have contributed 660,000 rubles, and a farther sum of 350,000 is required to complete the original design. Within the city the Russians are erecting an asylum for female pilgrims, which in every way will be worthy of the wealth and power of their nation. In excavating to lay the foundation of this building, the workmen descended through the rubbish thirty-five feet, when they came upon the remains of porticoes and pillars which once formed part of the principal entrance to the Church of the Holy Sepulchre in the time of Constantine the Great. It is an event of thrilling interest to the archæologist and Biblical scholar; and were a commission appointed by the several Christian nations of the earth to secure the consent of the Turkish government, and to superintend the excavation, ancient Jerusalem might be uncovered, the palaces of her kings exhumed, and the paths trodden by the world's Redeemer pressed by the willing feet of his devoted followers.

For more than forty years the light of a pure Christianity has been shining upon the city of David, dispelling the mists of error, revealing new forms of moral beauty, and lighting up the path of life. In 1841, the European mission to Jerusalem was modified and its several branches united under a common head, whose episcopal supervision includes Mesopotamia, Chaldea, Syria, Palestine, Egypt, and Abyssinia. Uniting in this religious compact, England and Prussia agreed that the diocesan bishop should be nominated alternately by the sovereigns of the two kingdoms, with the right of veto invested in the Archbishop of Canterbury as to the Prussian nominee. The only stipulations in the contract are the right to alternate with the British sovereign in appointing the incumbent of the Episcopal see, and the use of the cathedral when not occupied by the English Christians. True to her traditional policy to gain all things and lose nothing by her treaties, England consented, and the treaty was ratified. To support the bishop, the late Frederick William of Prussia funded $75,000, and England contributes annually a sum equal to the interest on the above amount.

The foundation stone of the new Protestant Cathedral was laid by Bishop Alexander in 1842, on Mount Zion, and consecrated to God on the 1st of January, 1849. To comply with the exacting conditions imposed by the Turkish government, the church was built in connection with the English consulate. It is now called "Christ Church," and is an elegant Gothic structure of yellow limestone, capable of accommodating 300 persons. Attached to it is a large plat of ground, occupied by residences and offices for the clergy and agents of the mission. Bishop Gobart, the present incumbent of the see, is a man of genuine Episcopal dignity; his face is kind and intelligent; his heart has the pathos of a woman's. His Easter sermon was simple, tender, evangelical. He enlists your attention by the tenderness of his tones, and melts you to tears by the depth of his emotion. He is a Christian of large charities, maintaining out of his ample income several schools in different parts of Palestine. He is assisted by the Rev. Mr. Hefter, an eminent scholar and a thorough gentleman, and by the Rev. Dr. Sandriczki, who has the general oversight of the literature of the mission. Near the church on Mount Zion is the Bible House, well supplied with the precious Word of Life. Not far from it is the female school, containing thirty native pupils; and beyond the wall on Zion, in a substantial stone building, is the male department, in which eighty boys were being educated for Christ by five Christian teachers.

In connection with the Prussian consulate is Pastor Valentiner, chaplain to Dr. Rosen, one of the most learned men in Palestine. Under the auspices of the consulate is a school for children and a hospital for poor pilgrims. The building is pleasantly situated on Mount Zion, and contains forty-one girls and as many boys, who are taught five different languages, with other branches of knowledge. These children are required to remain, by contract, from five to eight years, and, if the contract is broken by their parents, they are to pay the amount of expense incurred. The pupils represent nearly every nation, whose pilgrim parents have either abandoned them in a strange land, or died far from home. The "House of Charity" is governed by six deaconesses, principally Prussians. They dress in a simple blue gown and a clean white cap. They are excellent women and efficient teachers. The rules of their order require them to remain single during a fixed term of years, at the expiration of which most of them marry. Their home is often the scene of the most thrilling events. Shortly prior to our arrival in Jerusalem, a Turk had reached the city, and, having squandered his money in pleasure, was compelled to abandon his two slave girls—one a beautiful Circassian, the other a dark Abyssinian. Touched with their sad condition, the kind deaconesses received them to their "House of Charity." The former, after a brief time, embraced religion, was baptized, and died happy. The latter appeared stupid, and, when addressed on the subject of religion, declared herself "a donkey." She had attained her fourteenth year, and, after six months under the tuition of those Christian women, who watched her last moments with the fondness of sisters, she died of scrofula. Every effort to enlighten her mind had been unavailing, eliciting her only reply, "I am a donkey." But, to the surprise of all, on the night of her death she requested baptism at the hands of Pastor Valentiner, to whose inquiry why she desired the holy rite administered to her, referred him to the death of the Circassian slave, whose experience she had watched, and whose last joyful accents she had carefully cherished. Expressing as her last wish on earth to go where slaves are free and where woman is loved, she passed from earth to heaven.

CHAPTER VII.

Road to Jericho.—Delay.—Caravan.—Robbers.—Ladies.—Scenery.—Waters of Enshemesh.—Wilderness of Judea.—Scene of Christ's Temptation.—Thieves of Jericho.—Parable of the Good Samaritan.—Brook Cherith.—Wild Region.—Elijah fed by the Ravens.—First View of the Plain of the Jordan.—Evening at Jericho.—Ruins of the ancient City.—Historical Events.—Fountain of Elisha.—'Ain Dûk.—Castle of Doch.—Jericho of the New Testament.—Scene of Herod's Death.—Town of Riha.—Site of Gilgal.—Great Events.—Sunrise on the Plain of Jericho.—Richness of the Plain.—Quarantania.—Description of Turkish Soldiers.—The Ride.—Banks of the Jordan.—Sources of the Sacred River.—The ten Fountains.—The three Lakes.—Descent and Sinuosities of the River.—Glen through which it flows.—Flowers and Trees on its Banks.—Birds in its Shrubbery and Beasts in its Thickets.—Its Color.—Depth.—Rapidity.—Twenty-seven Rapids.—Falls.—Islands in the River.—Roman Bridges.—Brook Jabbok.—Jacob and the Angel.—War Scenes.—Entrance of the Jordan into the Dead Sea. — Meaning of Jordan. — Pilgrim's Ford. — Charming Scenery.—Mountains of Moab.—Vision of Balaam.—Vision of Moses.—His Death.—Crossing of the Jordan by the Israelites.—Probable Place.—Overflowing of the River.—Causes.—Translation of Elijah.—Cure of Naaman.—Baptismal Stations of John the Baptist.—Bethabara.—Enon.—Scene of Christ's Baptism here.—The Argument for it.—Journey to the Dead Sea.—Robbers.—Features of the Sea.—Delightful Bath.— Dimensions of the Sea.— Its Bed coeval with the Upper and Lower Valleys.—Sea larger than formerly.—No Outlet.—Its Waters evaporate.—Peninsula.—Island.—Surrounding Mountains.—Hot Springs of Callirrhoe.—Sublime Chasm.—Castle of Machaerus.—Wild Glen.—River Arnon.—Scenery. —City of Kerak.—Ruins of Zoar.—Location of Sodom.—Manner of its Destruction.—Mountain of Salt, cause of the saltness of the Sea.—Lot's Wife.—Ruins of Masada.—Besieged by Flavius Silva.—Tragical Death of 600 Sicarii, their Wives and Children.—Fountain of the Kid.—David and Saul.—Maon.—The Home of Abigail.—Journey to Bethlehem.—Wilderness of Engedi.—A Night with the Monks of Mâr Sâba.—The Monastery.—Bethlehem.—Its Names.—Antiquity.—History.—Convent of the Franciscans. — The Stable of the Nativity. — Present Condition.—Pictures.—The Manger.—Tomb of St. Paula.—Cell of St. Jerome.—Basilica of St. Helena.—Evidence that this is the Birthplace of Christ. — Stable in a House.— Situation of Bethlehem.—Population.—Beautiful Women.—Herodium.—Tomb of Herod the Great.—Cave of Adullam.—Hiding-place of David.—Its Wonders.

THE road from Jerusalem to Jericho leads from St. Stephen's

Gate down the steep sides of Moriah, across the Valley of the Kidron, over the southwestern shoulder of Olivet, near the village of Bethany, through the wilderness of Judea, and, descending the Mountain of Quarantania, terminates on the great Plain of Jordan. It is another illustration of the accuracy of the sacred writers in their topographical allusions, and another proof that only those who were familiar with the land—who had traversed its highways and noted its natural features, could have written descriptions so minute, and, withal, so incidental. In his parable of the "Good Samaritan," the Savior casually states, "A certain man went down from Jerusalem to Jericho;" which not only indicates the relative position of the latter place to the former, but also the descent of nearly 4000 feet from the Jewish capital to the city of Herod the Great. To the careful and candid observer, such internal evidence of the Bible is ever forcing itself upon his attention, and calling forth expressions of wonder and admiration for the truth-telling chroniclers of our Lord's life and ministry.

The "latter rains" had delayed our departure for the Jordan, and a farther delay had been caused by the high March winds, which had so dried the surface of the earth, and had filled the air with dust to such an extent, that for the space of a whole day the Mount of Olives was invisible even to one standing upon the wall of the city. But the charms of a Syrian spring morning soon returned, and at an early hour we were in the saddle, waiting impatiently for the caravan to rendezvous at the Garden of Gethsemane. It was a day peculiar to the Promised Land, for the blandness of the sky and the softness of the air. The foliage on shrub and tree wore every shade of green, and the lovely flowers that covered vale and hill-side recalled the beautiful lines of Shelley:

> "And the spring arose on the garden fair,
> Like the spirit of love felt every where;
> And each flower and herb on earth's dark breast
> Rose from the dreams of its wintry rest."

Our dragoman had agreed to furnish horses, tents, board, and military escort for the journey at six dollars a day *per capita*. The escort is indispensable, for he who goes down to Jericho without a guard "falls among thieves," and, though it is only a question of time when the traveler is robbed, whether prior to the tour or afterward, yet, for the sake of convenience, the former is preferable. He is robbed before the journey by the government, which insists that every pilgrim must pay for its protection; he is robbed on the journey by the organized banditti of the Ghôr, whose depredations the government winks at, if it does not connive with the thieves themselves.

It was ten o'clock A.M. when the caravan moved. Happily for the social amenities their society afforded and the smiles of joy their presence never failed to impart, we were joined by the talented and amiable wife and daughter of a distinguished New Yorker,[1] who was making the tour of Palestine. Mounted on their swift Arabian horses, and tilting their long burnished spears, the Arab guard led the way, followed by the ladies on gentler horses, while the heavy-laden mules, carrying tents, baggage, and cuisine, brought up the rear. On our right lay the Valley of Jehoshaphat, with its monumental tombs; on our left were the terraced slopes of Olivet, green with verdure and bright with flowers; while before us rose the rugged Hill of Offense. Crossing the shoulder of the Mount of Olives, the path sweeps abruptly to the east, and, after winding round the head of the small valley that furrows the hill-side, descends eastward past the place where the Redeemer paused to weep over Jerusalem, and just beyond skirts the town of Bethany. Descending between rough and barren hills, we entered a rocky glen, and in half an hour came to the fountain of El-Haud, the "waters of Enshemesh,"[2] marking the boundary-line between Judah and Benjamin. It is the halting-place of caravans, and its cool, sweet water, flowing into a stone trough beneath a Saracenic arch, is alike refreshing to man and beast in a region so waste and arid. Continuing down the glen for more than an hour, we turned to the left, and soon began the ascent of a wild ravine, the sides of which are limestone, streaked in graceful curves with dikes of porphyry. As the farewells of cultivation, and half rebuking Nature for her general sterility, a stray flower peeped above the rocks, and a stunted tree stood in silent desolation on the hill above. Gradually ascending over chalky hills, our path lay through the bleak Wilderness of Judea. At noon we reached the summit of the central ridge between Enshemesh and Jericho. Neither pen can describe nor pencil sketch the forbidding aspect of this dreary spot. The hills are broken into a thousand rugged,

[1] J. D. Phelps, Esq.   [2] Josh., xv., 7.

barren peaks, and in color are a mixture of yellow and of a dull red and white. The intervening valleys are dry and stony, and on all that blighted soil there is neither shrub, flower, blade of grass, nor any living thing to relieve the dreariness of the accursed scene. Fit abode for the devil and his angels, the counterpart of Pandemonium, it was hither the Spirit led the suffering Son of God to encounter the Evil One.[1]

For twenty centuries this region has borne a thievish character, and the lapse of time has not changed its reputation. As in the days of our Lord, it is still infested with robbers, who, from their undiscovered dens, or from behind some craggy bluff or beetling cliff, level their long gun at the unwary traveler. Suggested by the dangers of the route, the desolation of the spot, and the remains of an ancient caravansary, tradition has identified it as the scene of the parable of the "Good Samaritan." Hard by the roadside are broken walls, fragments of an arch, and deep vaults, said to mark the site of that inn to which the "certain man was brought who went down to Jericho and fell among thieves."[2]

Resuming our journey, we began rapidly to ascend, and soon came upon portions of an old Roman road dating back to the reign of Herod the Great. Winding downward amid chalky hills and through narrow rocky defiles, we at length reached the brow of that sublime gorge through which the brook Cherith flows. Like a silver thread, the stream is seen flowing between banks bright with oleanders. It is here Elijah was fed by the ravens while the famine raged in Palestine. Rising like massive walls five hundred feet high on either side, the mountains cast their deep shadows into the profound chasm below. In their precipitous sides the anchorites have burrowed their solitary cells, and on the loftier crags the Syrian eagle builds his eyrie. Increased by the sombre foliage of the stunted shrubbery clinging to the rocks, there is a solemn grandeur in this mountain gorge, reflecting the sturdy character and rugged life of the great prophet of Tishbeh. Skirting the very verge of the cliff, the winding path descends five hundred feet to the bottom of the glen, where the white rocks reflect the heat like the blast of a furnace. Bearing the Arabic name of El-Kelt, we soon reached the verdant banks of the prophetic brook. The waters are clear, cool, and sweet, but

[1] Matt., iv., 1.   [2] Luke, x., 30-37.

in early autumn, as in the time of Elijah, the stream becomes dry, and as then, so now, the black-winged raven croaks in its

RAVEN.

flight over the deep ravine.¹ The Cherith flows through the Valley of Achor over the Plain of Jericho, and, meandering as it advances, is lost amid the shrubbery surrounding the castle of Riha. Refreshed by its delicious waters, we ascended the northern bank of the streamlet, and were soon in the Vale of Achor, where Achan was stoned to death.²

Like the enchantment of a mirage, the Plains of the Jordan, green and well-watered, now burst upon our view, and beyond appeared the trans-Jordanic mountains. Following the sinuous banks of the Kelt, we reached the foot of the descent late in the afternoon, and, turning northward, pitched our tents near the Fountain of Elisha. The sun had gone down behind Mizpeh and Gibeon; the shadows of Quarantania lay darkly on the plain; the bleating flocks on the distant hill-side had gathered round the shepherd of the Ghôr; the stars came out one by one from their empyrean abode, and we lay down to slumber amid the ruins of ancient Jericho.

Two cities, neither identical in site nor history, have borne

¹ 1 Kings, xvii., 3-7.   ² Josh., vii., 21-26.

the name of Jericho—one belonging to the age of the prophets, the other founded by Herod the Great and visited by our Lord. The remains of the former consist of six mounds of rubbish and two noble fountains, located half a mile from the foot of the mountain pass. These mounds vary in height from ten to forty feet, and in like proportions in their circumference. Around their bases and on their sides and summits are the débris of old buildings, such as heaps of hewn stone and fragments of pottery, and within them are the entombed dwellings and palaces of the ancient city, remaining for future excavations to uncover. Situated on this magnificent plain, the walls and towers of the older Jericho attracted the attention of the Israelites, who from the mountains on the other side of the Jordan looked down with delight upon this, the first city of Canaan which they had seen.[1] Hither came the spies to "search out the country;" here lived the friendly Rahab, who secreted the two Israelites under the "stalks of flax which she had laid in order upon the roof;" to the west are the mountains whither she sent them to elude pursuit;[2] and around these mounds stood the walls which were miraculously thrown down.[3] Dooming the city to perpetual destruction and infamy for the gross idolatry of the inhabitants, Joshua pronounced a curse upon him who should attempt to rebuild it, which 550 years thereafter was singularly fulfilled in the days of Ahab.[4] Here the embassadors of David, whom Hanun, king of the Ammonites, so shamefully treated, were ordered to remain "till their beards were grown."[5] Subsequently to the reconstruction of the city by Hiel, it became the seat of the famous school of the prophets.[6] From it Elijah and Elisha passed over the plain to the Jordan, and, crossing the river by a miracle, the former was translated, and the latter, returning to the city, reluctantly consented that fifty of the sons of the prophets should ascend the mountains of Moab to search for Elijah.[7] Delighted with its pleasant situation, and desiring to make it their permanent abode, the young prophets requested Elisha to heal the fountain and restore fertility to the land; and after the miracle, the effects of which are apparent to this day, the successor of the renowned Tishbite left Jericho for Bethel.[8]

---

[1] Num., xxxiii., 47, 48.   [2] Josh., ii.   [3] Ib., vi., 1–25.
[4] Ib., vi., 26; 1 Kings, xvi., 34.   [5] 2 Sam., x., 5.   [6] 2 Kings, ii., 5.
[7] Ib., ii., 6–18.   [8] Ib., ii., 19–24.

The fountain which the prophet healed is now called 'Ain es-Sultân, and gushes forth from the base of a double mound. The water is cool and sweet, and, after pouring into a large semicircular reservoir, flows in random streamlets to the Jordan. Less than three miles to the northwest is the more copious fountain of 'Ain Dûk, supplied from two springs bursting out of the southern bank of Wady en-Narwaimeh. The water is conducted by an aqueduct along the base of Quarantania to sugar-mills half a mile distant from 'Ain es-Sultân; but, as the mills are now in ruins, this fine stream performs no higher work than to water a few gardens of cucumbers in the vicinity of its source and along its course. Around these springs are strewn the remains of the celebrated Castle of Doch, in which Simon Maccabaeus was murdered by his son-in-law Ptolemy.[1] Abandoning the site of the ancient city, Herod the Great founded the Jericho of the New Testament on the banks of the Cherith, a mile and a half to the south. Around it were the palm-groves and balsam-gardens which Antony presented to Cleopatra, and which the Idumean farmed of the Egyptian queen.[2] Selecting it as one of his royal cities, Herod adorned it with a palace, a hippodrome, and other magnificent buildings. Here he entertained Cleopatra in a sumptuous manner, and here he terminated his life. From this palace he was borne, amid unrivaled funeral pomp, over the southern plain, and up to the wild pass of Nukb el-Kuneiterah, to be interred on the summit of Herodium, in the splendid mausoleum which he himself had constructed at great expense during his reign.[3] More than thirty years after the death of this royal monster, Jericho was visited by Christ, in his frequent tours from the Land of Moab to Judea. Here resided the rich publican Zaccheus, with whom Jesus lodged; by the side of some of its thoroughfares blind Bartimeus sat, whom the compassionate Savior restored to sight; and from scenes so tender he ascended to Jerusalem, to make his triumphal entry into the Holy City.[4]

Not two miles to the southeast is the Arab town of Riha. It is small and filthy, and contains a few hovels occupied by from fifty to one hundred inhabitants, who are guilty of the sins of Sodom. Within a rude court-yard is the only reservoir

---

[1] Josephus, anti B., xiii., c. vii., s. 4; 1 Mac., xvi., 14, 15.
[2] Anti B., xv., c. iv.   [3] Ib., b. xvii., c. x.
[4] Luke, xix.; Mark, x., 46.

of the village, and near it stands a rough stone tower thirty feet square and forty high. It is the barrack of the Turkish garrison, stationed here for the protection of the government lands, for the defense of the peasants of the Ghôr, to collect the taxes imposed upon the miserable villagers, to punish offenders, and to serve as the escort of travelers *en route* for the Jordan and the Dead Sea. Though bearing the name of Jericho, it is more probably the site of ancient Gilgal. In view of the silence of historians on the point, it is impossible now to decide whether Gilgal was the name of a city or the designation of a tract of land, though the former is more in harmony with the scriptural account of the place. Accepting Josephus as authority, Gilgal was ten stadia, or less than a mile and a half, from Jericho, and fifty stadia, or more than six miles, from the Jordan.[1] The old Tower of Riha coincides in its location with this description, and may be regarded as indicating with sufficient accuracy the scene of so many memorable events. Few names in sacred history recall scenes more thrilling and momentous than Gilgal. Removing the twelve monumental stones from the bed of the Jordan, Joshua caused them to be placed here as the memorial of the miraculous dividing of the river;[2] around them the Israelites first pitched their tents within the Promised Land;[2] here they rolled away the reproach of Egypt by the renewal of the rite of circumcision;[3] here they kept the Passover for the first time in Canaan;[4] here Joshua saw, in a day-vision, the captain of the Lord's host "standing over against him with his sword drawn in his hand;"[5] and here the tabernacle was first set up in Palestine, where it remained till removed to Shiloh.[6] Four centuries later Samuel held his court nigh unto this ruined tower, and offered sacrifices for the people then assembled.[7] Here Saul of Gibeah was made King of Israel,[8] and two years thereafter, upon the very spot of his coronation, he lost his kingdom by acting "foolishly."[9] After the death of Absalom the tribe of Judah assembled here to hail the return of David.[10] And here, in the reign of Jehoram, Elisha healed the poisoned pot,[11] restored Naaman to health, and cursed Gehazi with leprosy for his cupidity.[12]

[1] Anti B., v., c. i., s. 4.   [2] Josh., iv., 1–20.   [3] Ib., v., 9.
[4] Ib., v., 10.   [5] Ib., v., 13–15.   [6] Ib., xviii., 1.
[7] 1 Sam., vii., 16; x., 8.   [8] Ib., xi., 15.   [9] Ib., xiii., 8–14.
[10] 2 Sam., xix., 15.   [11] 2 Kings, iv., 38–41.   [12] Ib., v.

The sun rose upon the Plains of Jericho after our first night's slumber among the Arabs of the Ghôr, reflecting a pale yellow light through dense masses of mist which obscured from view the summits of the distant mountains. Ascending the loftiest spur of Quarantania, a landscape of extraordinary character lay before me. Stretching from the northern shore of the Lake of Tiberias to the southern coast of the Dead Sea, the valley of the Lower Jordan unfolded to the eye its manifold and marvelous features. A hundred and twenty miles in length, ten in breadth, and 1312 feet below the level of the Mediterranean, it is among the greatest geological wonders of the globe. From sea to sea lofty mountains bound this great chasm on either side. Rising thousands of feet above the river terrace, the Moab range forms the eastern wall of the great valley, while the Heights of Galilee, the Mountains of Samaria, and the Hills of Judea run along its western border. Broken and barren, the sides of these mountains are furrowed with deep ravines, the frequented passes to the plains below. As far as the eye can reach, the deep, tortuous bed of the Jordan is seen along its eastern side, the turbid waters of which remain unseen till viewed from the second terrace of the stream. The broadest portion of the Jordan valley, the Plain of Jericho is not unlike in form a vast semicircle. Not ten miles long, it is less than eight broad from the roots of the western mountains to the banks of the river. On the south is the Dead Sea, on the east the Jordan, on the north are the Hills of Judea dipping into the rushing river, and on the west is Quarantania rising 2000 feet above its base. Level in the centre, but gently undulating toward the north and south, it has a soil of inexhaustible fertility; and abundantly watered by its numerous fountains, its groves of zukkûm, its beautiful willows, its verdant meadows, its flowers and rank weeds growing luxuriantly, sustain the scriptural allusion to "Jericho, the city of palm-trees,"[1] and the prophetic blessing, the promise of perennial fruitfulness.[2] Such was its fertility in the "Middle Ages," that the cultivation of the sugar-cane, with other products, yielded the nuns of Bethany an annual revenue of $25,000,[3] and by the application of scientific agriculture, would again become, in the language of Josephus, a "divine region."[4]

[1] Deut., xxxiv., 3.
[3] Robinson's B. R., vol. i., p. 562.
[2] 2 Kings, ii., 21.
[4] B. J., b. iv., c. x., s. 3.

PLAN OF JERICHO AND VIEW OF THE DEAD SEA FROM THE NORTH.

Called Quarantania to indicate the forty days during which the Son of God endured the assaults of the Evil One upon its summit, the Mount of Temptation is sterile and gloomy. The rocks are white and naked; the sides are perforated with the cells of hermits, who, retiring from society, hope by the rigors of a solitary life to obtain a better world; and the summit is crowned with a small chapel, the only monument of the Redeemer's triumph over the Prince of Darkness. In the lower caves some wild Bedouins, with their families, had taken refuge, and near them were shepherds keeping their scanty flocks.

The sun had mounted high above the thick mists, which at an earlier hour had veiled his brightness, when I returned to the encampment. Weary in waiting my return, the caravan had moved, and I was left alone among the "thieves of Jericho." The sight of a revolver extorted from a skulking Arab the direction the party had taken, and applying whip and spur, I dashed through the jungle on the banks of the Cherith, and in half an hour rejoined it. On reaching Riha we obtained an additional escort. Our military guard now consisted of six soldiers—five Bedouins and their sheikh. Though wild in their exterior, there was a rude grandeur in the soldiers of Riha. Each wore a loose garment of camel's hair, with openings in the side for the free play of the arms, a pair of rough sandals on his otherwise naked feet, and a bright-colored shawl of Broosa silk thrown carelessly on the head, and held firmly by an elastic cord, the ends of the shawl hanging loosely down. Each carried a brace of pistols and a pair of daggers in his girdle; over the shoulder was slung a long gun, by the side dangled a Damascus blade, and in the hand was borne a lance fifteen feet long. The saddle of each was large, with the bow terminating front and rear in a pommel. The stirrups were of sheet iron, fourteen inches long and seven wide, gently curving, the lateral edges turned upward. Each was mounted on a small but swift and spirited horse, and the captain of the band was followed by a pack of hounds used for hunting gazelles. Their speed was wonderful. Proud of their splendid horsemanship and willing to excite our admiration, these rude soldiers of the Desert gave proof of their marvelous skill and daring, darting forward with the suddenness and celerity of the thunderbolt over hill, through gully, over rocks, through briers, over streams, through thickets, tilting the spear as they rode, as if to plunge it into some advancing foe.

For half an hour our path lay through a jungle of thorny shrubs, beyond which was an open plain. The day was glorious; the air balmy; the sun shone through a gauze-like haze; the leafy songsters, from their sylvan coverts along the streamlets, "caroled the melody of their song." Our horses were fleet, our spirits buoyant, and over that noble plain we rode with unbounded delight. Both in kind and richness the soil varied as we advanced. Now it was barren and covered with a thin, smooth, nitrous crust, through which we sank as in ashes; again it was rich, bearing groves of fruit-trees, tufts of the feathery tamarisk, and beautiful oleanders, with their finger-like leaves and tulip-shaped flowers. At ten A.M. we reached the first terrace, or highest bank of the Jordan, composed of irregular hills of clay, and measuring twenty feet deep. Here our soldiers sallied forth, plunging into the dense thickets and sweeping like lightning around the hills to discover the robbers and save us from surprise. In fifteen minutes more we had descended to the second terrace, and five minutes thereafter we stood on the banks of the most sacred and renowned river in the world. Other rivers are deeper, broader, longer, but the Jordan is unsurpassed in the peculiarities of its source, the sinuosities of its channel, the glories of its history. Springing from the heart of anti-Libanus, ten crystal fountains pour their eternal waters into its descending current. From the base of snow-capped Hermon three noble fountains send their united contributions southward, feeding the River Hasbâny. Situated forty miles to the north from the head of Lake Tiberias, the first is the Fountain Fuarr, at Hasbeîya, and is the remotest perennial source of the Jordan; the second is called Sareid, located south of Kefr Shubah; the third is Luisany, near El-Ghujar. Eighteen miles to the south from Hasbeîya is the largest permanent fountain in the world, known as El-Leddân. Its pure waters gush forth from the foot of the green hill of El-Kâdy, and, after forming a pool, they flow southward in a broad stream, increased in its course by many rills creeping from beneath noble oaks, and at length it joins the Hasbâny seven miles north of Lake Merom. Four miles to the east from El-Kâdy is the Fountain of Banias, next in size to that of El-Leddân, but which, unlike the latter, originates in many rivulets, which, uniting, rush on to a confluence with the Leddân, and, a mile below the junction, join the Hasbâny. Farther to the south the fountains of Derdara, Ruahiny, and those of Belât, Blâta, and El-Mellâhah, unite with the same stream, which, after flowing southward for six miles over the lovely Plain of Hûleh, spreads out into Lake Merom, on whose shores Joshua achieved his final triumph over the banded kings of Canaan.[1] Four and a half miles in length and three and a half in breadth, this gem of the lakes is the first gathering together of the waters of the Jordan from their perennial springs. The lake having a triangular form, the river issues through the apex, and, after running nine miles with a fall of 650 feet, expands into the Sea of Galilee, which is thirteen miles long and six wide. The inlet to the sea is seventy feet broad, and the waters, flowing between alluvial banks, are lazy and turbid. Purified in their passage through this second reservoir of the Jordan, they find an outlet in the southwest corner of the sea. Here the river is more than ninety feet wide, the banks are high and round, and the contiguous mountains rugged and barren. Half unwilling to leave the parent waters to take the headlong leap over twenty-seven rapids to the Sea of Death, the Jordan turns back upon itself; but, forced at length to return by the unyielding rocks, it cuts a channel westward, then west by south, when, impelled by the unchanging law of gravitation, it rushes madly southward, foaming and leaping downward 700 feet in less than sixty miles. Though, between the seas as the crow flies, the actual distance is not more than sixty miles, yet, owing to the infinite multiplication of its windings, it is more than 200 miles in length. The tortuous glen through which it flows varies in breadth from 200 to 600 yards, and in depth from fifty to eighty below the surrounding plain. The sides of the glen are abrupt and broken, composed of marl and clay intermixed with limestone. Where it is widest, the bottom is mud covered with reeds; where it is narrowest, it is rock and sand. Along its banks grow in rich profusion the scarlet anemone, the yellow marigold, the waterlily, the feathery tamarisk, the pink oleander, the Syrian thistle with its gorgeous purple blossom, and cane-reeds, oaks, willows, and wild pistachios. Amid foliage so rich and rare are birds of exquisite plumage and variant song. Disporting in the wa-

[1] Josh., xi., 6-10.

ter are herons and ducks; dancing from bower to bower are sparrows, swallows, and nightingales; wheeling their tireless flight over stream and shrub are eagles, partridges, hawks, and snipes, while storks spread their vast wings along the banks, and

> "The moping owl does to the moon complain
> Of such as, wandering near her secret bower,
> Molest her ancient solitary reign."

In the deep, impenetrable jungle, extending for miles in depth along either bank, is now, as formerly, the hiding-place of the leopard, the wild boar, and tiger. In color the Jordan is not unlike the Tiber. In breadth it varies from eighty to 240 feet; in depth it is from two to sixteen feet; in motion it flows from two to twelve knots an hour, bearing on its yellow bosom, as it rolls to the sea, the débris of northern forests. In its descent there are wild cascades, down which the foaming torrent leaps eleven feet, at the rate of twelve miles an hour. Throughout its sinuous course there are twenty-seven rapids, some of which are 900 feet long, and the shallow waters foam as they pass over the large boulders of sandstone and trap. Below the longest rapid there is a series of five falls, having a descent of eighteen feet, with rapids between them; and at El-Bûk'ah there is a whirlpool grand and dangerous. At intervals, where the channel is deep and free from rocks, a boat might glide with ease and pleasure. In the broader portions of the river bed there are islands, some barren, others verdant and flowery. Near the four well-known fords are the remains of old mills, with their sluices, and the ruins of ancient bridges of Roman construction, pointing us back to a better civilization, and reflecting the genius, industry, and utility of a former age. At Semakh, a mile south of the Lake of Tiberias, are the abutments of a fine bridge of ninety feet span, and at Zurka are the remains of a nobler structure.

Midway the two seas the Brook Jabbok flows into the Jordan. Descending through a deep ravine, amid the loftiest of the Ajlûn range, its volume is swelled by the mountain torrents, rendering it at times impassable. Its banks are fringed with tamarisks and oleanders, the clustering flower of the latter imparting a gorgeous aspect to the scene. As three thousand years ago the Jabbok was the boundary between the kingdoms of Sihon and of Og,[1] so this modern Zurka is the dividing line between the province of Belka and that of Ajlûn.

SHOOTING THE RAPIDS.

Somewhere on its banks occurred one of those thrilling events so common in the patriarchal history. Coming from the distant home of Laban, enriched with the rewards of twenty years' industry, and blessed with a numerous family of children and servants, the patriarch Jacob halted on the northern bank of the Jabbok, and that night wrestled with an angel. And as the light of the coming day dawned, down the glens and sides of the southern mountain the chieftain of Seir came, with his

[1] Josh., xii., 2-5.

four hundred warriors. Hoping to appease Esau's anger by the gentleness of his manner, Jacob crossed the brook, and, forgetting the enmities of boyhood, the twin brothers embraced and were reconciled. Parting, Esau returned to his mountain home, and, fording the Jordan here, Jacob ascended by the beautiful Tirzah, and dwelt in the Vale of Shechem.[1]

Centuries later, this brook was the scene of events less peaceful. Obeying the heroic Gideon, the men of Ephraim took possession of this ford and slew the fugitive Midianites;[2] and ninety years thereafter the Gileadites under Jephthah, descending from their native mountains, held the passage of the stream, and slew every Ephraimite whose betraying tongue could not correctly pronounce the password Shibboleth.[3]

The Pilgrim's Ford, opposite Jericho, is no less enchanting in its natural scenery than it is memorable for its sacred associations. A hundred feet wide and twelve deep, the Jordan sweeps by at the rate of six knots an hour. From this point to the Dead Sea the river retains its general peculiarities of sinuosity, of color, of rapidity, of banks, and foliage. The inlet to the Asphaltic Lake is three feet deep and 540 wide, and here is the third and largest reservoir of the Jordan—its first and only stage of rest. Here it ends.

This being an ancient ford, the western bank is worn down to the water's edge by the tread of many generations. On either side willows bend their graceful limbs to touch the rapid stream, tamarisks wave gently in the soft zephyrs, oleanders bloom amid foliage of lighter and deeper green, and the crystal streamlet from Riha flows into the turbulent Jordan among trees of statelier form. A little to the south the banks are steep, and the bottom is soft and covered with weeds and lacerating briers. Directly opposite, the Mountains of Moab rise in all their rugged grandeur, with their sides broken by deep ravines and their summits veiled in a purple haze. Forgotten in the lapse of time, yet somewhere on those loftier peaks were the high places of Baal,[4] the "field of Zophim,"[5] and the "top of Peor,"[6] whither Balak led Balaam to curse Israel. From those summits of vision the prophet of Pethor looked down upon the Lord's chosen people, but could not "count

---

[1] Gen., xxxii., xxxiii. [2] Judges, vii., 24, 25. [3] Ib., xii., 5, 6.
[4] Num., xxii., 41. [5] Ib., xxiii., 14. [6] Ib., xxiii., 28.

the dust of Jacob."¹ He beheld them "crouching like a lion,"² and, in the rapture of his song, exclaimed, "How goodly are thy tents, O Jacob, and thy tabernacles, O Israel."³ Under more auspicious circumstances, a greater than Balaam surveyed the Land of Promise from Pisgah's top.⁴ Turning northward, "his eye that was not dim" swept the land of Gilead unto the icy crown of Hermon; turning westward, he beheld the distant hills of Naphtali standing out against the sky; nearer, he saw the possessions of Ephraim and Manasseh; directly before him was the Land of Judah and Benjamin, the City of the Great King, and the blue waters of the Mediterranean beyond; while at his feet lay the rich plain of Jericho, the "city of palm-trees," the first conquest of the triumphant arms of Joshua. In his tent, or in some retired glen, or on some solitary peak, the son of Amram wrote most of his inspired history; and yonder, when the work of his wondrous life was finished, when the farewell view of the goodly Canaan had been completed, when he had given his final blessing to Eleazar the priest, to Joshua the warrior, "Moses, the servant of the Lord, died there in the land of Moab, according to the word of the Lord; and he buried him in a valley in the land of Moab, over against Beth-peor; but no man knoweth of his sepulchre unto this day."⁵ A tomb so vast was worthy of the world-wide influence of his life, and the Mountains of Moab are the appropriate monument of a character so pure and a name so great.

The tradition that identifies this ford as the place where the Israelites crossed the Jordan is supported by the clear and simple statement that they "passed over right against Jericho."⁶ The crossing, however, could not have been confined to this limited space. Here probably the priests crossed, while the multitude sought a passage at every feasible point between the city of Adam, thirty miles to the north, and the Dead Sea, five miles to the south. To facilitate the crossing, this long section of the river-bed became dry, which was necessitated both by the millions of people to cross, and also by the impassableness of many portions of the banks. The rendezvous was opposite Jericho, and as the swarming millions came up the western bank, they turned northward and southward toward a

¹ Num., xxiii., 10. ² Ib., xxiii., 24. ³ Ib., xxiv., 5.
⁴ Deut., xxxiv., 1–3. ⁵ Ib., xxxiv., 5. ⁶ Josh., iii., 16.

common centre. Bearing the ark of the covenant, the priests led the van, and as their feet touched the water, "the waters which came down from above stood and rose up upon an heap very far from the city of Adam, that is, beside Zaretan; and those that came down toward the sea of the plain, even the salt sea, failed and were cut off, and the people passed over right against Jericho."[1] Unlike the dividing of the Red Sea, this was the cutting off or damming up of the waters on the north; and the miracle is the more wonderful, as at that time the river was more than ordinarily full. The incidental allusion that the "Jordan overfloweth all his banks all the time of harvest"[2] is equally true at the present day. In the tropical climate of the Jordan Valley the harvest is many weeks earlier than on the mountains 1300 feet above it. Barley harvest occurring here in the middle of March and wheat harvest about three weeks later, it is evident that the allusion refers to the harvest-time of the Jericho plain. At this time of year the Jordan annually rises to the fullness of its banks, and not unfrequently overflows them; and, though occurring in the dry season of the year, the rise is owing to the melting snows on Mount Hermon, and also to the heavy winter rains, which, having previously fallen on the Hermon range, and by March having percolated the sides of the mountains, begin to swell the springs within them, which, being the sources of the Jordan, then commence and for weeks continue to pour an increased volume into the river channel, permitting the traveler of to-day to behold the filling up and overflowing of the sacred river as it overflowed all its banks three thousand years ago.

More than five centuries later, the Jordan was here twice divided in one day—once for the safe passage of Elijah and Elisha to the land of Moab, and again for the return of the latter to Jericho;[3] and, two years subsequently, here the proud Naaman bathed his leprous person and was made whole. To one unacquainted with the three rivers mentioned in connection with his cure, there is the appearance of pride and contempt in his language; but in recalling, in the moment of disappointment and chagrin, the clear waters of the Abana and Pharphar, in contrast with the yellow, turbulent waters of the Jordan, the Syrian warrior but indicated the correctness of his

[1] Josh., iii., 16.   [2] Ib., iii., 15.   [3] 2 Kings, ii.

taste in preferring the "rivers of Damascus to all the waters of Israel."[1] But after a cure so miraculous, notwithstanding its inferior beauty, the Jordan must have been to him the noblest and most sacred of rivers.

As the baptismal station of John the Baptist, and the scene of our Lord's baptism, the Christian contemplates this traditional spot with deeper, sweeter interest. But, however sincere and intense may be the desire to identify the scene of an event so hallowed, it is difficult to ascertain with certainty where that greatest of all baptisms occurred. In general terms, St. Luke describes John as coming into "all the country about Jordan;"[2] but, with great precision, St. John designates two stations of the great Baptist: "Bethabara, beyond Jordan,"[3] and "Ænon, near Salim."[4] Signifying "The House of Passage," Bethabara may have been the name of some well-known ford; but the most eminent critics agree that Bethany should be inserted in the text in the place of Bethabara.[5] Finding it difficult to discover a Bethany beyond the Jordan, Origen, in the early part of the third century, changed the reading, and others, following his version, place Bethabara near the Brook Jabbok, on the east, and Ænon on the west, eight miles southeast from Bethshean.[6]

Such locations, however, leave Southern Palestine without a baptismal station. Born in the south, and from his Judean home called to the great work of his mission, John's ministry was commenced in the "wilderness of Judea."[7] His first hearers were those of the Jewish capital and of its adjacent towns: "Then went out unto him Jerusalem, and all Judea, and all the region round about Jordan."[8] Preferring a journey of six hours to one of two days, the people of the south would naturally descend to this traditional ford, where the Baptist as naturally would be waiting to receive them. And where else should Jesus be baptized but where his ancient people had crossed the "swellings of Jordan," and nigh unto the capital of his kingdom, whose citizens had just received his forerunner?

Having prepared the way of the Messiah in Judea, and to accommodate the multitudes of the north, and prepare them

---

[1] 2 Kings, v., 12. [2] Luke, iii., 3. [3] John, i., 28. [4] Ib., iii., 23.
[5] Clark's Comment. on John, i., 28. [6] Stanley's Palestine, p. 304, 305.
[7] Matt., iii., 1. [8] Ib., iii., 5.

for the reception of the promised Christ, John ascended the river to the mouth of the Jabbok, where he baptized the inhabitants of Samaria; and ascending thirty miles farther, to the ruined bridge of Semakh, he baptized the people of Galilee. His mission accomplished in Southern, Central, and Northern Palestine, and compelled to leave the Jordan at that season of the year to seek water suitable to drink, John removed to the fountains of Ænon, eight Roman miles southeast from Scythopolis, where there was "much water," and where he baptized "strangers," and those who had failed to attend his ministry at the river. His latter days were spent in the north, and mostly in Tiberias, the royal city of Galilee, where, true to his high calling, he reproved Herod Antipas for his connubial infidelity, for which he was imprisoned and beheaded in the Castle of Machaerus, near the scene of his earlier labors.

The sun was rapidly approaching the zenith when we left the ford for the Dead Sea. To avoid a detour, and also to shun the banks of the river, which, from their softness and steepness, are never safe, we crossed diagonally the great plain extending to the sea. The heat was intense; not a breath of air was stirring; neither shrub nor flower appeared to gladden the eye; no fountain was nigh to moisten our parched lips. A deep purple haze veiled earth and sky, obscuring the view of Moab and the peaks of Engedi; and over that vast plateau of unrelieved desolation was spread a white sulphurous crust, reflecting the light and heat. Near the mouth of the Jordan a band of Bedouin ruffians were holding an ominous consultation, and keenly watching our movements. From the head of the caravan came the shrill voice of the sheikh to "close ranks," while two soldiers dashed into the jungle to ascertain the design of the council. Intimidating the robbers by threats, they returned, assuring us that no attack would be made, but advising us to keep close together. At noon we stood upon the northern shore of the Dead Sea. Owing to the thick haze that obscured the mountains, it seemed shoreless. The smooth waters lay like molten silver, silent and motionless, sparkling in the sunlight and dazzling to the sight. It was death robed in light. The waters are clear as crystal and exceedingly brilliant, and, though intensely salt, they are so soft that a bath in them is like bathing in oil. When midway my person I

DEAD SEA.

began to rise, and yielding to the soft hands that bore me up, I reclined as upon the softest down. To sink was impossible; to float required no effort; to read, converse, sleep, was easy. Where the cuticle was bruised or broken a smarting sensation was experienced, and for ten hours after the bath the hair remained stiff and the body felt as if it had been lubricated with oil. Gently sloping toward the sea, the northern coast consists of sand and blackened pebbles, and over its entire breadth are strewn quantities of drift-wood, such as willow twigs, broken canes, and poplar branches, thrown up by the violence of the waves when the sea is in commotion. Higher up is a terrace of bitumen, soft and slippery, and not unlike black clay. Neither shrub, flower, nor blade of grass, nor shell, can be found on all that lengthened beach.

Occupying the lowest portion of the Jordan Valley, the Dead Sea is forty miles long, from five to nine wide, and from two to 1308 feet deep. Its greatest depth is 2620 feet below the level of the Mediterranean, and 5220 below the site of Jerusalem. Having its greatest width midway the sea, from Ain Jidy to the River Arnon, it is most shallow at its southern extremity, and deepest in its northern section, southwest from the thermal waters of Callirrhoe. Not many yards from the eastern cliffs it is more than one hundred and seventy fathoms deep.

Geologically considered, the profound cavity containing this inland sea must be coeval with the conformation of the Jordan Valley on the north and the Valley of 'Arabah on the south. This mighty chasm must always have been the bed of a great lake, receiving the waters of the Jordan and the mountain torrents, together with those of the living springs which abound along the margin of the vale. Though much smaller then than now, both Abraham and Lot must have looked down upon its waters. Originally confined within its deeper bed, it has passed its primal limits by some convulsion or atmospheric phenomena as yet unknown. The great difference in its depth, from a third of a fathom to two hundred and eighteen fathoms, together with the record of Moses that the "plain of Jordan was well watered every where before the Lord destroyed Sodom and Gomorrah, even as the garden of the Lord, like the land of Egypt as thou comest unto Zoar,"[1] sufficiently

[1] Gen., xiii., 10.

indicates that the more shallow portions now overflown were once the rich green fields so tempting to the eyes of Lot.[1] According to authentic history, this vale was one of the cradles of the earliest civilization, not only containing the five royal cities that were destroyed, but also the cities of the Phœnicians, who, afterward removing to Tyre and Sidon, rose to greatness in art, science, and commerce. Its present desolation is due to natural causes, some of which are still apparent, and though its waters must always have been more or less salt, and its coasts must always have abounded in bitumen pits, yet these are not inconsistent with the richness of its plains, as attested by sacred and profane writers.

Though the receptacle of the perennial Jordan and of springs that never fail, and though without an outlet its mighty caldron is never filled to overflowing, and its waters have but a slight perceptible rise and fall. Situated 1312 feet below the level of the Mediterranean, and shut in by high barren mountains of limestone, its supply never exceeds the demand made by its rapid evaporation. With the Gulf of Akaba thirty-five feet above the Mediterranean, it is inconceivable how the Dead Sea could ever have flowed southward over the plain of 'Arabah to mingle its waters with those of the Red Sea; and this impossibility is the more apparent from the fact that the waters of 'Arabah flow into the Dead Sea from a water-shed midway between the two seas. Such curious facts at once disprove the hypothesis either that there is a subterranean outlet on the south, or that, prior to the fall of Sodom, the waters of the Jordan flowed in a river channel through the "Vale of Siddim" to mingle with those of the Indian Ocean. Evaporation was then, as now, the only outlet.

With the exception of a few semicircular plains, the "Salt Sea" covers the entire breadth of the vale, in many places the mountains dipping into the waters without a footpath along the shore. At the northwest corner there is a neck of land extending into the lake, which, when the water is low by increased evaporation, is a peninsula, but at high water its extreme point is a small island, covered with ruins of great antiquity, consisting of heaps of unhewn stones, some of which retain their original position in the foundation of a building whose history is unknown; and at the southeast angle of the sea, near

[1] Gen., xiii., 10.

the ravine of Kerak, is a low, broad promontory or cape, extending four miles to the north up the centre of the lake. Wherever a brackish fountain trickles down the hill-side, and flows over those little plains formed by the receding mountains, there shrubs grow, flowers bloom as in more genial climes, birds sing sweetly as in more enchanting bowers, and the Arab, with the traveler, pitches his tent, unaffected by the fancied deadly exhalations from the poisonous sea, which only exist in the stories of poet and romancer.

The mountains that bound the Asphaltic Lake on the east and west are as remarkable for their native grandeur as for their historic associations. Those on the east are portions of the Moab and Edom ranges; the one descending from the north and the other ascending from the south, are separated midway the sea by the sublime chasm of El-Mójib. The former is composed of sandstone, with sections of limestone, and with dikes and seams of trap rock, over which are scattered quantities of post-tertiary lava, pumice-stone, and volcanic slag; the latter is in part sandstone with strata of limestone; while at the extreme south there is a post-tertiary deposit of carbonate of lime, with sandstone disintegrated, and with a mixture of sulphur and gypsum. Rising from 2000 to 3000 feet high, the eastern range is rugged and barren, and, from a peculiarity in the atmosphere, is perpetually veiled in a purple haze. The sides are broken by twelve ravines desolate and wild. Less than ten miles from the northeast angle of the sea, at the mouth of Wady Zŭrka Ma'in, are the warm springs of Callirrhoe, sending forth, between grand and lofty sandstone cliffs, a copious stream, in whose thermal waters Herod the Great sought, in vain, relief from his loathsome disease. It is twelve feet wide, ten inches deep, and has a temperature of 95° Fahrenheit. Its banks are lined with canes and tamarisks, and the pebbles are tinged with the sulphurous waters. The chasm is 112 feet wide, and from eighty to 150 high, through which the torrent sweeps to the sea at the rate of six knots an hour. High up the ravine is a pretty cascade, with a perpendicular fall of six feet, and below it the foaming waters rush over a succession of rapids. In this sublime glen purple flowers bloom, and ravens and butterflies wing their tireless flight. On the very brow of the northern cliff stood the famous fortress of Machaerus, where John the Baptist was beheaded.[1] Two miles to the south, on the borders of a little streamlet, is a grove of thirty date-palm-trees; three miles farther is a bright cascade, whose sparkling waters leap into the sea from the very mountain summit; and five miles beyond is the ancient river Arnon, on whose banks Balak met Balaam,[2] and which was the southern boundary-line of the Amorites, whose dominion ran northward to the Jabbok. This tract of land Moses conquered from Sihon,[3] and for it the Ammonites fought with Jephthah[4] while it was possessed by the tribes of Reuben and Gad.[5] The Arnon is a tributary to the sea, eighty-two feet wide, four deep, and one hundred wide at its mouth. The vast fissure through which it falls is ninety-seven feet wide, and varies from 100 to 400 feet high. The cliffs are red, yellow, and brown sandstone, and, worn by the winds and rains, resemble Egyptian architecture. In graceful curves the ravine winds inward, and in its profound depths are huge boulders, which have fallen from the summit above. Along the border of the torrent a few shrubs grow, and gazelles descend to drink of its limpid waters. Fifteen miles to the south, on a summit 3000 feet above the sea, stands the ancient city of Kerak, containing more than 3000 inhabitants, about equally divided into Christians and Moslems, which is renowned in the history of Jewish wars as the city whose king, in a moment of desperation, rather than surrender to King Jehoram, offered up his eldest son upon the town wall as a burnt-sacrifice, so disgusting the Israelites as to compel them to raise the siege.[6] From the mountain of Kerak a wild ravine leads down to the reputed ruins of Zoar, near the shore, to which Lot fled when commanded to fly to the mountains above.[7]

To the southwest from the ruins of Zoar stood Sodom and Gomorrah, with their companion cities of the plain. Covering a large area of what was once dry land, the sea is here exceedingly shallow, and the plains bordering on the southern coast give evidence of their former fertility. These cities must have occupied this section of the vale, or it would have been impossible for Abraham to have seen the conflagration from Hebron, sixteen miles to the northwest.[8] But not a vestige of those

---

[1] Josephus, b. xviii., c. v. [2] Num., xxii., 36. [3] Judges, xi., 19.
[4] Ib., xi., 13. [5] Josh., xiii., 8. [6] 2 Kings, iii., 37.
[7] Gen., xix., 17-20. [8] Ib., xix., 28.

renowned cities remains to designate the scene of their glory and shame. The "rain of fire" was probably a shower of nitrous particles ignited by the electric flash, which, as it fell, kindled to a flame the buildings of the cities, constructed of bituminous stones and cemented by green asphalt. Formed of such combustible materials, the conflagration of the towns must have raged with unwonted fury, and the descending fire, wrapping vale and mountain in a winding-sheet of flame, must have precluded the possibility of escape. But the preservation of Zoar amid the general burning was a miracle of the highest order. Standing within the vale and hard by the neighboring towns, but without the smell of fire about its dwellings, it must have presented a singular spectacle, surrounded by an invisible wall against which the burning waves madly dashed in vain.

The mountains on the western side of the Dead Sea, like the hills of Judea, are limestone, of a white, red, and yellow hue, and, rising from 1000 to 2000 feet high, their sides are barren and rugged, and broken into wild ravines. At intervals the hills recede, forming on the shore semicircular plains, which, being watered by brackish fountains, are converted into salt marshes. Along the western coast large quantities of pure sulphur, asphalt, and pumice-stone abound. In the southwest corner of the vale, extending five miles to the northwest, is a rugged ridge of hills composed entirely of mineral salt. From a marshy delta, coated with salt and bitumen, a grand ravine leads up to this saline ridge, called by the Arabs Jebel Usdum. The winter torrents have cut deep furrows in its sides from summit to base, and the combined action of the rains, and the burning siroccos that sweep over mountain and plain, have rounded the faces of the cliffs. The peaks rise in tiers, while their roots, in lesser hills, project toward the sea. Far up the ravine, between two higher cliffs, is a lower ridge, not unlike a pedestal, on which is a singular pillar of pure solid salt, round in front and angular behind. Resting on a pedestal sixty feet high, the solitary column rises forty feet higher, connected with the hill behind by an immense bar of salt. This is the only resemblance to "Lot's wife" in the vale, but can not be her, as its position is in the wrong direction from Zoar. But the presence of such a mountain of salt, whose base beneath the surface is washed by the waves, and from whose summit large blocks of salt are carried down by the rains into the water, sufficiently accounts for the extreme saltness of the sea. On the marshy flats at its base is the " Valley of Salt," where David slew " eighteen thousand Syrians,"[1] and where Amaziah, at a later period, slew " ten thousand Edomites."[2]

Situated on the brow of a lofty cliff 1500 feet above the sea, and twelve miles north from Usdum, is Masada, the last refuge of the Jews after the destruction of Jerusalem by Titus, and the scene of the noblest heroism and of the most bloody tragedy in the annals of war. Separated by a deep ravine from the surrounding mountains on the north and south, and attached to them on the west by a narrow ridge two thirds its height, is a naked rock, having a perpendicular face toward the sea, and rising 700 feet high. Standing two miles from the shore, it is not unlike a pyramid in form. Though the summit is jagged and peaked, it contains a level area for building purposes 3000 feet in length and 1200 in width. Portions of four buildings are standing. On the south are the remains of an ancient gateway with a pointed arch; on the north stands a tower with a double wall of great strength, and near it is a quadrangular ruin. Within the ancient wall, which once completely encircled the rock, are three large cisterns, hewn in the solid rock, and covered with white cement. The largest of them is forty feet broad, 100 long, and fifty deep. Adjacent to the wall are the remains of the old Roman camps, constructed by the besieging army of Flavius Silva, apparently as complete as when abandoned centuries ago.

Reared in the second century B.C. by Jonathan Maccabaeus as a strong defensive work, the fortress of Masada was enlarged and rendered impregnable by Herod the Great. Designed by him at once for a palace and a fortress, he strengthened the position, and connected with his royal apartments baths, adorned with porticoes and colonnades. Confident of its impregnability, here the Idumean king deposited his rarest treasures against the day of danger.

Prior to the fall of Jerusalem, the Sicarii, who had sworn never to submit to the Roman arms, obtained by treachery the possession of this fortress. Commanded by the bold and skillful Eleazar, 600 of these patriots, with their wives, children, and servants to the number of 967, retired to Masada as the

[1] 2 Sam., viii., 13.   [2] 2 Kings, xiv., 7.

last refuge of the Jewish nation. The strong-holds of Machaerus and Herodium had yielded to the powerful arms of Lucil-

MASADA.

ius Bassus, and now Flavius Silva, his successor, laid siege to Masada. Cutting off all hope of succor from without, and of escape from within, by circumvallation, the Romans reared for the intended assault a mound of earth and stones, on which they planted an iron-cased tower commanding the walls of the fortress, and from which they drove the Jews from their ramparts. Successful in gaining a position so advantageous, the Romans retired for the night with the intention of storming the fortress the following morning.

Conscious of his inability to continue a successful defense—convinced that any attempt to escape would prove disastrous—satisfied that death awaited the garrison, ravishment their wives, and slavery their children, that night Eleazar called his faithful band around him, and proposed self-destruction as the terrible alternative. Appalled by the thought of murder and suicide, the heroic Sicarii, whose souls had never known the sensation of fear, for a moment hesitated; but, upbraided for the want of true courage by their leader, a frenzy seized them, and, each one grasping his wife and children in his arms, after lavishing upon them the fondest tokens of affection, they plunged their daggers to their hearts, leaving the bleeding bodies lifeless upon the ground. Resolved not to survive a calamity so insupportable, they prepared for their own destruction. Gathering the immense treasures of the palace together, they consigned them to the flames; then, choosing by lot ten of their number to dispatch the rest, each soldier threw himself down by his wife and children, and, grasping them in his arms, offered his neck to the sword of his companion. Drawing lots who should be the last survivor of the ten and the executioner of the nine, the lot fell on one who in turn was to dispatch himself. The nine slain, all the victims were examined to ascertain whether life was extinct; then, applying the torch to the palace, and surveying for a moment the raging flames and the dead, in families, stretched upon the ground, he lay down beside his wife and child, and the last of the Sicarii dispatched himself.

The morning dawned; the command was given; the Romans rushed to the assault; but, on scaling the ramparts, no foe appeared, no sound was heard, and, lifting a shout of triumph, they rushed to the palace. Their approach had startled from their retreat a sister of Eleazar, an elderly woman, and five children, who, learning of the intended slaughter, had secreted themselves in the vaults of the fortress. When they refused to credit her story, the sister of Eleazar led the conquerors within the court-yard of the palace, and pointed them to the dead who were too brave to be Roman slaves.[1]

Fifteen miles to the north from the Plain of Masada is the Fountain of the Kid. This beautiful spring is four hundred feet up the mountain side. Bursting from a limestone rock, and rushing down over precipitous rocks, and amid acacias and flowers, it fertilizes a small plain extending to the beach, and cultivated by the Bedouins of the Ghôr. Near this fountain David was secreted when pursued by Saul, and in a cave near

[1] Josephus, B. J., b. vii., c. viii.

by he "cut off the skirt of Saul's robe privily."¹ Up this pass the children of Ammon ascended to attack Jerusalem in the days of Jehoshaphat.² Originally celebrated for its vines and aromatic plants, Solomon compares his beloved to a "cluster of camphire³ in the vineyards of Engedi."⁴ Around this fountain now grow the "apples of Sodom." The fruit grows in clusters upon a tree fifteen feet high and two in girth, is of a yellow color, and has such a blooming appearance as to tempt the traveler's appetite; but, on being pressed, it explodes like a puff-ball, leaving in the hand nothing but the rind and a few dry fibres.

On the summit of an adjacent hill are the ruins of Maon, the residence of the churlish Nabal and his beautiful wife Abigail, and a mile to the north is the large fountain where this "son of Belial" held his annual feast, to whom David sent his famishing troops to ask permission to enjoy the festival as a reward for services which he had previously rendered to the ungrateful Nabal.⁵

The shrill call of the Bedouin sheikh roused me from my reverie as I sat on the small island in the sea recalling the past and receiving imperishable impressions of the changeless features of the "Vale of Siddim." That night we were to sleep with the monks of Mâr Sâba, and the journey thither was long, toilsome, and dangerous. Filling a can with seawater, and gathering mineral specimens from the beach, we mounted. The path lay across an undulating plain to the right of Ain Jehâir, whose brackish waters nourish a thicket of canes and a few pale flowers. Ascending the rugged pass of Nukb el-Kuneiterah, one skirted for an hour the verge of a yawning ravine, the precipitous sides of which were as dangerous as the view below was grand and awful. Reaching in less than two hours the summit of the highest ridge, the Wilderness of Engedi lay before us, and through openings in the distant cliffs we caught farewell glimpses of the Dead Sea. Passing an encampment where the children were nude and the women unveiled, we were glad to drink of Arab *leben*, or soured milk, a beverage similar to that which Jael gave Sisera,⁶ which was brought to us in a goatskin bottle. Descending

¹ 1 Sam., xxiv., 1-7.   ² 2 Chron., xx., 1, 2.
³ Species of fragrant grape.—THOMPSON.   ⁴ Cant., i., 14.
⁵ 1 Sam., xxv., 1-12.   ⁶ Judges, iv., 19.

hills gray and barren, and crossing verdureless plains, we reached the Vale of the Kidron as the last rays of the sun were tipping the higher peaks of Moab. Wild and grand, the perpendicular sides of the gorge are more than 300 feet high. The limestone rocks are blackened with age, and perched on the highest portion of the ridge is the famous Convent of Mâr Sâba. Approaching night had now thrown a deeper shadow in the ravine below; the skies reflected subdued light, and from the transparent blue the stars began to shine. The fatigue of the day had left the mind pensive, and the silence of the hour was unbroken except by the chirping of some invisible songster. Winding round the brow of a bold cliff, the gray towers of the ancient monastery stood out against the evening sky, and from the uppermost turret a solitary monk in dark flowing robes was watching our approach. The ponderous iron gate of the convent was thrown open, and, led by one of the fraternity through an interior court-yard, where orange and lemon trees scattered their rich perfume, we entered the "Pilgrim's Room."

Like many other religious establishments, the monastery of St. Sâba rose from the devotion of a single hermit. Attracted by the solitude of the spot and the wild grandeur of the situation, some time in the year 483 A.D., St. Sâba, a native of Cappadocia, and a man of extraordinary sanctity, founded the convent which bears his name. His triumph over the "Lion of the Kidron" attracted his fellow-anchorites to the glen, to the number of 14,000, to share his glory and devotion. From the cells which they excavated in the rocks gradually rose the walls, towers, chambers, and chapels of the edifice; and so curiously are the several parts arranged, that it is difficult to determine the masonry from the native rock. Crowned with a dome and clock-turret, the church stands on the brink of the highest cliff, supported by enormous buttresses rising from the bed of the Kidron. The interior is after the Byzantine order, adorned with pictures, ornamental lamps, and sacred banners. Near the church is the charnel-house, where the bones of the pious have been carefully preserved from the time of the patron saint to the last brother deceased. The bodies of the dead are deposited in vaults till the flesh has wasted away, when the skeleton is broken to pieces, and the bones are piled up in ghastly array, arm with arm, leg with leg, skull with skull.

CONVENT OF SANTA SABA.

Though enlarged and beautified by monkish industry, the cave in which St. Sàba lived still retains its native rudeness. Among the pictures which adorn the walls is one representing the beheading of John the Baptist. The artist has transferred to the canvas the horror of the murder and the turpitude of the crime which led to the execution. In the background is seen the martyr's cell, with barred window and iron door. Robed in green garments, the headless body of John lies prostrate upon the marble pavement, while over it stands the fierce executioner, holding in one hand his sword still dripping with blood, and in the other the bleeding head. With an air of triumphant revenge Salome is approaching, attired in ermine and adorned with a coronet of jewels, and bearing on her hands a charger to receive the dissevered head of the faithful minister of truth and purity.

The morning was far advanced when the iron gates of Mâr Sâba opened for our departure. The day was charming, and the ride to Bethlehem was one of extraordinary delight. The spring clouds, like softest gauze, screened us from the otherwise burning rays of a Syrian sun, and a gentle breeze from the Mediterranean came over the hills of Judæa "fresh as the breath of morn." It being early spring-time, Nature smiled in all her virgin beauty. Grasses and grains were ripening; flowers every where were in bloom; herds of cattle and flocks of sheep were feeding on the hills, and high up in mid air three eagles screamed as they soared above us.

In an hour from the monastery Jerusalem was seen to the north, and half an hour beyond I for the first time saw Bethlehem nestling among the Judæan hills. A flood of childhood's memories rushed back to mind, unsealing the fountain of emotion as when in boyhood I was accustomed to read the story of the new-born King. On the south lay the Plains of Bethlehem, where shepherds were watching their flocks—some chanting a pastoral song, others playing upon their rude flute. The sterility of the wilderness had given place to cultivated fields, and along the wayside grew a pretty blue flower, of a stellar form, called by the monks the "Star of Bethlehem." Passing through the small village of Beit Sahûr, we turned westward, and, ascending a well-made road, in half an hour we passed beneath the ancient portal of the City of the Nativity. The streets were crowded with people, and along the main thoroughfare were merchants selling fruits, flowers, grains, vegetables, cutlery, saddlery, clothing, furniture, and ornaments, and mechanics of all kinds were pursuing their respective vocations.

So long as childhood continues, Bethlehem will be cherished by the young, and recalled with delight by those of riper years.

VIEW OF BETHLEHEM.

The synonym of helpless infancy, mothers will revert to it with hope, and the children of each generation will claim it as their common heritage. As here the young mother pressed her tender offspring to her bosom for the first time, Bethlehem must ever remain the symbol of domestic affections and privacies.

Originally called "The House of Bread," and now "The House of Flesh," its Arabic name, Beit Lahm, contains the significance of its wondrous history. To distinguish it from Bethlehem belonging to the tribeship of Zebulun,[1] it is called by the sacred historian "Bethlehem of Judah;"[2] to preintimate its fruitfulness, it was prophetically designated Ephratah;[3] to illustrate its rising glory "among the thousands of Judah," it was announced as the birthplace of Him "whose goings forth have been from of old."[4] In antiquity coeval with the oldest cities in the world, its identity is unquestioned. Stretching backward thirty-six centuries, its authentic history opens with the mournful death and burial of the beautiful Rachel;[5] and rendered imperishable by the sepulchral monument to that beloved wife, 600 years later it was the scene of the touching story of Boaz and the youthful widow of Chilion.[6] Giving birth to Obed, the father of Jesse, Bethlehem, less than 100 years subsequent to the marriage of Ruth and Boaz, was the birthplace of David,[7] where, at the tender age of seventeen, he was anointed king over Israel; and, in honor of events so illustrious, it thereafter was called the "City of David." During the reverses which befell Saul of Gibeah it was captured by the Philistines, and David, having been declared a public enemy, was compelled to fly to the cave of Adullam.

After 1000 years of comparative oblivion, Bethlehem suddenly emerged from obscurity into brighter and more enduring glory. Summoned by the Emperor Augustus to their native city to be taxed, Joseph and Mary came from the hills of Nazareth, and, reaching the town at the close of the day, after a journey of eighty miles, the mother of the Messiah was compelled to lodge in the stable, "because there was no room for them in the inn."[8] That night the Prince of Peace was born; the race commenced its life anew; angels sang the song of the nativity; wondering shepherds hastened to pay homage to the new-born King; a lone but marvelous star arrested the attention of the magi of Arabia Felix; and Bethlehem rose to be "greatest among the thousands of Judah."

[1] Josh., xix., 15.
[4] Ib.
[7] Ib., iv., 17-22.
[2] Matt., ii., 1.
[5] Gen., xxxv., 18-20.
[8] Luke, ii., 7.
[3] Micah, v., 2.
[6] Ruth, iv., 13.

An event so great and memorable has rendered the city of the Savior's birth a holy shrine, at which the devout of all ages and countries have bowed with unspeakable delight. And, in commemoration of the event, and to rescue the site from oblivion, the Emperor Constantine, in the commencement of the fourth century, ordered the erection of a magnificent basilica over the "Grotto of the Nativity," which is now the oldest monument of Christian architecture in the world. Separated from the town by a long esplanade, the church occupies the eastern brow of the hill on which the city is built, and, together with the three convents abutting from its sides, forms an enormous pile of limestone, vast in dimensions, irregular in outline, and, though it is destitute of external architectural grandeur, the size, strength, and commanding position of the edifice render it the chief attraction of the place. The Greeks, Latins, and Armenians hold joint possession of the basilica, and adjoining it are the monasteries for the entertainment and devotion of their respective orders.

It was late one evening in the month of April that I rapped for admission at the iron door of the Latin convent. The Franciscans received me kindly, and, after a generous meal, an aged monk led me to my apartments for the night. The convent bell called me early from my slumbers, and, ascending to the broad, flat roof of the monastery, I enjoyed an extensive view of the surrounding country. The sky was soft, the air pure, and the sun was just rising above the mountains of Moab. The shepherd's shrill voice mingled with the tinkling of bells as he led his flock in search of pasture, and the leaves of orange, fig, and olive trees shone like jewels as the dewdrops thereon reflected the morning light. Far away to the east are the Plains of the Jordan, the mountains of Gilead, Moab, Ammon, and Seir; on the north the Hills of Judea are bleak; on the west they are green as far as the eye can reach toward the "Great Sea;" on the south are the Gardens of Urtas and the Pools of Solomon. With a mind attuned by such a scene, I read the romantic story of Ruth and Boaz, the history of David's coronation, and the more tender narrative of the Savior's birth. The past returned with all the reality of the present, and history repeated its wondrous deeds before the eye of a sublime faith. But the charm was broken in a moment by the chant of a funeral dirge. Just beneath me, and

CAVE OF THE NATIVITY.

near the convent wall, a long procession of women was approaching, following to its final rest the lifeless form of some daughter of Bethlehem. It was a singular hour for a burial. Except the men who bore the corpse, there were no others present. Fifty women robed in white gathered about the grave, and, as a symbol of the abundant happiness of departed spirits, each one bore upon her head a basket of bread, and, leaving it upon the tomb, they all retired.

Descending through the long halls of the monastery, we found the monks differently engaged; some were arranging their scanty toilets, others repeating their prayers. On each door is a rude picture illustrating the faith of the inmate, and the subject he desired to be most frequently reminded of. On one is a coffin; on another are the lambent flames of Purgatory; but on most is the serene face of Mary. My guide rejoined me in the hall of the refectory, and led me to the stable of blessed memory. Passing through the Latin chapel, where a priest was celebrating mass, we descended a flight of narrow winding steps, cut in the native rock, at the foot of which is the sacred grotto. Thirty-eight feet long, eleven wide, and two deep, it has the appearance of having been the cellar of a Syrian house, which, according to a custom still prevalent, serves as a stable. Near the eastern end is the supposed place of our Lord's birth, marked by a white marble slab, in the centre of which is a large silver star, encircled with an inscription in Latin, "Here Jesus Christ was born of the Virgin Mary." Sixteen silver lamps shed a perpetual light upon the shrine; from golden censers incense unceasingly ascends, while the walls are covered with silk embroidered with gold. To the south is the substituted manger, the original having been carried to Rome and deposited in the church of Santa Maria Maggiore. Above it is a fine picture of the birth-scene by Maello, and near it is a better one of the Magi. A narrow passage leads to the small grotto where Joseph is said to have stood at the moment our Lord was born, and in it is a picture representing the angel warning him to take the young child and his mother and escape into Egypt. The angel's face is expressive of intense earnestness; the countenance of Joseph is calm and thoughtful; while Mary tenderly but firmly clasps her infant to her bosom.

Following a glimmering light, we entered a large sepulchral

vault containing the dust of the departed members of the fraternity, and from it passed to the "altar of the infant martyrs" slain by Herod. A picture above it commemorates the death of "twenty thousand innocents," and the old monk groaned as he looked upon it. In an adjoining oblong chamber are altars dedicated to the memory of St. Paula and her daughter Eustachia, two eminent Roman ladies, who spent their days here in charity and devotion; and near the altars are their tombs, over which are the portraits of the saints. Their features are represented as sharp, their expression pensive, and over their heads an angel holds a wreath of glory. Not far from these sepulchres is the tomb of Jerome, and in the north end of the same chamber is the study of that eminent scholar. Here, in a cell twenty feet square and nine deep, around which runs a stone seat, he spent most of his life, producing those great works which have given immortality to his name. Here, in the severities of monastic life, he smote his body with a stone while imploring the mercy of the Lord. It was here he fancied he heard the peals of the trump of the last judgment incessantly ringing in his ear. On the wall hangs a portrait of this great man. The head is round and bald, the face beams with intelligence, by his side hangs a crucifix, and behind him stands an angel sounding in his ear the trumpet of the last day.

Reascending the narrow staircase, we passed into the magnificent Basilica of St. Helena. In length 120 feet by 110 wide, the interior consists of a central nave and four lateral aisles, formed by four rows of twelve Corinthian columns in each row, twenty feet high and two and a half in diameter, supporting a horizontal architrave. According to tradition, these pillars were taken from the porches of the Temple at Jerusalem. Originally the roof and rafters were formed of cedar from the forests of Lebanon, but at present they are of oak, the gift of King Edward IV. when the church was last repaired. The gold, marble, and mosaics which once adorned the walls of this noble edifice have been removed, and by the mutual jealousies of the rival sects this grandest of Eastern basilicas is in a neglected state. The aspect of the interior is greatly injured by a partition wall separating the choir from the body of the church, which in turn is divided into two chapels, one belonging to the Greeks and the other to the Ar-

INTERIOR OF THE CHURCH OF THE NATIVITY.

menians; on the north side of the choir is the Chapel of St. Catharine, occupied by the Latins.

Though we reject the unwarrantable grouping together in a single grotto of so many "holy places" as unfounded in fact, and especially the particular spot where Christ was born, there is no reason for the rejection of the cave itself. Its history runs too far back to have its identity affected by the flood of monastic legends which followed the conversion of the empire, and the historical chain is unbroken from the death of the Apostle John to our own day. A native of Nablous, and born in the beginning of the second century, Justin Martyr describes the birthplace of Jesus " as a grotto in Bethlehem;" one hundred years later, Origen refers to the fact as recognized by Christians and pagans; and, a century after him, Eusebius mentions it as an accepted traditional spot, and as so regarded prior to the time of St. Helena's visit. Crediting the tradition, the mother of Constantine caused to be erected the present basilica in the year 327 A.D., and fifty years after its erection, Jerome of Dalmatia, with Paul and Eustachia, settled in Bethlehem, where the great "Father of Church History" expired, in 420 A.D., in his ninetieth year. Though the city fell into the hands of the Moslems at a later period, and the church was stripped of its ornaments, yet the cave remained undisturbed; and, on their approach to Jerusalem, the Crusaders retook Bethlehem, and in 1110 A.D., Baldwin I. elevated it to the dignity of an episcopal see; and, notwithstanding the vicissitudes through which it has passed, it is now a thoroughly Christian town. Unlike the tradition identifying our Lord's tomb, the traditional history of his birthplace is unmixed with monkish miracles, and the preservation of the site is as simple as it is natural.

In a land where the customs of the people never change, all the incidents of the story of the birth of the Savior are confirmed by modern usage. It is no evidence of the poverty of Joseph and Mary that they failed to obtain lodgings in the inn, as the decree of Augustus had called home all citizens belonging to the town, which, being small, was filled to overflowing; nor is it proof of the humbleness of the holy family that they were compelled to lodge in the stable, as to this day, both in Bethlehem and in other Syrian cities, kitchen, parlor, and stable are frequently under the same roof, and often without a partition between them. In going from Jerusalem to Nablous, I stopped with a Christian at Beeroth, near Bethel. His dwelling was a one-story house. Within was a raised platform not two feet high, on which was arranged the furniture of his home; at the foot of the platform was a space four feet wide, and extending the whole depth of the building, which was the stable, and in one corner stood his ass. And in a neighboring house a woman was kneading dough on the platform, and a little girl was holding an infant, and two feet from them stood the ass, with his elongated head thrust into a stone manger excavated in the solid rock. This order of domestic architecture throws light upon the apparent discrepancies of Matthew and Luke. The former mentions a house in connection with our Lord's birth;[1] the latter a manger, thereby supposing a stable.[2] But the historians refer to two distinct events—St. Luke, to the night of the Savior's birth; St. Matthew, to the visit of the Magi, which occurred some time later. Mary and her son may then have found room in the inn; or, if the visit of the wise men was simultaneous with that of the shepherds, St. Matthew alludes to a house with a stable under the same roof, and the entrance to which was through the main door of the dwelling.

Bethlehem may be viewed with a pleasing confidence as the city where "God was manifested in the flesh," and that from a place so humble influences have gone forth affecting the present condition and future hopes of the entire race. Since that wondrous child was born, empires have passed away and generations have descended to the grave. Of that renowned empire, whose proud emperor summoned Mary to perform a journey of eighty miles in the rains of December, not a fragment remains; and of the Herods who waylaid his infancy and persecuted his manhood, not a descendant reigns over an inch of the broad earth. But the kingdom of Christ endures, his subjects people both hemispheres, and the song of the Bethlehem songsters is yet to be the anthem of a redeemed world.

The situation of Bethlehem is peculiar. Located on a narrow ridge projecting eastward from the central mountain range, and breaking down in the form of terraced slopes, it is bounded on the east, north, and south by deep valleys. Constructed of white limestone, well built, square in form, and crowned with small domes, the buildings rise above each

[1] Matt., ii., 11.   [2] Luke, ii., 7.

TOMB OF HEROD THE GREAT—HERODIUM.

other in somewhat regular gradations. The streets are few and narrow, and though the city is not surrounded with a wall, it has two gates, which are closed at night. Sweeping in graceful curves around the ridge, and regular in their ascent as stairs, the well-kept terraces are adorned with the vines of Eshcol, and with fig and olive-trees. Extending from the base of the hill toward the south and east are the fertile plains where Ruth gleaned, and where the glory of the Lord shone around the peaceful shepherds.

Numbering over three thousand souls, the modern Bethlehemites are superior in their appearance to the citizens of any other town in Palestine. The men are of light complexion, with finely developed forms, and, in their affable demeanor and noble bearing toward the "stranger within their gates," are not unworthy descendants of Boaz. In the regularity of their features, the freshness of their complexion, and the sweetness of their countenance, the women are not unlike those of America; and as if the Savior had bequeathed the beauty of his childhood to the children of his native city, they are exceedingly fair. So thoroughly Christian in sentiment are the inhabitants, that no Moslem is allowed a residence within the town. The Cross is unrivaled by the Crescent, and Christ reigns supreme where he was born. While most of the people are either peasants or shepherds, others are the manufacturers of "pious wares," such as beads, crosses, rings, crucifixes, and models of the Holy Sepulchre, wrought out of olive-wood and mother-of-pearl.

Five miles to the southeast from Bethlehem is Herodium, the tomb of Herod the Great. Cherishing an ambition that knew no bounds, and rivaling Solomon in the magnificence of his reign and in the splendor of the cities of his kingdom, Herod sought renown in life by the power of his name and the perpetuity of his fame in death, by rearing for himself a mausoleum which he vainly hoped would have continued complete to the latest generation. Conscious of the vicissitudes to which his empire city was subject, and knowing that as he himself had rifled the sepulchre of David, his in turn might be plundered, he prepared for himself a tomb of great strength, far from human habitation. A ride of more than an hour brought us to the grave of this most execrable of monarchs. Being the last position held by the Crusaders after the fall of Jerusalem, the hill bears the traditional name of "Frank Mountain;" but, from the supposed luxurious life of Herod, the Arabs call it Jebel Fureidis, or "Little Paradise Hill." Josephus, however, designates it Herodium, after the founder of the city which crowned its summit. According to him, it is sixty stadia from Jerusalem, and was designed by Herod to be a military outpost, protecting the inhabitants of the inland towns from the depredations of the Bedouins of Engedi, and also to serve as a palatial retreat for the king and his court. Having subserved the double purpose of war and pleasure, it at length fell before the powerful arms of Lucilius Bassus.[1]

Rising in the form of a truncated cone 400 feet from the crest of a round isolated ridge, it resembles, when viewed from the plain below, some grand catafalco. The ascent is up a circular path, and the view from the summit imposing. Through openings in the cliffs the Dead Sea is seen to the east; two miles to the southwest is the small town of Tekoa, the home of the wise woman whom Joab called to plead before David in behalf of Solomon,[2] and the birthplace of the Prophet Amos;[3] and to the northwest are the white walls and domes of Bethlehem. At its northern base is a reservoir 200 feet square, from the centre of which rises a mound of earth like an island in a lake, and near it are traces of the aqueduct, which conveyed the water from a great distance. The summit is an area 750 feet in circumference, surrounded by a ruined wall of large hewn stones, with a massive square tower at each angle. Within this inclosure are many vaults, and the walls of what appears to have been an amphitheatre. The latter is in the form of a three-quarter circle, and on the south side are three large blocks of limestone, so arranged as to suggest the idea that they were the royal seats from which Herod and his courtiers beheld the dramatic and equestrian feats so pleasing to Oriental kings. To the northwest of this structure is a large vault, which I succeeded in entering by creeping through a narrow opening. The roof is a beautiful raised dome, with a circular keystone in the centre, and on the sides are doors leading to other chambers. On the very summit of the hill is the Tomb of Herod. It is a vaulted chamber of hewn limestone, fifteen feet long, twelve wide, and ten deep. Dying at Jericho, the royal mon-

[1] Anti B., xv., b. ix., c. iv.; B. J., i., b. xxi., c. x. ; Ib., iv., b. ix., c. v.
[2] 2 Sam., xiv., 1-20.   [3] Amos, i., 1.

ster was here interred, amid the scene of his crimes and folly. Profound silence now reigns where once the noise of revelry was heard, and, unhonored and unlamented, the dust of the proud Idumean is trodden by the foot of the transient traveler and the wild Arabs of Engedi, while in sight of his sepulchre the domes and towers of the city in which he sought to slay the "young child" rise up toward the throne of the world's Redeemer as the monuments of the birthplace of Him who "liveth for evermore."

One of the wildest, roughest roads in Palestine leads from Herodium to the Cave of Adullam, where David and his men were secreted when pursued by Saul, and where "every one that was in distress, and every one that was in debt, and every one that was discontented, gathered themselves unto him, and he became a captain over them, and there were with him about four hundred men."[1] From this cave his three "mighty men" broke through the lines of the Philistines who garrisoned Bethlehem, and, drawing water from the well that David loved so much, and which still exists, brought it in triumph to their chief;[2] and from here he took his parents across the Jordan, to place them in the care of his kinsmen of Moab.[3]

Descending over ledges of rocks to the bottom of a deep ravine, dry and barren, and walled in by perpendicular mountains 1000 feet high, we found ourselves in one of the grandest gorges in the Wilderness of Judea, where the solitude is unbroken by human habitation. In the face of the rocks are vast caverns, partly excavated by the winds and partly by the band of robbers whose dens they were. Winding round rocky projections and crossing wilder ravines, we reached at noon the foot of the ascent of the opposite mountain range, in the side of which, 400 feet above us, was the cave of Adullam. Compelled by the intense heat and the impossibility of finding a path to leave our horses, we advanced single file, now leaping yawning gulfs, now clambering over smooth-faced rocks, and again skirting some dangerous precipice.

It was past noon when the advanced guide cried out "Kureitûn!" In front of the cave were three immense boulders, over whose smooth slanting sides only goats could apparently pass; but we had endured too much to be thwarted by such obstacles. One leap brought us flat upon the first rock, anoth-

[1] 1 Sam., xxii. 1-3. [2] 2 Sam., xxiii. 14-17. [3] Ib., xxii. 3, 4.

er on the second, a third into the mouth of the cave. Turning round, I looked down upon a scene of complete desolation. No mountain pine waved its green foliage as in Alpine solitudes; no waterfall delighted the ear with its music; no feathered songster awakened the slumbering echoes of the glen. Entering the cave through a passage-way six feet high, four wide, and thirty long, but which soon contracted to such dimensions as to compel us first to stoop and then to creep, we at length found ourselves in the hiding-place of David. Owing to the curve in the entrance, no sunlight ever penetrates this dismal abode. Lighting our candles, we began to explore. We found the interior divided into chambers, halls, galleries, and dungeons, connected by intricate passage-ways. The chief hall is 120 feet long and fifty wide; the ceiling is high and arched, ornamented with pendents resembling stalactites, and from the walls extend sharp projections, on which the ancient warriors hung their arms. The effect was grand as our tapers revealed each irregular arch, graceful pendent, and sharp projection, giving the whole the appearance of a grand Gothic hall. Lateral passages radiate in every direction from this chamber, but ultimately converge in a central room. Threading one by one these labyrinthian alleys,. I became separated from the guide, and felt no little trepidation till I heard him respond to my call. The darkness and silence were oppressive, and the seclusion and intricacies of the cave would have baffled any attempt of Saul to capture the object of his pursuit. From the side of the first chamber we reached a pit ten feet deep, and from it a low, narrow alley, 210 feet long, leads to another hall, the inner *sanctum*, where David held his secret councils. On the walls are the names of a few explorers, and among them that of a romantic Irish lady. Though this appeared to be the end of the great cave, yet the guide spoke of a secret passage to Tekoa and Hebron.

 The only difficulty in identifying this cave with the one David occupied is the fact that two Adullams are mentioned in the Bible—one on the borders of Philistia, and the other among the cities of Judea. A hundred feet above the cavern are the ruins of a city, probably the site of the Judæan Adullam, from which the cave takes its name. And three scriptural facts seem to place the question beyond dispute: David's escape from Gath,[1] the reception of his father's house,[2] and the draught of water which his "mighty men" obtained for him at the peril of their lives,[3] all of which favor this location rather than the one in an enemy's country.

[1] 1 Sam., xxii., 1.   [2] Ib.   [3] 1 Chron., xi., 15.

CHAPTER VIII.

En Route for Hebron.—Travelers.— Beautiful Scenery.—Ancient Travelers. —Evening.—Gray's Elegy.—Search for Lodgings.—Hebron.—Its Name. —Origin.—Home of Abraham.—History.—Location of the City and its Environs.—Pools.—Cave of Machpelah.—The Mosque over it.—Tombs of the Patriarchs and their Wives.—Prince of Wales.—Isaac still Lives.— Identity of the Cave.—Evidence.—United in Death.—Beersheba.—Its ancient Wells.—Events of the Past.—Changeless Customs.—Abraham and the Angels.—Dining with an Arab Sheikh.—Grapes of Eshcol.—Abraham's Oak.—Ruins.—Pool of Solomon.—His Aqueduct.—Plains of Rephaim.

It was four o'clock, one Friday afternoon in the month of March, when we issued from the western portal of Bethlehem on our way to Hebron. We had dined at a small German inn within the town, and from the proprietor I had obtained a spirited horse, though at an exorbitant price. The descent from the hill on which the city stands is rapid and difficult. In less than half an hour we reached the Pools of Solomon, but the day was too far advanced to examine them with care. Many travelers were on their way to northern cities, some on camels, some on asses, some on foot. Salutations were exchanged as we passed each other, and their appearance indicated both kindness and thrift. The men were attired in loose flowing robes, with sandals and turbans; the women in blue garments, and a white sheet enveloping their person; a thin veil was drawn closely around the lower part of the face, just above which their black lustrous eyes were peering. It was a strange sight to an American to see men riding and women walking; but in the land of Sarah, Rachel, and Mary, where the highest honor ever bestowed upon our race was conferred upon a woman, her degradation is no less true than sad.

Beyond the Pools the country rapidly improved in fertility and beauty. Though hilly, the land was not mountainous; and though the relative position of hill and valley was not regular, yet this confusion added interest to the scene. The vales

HEBRON.

were green with grains and grasses; the hills were covered with groves of fruit-trees; and along the highway were wells and fountains of cool water. As we advanced the scenery became picturesque. Now the valleys ran tortuously between the mountains; now ridges of Jura limestone rose on either hand; now dwarfed oaks and wild flowers covered hill and vale, while every where were visible ancient terraces and ruined towers, the evidence of former cultivation and of a larger population. But the pleasures of the journey were lessened by the condition of the roads, which were crooked and uneven, broken and stony. Sections of the old Roman highway remain, but by the neglect of twelve centuries this once famous road, over which the Roman chariot rolled, has been so damaged that those "royal road-makers" would now disown it as the work of their hands. Yet even an inconvenience so great was forgotten in the recollection that over this same road Abraham had passed with Isaac to the Land of Moriah, Jacob had fled from the face of Esau, David had ridden in triumph to Jerusalem, and the Holy Family had hastened to Egypt to escape the murdering minions of Herod.

The day was far gone as we neared the home of the Patriarchs. The sun was fast sinking into the blue waters of the Mediterranean; the Hebron Hills were casting their lengthening shadows over the vineyards of Eshcol, and the wild flowers, blooming along the path, were closing their tiny petals "beneath the kisses of night." It was such an hour and such a scene as the plaintive bard has embalmed in immortal verse:

> "The lowing herd winds slowly o'er the lea,
> The plowman homeward plods his weary way,
> And leaves the world to darkness and to me.
> * * * *
> "Now fades the glimmering landscape on the sight,
> And all the air a solemn stillness holds,
> Save where the beetle wheels his droning flight,
> And drowsy tinklings lull the distant folds."[1]

A solitary light shone from the minaret of Hebron as we entered its ancient portal. "Strangers in a strange land," we sat down upon the stone pavement, waiting the return of our dragoman, whom, in the absence of a hotel, we had dispatched to search for lodgings in a private dwelling. Weary and hun-

[1] Gray.

gry, we waited till nine o'clock for his return, being closely watched by the Hebronites, and, in turn, we watched the progress of a little courtship between a pretty Jewess and a young Israelite—she coquettishly peeping through a latticed window, he standing beneath it, catching the smiles and accents of love.

A Polish Jew had been persuaded to receive us into his house, but as it was Friday night, the beginning of the Jewish Sabbath, the family refused to prepare us food, or do any thing for our comfort which required work. Our host's name was Jonah, a most unpromising fact. According to the style of Polish Jews, he wore yellow robes trimmed with fur, and a high round fur cap. His wife was elegantly attired, and was a person of more than ordinary beauty, which was not true of the other ladies of the family. Their house was near the Cave of Machpelah, and built of gray limestone. The room we occupied was in the second story; the ceiling was arched, and on the sides of the apartment was a raised platform, which served us as a couch. We had eaten nothing since we left Bethlehem; our host's religion would not allow him to relieve our hunger, and, while we sent for a little Mohammedan maid to prepare the meal, I thought on our Lord's parable of the ass in a ditch on the Sabbath-day.

Hebron comes from Kirjath-Arba — city of Arba — from Arba, who was father of Anak, and progenitor of the giants called Anakims. At a later period it received the name of Mamre, in honor of Mamre, the Amorite, the friend and ally of Abraham. It now bears the Arabic name of El-Khulêl, "The Friend of God," evidently referring to the "Father of the Faithful." Hebron is older than the oldest authentic history. According to Moses, Hebron was built seven years before Zoan in Egypt.[1] But when was Zoan built? Seven years after Hebron! This indefinite answer leaves us to infer that Hebron is among the oldest cities in the world, having a greater antiquity than Damascus. Though its earliest history is obscure, its identity with the home of the patriarchs is unquestioned. Subsequently to his separation from Lot at Bethel, Abraham pitched his tent on the Plains of Mamre.[2] Hither came the fugitive from the battle of the kings, and informed him of the capture of his nephew.[3] From these peaceful pasture-fields he went forth with 318 trained servants, born in

[1] Num., xiii., 22.   [2] Gen., xiii., 18.   [3] Ib., xiv., 13.

his own house, and, pursuing the victors unto Dan, there retook his relative.¹ It was here, while sitting in his tent door, as old men are accustomed now to sit, that three angels in human form came to his tent, one to promise him a son, the others to pass on and destroy the "cities of the plain;"² and, ascending the eastern hill early the next morning, he saw the smoke of the country that went up as the smoke of a furnace.³ Here, in harmony with the renewal of a covenant previously formed, and in obedience to the Lord's command, he and all the males of his house were circumcised. Here is the scene of the unhappy story of Hagar and Ishmael,⁴ and, years later, of the birth of Isaac. Here Sarah died, and in the cave of Machpelah Abraham interred his beloved wife.⁵ Years after, the prince of patriarchs was laid by her side; and, in the termination of generations, Isaac and Rebecca,⁶ Leah and Jacob,⁷ descended to this abode of death. Two and a half centuries subsequent to the demise of Jacob, the good Caleb rested in peace and honor in Hebron;⁸ and, 400 years later, David here inaugurated a long and prosperous reign, and held his court during seven and a half years.⁹ But in less than 1000 years thereafter the home of the patriarchs and the seat of royalty became the theatre of the most horrid tragedies of war. Here, beside the graves of their fathers, and beneath the noble oaks on the ancestral plain, thousands of Jewish captives were brought from Jerusalem by the victorious Romans and sold into slavery.

Having an elevation of 28,000 feet above the sea, the modern town of Hebron is beautifully situated in the Valley of Eshcol. Extending north and south, and spreading out over the slopes of the neighboring hills, the city is divided by gardens into two sections, the main portion lying on the eastern slope, surmounted by the lofty wall of the Haram. To the north, on the declivities of the western hills, is a large cemetery. The graves of ordinary persons are marked by a circle of stones, while the tombs of distinguished individuals are designated by heaps of small stones, thrown together by friends and admirers to perpetuate their memory. The hills that bound the city on the east and west are not high, but graceful and roll-

---

¹ Gen., xiv., 14. ² Ib., xviii. ³ Ib., xix., 28.
⁴ Ib., xvi., xvii. ⁵ Ib., xxiii. ⁶ Ib., xxxv., 29.
⁷ Ib., l., 13. ⁸ Josh., xv., 13. ⁹ 2 Sam., ii., 11.

ing. To the northwest they are thickly covered with olive-groves, orchards of fruit-trees, and vineyards, each with a watch-tower for shelter and protection. There is nothing in the architecture of the town to awaken admiration. Like the buildings in the suburbs of Damascus, the dwellings are of gray limestone, with flat roofs, and surmounted by one or two domes. Unlike Jerusalem, the city has no walls, though at the entrance of the chief thoroughfares there are gates, which are closed at night, and carefully guarded during the day. The streets are nothing more than paved alleys, and would be vastly improved by an occasional cleansing. Though subject to Mohammedan control, Hebron is a thoroughly Jewish city. The population is estimated at 10,000, 500 of whom are Polish Jews. There is not a resident Christian in Hebron. The citizens live by cultivating fruit-groves and vineyards; by a small mercantile trade; and by the manufacture of water skin-bottles and colored glass trinkets, such as rings and bracelets, which find a ready market among this simple-hearted people.

In a country where water is scarce, and the mechanical art is in a rude condition, the pools and fountains of the wiser and more opulent ancients are preserved with care. The traveler is therefore not surprised to find himself standing beside fountains as old as the reign of David. In the southern part of the vale, where the buildings stretch across the valley from east to west, is the pool over which were hanged the murderers of Ishbosheth.[1] It is a square tank, solidly built of large hewn stones, measuring 130 feet on each side and fifty deep; and in the northern section of the town there is another reservoir, eighty-five feet long, fifty-five broad, and eighteen deep.

But the chief attraction in Hebron, alike to the Christian, the Jew, and the Moslem, is the cave of Machpelah, now bearing the Arabic name of El-Khulil—"The Friend of God." Approaching it with a reverence almost religious, with head uncovered, and with emotions excited by the hallowed associations of the place, I had hoped to have entered its precincts, and to have read the Bible story of its purchase and of the interment of the patriarchal families, but a Moslem fanaticism, as inhuman as it is irreligious, drove me from the sacred inclosure. What a stinging rebuke to such conduct is found in the courtesy, the justice, the goodness displayed by Abraham

[1] 2 Sam., iv., 12.

in the purchase of the field from the sons of Heth! His memory should soften religious asperities; his character should pacify the rage of fanaticism; his spirit should harmonize the discordant elements of sectarian strife; but a Moslem is too selfish, too bigoted, too depraved to rise to such sublime conceptions.

The field containing the cave of Machpelah is located on the higher slope of the eastern hill, and is now inclosed by a massive wall fifty feet high, the lower portion of which, to the height of forty feet, is of Jewish construction, and the upper part is of Saracenic origin, with a minaret at each angle. The wall has an ancient appearance, being constructed of large beveled stones hewn smooth, and extends north and south 200 feet, and 115 east and west. The exterior is ornamented with square pilasters, sixteen on each side, eight at each angle, which, without capitals, support a cornice extending the whole length of the structure. The wall is solid, without window or aperture except at the angles of the northern end, where are the chief entrances, reached by broad flights of steps, of gentle ascent, leading to the court within. Within this mural inclosure stands a mosque, once a Byzantine church, which, like the Church of St. Sophia in Constantinople and the Church of Justinian in Jerusalem, has been essentially altered and dedicated to Mohammed. Beneath it is the cave of Machpelah, and within it are the monumental shrines of the patriarchal dead. Within a small chapel, on the right, is the cenotaph in honor of Abraham, and directly opposite, in a similar recess, is the shrine of Sarah. Each is inclosed by an iron railing, and guarded by a silver gate. That of the father of the faithful consists of a coffin-like-structure, six feet high, built of plastered marble, draped with three carpets of a green color, embroidered with gold, while over that of Sarah is spread a pall. On the sides of the mosque, midway the building, and immediately opposite each other, are the monumental tombs of Isaac and Rebecca. Like those of their parents, they are placed within chapels, in the walls of which are windows, protected by iron bars. In a separate cloister, opposite the entrance of the mosque, in corresponding recesses, are the tombs of Jacob and Leah. Over that of the former are green-colored carpets of a coarse texture; against that of the latter recline two war-banners of the same hue.

Regarding these tombs with a superstitious veneration in keeping with the spirit and teachings of their religion, and with a fanaticism that would lead to the instant death of an intruder, the Moslems reverence them as among their holiest shrines. Until the year 1862, admittance was absolutely refused to Jew and Christian, except to architects, who were allowed to enter to repair the structure; but, thanks to the intelligence, the power, and perseverance of the Prince of Wales, the bar of seclusion from this most sacred and interesting place has been removed; and though at present the relaxation is slight, yet the ultimate effect of the prince's visit must be the removal of all restraint, at least so far as to admit the ordinary traveler to the sacred inclosure, as he is now admitted to the Mosque of Omar, for a small fee, which formerly was as sacredly guarded. Moslem cupidity can not brook the temptations of gold.

Canon Stanley, who accompanied the prince, has recorded, with his usual elegance of diction, some thrilling illustrations of the superstition and almost religious awe with which the guardians of the Mosque regard these patriarchal shrines. "The princes of any other nation," said the chief santon, "should have passed over my dead body sooner than enter; but to the eldest son of the Queen of England we are willing to accord even this privilege." And, as the party entered the silver gate guarding the tomb of Abraham, the priest ejaculated, "O Friend of God, forgive this intrusion." Maintaining even in death their rigid rule of the exclusion of male visitors from the society of their females, not even the Crown Prince of England was permitted to approach the cenotaphs of Sarah and her female descendants. The patriarchs being regarded as still existing in a state of suspended animation, and capable of resenting any indignity offered to their sepulchres, or the presence of any unwelcome visitor, the prince's party was denied admittance to the tomb of Isaac, who, according to the santon, being unlike his kind-hearted father, and more easily exasperated, would arise and drive out any but those congenial to his spirit.

Beneath the Mosque is the sacred cave where rest in peace the remains of the eminent dead, and where to this day may still repose intact the embalmed body of Jacob. Machpelah signifying "double," the cave consists of two compartments, separated by a wall of native rock. To its sepulchral vaults there are three entrances—one in the northwest corner, close to the western wall; a second in the court, opposite the entrance-gate of the Mosque; and a third near the shrine of Abraham. Believing, like the Catholics, in the intercession of saints, the Moslems throw their petitions to the patriarchs[1] through the latter aperture.

Of the identity of this spot with the cave of Machpelah there can not be a reasonable doubt. In the days of Josephus it was marked by a memorial erected by Abraham himself, and from his time both Jews, Christians, and Moslems have in turn been the faithful guardians of the patriarchal tomb. Its identity is avouched by the belief of the Jews themselves, and around its venerable walls the despised descendant of the illustrious patriarchs now chants his prayers, and laments the departed glory of the once mighty kingdom of his renowned ancestors. Threatened with instant death should his devotion or temerity lead him to cross the threshold, he is only permitted, on certain occasions, to look through an aperture in the massive wall upon the spot where rest in peace those who were mighty in their day and generation, but who, in the helplessness of death, can bring no relief to a posterity who have abandoned their altars, and rejected the long-promised and now exalted Messiah.

There was something touching in the thought that I stood beside the family vault of those who had long lived together in the happy estate of matrimony, and there was even enjoyment in the reflection that God had vindicated the duality and unity of marriage in the grave. Here, side by side, sleep Abraham and Sarah, Isaac and Rebekah, Jacob and Leah. Hagar and Keturah are not with Sarah, and Rachel is not with her sister Leah. Is this separation in death God's reproof to Jacob for his dissatisfaction with Leah? Though the reasons that determined him to inter his beautiful Rachel in a common field by the roadside are unknown to us, and though Hebron is less than twenty miles distant from Ephrath, yet it is somewhat remarkable that in after years she was not exhumed and laid in the family tomb of Machpelah. Was Jacob unwilling to divide his grave with the daughters of Laban?

[1] See Stanley's Account of the Visit of the Prince of Wales, Appendix II. to his History of the Jewish Church.

or, conscious of the purity and singleness of his affection for Rachel, would he have her alone even in death? By the highway her solitary tomb remains, and, as if impressed with the patriarch's wish, his descendants have made no interments on the spot.

Inseparably connected with Hebron is Beersheba, which is less than forty miles to the south. The road thither is hilly, and the journey toilsome; but, on approaching the well that Abraham dug, the pasture-fields of the patriarchs stretch out before the eye in all their native beauty and richness. Covering an area half a mile in length and a quarter of a mile in breadth are fragments of pottery, remains of foundations, and traces of a stone wall, the date of which is unknown, called by Moses Beer-sheba, "Well of the Oath," because of the covenant between Abraham and Abimelech, and by the Arabs Bir es-Seb'a, "Well of the Seven," because of the seven ewe-lambs the former gave the latter: the modern name corresponds with the Bible designation. Having a diameter of twelve and a half feet, and a depth of forty-four feet to the surface of the water, this well is excavated in the living rock, and contains an abundance of pure fresh water.

Around this well what thrilling memories cluster! Departing from Hebron after the conflagration of Sodom, Abraham planted here a grove, whose fruit he gathered, and beneath whose shade he worshiped.[1] Here Isaac spent his happy youth, rejoicing in the smiles of honored parents, and here his father received the command to offer the child of promise as a burnt-offering.[2] After the demise of his mother, here Isaac received his bride Rebekah; and Beersheba became the scene of that sad episode in domestic life, the fraud of Jacob in obtaining Esau's birthright.[3] Here, in manhood, those brothers were estranged by a mother's folly, and from this ancestral abode Jacob fled to Haran.[4] After the lapse of seventy-five years he was here again, and offered sacrifices prior to his departure into Egypt, whence he was brought back with funeral honors such as only kings receive.[5] Threatened by the infatuated Jezebel, hither Elijah fled, and, sitting beneath the shade of a juniper-tree, requested for himself that he might die.[6] And here was the southern boundary of the Promised Land, whose

[1] Gen., xxi., 33. [2] Ib., xxii., 1-19. [3] Ib., xxv., 27-34.
[4] Ib., xxviii. [5] Ib., xlvi., 1. [6] 1 Kings, xix., 1 4.

uttermost limits, in the earlier history of the nation, were from "Dan to Beersheba."

In a land where social and domestic customs never change, the scenes of historic associations possess an interest that never fails. The advanced civilization of Europe has there left to the traveler the ruins of renowned cities, without perpetuating the customs of their citizens. The temples, palaces, and dwellings of the Greeks and Romans remain, attesting the genius, elegance, and wealth of their age, but the social habits of the inhabitants of Athens and Rome bear no resemblance to those of their superior ancestors. In Italy and Greece one feels himself in an ancient country surrounded by a modern people, and, to re-live the past, he must forsake the present. But in the East, where a "thousand years are but as one day"—where the stereotyped life of the patriarchs is the every-day life of the Arabs—where intonations of voice, peculiarities of gesture, modes of salutation, styles of dress, habits of business, customs of domestic life, and where the tent, the meal, the fold are the same, the only difference is in the change of the persons who now occupy the homes of those whose memory we cherish, whose examples we imitate, and whose faith we aspire to attain. Accustomed to the slow and regular processes of nature, possessing power rather than capacity, and clinging to experience as something immutable, those who live by the cultivation of the soil look with suspicion upon novelties, regard innovations with dread, and are the last to change. The incoming of Franks into Eastern cities insensibly affects the manners of society; but here, on the patriarchal pasture-fields of Mamre and Beersheba, the domestic life of to-day is the same as it was 4000 years ago.

In crossing the great Plain of Wady esh-Sheikh, in Arabia, *en route* for Mount Sinai, Sheik Hassan, the chief of a tribe of Tawarahs, invited us to dine at his tent. It was noon when, from the backs of our camels, we espied the encampment to the southward. Nine tents of camel's hair were arranged in a line, supported by rude poles. Those for the females were impenetrable to the eye of strangers, while those for the males consisted merely of a roof, with the sides and ends open. On reaching the tent prepared for our reception, our camels knelt, we dismounted, and the sheikh's father, a man of eighty years, rose to greet us, and bowed himself to the ground in an at-

17

titude of profound respect.¹ Mats were spread for us to sit upon, and water was brought to wash our hands and feet.² To the east of this tented home Hassan's daughters were keeping his flocks, as Rachel had kept those of Laban nearly forty centuries ago.³ A young man was sent to the fold to fetch a kid, tender and good, and, having dressed it, carried it into the tent to Hassan's wife, who cooked it with milk and rice. The rice and meat were brought on two large wooden plates into our tent, and set before us on a small stool less than a foot high. Without knife, fork, or spoon, we returned to the days before the invention of such instruments, and with our fingers began to eat, while the sheikh respectfully stood up, attentive to our wants.⁴ It being a breach of Arab etiquette to inquire after the health of a wife, we were not permitted to ask for Sarah as the angels did.⁵

Had the dinner Abraham prepared for the three angels on the plains of Mamre been dramatized, the correspondence could hardly have been more exact. The tent-life; this distant field; the pressing invitation to dine; the water for the ablution of our hands and feet; the going to the field for a kid; handing it to a servant to dress it; the meal itself; the sheikh standing up while we ate; the seclusion of the females gave a lifelike reality to the sacred story.

Like the patriarchs of old, these Bedouin sheikhs lead a predatory life, moving their tents from place to place, according to the climate, and the demands of their herds and flocks. But in wealth, in hospitality, in reputation, in purity of character, in devotion, in intellect, in nobility of nature, the modern Arab chief holds no comparison with the exalted nature, the high-toned character, and the Christian-like piety of the prince of the patriarchs.

As in the days of the Hebrew spies, the Vale of Hebron is still famous for the delicious grapes of Eshcol.⁶ Extending up the valley for more than a mile, and covering the sloping hills on either side, these celebrated vineyards are cultivated with care, and are a source of considerable revenue to the proprietors. Unlike our vineyards, those of Eshcol have no arbors. The vines are planted in rows, from eight to ten feet apart in each direction. When they attain a height of six feet they

---

¹ Gen., xviii., 2. ² Ib., xviii., 4. ³ Ib., xxix., 6.
⁴ Ib., xviii., 8. ⁵ Ib., xviii., 9. ⁶ Num., xiii., 16–26.

are attached to a stake, placed in a sloping position, and the shoots extending from vine to vine form a long and graceful festoon. Occasionally two opposite rows are purposely inclined toward each other, forming with their branches a natural arbor. After vintage, in late autumn, all the shoots are pruned off, and the stocks are cut down within a few feet of the ground, leaving an ungainly and apparently dead trunk; but the returning spring brings forth again the tender leaf, and the coming summer matures the luscious grape for the autumnal vintage. In each vineyard there is a lodge, or stone tower, from which the watchman keeps guard against the depredations of beasts and the incursions of robbers. During the vintage season the town is deserted; the people retire to these towers, each one sitting beneath his own vine and fig-tree,[1] and dividing the time between the gathering of the fruitage and the enjoyments of the annual festival. As the Moslems, who are the principal proprietors, are not allowed by their Koran to make wine, the grapes are either dried into raisins, or they are first pressed, and the juice is then boiled down into a sirup called dibs, not unlike molasses, but of a more delightful flavor and delicious taste. It was to these vineyards the spies came, and from them they carried bunches of the grapes to Moses and their brethren as evidence of the fruitfulness of the Promised Land. Their journey was long, fatiguing, and perilous. Leaving Kadesh Barnea, in the Desert of Paran, they entered the Jordan Valley, and followed the river northward to Lake Tiberias, and, winding round its northern shore, entered the upper valley of the Jordan, pursuing their journey as far as Rehob, near Dan, as men come to Hamath; thence returning through the midst of the land by Tabor, across the great plain of Esdraelon, over the hills of Samaria, through the vale of Shechem, by Jacob's well, over the heights of Benjamin and Judah, by Shiloh, Bethel, Jerusalem, and Bethlehem, to Hebron. Here flows the brook Eshcol, from which they drank, and from the vines along its banks they cut down a branch with one cluster of grapes, "and they bare it between two upon a staff." To those who live in more northern climates, this story of the enormous size and great weight of a single bunch of grapes must seem incredible; but, whatever may be the degeneracy of the Syrian grape, through centuries of neg-

[1] Micah, iv., 4.

feet, the proof is abundant that in southern latitudes grapes grow to an enormous size. According to Pliny, a bunch of African grapes was larger than an infant. Paul Lucas mentions bunches which he saw in Damascus weighing forty-five pounds each, and in Naples I have eaten grapes each one as large as a plum. The mode, however, adopted by the spies to carry the bunch from Eshcol to Kadesh Barnea was probably not rendered necessary by the size of the cluster so much as by the desire to preserve it entire for the benefit of their brethren.[1] Watched by the keen eye of the vine-dresser, we entered the vineyard, and were impressed with the exact correspondence between the one before us and the one described by our Lord: There was a certain householder, which planted a vineyard, hedged it round about, digged a wine-press in it, built a tower, and let it out to husbandmen.[2] There were the vines; around them was the hedge; within it was the press; yonder stood the tower, and by my side toiled the husbandman. Within the same vale are groves of olives, and orchards of figs, and apricots, and quinces, and pomegranates. The latter fruit, so frequently referred to in the Bible, is as sweet to the taste as it is pleasant to the eye. In form and size it is not unlike an orange, and in color inclines to a pale yellow, tinged with a red blush. They grow upon a thorny bush, with a tulip-shaped flower of a brilliant red color, and form one of the luxuries of the East both to the native and to the stranger. But the noblest of all the trees of Hebron is the remarkable oak of Abraham. It stands in the midst of the vineyards, in a clean, smooth spot, covered with soft, fresh grass, and near a well of cool water. It is an oak of the evergreen species, measuring twenty-three feet in girth, and its magnificent branches spread out over a circle ninety feet in diameter. Six feet from the ground the trunk separates into four huge branches, and, higher up, these in turn spread out into many more. Standing alone, it appears to greater advantage, and its lengthened arms, loaded with exquisite foliage, affords delightful shade to the weary traveler. Here, on their festive days, the Jewish maidens and the young men of Hebron assemble beneath this ancestral tree to enjoy the rural pleasure of the song and dance. Though of great age, it is still sound and majestic, and with it tradition associates many thrilling

[1] Num., xiii. [2] Matt., xxi., 33.

memories. Standing on the Plain of Mamre, it probably marks the spot where Abraham pitched his tent and entertained the angels. Though hardly credible that this terebinth should have remained green and vigorous during the lapse of nearly forty centuries, yet it may be cherished as the last representative of the sacred forest of Mamre. Fond of contrasts, and never happier than when the extremes of fortune and the ends of time meet in the same scene, the Oriental legendaries point to this noble oak as the slave-mart where the descendants of Abraham were sold by their Roman masters into captivity.

Plucking a leaf from the famous oak and a sprig from the vines of Eshcol, we mounted our horses, and in less than an hour reached the ruins of Remit el-Khulîl, the house of Abraham. Occupying the summit of a mountain ridge, from which the blue waters of the Mediterranean were distinctly seen, they consist of massive stone walls, of rounded columns now broken, of arched vaults now in ruins, and of a noble well hewn out of the solid rock. The two remaining walls are constructed of well-dressed stones, measuring fifteen feet in length, and are in good condition. The wall facing the south extends east and west 290 feet, while the other, running at right angles with the former, is 160 in length. The well is a perfect circle, with a diameter of ten feet. Its sides are faced with smooth dressed stones, from out the joints of which exquisite ferns were growing. The water is deep, clear, and sweet, reflecting the sun by day, and the moon and stars by night. An unsolved mystery still hangs over the ruins of Remit el-Khulîl, if ruins they be. Their founder and their age are alike unknown. The Jews point to them as marking one of the halting-places of Abraham; the Latin fathers of church history ascribe them to Constantine the Great; while others attribute them to some unknown person, who would have reared for himself a castle and a palace, but was unable to finish the designed plan.

Resuming our journey, in half an hour we passed on our right a mosque, whose solitary minaret rose gracefully in honor of the Prophet Jonah, while to the left, a mile beyond, was a crumbling tower with pointed arches, and near it an immense fountain, where shepherds were bathing. On either side of the road were excavated tombs, now the haunt of the hyena and jackal. The mosque probably marks the site of Halhul, and the tower the site of Beth-zur, enumerated by Joshua as among the cities of Judah.[1] Fifteen miles to the north from Hebron the valley of Urtâs crosses the road at right angles, and to the right of the highway are the celebrated Pools of Solomon. To these, and to the lovely gardens which once environed them, he refers in Ecclesiastes, ii., 5, 6: "I made me gardens and orchards, and I planted trees in them of all kinds of fruits. I made me pools of water, to water therewith the wood that bringeth forth trees." Nowhere in the environs of Jerusalem could the wise king have attained the consummation of his wishes to greater advantage than here. Under the horticultural care of a Christian Jew, the valley of Urtâs has been transformed into a charming garden. What were once rocky hills are now terraced from base to summit, covered with olives, figs, and almonds, while in the bed of the valley are grains and grasses, flowers and vegetables, growing in rich abundance. With his inexhaustible resources, what a scene of beauty must the vale of Etham and the neighboring hills have presented in the days of Solomon's strength and glory! But Time, that inexorable destroyer of human works, has effaced every trace of his wonderful genius save the pools that bear his name. Both history and tradition point with unmistakable accuracy to the imperial founder of these great fountains. With his accustomed love of detail, Josephus refers to the rivulets and gardens of Etham, situated fifty stadia to the south from the Holy City, whither Solomon was wont to retire for rural delights; and the Rabbins, with even greater minuteness, describe the aqueduct which conveyed the waters of Urtâs to Jerusalem.

These pools consist of three immense reservoirs, situated in a straight line one below the other, and so constructed that the bottom of the first is higher than the top of the second, and the second than that of the third. They are in part excavated in the rocky bed of the valley, and in part built of square hewn stones covered with cement, and are entered by stone steps excavated in the rock. Measuring 380 feet in length, 236 in breadth, and twenty-five in depth, the upper pool is the smallest of the three. A hundred and sixty feet to the east is the middle pool, which is 423 feet long, thirty-nine deep, and varies from 160

[1] Josh., xv., 58.

to 250 wide. Two hundred and forty-eight feet farther east is the lowest and largest reservoir, being 582 feet in length, from 148 to 207 in width, and fifty feet in depth, and, when full, capable of floating one of our largest men-of-war. The eastern end of the lowest pool is supported by immense buttresses, in one of which is a chamber, and in the north wall of the first tank is a filter—a wise precaution. Forty rods to the northwest, in an open field, are the perennial sources of these great fountains. Twelve feet below the surface are two vaulted chambers, the larger of the two being thirty-seven feet long and twenty wide. Springing up at four different places through the bottom of these chambers, the water is conducted by little ducts into a large basin, from which it flows through a subterranean canal to the northwest corner of the first pool, where it is divided, a portion of it flowing into a deep vault near the old castle, and thence being conducted into the first pool, while the remainder is carried by an aqueduct along the hill-side, which is so arranged as to send a portion of its water into the second and third pools, and then, descending rapidly, joins the aqueduct leading from the lowest pool, from which point the water is conducted, via Bethlehem, by a sinuous channel to Jerusalem. I know not which to admire more—the genius of the architect that conceived such a complicated work, or the public spirit of the king who supplied the means for its execution. The original design was to supply the Holy City with pure cool water, and also the Temple service, which demanded such large quantities. And to obtain a constant and unfailing supply, these tanks bore to each other a mutual relation. When the fountain yielded more than was necessary, the surplus was carried into the pools, and when the yield was not equal to the demand, the deficiency was supplied from the pools themselves.

The wind blew hard from the northwest as I traced up the hill-side the ancient aqueduct, repeating those impressive words of the great proverbialist, "Vanity of vanities, all is vanity." Like the melancholy strains of a dirge, the winds moaned as they swept round the mountain brow, and the waters sighed as they languidly fell from pool to pool. Was it not the requiem of his departed glory? A solitary descendant of his mighty kingdom now grubs a living where once his royal gardens stood, of whose beauty he sang in all the tenderness of the Canticles; and the robber of the desert and the wild Bedouin of the hills now bathe in those fountains which once sent murmuring streamlets along verdant banks and flowery beds, and supplied the imperial table with the cooling beverage.

The aqueduct is constructed of red earthen pipes, covered, for protection, by common limestone flagging. In many places the flagging is removed and the pottery broken, to accommodate the traveler with water. To preserve a proper level, it sweeps around the hills and heads of the valleys; and, though fatiguing to follow its windings, it repaid the toil, as illustrating the fact that, while the ancients could construct the most complicated works of masonry, they were ignorant of the simple method of conducting water over a level higher than its source. Having followed the aqueduct two miles, we crossed the wild valley of Ta'āmirah, and reached Bethlehem in time to enjoy a Christian wedding. Ten pretty maidens had assembled at the door of the bride, and were singing a simple but sweet melody, accompanied with the clapping of hands. Unlike the music of the Moslems, there was a warmth in these bridal songs thrilling and joyous. From a scene so happy we passed through the town, and, a mile from the ancient gateway to the northwest, we came to the tomb of Rachel.

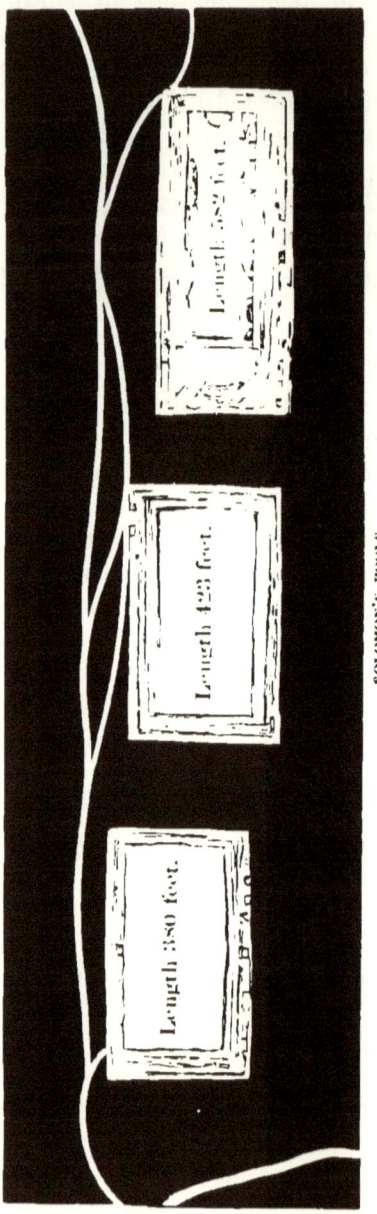

"And they journey from Bethel; and there was but a little way to come to Ephrath; and Rachel died and was buried in the way to Ephrath, which is Bethlehem. And Jacob set a pillar upon her grave; that is the pillar of Rachel's grave unto this day.[1]" The pillar reared to the memory of a beloved wife has given place to a small white square building, surmounted by a dome. It is a Mohammedan wely. Standing by the side of the great road from Jerusalem to Hebron, the site has never been lost, its identity never questioned. Jew, Christian, Moslem, equally revere it, and never pass it without some token of affectionate remembrance. Gathering a few wild flowers growing near the dust of Rachel, we resumed our journey toward Jerusalem. In half an hour we reached the convent dedicated to Elijah, called Mâr Eliâs, and here came upon the new and noble macadamized road, extending from Bethlehem to Jerusalem, constructed by the monks of Mâr Eliâs, which is the first of the kind in Palestine, since the construction of a similar road by the French, running from Beîrut to Damascus. The wind had increased to a tornado as we swept by the Plain of Rephaim. It was the last object of Biblical interest to heighten the joy of a long and interesting tour. Stretching from the rocky brow of Hinnom to the Convent of Elias, it gradually declines to the narrow Valley of Roses. A mile in length, it is one of the richest plains in the Holy Land. It is remarkable in sacred history as the camp of the Philistines in the days of Saul, and as containing a mulberry-grove, now gone, in the tops of the trees of which David heard a "sound of a going,"[2] which to him was the signal of war and the pæan of victory.

[1] Gen., xxxv., 16–20.   [2] 2 Sam., v., 24.

CHAPTER IX.

Land of the Philistines.—Its Limits.—Fell to the Lot of Simeon and Dan. —Origin of the Philistines.—The meaning of the Name.—Their royal Cities.—Their God and Goddess.—Journey thither.—Valley of Roses.— Baptism of the Eunuch.—Home of John the Baptist.—Slaughter of the Jews in the City of Bether.—Site of Bethshemesh.—Home of Samson.— Village of Zorah.—Field where the Angel appeared.—Town of Timnath. —Lair of the Lion.—Home of Delilah.—Oriental Weddings.—Valley of Shochoh.—Scene of the Conflict between David and Goliath. —Correspondence between Scripture and the natural Features of the Place.—The Valley.—The Brook.—The smooth Stones.—The Sling. —The Mountains.—The Champions.—The Victory.—Home of Goliath.—Gath.—David's feigned Insanity.—Road to Eleutheropolis.—Its Location.—Great Caves.—Site of Lachish.—Its great Battle-field.—Sennacherib and Hezekiah.—Byron's Hebrew Melody.—Gaza.—Palm-groves.—Direction of the Road.—Site of the City.—Modern City.—Ancient Ruins.—Christian Church.—Home of Giants.—Gates that Samson carried away.—His Prison.—The great Feast.—Samson called.—His Presence alarms the Multitude.—Feats of Strength.—Death Scene.—He is a Failure.—Alexander the Great wounded at Gaza.—A Moslem City.—Ascalon.—Route thither. —Stood near the Sea.—Ruins.—Desolation.—History.—Adorned by Herod.—Captured by the Crusaders.—Road to Ashdod.—Beautiful Gardens. —No Ruins.—Dagon and the Ark.—Road to Joppa.—Villages.—Joppa on the Sea.—Its Antiquity.—Floats of Pine and Cedar.—House of Simon. —Substantial Structure.—Peter's Vision.—Appearance of the Town.— Gate of the City.—Population.—Jews.—Nubian Magician.—Magnificent Orange-groves. — Ramleh. — Franciscans. —Traditions —Antiquities.— Tower.—View.—Ludd.—Eneas cured of Palsy.—Church of St. George. —Beautiful Ruin.—Nether Bethhoron.—Wretchedness.—Upper Bethhoron.—Battle-field of Gibeon.—The Battle.—Wonderful Correspondence. —Testimony of the Rocks.—Ajalon.—Sun and Moon stand still.—City of Gibeon.— Modern Town.—Gibeonites.—History.—Death of the Gladiators.—Pool of Gibeon.—Murder of Amasa.—Solomon's Dream.—"The Look-out." — Mizpeh. — National Rendezvous.—Ebenezer Stone.—Saul chosen King.—Minaret.—Vast and magnificent Prospect.

PHILISTIA is among the richest sections of Palestine, and is scarcely surpassed in fertility by any other portion of land upon the globe. Consisting of that vast maritime plain extending from Joppa on the north to Gerar on the south, it is washed by the Mediterranean on the west, and is bounded on the east by the Mountains of Judea. Originally occupied by the Avims, the descendants of Cush,[1] it subsequently became the possession of the Philistines. In the division of the land it fell to the tribes of Simeon and Dan, who, however, were never fully able to subdue their allotted provinces. At present it is inhabited by Moslem Arabs, whose humble towns occupy the sites of more renowned cities. On the origin of the Philistines the learned are not agreed. In the absence of authentic records and of distinctive customs, it is difficult to decide whether they came from the hills of Cappadocia, the islands of Cyprus and Crete, or from Lower Egypt. Their national name, signifying "strangers," implies their foreign birth. Nor is it definitely known whether they came in possession of their new territory by conquest, or by alliances formed with the aborigines of Canaan, who, in process of time, were absorbed by the more rapid increase and superior strength of their allies. Rising to greatness from an humble beginning, their history forms part of the inspired narrative, and the whole country now bears the name of Palestine, or "the Land of the Philistines." Dividing their possession into five lordships, they founded as many royal cities, which are known in Scripture by the names of Gaza, Ashdod, Askelon, Gath, and Ekron. Idolaters in faith and practice, their chief divinity was Dagon, the "Fish-god," whose dominion over men, beasts, and fowls was represented by the triple formation of his body. He had a human head, a horse's neck, and trunk and limbs covered with the feathers of different birds. His wife Derceto, "the Fish-goddess," or Syrian Venus, had the form of a beauteous maid from her waist up, and thence downward resembled a fish.

As the home of Samson, and the scene of many a romantic story, Philistia has a history of thrilling interest. It was therefore with no ordinary delight that we left the Holy City to explore a region where have occurred so many grand historic events. Skirting the northern border of the Plain of Rephaim, we were soon under the shadow of the Convent of the Cross. Turning to the right, we entered the Valley of Roses, called by the Arabs Wady el-Werd. For more than half a mile the bottom of the glen is covered with rose-bushes, cultivated for

[1] Deut., ii., 23.

the manufacture of rose-water, which is used in the East in large quantities. Descending Wady el-Werd, we soon reached Philip's Fountain, where, according to a recent tradition, the Evangelist baptized the Ethiopian eunuch.[1] 'Ain Haniyeh is a pretty fountain gushing out from a semicircular apse, ornamented with pilasters, and is situated in a wild glen by the wayside, on the ancient road to Gaza. On the summit of a neighboring hill to the north stands the quiet hamlet of 'Ain Kârim, the birthplace of John the Baptist. It is in the "hill country of Judea," and is the scene of the meeting of those pious cousins, the destined mothers of the Messiah and his harbinger.[2] High up on a wild ridge to the south is the city of Bether, where the pretended Christ, called Bar-cochba, the "Son of a Star," made his last and fatal stand against the Romans under Adrian. It was then a Jewish city of wealth and learning, and, after a siege of three and a half years, was forced to surrender. Eighty thousand of its unfortunate citizens fell beneath the conqueror's sword; and such was the dreadful slaughter, that, according to the historian, the horses waded in blood up to their bridles.

Following the Sultâny, or "Queen's Highway," our path lay among the "hills of Judea," clad with vines and covered with corn. Approaching the large town of Beit 'Abab, we turned to the west, and at high noon reached the ancient city of Bethshemesh. Thistles and marigolds now cover the ruins of the Philistine village, to which the Ark of the Lord was brought from Ekron, and where fifty thousand people were slain for their temerity in looking into the ark, contrary to the Lord's express command.[3] We were now in the country of Samson. Around us rose his native hills, and beneath us stretched the valleys of his childhood, while here and there appeared the scenes of many memorable deeds of his riper years. On the summit of a neighboring hill to the right, which rises steeply from the Valley of Sûr'ah, is the village of Zorah, where he was born,[4] and adjoining it is the field where the angel of the Lord appeared unto Manoah and his wife. Beyond an intervening ridge, and less than two miles to the westward, is Timnath, situated on a plain, the place where Samson married his Philistine wife.[5] It was in one of the vineyards in the adjacent

[1] Acts, viii., 27-29.   [2] Luke, i., 39.   [3] I Sam., v. and vi.
[4] Judges, xiii., 2.   [5] Ib., xiv., 1.

glen that, as he hastened to his betrothed, he turned aside to slay the lion of Timnath who roared against him,[1] and from whose dead carcass, on a subsequent occasion, he took the honey which, on his wedding-day, was the subject of that perplexing riddle, "Out of the eater came forth meat, and out of the strong came forth sweetness."[2] It was there the wife of his bosom was afterward given to another, and, to avenge himself, he went forth to destroy the corn-fields of his enemies, which dotted the Plain of Philistia.[3] From the base of his native hill extends the Valley of Sorek, the home of Delilah,[4] and where the man with a divine secret, yielding to the entreaties of a woman, fell asleep in the lap of false affection, to awake to weakness and to shame. Along this same vale the road leads to Gaza, whither the blind captive was led, bound with fetters of brass, to grind in the prison-house of the Philistines.[5] And now, after the lapse of so many centuries, all the incidents of his wedding are illustrated by existing customs and confirmed by facts. Wives are procured now, as then, by the intervention of parents; marriages are attended by the same display; and on such occasions riddles are propounded by the bridegroom, and other sports practiced. In the wild glens of this region, and on the rugged hills, are foxes or jackals, and through the corn-fields on the rich plains below another Samson might send them on their burning mission.

Passing on toward the scene of his death, we turned to the southeast in search of the Valley of Shochoh, where David slew Goliath. A ride of six miles brought us to Beit Nettif, a small village crowning a lofty cliff. Impelled by curiosity, the people gathered around us in crowds to examine our garments and riding equipage. Compelled to take a guide to the romantic valley, we secured the services of a white-turbaned Arab, who, after tenderly kissing his child and bidding his wife adieu, led us through the town, and, to save a detour, up the roughest, steepest mountain in the Holy Land. Skirting the verge of a dangerous precipice on the north, we turned southward, and in less than an hour entered one of the most picturesque ravines in Southern Palestine. Rising grandly on either side, the rocks were festooned with delicate shrubs, and from a thousand rills the water glided, forming a brooklet be-

---

[1] Judges, xiv., 5, 6.   [2] Ib., xiv., 14.   [3] Ib., xv., 4.
[4] Ib., xvi., 4.   [5] Ib., xvi., 5-21.

low. Midway the ravine there is a fountain gushing out of the mountain's side, around which are a few Arab huts. The glen contracted as we ascended, and at its terminus the country opened and declined toward the south. Rapidly descending a mountain path, we were soon in the Valley of Elah, where David achieved his celebrated victory. Here, as elsewhere in our travels, we had proof of the harmony existing between the inspired narrative of the event and the topography of the scene of its occurrence.

Running north and south, the bed of the valley measures a mile in width, and was covered with grain and flowers. Through its centre extends a torrent bed, lined with smooth pebbles, and fringed with acacia-trees. Though not high, the mountains on either side are bold and well defined. On their summits the contending armies were drawn up in battle array, watching each other's movements. To make an assault, the intervening valley must first be crossed, which would give to the defense an immense advantage. Unwilling to lose a good position and invite such a fearful slaughter, the armies were disinclined to make an attack. Impatient at the delay, there was one brave spirit among the Philistines who offered to stake the issues of the war upon a single-handed combat. Descending, day after day, for forty days, the left bank of the valley, Goliath of Gath threw down the gauntlet and cried out, "I defy the armies of Israel; send me a man, that we may fight together." His giant form, his proud, defiant tone, his powerful weapons, sent dismay to the heart of Israel, and neither the once heroic Saul, nor any of his warriors, had the courage to accept the challenge. With all the appearance of an accidental event, David that day reached the camp with provision for his three brethren who were in Saul's army. Rising above the contempt of Eliab, rejecting the king's armor, but trusting in that higher power which had led him to the scene and ordained him for the fight, David went forth to retrieve the honor of his country, and vindicate the supremacy of Jehovah over the idol Dagon. Like Syrian shepherds of to-day, he carried a staff, a scrip, and sling, for the defense of his fold. Confident of his ability to employ with success the instruments which he had been accustomed to all his life, David descended, in the presence of the embattled hosts, and from the flowing brook he stooped to gather five smooth stones for the conflict. The apparent advantages were with the Philistine; but the Unseen, who was with David, was more than he who was against him. Goliath had size, strength, experience, armor, and weapons. David was young, small, and armed only with a sling; but he had spirit, courage, and faith. What to him would forever have remained the romantic stories of a shepherd's life, now suddenly becomes the source of inspiration and the ground of hope. Among his native mountains a lion and a bear had attacked his fold, and when, in attempting to rescue the lamb, the wild beasts rose up against him, he smote the one and the other, "and this uncircumcised Philistine shall be as one of them, seeing he has defied the armies of the living God." Those champions met, one in the pride of his strength and military prowess, the other in the name of the Lord of hosts; one full of contempt for his antagonist, the other conscious of a just cause. The polished armor, the brazen shield, the burnished helmet, and immense spear of Goliath, glittered in the sunlight; the ruddy cheeks of the shepherd boy glowed with a heroic spirit, which was his only helmet, and a brave heart within him, beating calmly, was his only shield. Swung by unerring skill, and guided by an invisible hand, the smooth stone from the Brook Elah penetrated the brain of the giant, and David stood in triumph upon his fallen body, amid the shouts of victory and the benedictions of his countrymen.[1]

Seven miles to the northwest, on the same road over which the routed Philistines fled, is Gath, the native city of Goliath. The conspicuous hill on which it stood rises 200 feet above the Plain of Philistia, and is now crowned with an old castle, a Mohammedan tomb, and a few huts, which compose the modern town. Besides being the birthplace of the famous warrior, it is also the scene of a singular episode in the life of David. Compelled to fly from the presence of Saul, he stopped at Nob, where, having obtained from Abimelech a supply of food and the sword of Goliath, he came to Gath, either in the hope of not being recognized, or, as a fugitive from Saul's court, of receiving a welcome from the Philistines, with whom the king was then at war. Disappointed in both, and discovering that his fate was sealed, "he feigned himself mad in their hands, and scrabbled on the doors of the gate, and let his spit-

[1] 1 Sam., xvii.

tle fall upon his beard." Madmen being privileged characters then, as they are now in the East, he was permitted to roam at large; and, embracing a favorable moment, he fled to the cave of Adullam, where he gathered a small army around him, and resisted the repeated attempts of Saul to take his life.[1]

From Gath the road runs toward the southeast, and the next important place is Eleutheropolis, six miles distant. The path is rugged, and alternately crosses stony ridges and small valleys. The village occupies a nook in a green valley, and is surrounded by low hills. Though the ancient city is destitute of special Biblical interest, yet its ruins are extensive and unique. Within an inclosure 600 feet square are the remains of a castle, filling one third of the entire space. The interior contains arches, vaults, and marble shafts. Two hundred yards up a ravine, extending eastward, are massive foundations, and a fine well, more than seventy feet deep; but the chief attraction is the great caves, unequaled in extent by any in Syria. The largest of these caverns is 100 feet high and sixty-five in diameter. Lateral galleries connect it with adjoining caves, which are surmounted with domes, and ornamented with cornices. In another portion of the town is a vast range of bell-shaped chambers, connected by arched doorways and subterranean passages. While a few of them are entirely dark, most of them are lighted by a circular aperture in the top. Some regard these caverns as the work of Idumean Troglodytes, while others suppose them to have been excavated for cisterns; the former is the more probable theory.[2]

Thirteen miles to the southwest is the site of Lachish, called by the Arabs Um Lâkis. The intervening country is rocky and undulating, and occasionally dotted with deserted villages. The hill on which the city stood is low and flat, and is strewn with fragments of marble columns and blocks of hewn stones. Lachish was among the cities of Judah captured by Joshua,[3] but derives its chief significance from having been fortified by Rehoboam,[4] and afterward besieged by Sennacherib. It was while the latter was encamped here that King Hezekiah sent unto him, saying, "I have offended; return from me; that which thou puttest on me I will bear." To meet the demand for 300 talents of silver and thirty talents of gold, Hezekiah

[1] 1 Sam., xxi. 10–15.
[2] Robinson.
[3] Josh., x. 31, 32.
[4] 1 Chron., xi., 5–12.

emptied his own treasure and that of the house of the Lord; and, to supply a deficiency that remained, "he cut off the gold from the doors and pillars of the Temple." But, not satisfied with a sum so large, Sennacherib sent three of his generals to Jerusalem to demand the immediate and unconditional surrender of the city. One of the three was Rabshakeh, whose blasphemous speech offended Heaven, as his proud and defiant words had overwhelmed the king with consternation and fear. That night God heard Hezekiah's prayer, and vindicated his own insulted majesty. From his throne "the angel of the Lord went out, and smote in the camp of the Assyrians an hundred fourscore and five thousand." The next morning Sennacherib departed for Nineveh, where he was assassinated by two of his sons while worshiping in the temple of Nisroch, his god.

In one of his noblest odes, Byron has described the destruction of the Assyrian host:

> "The Assyrian came down like the wolf on the fold,
> And his cohorts were gleaming in purple and gold;
> And the sheen of their spears was like stars on the sea,
> When the blue wave rolls nightly on deep Galilee.

> "Like the leaves of the forest when Summer is green,
> That host with their banners at sunset were seen;
> Like the leaves of the forest when Autumn hath blown,
> That host on the morrow lay wither'd and strown.

> "For the Angel of Death spread his wings on the blast,
> And breathed in the face of the foe as he pass'd;
> And the eyes of the sleepers wax'd deadly and chill,
> And their hearts but once heaved, and forever grew still.

> "And there lay the steed with his nostril all wide,
> And through it there roll'd not the breath of his pride;
> And the foam of his gasping lay white on the turf,
> And cold as the spray of the rock-beaten surf.

> "And there lay the rider distorted and pale,
> With the dew on his brow, and the rust on his mail;
> And the tents were all silent, the banners alone,
> The lances unlifted, the trumpet unblown.

> "And the widows of Ashur are loud in their wail,
> And the idols are broke in the temple of Baal;
> And the might of the Gentile, unsmote by the sword,
> Hath melted like snow in the glance of the Lord!"

The bleakness of the scenery from Lachish to Gaza is relieved by groves of palms, olives, and willows, together with the gardens which surround the half dozen intervening villages. The peasants of these towns are industrious, and the glee of the children indicated their happiness, notwithstanding their nudity. The road crosses diagonally several deep torrent beds, which drain the upland country, and which continue their courses through the white sand downs to the sea. The approach to Gaza is among sand-hills and through olive-groves, and, after a ride of twelve miles from Lachish, the traveler finds himself in this renowned Philistine city. Situated three miles from the sea, Gaza is a city of 15,000 inhabitants, 300 of whom are Christians and the rest Moslems. Around it, like a green belt, are gardens of apricots, mulberries, and palms. On its western side runs the same road which was trodden by the Pharaohs thousands of years ago, and which leads to the pasture-fields of Gerar. Between the town and the sea is a range of hills, of drifting sand, two miles wide. On the east of the city are barren hills, the highest of which is crowned with a Mohammedan wely, and is probably the hill to the top of which Samson carried the gates of Gaza.

Rising from amid the rude buildings of the town is the great mosque, which was once a Christian church, and dedicated to John the Baptist. It has a peaked roof and an octagonal minaret. The interior is 130 feet long, and is divided into a nave and two aisles by rows of Corinthian columns. Modern Gaza has neither walls, gates, nor fortifications of any kind. Though thus exposed to the attacks of the predatory bands of Bedouins, yet the inhabitants are seldom molested, for no other reason, perhaps, than the fact that they themselves in part are freebooters.

With an antiquity that ranks it among the oldest cities in the world,[1] Gaza was originally inhabited by the Hivites, the descendants of Canaan,[2] who in the lapse of time were dispossessed by the Philistines, who elevated it to the dignity of a royal city. In the days of Moses it was the home of those giants known as the Anakims, whose formidable stature and warlike character alarmed the Hebrew spies, and, though subsequently captured by the tribe of Judah, it was repossessed by the sons of Anak, who enslaved the Israelites.[3] But Gaza appears most prominent in sacred history as the scene of many remarkable events in the life of Samson, and from him it has

[1] Gen., x., 19. [2] Josh., xiii., 3. [3] Judges, xiii., 1.

GAZA.

derived an imperishable name. In his happier days he here performed one of the most astonishing feats of his supernatural strength. Besieged by his enemies, he arose at midnight and carried the gates of the city upon his shoulders to the top of a hill that is before Hebron.[1] It was prior to his alliance with Delilah, and when in full possession of his marvelous strength, that he thus bade defiance to a whole race of giants. But, deceived by the duplicity of an unworthy wife, he afterward became, in the very city of his triumph, a blind, fettered, imprisoned captive, the sport of woman, and the ridicule of man.

Dreading him more than an army with banners, the Philistines had taken every precaution to secure their powerful and determined foe. Having consigned him to eternal darkness by the destruction of his eyes, they fastened his limbs with fetters of brass, and, thrusting him into a loathsome dungeon, appointed him to the menial work of an Eastern woman.[2] But He who had chosen him to be the champion and avenger of his people restored his strength, and with its restoration the day of vengeance returned. Deeming his capture a public good, the Philistines assembled to offer thanksgiving to their god Dagon. The day dawned without a cloud, and the sun rose in beauty upon the Plains of Philistia. At an early hour the streets of ancient Gaza were thronged with an excited multitude, who were hastening to the great sacrifice, and rejoicing in the capture of the giant of Zorah. The grand temple of their idol crowned the loftiest of their hills. Its broad flat roof was supported by arches resting on pillars. Two central columns, massive and strong, and standing near each other, were the key to the whole support. On the roof of the spacious temple, and also within the sacred fane, the lords of the Philistines, with their wives, had assembled to honor their god and enjoy the sports of the occasion. Though it was no part of their original purpose that Samson should add to the joy of the day by exhibitions of his strength, yet, as one pleasure never fails to excite a desire for another, and as a succession of pleasures demands the most extravagant delights, so, in the delirious excitement of the moment, the blind captive is called to make them sport. They had heard of the return of his strength, and he being now sightless, they could witness exhibitions of his power without fear of injury to themselves, as

[1] Judges, xvi., 2-3.   [2] Ib., xvi., 21.

in former days, so long as they remained beyond his reach.
Josephus supposes they made him a laughing-stock, and insulted him in their cups; but, rather, they forced him to perform prodigious exploits of physical strength, which accounts for his weariness, and his excuse to lean against the pillars. Led by a little Philistine boy, he came from his gloomy dungeon. The transition from darkness to light had no effect upon his sightless eyeballs. Recalling the havoc he had made among their countrymen at Lehi, and not knowing what plans of revenge were then the subject of his thoughts, many ran at his approach, while all sought to avoid his grasp. As he advanced he was greeted with shouts of ridicule and peals of laughter. Removing the brazen fetters to give full play to his mighty limbs in the contemplated performance, a guard of Philistine giants encircle him, to pierce him with spear and javelin should he attempt to avenge his misfortune. Without knowing the manner in which he acted, we are left to imagine how he made sport for his enemies. What massive block of marble did he lift? what new lion of Timnath did he grapple with? what gate with posts and bar did he carry on his shoulders? what new cord or green withes did he snap asunder, as "tow is broken when it toucheth the fire?" what new Delilah wove his fresh-grown "locks with the web, and fastened them with a pin to a beam," that he might bear away web, pin, and beam?

Deceived by the docility of his spirit and the obedience of his behavior, he is called within the temple itself. At length, wearied with the great exertions he had been required to make, he unsuspectedly requested of the lad that led him, "Suffer me that I may feel the pillars whereupon the house standeth, that I may lean upon them." Sweating, panting, weary, the captive leans for rest against the marble columns, while, in fancied security, the people shout, joke, laugh, rending his very soul. A blind man's eye reveals no heart-secret. Samson repents a misspent life, and, conscious that his strength was Heaven's gift, he prays, "O Lord God, remember me, I pray thee, and strengthen me, I pray thee, only this once, O God, that I may be at once avenged of the Philistines for my two eyes." Then, seizing the two pillars, "he bowed himself with all his might," and in a moment the roof fell in, precipitating those on the top into one broken, dying mass with those within, and, slaying more in his death than in his life, the victor and the vanquished slept the sleep that knows no waking.

I wept when I remembered the son of Manoah. He was a child of Providence. His was a miraculous birth. Chosen to punish idolatry, to deliver his country, and judge a nation, Samson was an army of *one*. God had purposed to accomplish through him what he had done by the mighty forces of Joshua, Deborah, Gideon, and Jephthah, and to illustrate his own divine power in subduing the enemies of his church by the arm of a single man. It was a thought worthy of a God. As in other ways of the Almighty, the secret of Samson's power was hidden. Unlike Goliath, he was an ordinary man in stature: there was nothing in his physique that indicated his wondrous strength. It was this that confounded his foes, and impelled them to solicit Delilah with a bribe to ascertain the secret of his power. As his strength was not in his muscles, so it was not in the seven locks of his hair. When asleep and at ordinary duties he was as other men, but when the Philistines were to be punished, the Spirit of the Lord came upon him. So long as he retained the solitary virtue of secrecy, and allowed his beard and hair to grow untrimmed, it pleased the Lord to use him as he did Jephthah and Cyrus, and as he does a thunderbolt or a volcano, to punish the wicked; but when he preferred the smiles of a woman to the benedictions of heaven, he became as other men. Though a failure in life, he was faithful in death; and for the faith of his dying act, St. Paul records the name of Samson among the illustrious believers.[1]

The subsequent history of Gaza is replete with memorable events. Being the key to Palestine to those on the south, and the key to Egypt to those on the north, it has been frequently subjected to the calamities of war. Besieged by Alexander the Great, its defenders surrendered their city with their lives; and in the fearful conflict the great warrior received a wound in the shoulder, which threatened to terminate his eventful career. In the first century of our own era it was twice destroyed, and, though subsequently rebuilt, it never attained its ancient splendor. Though early visited by the teachers of Christianity, yet in the fifth century it contained eight temples dedicated to the worship of heathen gods. In 634 A.D. it yielded to the conquering arms of Mohammed, and afterward

[1] Heb., xi., 32.

became the birthplace of Esh-Shāfa'y, the founder of one of the largest of the Mohammedan sects. In 1152 A.D. the Crusaders found the city deserted, and, erecting a strong fortress on the highest hill, intrusted its defense to the Knights Templars.[1] Captured and sacked by Saladin in 1170 A.D., with the exception of a brief interval, it has remained, as it is now, a Moslem city.

Askelon is on the sea, twelve miles to the north from Gaza. The great route thither runs along the eastern side of the sand downs which separate it from the shore, and, continuing northward, passes through several Arab towns, surrounded with orchards of figs and groves of palms. Despite the incessant efforts of the villagers, the drifting sand is annually approaching their homes, and, if not resisted by a more formidable barrier, will completely destroy their gardens and overwhelm their dwellings. It is not uncommon to see trees so buried that only a green twig is visible, indicating the position of the tree, while the branches of those not yet entombed are dusted with the flying sand.

As one of the five royal cities of the Philistines, Askelon was celebrated for the grandeur of its architecture. It occupied an area not unlike in form an amphitheatre. Along the shore extend a series of bold cliffs, a mile in length and eighty feet high. From the northern end of this range a lofty ridge sweeps round like a semicircle, first to the eastward, then to the southward, and finally, bending westward, runs to the sea. Within this space are the ruins of the city, and on the top of this curving ridge the wall was built, defended by strong towers, the immense fragments of which, thrown together in confused heaps, suggest a destroying angel more powerful than the hand of man. On the east are the remains of a large castle, and near it is the chief entrance to the city. Not far from a ruinous wely are the traces of a noble avenue, which was once lined with columns, and within 200 yards of it is a low excavated area, on which are thirty large granite and marble shafts. Beneath mounds of sand there must be other remains, perhaps of temples and palaces, but at present not even the outlines of a building can be traced. Whether viewed in its ruins, or as defenseless against the encroaching waves of sand, Askelon wears an air of dreariness as indescribable as it is

[1] Robinson.

RUINS OF ASKELON.

ASHOOD.

sad. On her rests the burden of prophecy: "Askelon shall be a desolation.[1] Askelon shall not be inhabited."[2]

Though it was allotted to the tribe of Judah, the Philistines held possession of their city throughout the whole period of the Jewish monarchy. Its significance in sacred history is derived from its gross idolatry, and the fearful judgments denounced against it by the prophets, rather than from any great events having occurred within its limits. But, beyond the inspired record, it has a history in which figure many illustrious characters. Regarding its maritime location as invaluable, Herod the Great adorned the city with baths, porticoes, and fountains, and after his death his sister Salome resided there in a palace which her brother had built. Suffering greatly in the wars between the Jews and the Romans, the original citizens became the allies of the latter, and Askelon was the scene of a horrid massacre, in which 2500 Jews were put to death. In after years the Christians and the Moslems lost and won in turns this important sea-port town. Captured by Baldwin III. in 1152 A.D., it subsequently reverted to the Moslems, but yielded again to the Crusaders, under Richard Cœur de Lion, in 1191 A.D., who compelled Saladin to abandon this stronghold; and when, in turn, the Christians were expelled, Askelon began to wane, and to-day it is an uninhabited town.

Less than 100 yards to the northeast stands the wretched village of El-Jûrah, the modern representative of the royal city. Through its gardens the road leads to Ashdod, eight miles to the north. Two miles on the way is the town of Mejdel, the largest and most flourishing of all the villages on the Plain of Philistia. The buildings are large and well constructed, the streets are wide and clean, and the scenery and gardens around it are exceedingly beautiful. Passing through the village of Hamâmeh, the path runs along the sandy downs, and, after ascending a low ridge, enters Ashdod on the south. Its mud houses are located on the declivity of a hill, and near it is a lake 500 yards in circumference. Though once the capital of a lordship, yet Ashdod is without antique ruins, and the traveler is left to record its history amid the beautiful gardens, without the remains of temples and palaces to aid his recollection. It was here the Ark of the Lord was brought after the battle of Aphek, and the Philistines, deeming it a religious

[1] Zeph., ii., 4.   [2] Zech., ix., 5.

trophy, placed it in the temple of their idol, "And when they of Ashdod arose early on the morrow, behold, Dagon was fallen on his face to the earth before the Ark of the Lord." Elevating their deity to his place, the Philistines found him in the dust again on the second night. Smitten by the Lord with pestilence for their impiety, in their distress they sent the Ark to Gath.[1] Three centuries later Ashdod was dismantled by King Uzziah;[2] and it is afterward mentioned by Nehemiah, who reproaches the Jews for having there married heathen wives after their return from captivity.[3] Called by the Greeks Azotus, it was here that Philip the Evangelist was found after the baptism of the eunuch.[4] But Ashdod is conspicuous in profane history for having withstood a siege of twenty-nine years, when invested by Psammetichus, king of Egypt, which is the longest siege on record.

Twenty miles to the north, situated on the coast, is ancient Joppa. From Ashdod thither the route lies through one of the richest sections of the Plain of Philistia. It is a gentle depression coming down from the east, three miles wide, through the centre of which runs a deep, winding torrent bed. The soil is loamy, and yields the finest grain raised in Syria. Among the large and prosperous villages that dot its fertile sides are Batâneah and El-Burka; but beyond this oasis the land is stony and barren, and the wretched hovels of which the towns are composed, together with the squalidity of the peasants, recall the prophetic denunciation, "A bastard shall dwell in Ashdod, and I will cut off the pride of the Philistines."[5] Passing through Yebna, the Jabneh of the Bible,[6] and leaving Ekron,[7] five miles to the east the road crosses diagonally the great Wady Surâr, which drains the western section of the Judean Hills from Hebron to Bethel. Less than two miles from the sea are the remains of a Roman bridge which once spanned the torrent, and from this ruin the path declines westward to the coast, when, turning northward, it follows the beach to Yâfa.

Standing upon a rock whose western base is washed by the Mediterranean, Joppa is one of the oldest cities in the world. Though its authentic history begins with the partitioning of

[1] 1 Sam., iv., v.   [2] 2 Chron., xxvi., 6.   [3] Neh., xiii., 23-26.
[4] Acts, viii., 40.   [5] Zech., ix., 6.   [6] 2 Chron., xxvi., 6.
[7] 1 Sam., v., 10-12.

JAFFA FROM THE NORTH.

Palestine into tribal possessions, yet, according to Pliny, it existed prior to the Flood. Called by Joshua Japho,[1] by Luke Joppa,[2] by the Arabs Yâfa, and by the Franks Jaffa, it was originally allotted to the tribe of Dan,[3] but remained in comparative obscurity till the reign of Solomon, when it became the chief maritime city of his kingdom. Being the nearest harbor to Jerusalem, the floats of pine and cedar from Lebanon for the building of the first and second temples were landed here,[4] and hence transported to the Holy City on the back of camels. Centuries later, Jonah here embarked for Tarshish,[5] and in our own era here lived the benevolent Tabitha, whom Peter restored to life,[6] and here was the home of Simon, with whom the apostle lodged.[7]

The only antiquity to detain the traveler a single hour is the traditional house of Simon. Like all Eastern dwellings, it is constructed of stone, square in form, with a flat roof, and may have stood for centuries, as, without violence, it will endure for hundreds of years to come. Standing near the seaside, both the location and structure of the building are in harmony with the inspired narrative, and a venerable tradition points to it as once the residence of a tanner. The entrance is through a low gallery, before which the servants of Cornelius stood inquiring for Peter. Within is a small court-yard, containing a well of excellent water, and from the court a stone staircase leads to the roof, from which I enjoyed a commanding view of the sea, over whose blue waters had glanced the apostolic eye as Peter sat beneath those clear expanded heavens from which descended the symbolic sheet, opening to his Jewish understanding the purposes of the divine mind. Plucking a leaf from the solitary tree adorning the court, I entered the interior, which is now occupied by the Moslems as a place of prayer, and by whom it is revered no less for its antiquity than for its traditional sacredness. Excepting its gardens, Joppa is neither clean nor beautiful. The streets are narrow and irregular, and the best buildings have no claim to architectural elegance. Inclosed by a stone wall, the city has a single gate, opening toward the east. Near it, and around a pretty Saracenic fountain, are the famous fruit-bazars of Jaffa, where are sold the finest oranges and lemons in the world.

[1] Josh., xix., 46. [2] Acts, ix., 36. [3] Josh., xix., 46.
[4] 2 Chr., ii., 16; Ezra, iii., 7. [5] Jonah, i., 3. [6] Acts, ix., 36. [7] Ib., x., 6.

Here also is the seat of justice, where the cadi[1] tries all civil and criminal suits, sitting, as in Bible times,[2] in the gate of the city. As of old, Joppa is a sea-port town of considerable trade, and, if possessed of a good harbor, would be the most flourishing maritime city of Palestine. The products of its immense fruit-orchards, together with the silk and soap here manufactured, are exported in large quantities to the cities on the Mediterranean coast.

Possessing a population of 5000 souls, a fifth of whom are Christians, 200 Jews, and the rest Moslems, the basis of social and political distinction is religion rather than nationality. The Mohammedans have several mosques, the Jews a synagogue, the Latins, Greeks, and Armenians have each a convent, for the entertainment of pilgrims *en route* for the Holy City.

Under the direction of Dr. Barclay, who combines the two professions of physician and missionary, a society has here been formed called the "Abrahamic Coalition," the object of which is the gathering together in one large community all the indigent Jews in the East, and locate them on the Plain of Sharon, securing to each a small piece of land, and otherwise aiding the colonists in practical agriculture.

As illustrating the changeless character of Eastern customs, before the door of our inn stood a magician performing astonishing feats with serpents. A Nubian by birth, his face was black and glossy, his eyes small and snakish, and his countenance expressive of great cunning. With a smile, he drew from the ample folds of his bosom three large black serpents, which had been nestling next his naked breast; and caressing them in the fondest manner, he lifted them up to his neck, and allowed them to entwine themselves about his head. Subject to the will of their charmer, they obeyed his magical words, and the magician of Joppa vividly recalled the magicians of Egypt.[3]

Once more our faces were turned toward the Holy City. On leaving Joppa, our path for half an hour lay between enormous hedges of the cactus plant, inclosing orange and lemon groves, which cover an area of many miles in extent. The air was surcharged with the fragrance of those delicious fruits, and beneath the ladened trees lay heaps of lemons and oranges,

[1] Judge. [2] Ruth. xiv., 11. [3] Ex., vii., 12.

like apples in an American orchard. Charmed with a ride so delightful, we were soon upon the Plain of Sharon, stretching far to the northeastward, to the white and purple Hills of Benjamin. Passing the hamlet of Yasûr on our left, in thirty minutes we entered the pine-groves of Beit Dejân. The declining sun forewarning us of approaching night, we gave loose rein to our horses, and bounded over that glorious plain. As far as the eye could reach, crimson anemones, tufts of lily leaves, and white and yellow daisies covered the ground like a carpet of many colors, while here and there stood the shepherd's black tent, with herds and flocks around it, and on the evening air came the soft notes of his flute. In the starlight away to the east, like a dark column standing out against the sky of night, appeared the solitary tower of Ramleh. At seven P.M. we were knocking at the iron gate of the Latin Monastery, and, with a courtesy for which others have not given them credit, the Franciscan brothers received us to their retreat, while

RAMLEH, OR THE "LOOK-OUT."

their tall and graceful superior entertained us with an ease and dignity worthy a Christian gentleman. After an excellent dinner in the refectory, a quiet-looking friar led us, by the light of a single wax taper, across a dark court-yard to a small chamber containing four beds, neat and clean, as if the work of a woman's hand.

Ramleh is nine miles to the southeast from Joppa, and is one of the best-built towns on the Plain of Sharon. It is environed for miles with fig-orchards and orange-groves. Containing a population of 3000 inhabitants, the majority of whom are Greek Christians, tradition identifies Ramleh with the Ramah of Samuel, the birthplace of Nicodemus, and the native city of Joseph of Arimathea. Chosen by the Crusaders to be their southern rendezvous, it became the head-quarters of Richard of England in 1191 A.D. Its chief architectural attraction is a noble square tower 120 feet high, built of hewn stone, and standing a mile to the west from the town, amid the ruins of a large quadrangular inclosure. There is nothing, either in its construction or in history, to indicate whether it it is the campanile of a Christian church or the minaret of a mosque. A flight of stone steps, narrow and spiral, leads to the top, from which is obtained a view of surpassing beauty. In all its amplitude and richness, the Plain of Sharon spreads out before the eye, extending from the roots of Carmel on the north, to the promontory of Joppa on the south, and from the hills of Samaria and Judea on the east, to the Mediterranean on the west; while on every hand appear fields of grain, groves of fruit-trees, and towns, whose white domes shine in the sunlight like diamonds in a circlet of emeralds.

A ride of forty minutes through an embowered avenue brought us to Ludd, the Lod of the Old Testament,[1] and the Lydda of the New.[2] It is an Arab town of 2000 inhabitants, and, though unsurpassed by the beauty of its environs, it is neither remarkable for the elegance of its buildings nor the regularity of its streets. To the Christian, Lydda is interesting as the place where Peter cured Eneas of palsy, and where he was stopping when he was informed of Tabitha's death. To Englishmen it is memorable as the birthplace of St. George, England's patron saint, and as containing his tomb, in which he was interred near the close of the third century,

[1] 1 Chron., viii., 12.   [2] Acts, ix., 32.

after his martyrdom in Nicomedia, under the relentless Diocletian. According to William of Tyre, the Emperor Justinian reared a noble church over the ashes of the saint and martyr, which, at a later period, was destroyed by the revengeful Moslems. Rebuilt by Richard Cœur de Lion, it was partially destroyed again by the troops of Saladin. The walls and a part of the vault of the eastern niche of this monumental structure

CHURCH OF SAINT GEORGE.

remain, adorned with pilasters, capitals, and cornice. On the south side of the grand aisle is a pointed arch of great elegance, supported by massive clustered columns with marble Corinthian capitals, forming one of the most picturesque ruins in Palestine.

Forty minutes from Ludd we passed the town of Jimzu,[1] and just beyond the road branched, one path diverging to the right, running through Wady Suleimân, and the other ascend-

[1] 2 Chron., xxviii., 18.

ing the steep acclivities of Bethhoron the Nether. Though it is exceedingly rugged, yet, as it passes over one of the grandest battle-fields in sacred history, we chose the latter. Now began the toil of the journey. The verdure had disappeared, and the white limestone rocks protruded above the scanty soil, leaving only intervening patches of tillable land, which was being plowed as we passed. Disobeying the divine command, and disregarding the fitness of nature, a peasant was plowing with an ox and an ass,[1] and another with an ass and a camel. Passing Um Rush in two hours from Jimzu, we toiled up a mountain path, and at noon reached Lower Bethhoron. Memorable in Bible history as the second stage of the flight of the five kings of the Amorites, the roughness of the scene is in harmony with the horrors of war. The surface of the land is broken into circular rocky hills, around the base of which equally stony valleys wind. From the hill-sides the rocks protrude like terraces, rising with much regularity one above the other. The modern town is perched on a rocky ridge, and called by the Arabs Beit 'Ur et-Tahta. Amid its sterility a few half-naked peasants lay basking in the genial sunshine of spring, who greeted us as we passed with a lazy smile. Though located on the northwest border of Benjamin, the city belonged to Ephraim, and from that tribe it was taken and allotted to the Levites.[2] Passing over the roughest tract of land above the sea, in less than an hour we reached Upper Bethhoron. Bearing the Arabic name of Beit Ur el-Fôka, it is a small village, the huts of which are composed of large hewn stones once belonging to more pretentious buildings. Sturdy men sat smoking on the rocks, and near them women were playing with their children. Among the maidens were the sheikh's daughters, who wore about the head a circlet of silver coins. These ornaments are a maiden's dowry.

Surveying the surrounding country from the roof of the sheikh's house, the famous battle-field of Gibeon lay before me. Seven miles to the southeast is Gibeon, whose conical summit is just hidden by the loftier peaks of Benjamin. Less than three miles to the northwest is Lower Bethhoron, and five miles to the south, on the summit of a long, low ridge, is the small hamlet of Yâlo, the traditional site of Ajalon. Between the two hills is the green valley of Ajalon, now called

[1] Deut., xxii., 10.   [2] Josh., xxi., 22.

Merj Ibn 'Omeir, expanding, as it opens, into the Plain of
Philistia. Having formed a powerful coalition, the chiefs of
the Amorites, with the King of Jerusalem at their head, had
besieged the city of Gibeon. On the eve of the battle the Gibeonites sent to Joshua for relief, whom they had previously deceived into an alliance, and found him on the Plain of Jericho. Though despising a treaty founded in craft, yet appre-
ciating the obligations of an oath above a temporary inconvenience, and guided by the faint light of the stars, the Israel-
itish chieftain passed up the Plain of Jericho to Wady Färah,
and, turning westward, he reached the scene of the conflict,
after a forced march by night, in the early dawn of the next
morning. Falling with irresistible surprise and power upon
the confederate kings, "he slew them with great slaughter at
Gibeon." Flying before his victorious arms, the remnant went
"along the way that goeth up to Bethhoron." Outstripping
their pursuers, the Amorites continued their flight "in the going down to Bethhoron." Reaching the ridge on which we
stand with all his "mighty men" around him, Joshua beheld
the valley through which the fugitives were escaping, and, de-
spairing of overtaking them if the day was not prolonged, he
invoked the divine interposition in his behalf. Moved by a
sublime faith, he stretched forth the arm that bore the conqueror's spear, and, in the presence of all Israel, said, "Sun,
stand thou still on Gibeon, and thou, Moon, in the valley of
Ajalon." Respecting the faith of his servant and answering
his prayer, Jehovah interposed; "and the sun stood still, and
the moon stayed, until the people had avenged themselves upon
their enemies; and there was no day like that before it or after
it, that the Lord hearkened unto the voice of a man; for the
Lord fought for Israel." Receiving more than he had asked
for, a hail-storm came to his assistance, and after it had accomplished its terrible work, killing foes but sparing friends, Joshua and his warriors descended the declivities of Bethlehem, and
pressed the remnant of a once proud foe so hard as to compel
the five kings to take refuge in the great cave of Makkedah,
around which he encamped for the night, and on the morrow
hung the royal fugitives.[1]

"God's testimony is in the rocks." The correspondence between the inspired account and the facts as they now appear,

[1] Josh., x.

after the lapse of twenty-three centuries, illustrates the accuracy of sacred history. The night's march from Gilgal to Gibeon, a distance of less than twenty-five miles, was not only possible, but can now be accomplished by any ordinary pedestrian. The going up to Bethhoron the Upper, and the going down to Bethhoron the Nether, correspond with the altitude of the former from Gibeon, and the depression of the latter from Beit el-Fôka. The relative locations of Gibeon and Ajalon to Upper Bethhoron, and the probable position of the sun and moon in the heavens at that time, agree with the statement as to where Joshua was when he invoked the prolongation of the day; and his subsequent pursuit of the foe in the direction of Azekah, Makkedah, and Jarmuth is confirmed by the identification of those places.

There is nothing in the text indicating that the prayer of Joshua was offered late in the afternoon, and that, as Gibeon is on the east of Upper Bethhoron and Ajalon on the west, therefore the sun could not have stood still on the former nor the moon on the latter. It was probably not noon when he invoked the lengthening of the day. The sun had not yet passed the meridian of Gibeon, while over the western vale of Ajalon the faint crescent of an old moon still lingered, just as it appeared to me. Hence, standing between the two planets as they rode high in the heavens above him, and between the two cities on the earth, he gave forth his miraculous command with the utmost accuracy; while from the western sea came that fearful hail-storm driving up the valleys below, killing more than had been slain by the sword, and from the eastern border of the otherwise dark storm-cloud was reflected the light of the motionless sun and moon.

Leaving Upper Bethhoron, our path lay for some time along the old Roman road, sections of which remain as perfect as when the chariot of the proud Cestius was driven over it. Turning to the southeast, in two hours we reached the celebrated city of Gibeon. Like most Oriental towns, it crowns the summit of a conspicuous hill, which, being separated from the surrounding hills, rises in isolation from a noble plain. The encircling plains are unsurpassed in Southern Palestine for the richness of their soil, and their meadow-like smoothness and verdure. Covering many acres are vineyards, olive-groves, and almond orchards. Such is the peculiar formation of the

GIBEON.

hill on which the town is built, that the rocks protruding from the sides serve the double purpose of steps and terraces. Over the summit are scattered the small stone buildings of El-Jib, which in part are composed of materials of great antiquity. Without walls and gates, the city is destitute of fortifications, and the crooked, unpaved streets are accessible to all. The present inhabitants are an illustration that character, like names, is transmitted from one generation to another. In their address and shrewdness they resemble their ancestors. The Sheikh of Gibeon is a man of medium height, and, unlike his countrymen, is emotional, communicative, and exceedingly gracious. Pressing us to enter his khan,[1] he refreshed us with coffee, and, failing to persuade us to remain during the night, he accompanied us through the village, and received our gifts with flowing eyes and many bows. Nor are the children less crafty. Boys kissed our hand for paras, and for a piastre the maidens at the fountains let down their pitchers from their heads that we might drink. Reading the story of their ancestral cunning on the spot, we could easily fancy their fathers gathering together the emblems of deception to decoy the Israelites into an alliance that brought protection to themselves, but war to their allies; and with less difficulty their descendants could collect tattered garments, clouted shoes, rent wine-skin bottles, musty bread, and jaded asses, and with equal confidence declare themselves to be "embassadors from a far country."

Falling to the tribe of Benjamin in the division of the land,[2] Gibeon afterward became a Levitical city.[3] Subsequently to the destruction of Nob by Saul, it was the seat of the tabernacle till the completion of the Temple.[4] On the eastern side of the hill is a large well of delicious water. Springing up in a cave excavated in the solid rock, the water was originally conducted to a reservoir below, which measures 120 feet in length and 100 in breadth. Formerly it was called the "Pool of Gibeon," and around its peaceful waters the rival armies of Israel and Judah met in battle. It was here that Abner challenged Joab to terminate the strife by a gladiatorial fight between twenty-four chosen men—twelve representing David, and twelve representing Ishbosheth. But so equal were the champions in skill and power, "that they caught every man

[1] Inn.
[2] Josh., xviii., 25.
[3] Ib., xxi., 17.
[4] 1 Chron., xvi., 39.

his fellow by the head, and thrust his sword in his fellow's side; so they fell down together."[1] The death of all the combatants leaving the issue of the contest undecided, the two armies sprang to the fight on the adjoining plain, and, after a sore battle, Abner was defeated, and the claims of David to the kingdom of all Israel were confirmed by a decisive victory.[2] Thirty-three years after, by the "great stone which is in Gibeon," in the same highway now trodden by the feet of careless pilgrims, "Joab took Amasa by the beard with the right hand to kiss him," and, with a sword in the other, treacherously slew his cousin.[3]

But the glory of Gibeon is the dream and prayer of Solomon. Sanctifying the morning of a long and eventful reign by acts of devotion, he came from Jerusalem to worship the Lord. Upon a great altar which he had reared he offered a thousand burnt sacrifices, and that night in a dream he communed with the God of his fathers, and asking wisdom to govern his kingdom rather than wealth and honor, he received a wise and understanding heart.[4]

A mile to the south, beyond a green and lovely plain, is Mizpeh—"The Look-out"—one of the oldest watch-towers in Southern Palestine. With it stand connected many of the most thrilling events in Jewish history. Chosen in the infancy of the nation for the advantages it afforded as a point of observation in times of war, it subsequently became the national rendezvous, where the tribes were accustomed to meet to worship Jehovah, to make war, to conclude peace, and elect a king. Justly aggrieved at the insult offered the whole country by the citizens of Gibeah in refusing to surrender the young men who had committed the horrid crime on the person of the Levite's concubine, the eleven tribes here assembled, and, having vowed never to return to their homes till the inhabitants of Gibeah were punished, they marched forth to that series of battles in which thousands fell, and in which the tribe of Benjamin was well-nigh exterminated.[5] Two hundred and eighty-six years later, Samuel gathered the armies of Israel at Mizpeh to fight against the Philistines, and after their return from the slaughter of the foe he set up a memorial-stone and called it Ebenezer.[6] A quarter of a century there-

[1] 2 Sam., ii., 16.   [2] Ib., ii., 17.   [3] Ib., xx., 8-10.
[4] 1 Kings, iii., 5-12.   [5] Judges, xx.   [6] 1 Sam., vii., 6-12.

after the nation reassembled to choose a king; and here, for the first time in Israel, when the people beheld the majestic form of Saul, the son of Kish, on whom the lot had fallen, their loyal exclamations awakened the echoes of the surrounding hills—"God save the king!"[1] Fortifying it for the protection of his frontier, King Asa removed from Rama the materials with which Baasha had constructed his battlements, and with them built a strong fort. Five centuries after the coronation of Saul, Ishmael, of the royal family of Judah, here surprised and assassinated Gedaliah, the Chaldean governor, who, during the Jewish captivity, resided at Mizpeh.[2]

Called by the natives Neby Samwil, after the honored son of Hannah, the hill has an altitude of 600 feet above the surrounding plain. On its evenly-terraced sides the fig and vine grow luxuriantly. The summit is dotted with a few rude dwellings, composed of the remains of nobler edifices. The ruins of departed greatness are every where visible, and in the wall of a caravansary are imbedded shattered capitals and broken columns. In rude mimicry of happier days, the peasants have excavated small courts to the depth of several feet in the native rock in front of their unpretending homes. Rising, as if by way of contrast, from amid these hovels is a large but deserted mosque. Erected by the Crusaders, it was originally a Christian church. Constructed in the form of a Latin cross, the interior is ornamented with Saracenic arches. Within is the traditional tomb of Samuel, which, unlike the sepulchres of other prophets, has neither altar nor ornaments. Attached to the mosque is a graceful minaret, which rises 100 feet above the summit of the hill, from the balcony of which I obtained an extraordinary view of Southern Palestine. As far as the eye could reach, the land of Judea was spread out before me, broken by deep ravines and dotted with conical hills. To the north was Gibeon, and beyond appeared Alaroth, Beeroth, the dark peak of Ophrah, and the famous rock of Rimmon; lining the distant horizon to the northeast were Gibeah of Saul, Michmash of Jonathan, and the Hills of Gilead; over a forest of summits to the east were the Mountains of Moab—that ever-visible wall of limestone; beyond, the small hamlet of Hanina; to the southeast rose the domes and minarets of Jerusalem and Bethlehem, and the tomb-like form of Hero-

[1] 1 Sam., x., 23, 24.   [2] 2 Kings, xxv., 25.

dium; to the south were the vine-clad hills of Hebron and the home of Samson; while due west, and as far as the eye could penetrate north and south, was the white shore of the Mediterranean, with the blue waters of the sea mingling with the mists of the western sky. Such was the prospect from Mizpeh, which, in the mighty past, often met the eye of Samuel, Saul, and Solomon; and, though he occupied a stand-point a few miles to the eastward, but of greater altitude, such must have been the vision of Moses from the summit of Pisgah ere he entered into glory.

CHAPTER X.

Northern Palestine.—Gibeah.—Birthplace of King Saul.—Historical Events.—Thrilling Story of Rizpah watching her Dead Sons.—Identity of the City.—Field of the Arrow.—Parting of David and Jonathan.—Nob.—Massacre of the Priests.—The View.—Birthplace of Jeremiah.—Geba.—Pottage.—Benighted.—Yusef Shang, of Beeroth.—A Night of strange Experience.—Town of Beeroth.—Ancient Bethel.—Its Desolation. Site of the City.—Abraham's Altar.—Parting of Abraham and Lot.—The Fountain.—Jacob's Flight and Dream.—Idolatry.—Prophecy fulfilled.—Route to Shiloh.—Romantic Scenery.—Robbers' Fountain.—Wild Glen.—Robbers.—Their Dance.—Sinjil.—Shiloh.—Remains.—Site discovered in 1838.—Tower.—Damsels of Shiloh carried off.—Death of Eli.—Approach of the Robbers.—An Attack.—Resistance.—Again assailed.—Again resist.—Revolvers drawn.—Escape.—Overtaken.—Third Attack.—Revolvers in demand.—Sixteen against Four.—Serious Moment.—One of the Party whipped.—Narrow Escape.—Lebonah.—Ride to Nablous.—Grand View.—Evening on the Plain of Mukhrah.—Antiquity of Nablous.—History.—Its beautiful Situation.—Population.—Inside View of the Town.—Character of the People.—Christian School.—Origin of the Samaritans.—Remnant of the Nation.—Their Creed.—Their religious Peculiarities.—Their High-priest.—Their sacred Writings.—Vale of Shechem.—Its Length and Beauty.—Cursings and Blessings of the Law.—The Scene.—Great Congregation.—Twin Mountains.—Jacob's Well.—History.—Sweet Water.—Evidence of its Antiquity.—Jesus at the Well.—Woman of Samaria.—Accuracy of its evangelical History.—Well Sold.—Tomb of Joseph.—Symbol of his Life.—Ascent of Mount Ebal.—Twenty Lepers.—Ascent of Mount Gerizim.—Almond-groves.—Ruins on the Summit.—Holy of Holies of the Samaritans.—Traditions.—Not the Scene of the Offering of Isaac.—Samaritan Passover.—Impressive Moment.—Lambs slain.—The Feast.

The day was all that the most romantic tourist or thoughtful traveler could have desired, when, at three o'clock on Monday afternoon, in the month of April, we left Jerusalem for the last time, on our long tour through Northern Palestine. Passing out of the Damascus Gate, I ascended the rocky ridge over the grotto of Jeremiah, and looked down upon the Holy City with the fondness of one bidding adieu to the scenes of his childhood. A gentle breeze was blowing from the Western

Sea, and the flag of our country floated from the summit of Zion. The clattering of horses' hoofs on the pavements below told me my companions were coming, and, turning to the northwest, the "City of the Great King" faded forever from my view. Crossing the hill Scopus, we were soon on the great caravan route leading from Egypt to Damascus. For half an hour our path lay through an open and undulating country, when it passed between two conical hills—Shâfât on the west, and Nob on the east. Less than a mile beyond the latter is Gibeah, the birthplace of King Saul.[1] Called by the Arabs Tuleil el-Fûl—"the Hill of the Beans"—it resembles a perfect cone when viewed from a distance. Rising from a rich plain, it is an object of universal attraction. Terraced from base to summit, it presents to the eye a beautiful appearance, as the green circles of corn mingle with the white limestone soil. On the summit are the remains of a tower or palace, fifty-six feet long and forty-eight wide, and by some unknown force the huge blocks of stone have been thrown together in a form not unlike a pyramid.

Few places in the Holy Land fill so large a space in the inspired volume as Gibeah. Coming from Bethlehem on his way to Mount Ephraim, the unfortunate Levite at nightfall turned in hither, and was received into the house of a peasant. That night was committed an offense by the young men of the city, which resulted in one of the most terrible battles on record. To punish the offenders and avenge the insult, around this hill all Israel gathered for battle against the Benjamites, and, though the former were repeatedly repulsed, they at length triumphed and well-nigh exterminated the tribe of Benjamin.[2] Three centuries later, after the death of all the actors in that mournful tragedy, Gibeah rose to royal significance. Here resided Kish, unto whom was born Saul, than whom "there was not among the children of Israel a goodlier person than he; from his shoulders and upward he was higher than any of the people."[3] From here his father sent Saul to recover the strayed asses, and, while looking for the asses, he found a kingdom. Returning from Rameh after his coronation, he chose Gibeah as the seat of his new government.[4] From this first royal city in Palestine he went forth to fight

[1] 1 Sam., xi., 4.
[3] 1 Sam., ix., 1, 2.
[2] Judges, xix. and xx.
[4] Ib., x., 26.

his first battle, which was against the Ammonites, who had besieged Jabesh-gilead.[1] After his rejection by Samuel at Gilgal, hither Saul returned in disgrace;[2] and it was here, in those dark days of disappointment which followed, that an evil spirit came upon him, and, to soothe his troubled soul by the soft music of his harp, the shepherd-boy of Bethlehem was summoned to the king's presence.[3] Here the high-minded Jonathan conceived his more than woman's love for the son of Jesse.[4] Forgetting earlier attachments and David's well-earned renown, here, in a fit of passion, Saul threw his javelin at the youthful warrior.[4] Here he gave his daughter Michal in marriage to David;[4] and here the true-hearted wife rescued her persecuted husband from the murderous hand of her father, and deceived the king by placing an image in her bed.[5] Here the unwilling Michal was given to Phalti,[6] and from Gibeah Saul and his sons went forth to the fatal battle of Gilboa.[7]

Forty years after the death of the king the tragical history of Gibeah closed, as it had commenced, in a scene of blood. For an offense, the history of which is neither recorded by sacred or profane writers, the Almighty sent a famine of three years' continuance upon the land, and when David inquired of the Lord the cause, he was informed, "It is for Saul and for his bloody house, because he slew the Gibeonites."[8] Josephus supposes that Saul had violated the treaty which Joshua had made with the men of Gibeon, and had attempted to slay the entire population of the city. Wishing to relieve his kingdom from the miseries of a famine, David summoned the Gibeonites to his presence, to ascertain the nature of the redress they demanded. They demanded the surrender of seven of the descendants of Saul to be hung in Gibeah, and their request was granted. Five of the victims were the sons of Merab, whom Michal had brought up after her sister's death, and the other two were the sons of Saul by his wife Rizpah.[9] On the same day the sons and grandsons of Israel's first king were executed together, to expiate the offense of a father long since dead. Less fortunate than the offspring of Merab, the sons of Rizpah left a mother to mourn their untimely end. For tenderness

[1] 1 Sam., xi.   [2] Ib., xiv.   [3] Ib., xvi.
[4] Ib., xviii.   [5] Ib., xix.   [6] Ib., xxv.
[7] Ib., xxxi.   [8] 2 Sam., xxi., 1.   [9] Ib., xxi., 8.

of affection, for the depth of maternal grief, and for the lengthened period of watching and mourning, the story of Rizpah has no parallel in the literature of any nation. David's sorrow for Absalom was sincere, keen, and overwhelming, but the grief of Rizpah was the sorrow of a mother. "And Rizpah, the daughter of Aiah, took sackcloth and spread it for her upon the rock, from the beginning of harvest until water dropped upon them out of heaven, and suffered neither the birds of the air to rest upon them by day, nor the beasts of the fields by night." Such was the mournful spectacle that that brokenhearted mother presented to all who passed by, sitting beside the bones of her dead sons all through the long Syrian summer, from April till October, neither permitting the vulture to prey upon them by day nor the hyena by night. Time had assuaged her grief, and David ordered that the bones of her sons should be interred with those of Saul and Jonathan, in the country of Zelah, in the sepulchre of Kish.[1]

The identity of Gibeah as the scene of so many important events is sustained by evidence no less abundant than indubitable. In his description of the march of Titus to Jerusalem, Josephus informs us that the Roman general halted at Gibeah, thirty stadia from Jerusalem, which exactly corresponds with the distance between this hill and the Jewish capital. During the night a Roman legion, coming from Emmaus, joined the main army here, where is the point of junction between the two great routes from the north and west, and on the following morning the combined forces moved on to Scopus, from whence they beheld the Holy City. Three centuries later, Jerome, in describing the journey of Lady Paula to Jerusalem, represents her as coming up from Joppa *via* the two Bethhorons, with Ajalon and Gibeon on the right, and stopping at Gibeah, where "she called to mind the old story of the Levite and his concubine." Thus the crimes of a city perpetuate the memory of its site.

South of Gibeah is the field which contained the stone Ezel, where occurred the affecting interview between David and Jonathan, and where the latter discharged the signal arrow for the escape of the former. Behind one of the many jutting rocks which here lift their naked crowns on high the fugitive found a hiding-place, where he remained till, according to a

[1] 2 Sam., xxi.

previous agreement, Jonathan came, shot an arrow beyond a little lad, and cried, "Is not the arrow beyond thee?" which was the signal that Saul was intent on killing David. The two friends met, embraced, and wept; and, after renewing their covenant, Jonathan returned to Gibeah, and David fled to Nob. His presence excited the fears of the priest Abimelech, which he soon, however, allayed by a plausible story, and from his hand received the sword of Goliath, and the shew-bread to which our Lord alludes.[1] It was because of this kindness to a public enemy that Abimelech was summoned to the presence of the enraged king, and sentenced to death by him, with all of his father's house. Revering the sacred person of a priest, no Israelite would execute the royal sentence. The work of executioner fell to the lot of Doeg, the stranger, the shepherd, and the spy. Unappeased by the slaughter of eighty-five innocent priests, Saul smote the city of Nob with the edge of the sword.[2] Two places are designated as the probable site of this ancient Levitical city—one containing the famous tomb of El-Messahney, near the Tombs of the Judges, and the other a conical peak less than a mile to the south from Gibeah. The former has the advantage of an acknowledged Jewish sepulchre, while the latter has that of location.

The view from the summit of Gibeah is as interesting as it is commanding. Three miles to the southeast is Anâta, the Anathoth of the Bible and the birthplace of Jeremiah. Never large, it still retains its diminutive proportions. Standing on a low, broad ridge, surrounded by green fields, twenty huts occupy the site of this once priestly city. Of the ancient town all that now remains are portions of an old wall, a spacious cistern, and fragments of marble columns. It was hither Solomon banished Abiathar for attempting to raise Adonijah to the throne of his father David.[3] But Anathoth is chiefly significant as the native city of the greatest of prophets, whose courage was equal to his danger, whose fortitude never forsook him, and whose zeal for God was only excelled by the terribleness of his persecutions. In the darkest hour of his country's history, Jeremiah was called to lament the desolations of Zion, to reprove kings, and to die for the truth. Offended at the severity of his denunciations, his townsmen drove him from the place of his birth, and, flying to Jerusalem for refuge, his

[1] Matt., xii.   [2] 1 Sam., xxii.   [3] 1 Kings, ii.

fidelity to God, his unblanched courage in reproving royal crimes, and his horrid pictures of coming ruin, evoked the angry passions of those whom he would have reformed, and the plaintive bard of Israel was added to the long but honored list of martyrs.

Turning to the northwest, the tower of Geba of Benjamin was visible,[1] and three miles beyond were the rocks of Michmash, where Jonathan surprised and defeated the Philistines, and where are still to be seen the famous rocks Bozez and Seneh.[2] After glancing at other memorable places, which, together with those mentioned, we had previously visited, we descended from the summit of the hill, and at its base entered a noble field of lentiles or pottage, such as Esau sold his birthright for.[3] When young it resembles a pea-vine. It grows to the height of eight inches, and when harvested it is pulled like flax. It is cooked like beans, with the exception that the water is allowed to evaporate, when the softened grain is stewed with butter and onions, making a delicious dish, and one worth a birthright to a famishing hunter.

The sun was setting, and the shadow of the mountains darkened the plains when we resumed our journey. The lateness of the hour required dispatch, and Beeroth, the place where we were to spend the night, was six miles to the north. Unfortunately we were without a guide, and our path was simply a camel track, devious, stony, and uncertain. Though we knew the general direction of Beeroth, yet the number of small villages in the vicinity, the growing darkness, and the uncertainty of the road, baffled all effort to find the place. Overtaking an Arab belonging to Beit Untâh, he agreed for a present to serve us as guide. Not suspecting deception, we followed him nearly to his own town, which he assured us was the desired place. But knowing from our maps that Beeroth was to the right of the path, and Beit Untâh to the left, we refused to follow him farther. Truth is an unknown virtue in the Arab character, and he who confides in it leans upon a broken reed. For the paltry sum which a night's lodging would bring, this man was leading us astray.

A solitary light shone from a hut in Beeroth, when, turning eastward, we traversed plowed fields, leaped ditches, crossed ravines, and rued the day we had presumed to travel without

[1] 1 Sam., xiii.   [2] Ib.   [3] Gen., xxv.

a guide. Reaching a fountain, the waters of which sparkled in the starlight, we regained the path. Having a letter of introduction from Dr. Sandreczki, of Jerusalem, to one Yûsef Shang, a Christian Arab, and the scribe of the town, we inquired for him; but, to add to our mishaps, Yûsef was not at home. There we were, homeless, foodless, friendless, and in the dark. An old Arab dame, however (heaven pity her homeliness and reward her kindness!), knew where Yûsef was, and called him to our aid.

Yûsef Shang was a noble specimen of the Arab race. He was of medium height, well built, of full habit, with towering brow, large black eyes, handsome nose, a large, joyous mouth, and a heavy, flowing beard, which was white as snow, and beautifully contrasted the deep olive hue of his manly face. His countenance was at once benignant and intelligent. Besides, Yûsef was a clean Arab—a rarity worth a pilgrimage to see. His red boots, light-colored petticoat-trowsers, embroidered jacket, broad girdle, flowing robes of yellow Broussa silk, and a bright checkered turban, were neat enough for a picture. In his silken girdle he wore a brass inkhorn, a foot in length, with a small square bulb of the same material on the side near the end, rendered perfectly tight by a thin plate of the same metal, and containing in the long part a case for the reed pens, which are secured by a brass cap. His appearance recalled Ezekiel's description of the man clothed with linen, with a writer's inkhorn by his side.[1]

In the East there is a class of men, called scribes, who write for the common people. They sit at the corners of the streets, and persons wishing a letter written dictate the matter, while the scribe performs the penmanship. Deeming it an inelegance to write upon a table, the paper is placed upon the left hand, and the writer forms the graceful characters of the Arabic language, writing from right to left. Yûsef was such a scribe, and had risen to eminence in his profession. Having read our letter with an air of great consideration, he saluted us in the most gracious manner, and invited us to his abode. Following him through a narrow lane to the gate of his court, we dismounted, and, after removing saddles and saddle-bags, led our horses through a covered stone passage-way to the entrance of his dwelling. Yûsef's superb dress and elegant bearing had

[1] Ezek., ix., 2.

prepared us to expect an entertainment not unlike the festive scenes so wondrously described in the Arabian Nights. But never were two things more unlike, and never was the outside of the plates cleaner nor the inside filthier. His house was a wretched stone hut, entered by a low doorway. The interior consisted of a single room, divided into two apartments by a raised platform a foot high. The platform served the triple purpose of kitchen, chamber, and parlor, the walls and ceiling were dingy with smoke and dirt, and a few old mats spread upon the floor were the only furniture of his home. At the foot of the platform, beneath the same roof, was his stable, and in one corner stood Yûsef's favorite ass.

"Come in, come in, gentlemen," cried our host, "and bring your horses with you; there is plenty of room, and you are welcome." Leading my horse, I entered; but the ass brayed so furiously, and kicked with such rapidity and violence, that I was compelled to retreat. Despite my protest, Yûsef refused to turn his ass into the cold, and calmly suggested that I could take my horse on the platform with me. Refusing to turn Arab, I declined, and turned to procure quarters elsewhere. The power of money upon an Arab's soul is above calculation. Fearing that he might lose the customary present in return for his hospitality, Yûsef led his ass forth, braying and kicking as it went. Our host had previously sent the female members of his family away, lest the eye of a stranger should fall upon them, and left us the sole occupants of his dwelling. Spreading our blankets upon the platform, we commenced our frugal repast, but the fleas of Beeroth came upon us in such numbers as to force another retreat. We were again houseless. The sky was clear and the stars shone softly upon us, and we determined to sleep beneath the pure starlit heavens. Yûsef, however, succeeded in procuring for our use the council-room of the town, which was a large square apartment, with heavy arched ceiling, fireplace, and niche. The walls were black with the smoke of years, and the atmosphere stale and noisome. Here we spread our mats, and, with a saddle for a pillow, spent the night. The ground floor of the building was occupied by a family, who, for a few piastres, sheltered my horse. It was here I had an illustration of the story of Bethlehem. The same room served as a dwelling and a stable, divided by a platform, on which an Arab woman was kneading bread and a lad was tending an infant child. The occupants' ass having been turned out, I led my horse in. In one corner of the stable was a large stone manger, excavated in the living rock. Such, probably, was the internal arrangement of the inn at Bethlehem; and as the platform was occupied by other guests, Joseph and Mary lodged in the stable, and cradled the infant Savior in the stone manger.

Beeroth is situated on a rocky ridge, and contains a population of 800 Moslems and thirty Christians. It is mentioned in connection with the league formed between the embassadors of Gibeon and Joshua, but aside from this it has no scriptural significance. During the reign of the Latin kings it rose to importance, and the remaining ruins attest the antiquity of the site and the former elegance of the place. In the northwest part of the village is the old Gothic church, built by the Knights Templars centuries ago. It is a beautiful ruin, and reminds one of the ruined abbeys of Southern Scotland. The walls, the eastern apse, and the sacristy are standing, and inclose an area 100 feet long and sixty-three wide. The material is limestone well dressed, and the interior may have consisted of a nave, two lateral aisles, and three recesses in the eastern end. The finish of the architecture is exquisite. The apses are crowned with beautiful domed roofs, and the partition walls are ornamented with pilasters, the capitals of which are well preserved. The side walls are divided into sections by pilasters, and are decorated with a rich cornice. But it is now a green ruin. The grass grows where, of old, knights knelt in prayer, and where robed priests chanted their Ave Marias.

On leaving the church I witnessed a beautiful illustration of our Lord's parable of the "good shepherd." Three shepherds were leading their flocks to pasture, and, though near each other, there was neither confusion nor intermingling. Such is the richness of the native language in adjectives, that a shepherd gives to each member of his flock a name descriptive of some characteristic, which is as familiar to the sheep as to himself. A lamb had lingered behind picking the fresh grass of spring, and, though other voices were sounding at the time, the truant lamb heard its shepherd's voice and ran to the fold. "The sheep hear his voice, and he calleth his own sheep by name."[1]

Three miles to the north is ancient Bethel. As we advanced

[1] John, x., 3.

the country grew in richness and beauty, reminding us that we were approaching the favored inheritance of Ephraim. Passing a small fountain gushing from the foot of a cliff, in less than half an hour we knelt in prayer where, twenty-five centuries ago, Jacob slept to dream of angels. The silence of desolation now reigns where once was heard the voice of gladness. Quietly a few maidens came to the fountain, as in the days of the patriarchs, whose homes stand amid the débris of former glory. The ancient city occupied a low ridge between two small valleys, which converge on the southeast and run into Wady Suweinît, the great thoroughfare to Ai and Jericho. Portions of foundations, fragments of walls, and heaps of hewn stone cover an area of four acres. On the summit of the hill are the remains of a square tower, and to the south of it are the walls of a Greek church. Beyond the town, to the east, is the mountain on which Abraham pitched his tent and built an altar unto the Lord, having Bethel on the west and Ai on the east;[1] and there, three years later, he and his nephew stood, choosing different portions of the land for their respective flocks.[2] From the summit of that ridge, the whole plain of the Jordan, which so charmed the eyes of Lot, is seen; and the possessions of six of the tribes lay before the vision of Abraham, to whom the Lord on that occasion repeated the promise to give the whole land to his servant.

A few feet from the hill, located in the western valley, is the great Fountain of Bethel. It is inclosed with an oblong basin 314 feet long and 217 wide, which is constructed of large stones, many of which are yet *in situ*. The southern wall is still entire, but, owing to long disuse, the others are nearly gone. Grass now covers the bottom of the reservoir, and beautiful flowers bloom around the crystal spring.

It was probably in this lovely valley that Jacob had his wondrous vision. He had come from Beersheba, a distance of seventy miles. This long journey, however, is not in harmony with the common belief that the dream occurred on the first night after leaving his father's house. Urged on by the dread of an injured brother, he slept the first night beside the graves of his ancestors at Hebron, thirty-six miles from the patriarchal groves of Beersheba; rising early and passing through the vineyards of Eshcol, he rested at noon the next day at Beth-

[1] Gen., xii., 8.   [2] Ib., xiii., 10-14.

lehem, seventeen miles from Hebron, and near the spot where, twenty years later, he buried his beautiful Rachel; six miles beyond he passed Jerusalem on the right, the future capital of his mighty posterity; and late in the evening of the second day, the stranger and weary traveler reached Bethel, eleven miles farther northward. The gates of the city were closed, and, like the pilgrim Arab of to-day, he selected a stone for his pillow, and, wrapping his capote or cloak about him, lay down to peaceful slumber. In a land where customs never change, such beds and pillows are not uncommon now, and thus are explained not only the story of the fugitive, but also our Lord's command to the sick of the palsy, "Arise, take up thy bed, and walk."[1] The bed was simply a coarse thick cloak of camel's hair.

In this retired vale, and beside this same fountain, Jacob dreamed of the Invisible, and awoke exclaiming, "How dreadful is this place! This is none other but the house of God, and this is the gate of heaven." Here the shining ones came down, and here Jehovah calmed the troubled spirit of the sleeper by the promise of protection. Cheered by the gracious promises of the Almighty, Jacob awoke, and, as a memorial monument, set up the stone that had served as a pillow, and anointed it with oil to seal the covenant he had made. Whether he was the first to conceive of building a church to God, and whether that is the sense of the text, Bethel became a sanctuary for his descendants.[2] When he returned after an absence of twenty years, here the faithful Deborah died, and he buried her under an oak, to which he gave the name of Allon Bachuth—"the oak of weeping."[3] Destined to live in history in all coming time, Bethel became the scene of many great and thrilling events. It was the place where Samuel held his circuit court, in connection with Mizpah and Gilgal.[4] Subsequently to the death of Solomon, and the rending in twain of his vast empire, Bethel became the imperial rival of Jerusalem, and was polluted with an idol temple, in which Jeroboam placed a golden calf. It was against this abomination the prophet cried: "O altar, altar, thus saith the Lord, Behold, a child shall be born unto the house of David, Josiah by name; and upon thee shall he offer the priests of the high places that burn incense upon thee, and men's bones shall be burnt upon thee."[5] Offended at the bold-

[1] Mark, ii., 9. [2] Gen., xxviii. [3] Ib., xxxv. [4] 1 Sam., vii. [5] 1 Kings, xiii.

ness of the seer, the king sought to smite him, but in the attempt his arm was smitten with paralysis.[1] On this slope lived the old prophet who over-persuaded the Lord's servant to enter his house, contrary to the divine injunction, and by the wayside is the tomb in which both were interred.[2] Chosen for its central location, years later Bethel became a school for the prophets, and hither Elijah came on the day of his translation.[3] And three centuries and a half after the utterance of the prediction, Josiah destroyed the temple and altar of Jeroboam, but spared the tomb of the Judæan seer.[2]

To-day Bethel is a witness against herself. Her hills and valleys are barren, and her ruins are the evidences of her decay. God has forsaken her; his will is done; his word is fulfilled. "Seek not Bethel, nor enter into Gilgal; for Gilgal shall surely go into captivity, and Bethel shall come to naught."[3] The roll of twenty-five centuries has confirmed the prophetic announcement, and time and ruins are the credentials of the prophet. In vain we searched for the memorials of the past. Neither Abraham's altar, nor Jacob's pillar, nor Deborah's oak, nor Jeroboam's temple, nor the school of the prophets, could be found. These all have perished, and Bethel mourns her departed glory. The heavens are sealed; the ladder is withdrawn; the angels descend no more; and faith, hope, and charity are the only remaining steps by which to reach the heavenly world.

From the brow of a western hill, and through the dim distance of twelve miles, I saw the dome of Omar's Mosque, the lofty minaret of the Haram, and the Tower of Hippicus. With this last and unexpected view of Jerusalem we resumed our tour to the north. For a mile the country was broken, but beyond were olive-groves and fig-orchards, extending for miles on either hand. The path soon descended a steep, narrow, and rough torrent-bed, and, after an hour's ride, it entered the charming valley of El-Jib. Unsurpassed for the beauty and romantic character of its scenery, it abruptly contracts into a wild gorge, and, two miles from its mouth, it contains a gem of a fountain, called 'Ain el-Haramîyeh, or "The Robbers' Fountain." Here the glen is as lovely as it is wild, and as bloody in its history as it is dangerous to the unwary traveler. The mountains rise in solemn grandeur on the right and left,

[1] 2 Kings, ii.   [2] Ib., xxiii.   [3] Amos, v., 5.

shutting out the world, and casting a melancholy shade on the scene below. High up on a jutting cliff is an old castle, gray with age, and covered with moss and creeping vines. Through the bottom of the glen a fierce winter torrent has cut a deep and narrow channel, leaving a broad level space on either side. On the right runs the road to Shiloh; on the left is a small plateau, level and green, and extending inward to the mountain's base. Down the sides of the western cliff the water trickles, through trails of fern and over beds of velvet moss, into an artificial basin. The plateau is covered with grass, and beneath it is a large reservoir, now a garden. Charmed with the spot, desire inclined us to linger, but prudence warned us to depart. The waters of El-Haramîyeh have washed the bloodstained hands of many a highwayman, and the native of to-day hurries on conscious of danger nigh. A band of robbers were encamped upon the lawn when we reached the fountain. Some were whiffing their narghilehs; others were testing their strength in gymnastic sports, while around the captain of the band two girls were dancing to the music of timbrel and castanets. They returned our salutations, and, after drinking of the cool, sweet water, and plucking a few ferns as mementoes, we recrossed the channel, and began to ascend toward Shiloh. As we advanced the scenery assumed higher forms of sublimity. The mountains approached each other, and rose to the clouds; but when, in turn, the hills receded and the valleys opened, the former were terraced and clad with vineyards, and the latter planted with wheat and corn. Attired in gay costumes, peasant-girls were at work on the terraces, singing merrily; shepherds, with long guns thrown across their shoulders, were winding with their flocks around the loftier cliffs; while far away to the northwest, following the devious mountain-paths, were trains of camels and asses, whose tinkling bells awakened the echoes of the everlasting hills. More than once we dismounted to gather the tempting wild-flowers, and press the pretty anemones, poppies, amaranths, and white-thorn roses.

Reaching the head of the valley, we left Sinjil on the west to visit ancient Shiloh. Before us lay a broad fertile plain, running toward the Jordan, and in the midst of which stands the Arab town of Turmus 'Aya. To the north of the village the path leads up a gentle acclivity, and then, descending into a narrow valley, it gradually ascends through cultivated fields to the hill on which the renowned city of Samuel stood. At the southern base of the hill stands an old square tower, originally a mosque, and over it a large oak spreads its ample branches. The surrounding hills are round and naked, the valleys narrow and stony, and the landscape featureless and forbidding. Covering a low ridge, projecting from the central chain of mountains, are the scattered ruins of Shiloh. Consisting of heaps of hewn stone, with now and then a broken column, the remains are embedded in rank weeds and tall grass, and destitute of the ordinary attractions of a fallen city. Near them is an old ruined church, which, in the age of the Crusaders, served as a fortress. The walls, four feet thick, are supported by buttresses. Over the entrance is a sculptured *amphora*, between two wreaths, and within the inclosure are a few fallen Corinthian columns. Half a mile to the east, in a wild glen, is the famous fountain of Shiloh, issuing from the rocks, and flowing into a deep reservoir, where shepherds water their flocks.

From the days of Jerome to the year 1838 the site of Shiloh remained unknown, when the analogy between the ancient and modern names, together with a single verse in the Book of Judges, enabled a distinguished American traveler[1] to determine its long-lost site. Called by the Arabs Seilûn, he judged it the Arabic rendering of the more euphonious name of Shiloh, and, guided by the minute and accurate description of the location by the elders of Israel, he succeeded in identifying the place. Nothing can be more artless and correct than that remarkable passage, "Behold, there is a feast of the Lord in Shiloh yearly, in a place which is on the north side of Bethel, on the east side of the highway that goeth up from Bethel to Shechem, and on the south of Lebonah."[2] Though destitute of those monuments which have given historic significance to its name, the pleasures of a visit to this celebrated city are to be derived from the recollections of the past rather than from the grandeur of its antiquities.

Memorable as the place where the Tabernacle was first permanently set up in Canaan, and where the Ark remained from the days of Joshua till near the close of Eli's life, it was here the Israelites assembled to divide the land into tribal posses-

[1] Dr. Robinson.   [2] Judges, xxi., 19.

sions according to lot.¹ To fulfill a solemn vow, hither the pious Hannah brought her infant Samuel from Ramah to serve in the Tabernacle.² As the custodians of the Ark, from here Hophni and Phinehas went forth to the fatal battle of Ebenezer, and here by the wayside the venerable Eli expired when he heard of the capture of that Ark and the death of his sons.³ Here the son of a mother, overwhelmed with grief at such calamities, received the name of I-chabod, "The glory is departed from Israel."³ In a glen to the east of the town was held that feast at which the daughters of Shiloh were dancing when the 200 Benjamites rose suddenly from the encircling vineyards, and, rushing on the unsuspecting damsels, captured each man a bride, whom he bore in triumph to his home.⁴ Disguised like a peasant, hither came the wife of Jeroboam from Tirzah to inquire of the Prophet Ahijah concerning the life of her son.⁵

Having become the seat of impiety, the city fell under the curse of the Almighty, and, in the words of Jeremiah, it was doomed to its present shapeless and desolate condition: "Go ye now unto my place which was in Shiloh, where I set my name at first, and see what I did to it for the wickedness of my people Israel."⁶

It was amid the recollection of such events that the robbers of Shiloh made their appearance and commenced an unprovoked assault upon our party. We had been forewarned of the turbulent character of the people, and of the danger a visit involved. At Sinjil we had discussed the prudence of a detour to this place, and, though it was a bold and hazardous step, as the sequel proved, yet we resolved to advance. We were in search of the most important knowledge, and, trusting to a gracious Providence, we felt justified in making the attempt. Unfortunately, our servant at the time was at Nablous, awaiting our arrival there, and, being without escort or guide, we were compelled to employ a peasant whom we had chanced to meet in a neighboring field. He was a simple, inoffensive, unarmed man, and was of no advantage to us except to guide us to the site of Seilûn. Having seen us from their mountain fastnesses, the robbers rapidly congregated around the old stone tower, where, at the moment, we were reading the inspired story of

---

¹ Josh., xviii. ² 1 Sam., i., 24; ii., 1-18. ³ Ib., iv.
⁴ Judges, xxi. ⁵ 1 Kings, xiv. ⁶ Jer., vii., 12.

the place, and recording those reflections suggested by the hour.

Such another band of villainous-looking men Nature has scarcely ever suffered to dwell upon the earth. Some were without a nose, others without an eye, while all bore scars of previous fights, and wore a vicious countenance which promised us no good. Each ruffian was armed with a long gun and a missile not unlike an Indian tomahawk. One, more reckless than the rest, began the fray by plundering my saddle-bags; but, seeing with what determination I drew my revolver, he immediately desisted. Wishing, if possible, to avoid another collision, we attempted to cross a corn-field to the hill on which Shiloh's ruins lay scattered, but they seized us and drove us back. Knowing that every moment's delay diminished our chances of escape, we concluded to resume our journey— peaceably if possible, but forcibly if we must. But we had no sooner mounted our horses than the brigands seized the bridles and demanded our money. Another exhibition of our well-conditioned revolvers—which by them is a dreaded weapon— again saved us from their hands, and, putting spurs to our horses, we descended a narrow valley on the south of Shiloh, keeping an eye upon the robbers, who were after us at full speed. But the bottom of the valley soon became so rough that it was impossible to proceed faster than a walk. Having overtaken us, they still clamored for money, and evinced their purpose to renew the attack. At that moment my horse stumbled, throwing me on his head; but, springing back into the saddle, and jerking the reins with all the strength at my command, I saved him from going down. My haversack, however, had fallen off, and one of the ruffians, having picked it up, refused to return it without a reward. Fortunately, the small amount I gave him satisfied him, and to that man I owe my life. Among the plants I had gathered at Shiloh was one of curious structure, which I desired to preserve. Its large bright green leaves were so folded as to resemble an embossed star, but it was a deadly poison. Having dropped it, I called to the Arab to pluck another, but he refused, assuring me in Arabic that it was poisonous.

We now dismissed the peasant previously employed, giving him the promised sum. This proved our misfortune, as the robbers, becoming exasperated at the favor shown their neighbor, came upon us with renewed fierceness in a solitary mountain pass. They had the advantage in numbers, and a base indifference to human life. Sixteen against four gave us but little hope of successful resistance; but, unwilling to yield even against such odds, we determined to resist to the last. Rushing upon us with the utmost fury, they seized our bridles, and, raising their tomahawks over our heads, demanded our money or our lives. Refusing to give the former, we resolved to protect the latter. Having never seen the countenance of a bandit in the act of violence, I shall never forget the expression of the ruffian who assailed me. His face was livid with rage, and his solitary eye blazed with murderous intent as he grasped the bridle firmly with one hand and with the other raised the weapon of death over me. Undaunted either by his rage or threats, I held a parley with him for several minutes, he demanding, and I, in turn, refusing. Trying the power of religious fear, I pointed him to heaven, and repeated the sacred name of "Allah," but he smiled like a demon, and fiercely replied, "Give me your money!"

Our firmness would have saved us from violence had not a member of our party, in an unguarded moment, struck one of the brigands with a riding-whip, which precipitated the assault, and it was now baksheesh or death. Aware that by this act we had become the aggressors, we concluded to give each a few piastres. Happily for myself, I had not a piastre in change, but, borrowing half a one (two cents) from a companion, I gave it to the villain, whose fury had been cooled by firm looks, strong words, a Damascus blade, and a good revolver.

Grouping together, they counted the spoils, but, finding the booty less than they had expected, they attempted another pursuit, but we had eluded their grasp. Dashing down the glen, we reached in safety the small village of Lubbân—the Lebonah of the Judges,[1] grateful to divine Providence that, through Arab cowardice and Christian grace, no blood had been shed.

The day was now far spent. Three hours of hard riding were before us, and it was necessary to reach Nablous before sundown or the gates would be shut. Riding through ancient towns, over plantations of figs, and amid the most enchanting

[1] Judges, xxi., 19.

scenery, we passed, in less than half an hour, the hamlet of Sâwieh, perched on a lofty ridge on the left, and a short distance beyond we came to an old castle on the right, shaded by a noble oak, whose vast dimensions and majestic form recalled the famous oaks of Mamre. Descending into a deep valley running at right angles with the great northern route, on the north was Kubalân, and on the south Yetma, high up in the eternal hills, amid gardens of figs and olives, as if suspended in the air. Such a view is worth a pilgrimage to see. Toiling up the opposite side of the valley, in half an hour we gained the summit, and the beauties of Ephraim lay like a landscape of glory before us. Interjections were faint symbols of the joyous emotions awakened by the scene. The white limestone rocks and verdureless mountains of the south had given place to the vine-clad hills of the north, crowned with the benediction of the dying patriarch, "God make thee as Ephraim."[1] At our feet lay the great plain of El-Mukhnah, unbroken by fence or tower, dotted with groves, and rich in fields of wheat and corn. Spreading out more than a mile and a half in breadth, and extending more than seven miles north and south, it is bounded on the east by a range of low, dark hills, and from its western border rise Gerizim and Ebal, the former crowned with a small white chapel reflecting the setting sun. Far away to the northeast, rising like a column of alabaster against the calm blue sky of Damascus, was Mount Hermon, the symbol of a purer world. Rapidly descending into the plain below and turning northward, we soon passed the large town of Hawâra, built on the mountain slope, and inhabited by a turbulent community. Just beyond the village the road branches; the path to the left, after winding round the base of Gerizim and crossing a mountain spur, enters the Vale of Shechem near Nablous; the other path, continuing up the plain, leads to the city by way of Jacob's Well. Choosing the latter, we found it the best road in Palestine. After following the base of the mountain for a while, the path diverges to the centre of the plain and passes through the most enchanting scenery. Like a thing of beauty, the memory of that evening's ride still lingers in my mind. The deepening shadows of Gerizim had thrown their lengthened forms over the plains; shepherds were returning with their flocks; peasants

[1] Gen., xlviii., 20.

NABLOUS.

were plodding homeward their weary way; and in the dim twilight of departing day, and amid that solemn silence which awakens profound reflections, we reached the patriarchal well. Intending to visit this interesting spot again, we ascended the Vale of Nablous and entered the ancient city of Shechem just as the old gate-keeper was turning the ponderous key. Gladly dismounting after the exploits of such a day, we led our jaded horses over the flag-paved streets of the city, exciting the curiosity of an idle crowd of Shechemites, and affording them fresh materials for village gossip. It was nine o'clock when we found our host, who was the Christian school-teacher of the Protestant Mission. Receiving us with great politeness, he led us up a long flight of stone steps into a large clean room, where, after a simple repast, we spread our mats and blankets for the night.

Ranking with Damascus, Hebron, and Jerusalem in the antiquity of its origin and the importance of its history, Shechem, or the modern town of Nablous, is among the oldest cities in Palestine. Coming from Chaldea, Abraham pitched his tent on the fertile plains of Mukhnah, "in the place of Sichem, in the plain of Moreh."[1] Nearly two centuries later his grandson Jacob came from Mesopotamia to "Shalem, a city of Shechem, and pitched his tent before the city, and bought a parcel of a field, at the hand of the children of Hanor, for one hundred pieces of money, and erected there an altar, and called it El-Elohe-Israel."[2] Here Simeon and Levi plotted the murder of the whole male population of the town to avenge their dishonored sister, and, exposed by this act of indiscretion to the insults and attacks of the adjacent villagers, Jacob was compelled to remove to Hebron.[3] Retaining possession of these pasture-fields, hither he sent Joseph to search for his brethren, whom "a certain man found wandering in a field," and directed him to Dothan.[4]

Four hundred years afterward, having achieved the conquest of Ai, Joshua led his triumphant hosts over the Jordan into this vale; upon Ebal he reared the first Jewish altar in Samaria; and from this and its companion mountain caused to be read the blessings and cursings of the Law.[5] Two and a half centuries later, Abimelech seized this city and was proclaimed

---

[1] Gen., xii.   [2] Ib., xxxiii.   [3] Ib., xxxiv.
[4] Ib., xxxvii.   [5] Josh., viii.

king, which gave rise to the beautiful parable of Jotham.[1] Hither came Rehoboam to be crowned king of Israel; and in the same year here occurred the coronation of Jeroboam, under whom the twelve tribes revolted, and Shechem became the royal city of the new monarchy.[2] During the long captivity of the Jews in Assyria, Nablous rose to be the chief city of the Samaritans, who were destined to act such a conspicuous part in sacred history. Being instructed in the Jewish religion, they reared upon the summit of Mount Gerizim a rival temple to that in Jerusalem, and became the religious and political enemies of the Jews. Four hundred and fifty years after the erection of this temple, the Vale of Shechem was hallowed by the presence and teachings of Jesus and his twelve apostles. In the year 89 A.D. it was the birthplace of Justin, the philosopher and martyr, one of the earliest and most learned of the Christian fathers. From the days of the Roman conquest to the present time it has shared the varied fortunes of the Crescent and the Cross, and to-day is subject to the sceptre of the False Prophet.

Nablous is situated in one of the most delightful vales in Palestine. A garden-like valley opens from the Plain of Mukhnah and runs nearly east and west, with Ebal on the north and Gerizim on the south. Standing less than two miles up the vale, the city covers the roots of Gerizim, extending toward the opposite mountain. Of its 8000 inhabitants, 50 are Jews, 150 Samaritans, 500 Christians, and over 7000 Moslems. Its narrow streets, thronged with a busy multitude— its stone dwellings, crowned with small domes—its mosques, with their graceful minarets—and its numerous bazars, filled with fruit and other commodities, remind the traveler of Jerusalem; but the streets are less light and airy than those of the Holy City, as the buildings, projecting over them, supported by arches, impart to them a tunnel-like appearance. Except a spacious Saracenic doorway, now the portal of a mosque, a marble sarcophagus, now a water-trough, and a few prostrate columns of granite, limestone, and marble, there are no antiquities worthy of a moment's attention. The modern Shechemites are the chief cotton-growers, oil-makers, and soap manufacturers of Palestine. The valleys and hill-sides are covered with olive-trees, from the berries of which is ex-

[1] Judges, ix.   [2] 1 Kings, xii.

tracted the precious oil. In the adjacent fields cotton is raised in large quantities for home consumption and exportation. Regarded as the best quality grown in the dominions of the Turkish empire, thousands of bales are yearly exported to Europe. The present citizens of the town afford another illustration that the character of a people, no less than their names and social customs, are handed down from generation to generation. They are infamous for their turbulent and fanatical reputation in the past, and more street-fights occur in Nablous than in any other Syrian city. The rebellious spirit that rose three thousand years ago against the government of Rehoboam is still dominant, and the Shechemites are among the most troublesome of the sultan's subjects, obeying or rebelling as interest dictates or passion inclines. It required the powerful and cruel arm of Ibrahim Pasha to crush them, though not without a long and bloody struggle. Jews, Samaritans, and Christians live among those turbulent children of the Prophet only by sufferance, and the crimes of theft and murder perpetrated on them are seldom punished by the weak and timorous Turkish officials.

The Jews have a small synagogue within the walls, the picture of poverty and wretchedness. Of the 500 Christians, most are of the Greek Church, and worship in an edifice at once old and filthy. The Protestant Christian Mission is under the protection of the English and Russian governments, and is accomplishing much good in the education of the young. The mission school, under the care of our host, was held in a room adjoining the one we occupied. Accepting his invitation, we spent an hour with his pupils: there were present from forty to fifty boys, from three to fifteen years of age. Attired in Syrian costume, they were clean and pretty in their appearance, and modest and obedient in their behavior. Sitting on their heels, they were engaged in writing with a reed not unlike, in form and size, our common pencils. Calling up one by one, from the least to the greatest, the master exhibited specimens of penmanship which, as far as I was capable of judging of the graceful Arabic characters, were creditable to the young penmen. As they seemed anxious to know about the schools and children of America, I made them a brief speech, which was interpreted by our polite host.

From their wealth, social position, and historic importance, the Samaritans are by far the most interesting religious body in Nablous. The Bible account of their origin and history invests them with a peculiar charm, and imparts to the seat of their ancient empire an interest seldom equaled in the stories of romance. Hoping to effectually subdue Palestine to their powerful sway and restore it to the rites of idol worship, the Assyrian conqueror led the Jews of Samaria into captivity, and repeopled their depopulated cities with colonists from the distant East. During the long period that intervened between the captivity and the colonization, the bears, panthers, wolves, and jackals from the Heights of Hermon and the jungles of the Jordan had so far penetrated into the heart of the country, and had multiplied to such a degree, as to endanger the lives of the colonists. Being polytheists themselves, they ascribed the evil to the local divinities, whose worship they knew not how to perform. Complaining to their king, he sent them a Jewish priest, who taught them the name and worship of Jehovah. With a curtness that savors of irony, the inspired historian adds, "They feared the Lord and served their own gods."[1] National pride, and contempt for their origin and mixed religion, led the Jews, in after years, to despise the colonists, and being thus scorned by those from whom they had reason to look for truth and righteousness, the Samaritans in turn became exclusive. Multiplying in numbers and increasing in wealth, in process of time they erected a temple on the summit of Gerizim. To them this mount became their Moriah, and in the lapse of ages an invented tradition designated it as the scene of the offering of Isaac. By a better title it shared the solemnity and significance of Mount Sinai, as from its slopes Joshua proclaimed the Law; and the vale beneath became a second Rahah, since the hosts of Israel gathered there to hear the blessings and cursings of the divine commandments. With honest pride they contemplated their surrounding plains as the camping-ground of the patriarchs prior to their pilgrimage to the south, and as the scene of the coronation of the son of Solomon. Turning their attention to commerce, they became merchants in Egypt, and, traveling westward, in the fifth century they had a synagogue in Rome. Continuing to live under the varied fortunes and vicissitudes of empire, the existence of this present remnant is one of the most remarkable

[1] 2 Kings, xvii.

instances of the tenacity of national life in the annals of the world. Numbering 130 souls—the sum of all that remain of a once proud and mighty kingdom—they cling to their ancient seat of empire with undying fondness. Adhering to the Jewish law, which forbids marriage with foreigners, and numbering more males than females, not less than twenty men are doomed to involuntary celibacy. Industrious and thrifty, they dwell in their own houses, pursuing their vocations and maintaining their community with comparative ease. In their physique and apparel, in their intelligence and morals, in their social happiness and general behavior, they are the superior class among the citizens of Nablous. Possessing a solitary synagogue in the western part of the town, they observe their religious rites with much regularity. They have a school, under the direction of a shrewd, intelligent Samaritan. Their high-priest is a venerable man, who is assisted in the duties of his sacred office by two sons, the elder of whom will succeed his father to the office and rank he now holds. Besides a collection of hymns, they have in their possession the Book of Joshua in manuscript, with commentaries on the Law, and a copy of the Pentateuch in the original character. They claim for the latter that it is 3300 years old, and was written by "Abishua, the son of Phinehas, the son of Eleazar, the son of Aaron." Regarded as a treasure of incalculable value, it is preserved in a metallic case, and deposited in their synagogue under the care of the high-priest. The tattered, patched, and soiled parchment forms an immense scroll, the ends of which are attached to two rollers. Such is their superstitious reverence for this antique manuscript, that they deem it a pardonable offense to exhibit a duplicate as the veritable one, and many a traveler has left with the impression of having seen the five books of Moses written by the son of Phinehas. Though destitute of a temple, they ascend their sacred mount three times a year, and celebrate with much display the Feast of the Passover, the Day of Pentecost, and the Feast of Tabernacles.

The clouds that had overcast the sky, and the fogs which had hung upon the mountains like floating curtains in the morning, had been lifted up by noon, and Nature smiled in all the beauty of spring. Passing out of the eastern gate of the city, I entered the Vale of Shechem. It extends from the Plain of Mukhnah on the east to the city on the west, and is two miles in length and something over 200 yards in width. It gently ascends from Jacob's Well, and for half a mile its entire breadth is one vast and glorious grove of olive, fig, and almond trees, presenting at times the density of a forest. Beyond the orchards are vineyards and fields of grain, through which flows a crystal brooklet. Rising like massive walls from this garden valley are Mount Gerizim on the south and Ebal on the north, attaining an altitude of nearly 1000 feet. Standing midway the vale, and looking upon these celebrated mountains, one is impressed with their singular companionship. Of equal height, with rugged sides and flattened summits, they remind one of twin brothers. Equally renowned in sacred history, the honor bestowed upon the one was only equal to the glory conferred upon the other. If Gerizim was the mount of blessing and Ebal the mount of cursing, it was upon the latter that Joshua reared the first altar to the living God in Central Palestine. But, less impartial than history, Nature symbolizes the benedictions and maledictions of the law by causing flowers to bloom on Gerizim and thorns to grow on Ebal. Midway the vale are corresponding nooks in the mountain sides, resembling well-formed recesses, and increasing its breadth to nearly 400 yards. Standing out from the base of the mountains are perpendicular ledges of rock, not unlike grand pulpits, from which the whole vale is distinctly seen. Somewhere in this expanse the hosts of Israel assembled to hear all the words of the Law. Divided by the centre of the vale, the tribes of Simeon and Levi, of Judah and Issachar, of Joseph and Benjamin, were gathered around the base of Gerizim, and the tribes of Reuben and Gad, of Asher and Zebulun, of Dan and Naphtali, were congregated over against Ebal. Standing above the people on these great pulpits, which the Creator had reared for an occasion so august, the priests read the Law, while to each blessing and to each cursing the vast multitude responded their assent.[1] So firmly does Nature retain her ancient features, and so exact is the correspondence between the inspired account and the scene as it now appears, that, standing within this venerable church of God's own construction, thirty centuries unfold their mighty scroll, and the past comes back with the actuality of the present. Before the eye of a sublime faith the tribes reassemble, the priests take their stand, and in son-

[1] Deut., xxvii., 11-26; Ib., xxviii.; Josh., viii., 30-35.

JACOB'S WELL.

orous tones slowly and distinctly read, one by one, each command and each prohibition, while from either side, in alternate responses, beginning at the mountain base and rolling outward to the centre, rises the full, deep, responsive "Amen!" like the sound of many waters breaking in alternations of musical thunder against the opposite wall of the everlasting mountains. The area was sufficient for that grandest of human assemblies; and such is the profound silence of the vale, the human voice was heard then, as it is heard now, from mountain to mountain.

Viewed from this point, Gerizim is not unlike a cone with ridged sides and a broken base, while Ebal seems not so high nor steep, but rougher, with its top receding with gentle slope. In the centre of the vale opposite the nooks is the cool, clear, sweet fountain of 'Ain Depneh, whither, as of old, the maidens come for water, and around which shepherds linger with their flocks. In numberless rills the waters flow to the eastward, in pearly brightness and perennial music, the livelong day. From the fig and almond bowers birds of elegant plumage awaken the gentler echoes of the vale. Less than half a mile to the east of the fountain is the wretched hamlet of Belât, presenting a melancholy contrast between the beauty of nature and the deformity of man. Two hundred yards beyond, situated on the point of a spur from Gerizim, is Jacob's Well. On a mound of shapeless ruins, 20 feet above the Plain of Mukhnah, are fragments of granite columns, the remains of a Christian church. Measuring 75 feet in depth and nine in diameter, this patriarchal well is excavated in the solid rock with regular and smoothly-hewn sides. Originally, a vaulted chamber, 10 feet square and as many deep below the surface of the ground, formed the entrance to the well, the walls of which have fallen in, rendering access difficult. Leaping down into the ruined vault, I found two openings into the well through heaps of limestone blocks. Attaching a cord to a small tin bottle, I lowered it to the depth of 65 feet, but found no water; on lowering it, however, through the other aperture to the depth of 75 feet I reached the water, which was from three to five feet deep. Imagine my joy in drinking from the Well of Sychar, whose waters were sanctified by the lips of the gracious Redeemer! It is clear like unto crystal, having the softness of oil and the sweetness of honey.

Returning to the surface of the ground, and sitting beside the well whither the sons and daughters of the patriarchs had often come for water, and perchance where the Master had sat, I read its thrilling history as recorded by Moses and by John. With an accuracy that must claim the faith of every candid mind, all the facts of the sacred narrative are in harmony with the physical features of the scene. Stretching out to the north, east, and south is the parcel of a field Jacob bought of Hamor for a hundred pieces of money,[1] and on its western border is the well The three great religious sects agree as to its identity, and its site has been preserved in the memory and affections of man through an unbroken tradition to our own time. To one not conversant with Eastern customs it would appear improbable that a man as shrewd and prudent as Jacob would be at the expense and labor of excavating a well so near the living springs in the upper valley, which have always poured their irrigating waters down the Vale of Shechem. But the reflection on the prudence and economy of the patriarch is removed by the consideration of the well-known fact that in the East water is more valuable than land, and a higher value is set upon a well or spring than upon fields of pasture. "Pasture your flocks on my hills and plains, but let my wells alone," is the only request the Oriental makes of the stranger. In a land where water is scarce, every proprietor aims to have a well of his own, which he guards with peculiar vigilance. The custom of digging wells on a newly-purchased estate is as old as Abraham and Isaac; and as in their times, so now, there are more quarrels over wells of water than over fields of grain. Subject to the same social laws, Jacob but indicated his wisdom and conformed to an acknowledged usage in first purchasing a field and then digging a well. Accepting a tradition so venerable, I yielded to the full enjoyment which such a scene is calculated to afford, and the week I spent at Nablous I never wearied in my journeyings to drink of these delicious waters.

Interesting as were the patriarchal associations of the place, it was with unmingled delight I read the beautiful story of our Lord's conversation with the woman of Samaria. Had St. John written the incidents of the Savior's journey from Jerusalem to Sychar with a previous knowledge that his narra-

[1] One hundred lambs, or coins with the image of a lamb upon them. Gen., xxxiii., 19.

tive would be subjected to a searching criticism by the enemies of Divine truth, he could not have written with greater accuracy. As the facts of topography on which the traveler relies for the credibility of the story are recorded merely as incidents to the story itself, the correspondence between the statement and the fact is the more wonderful and convincing. Deeming it prudent to escape the snare of the Pharisees, "Jesus left Judea and departed again into Galilee." To reach his destination "he must needs go through Samaria." Reaching Jacob's Well at noon, he rested, it being on the direct road to Galilee by way of Tirzah, while his disciples, turning to the left, passed up the Vale of Shechem to the city to purchase refreshments. During their absence came the "woman of Samaria," with cord and pitcher, to draw water. He who had made the fountains of earth and sky requested, "Give me to drink." As at most Eastern wells there is neither wheel, chain, nor bucket, and surprised at his promise to give living waters, her reply was no less natural than truthful: "Sir, thou hast nothing to draw with, and the well is deep." Hoping to divert his attention from the irregularities of her life, she introduced the relative claims of the Jews and Samaritans to religious superiority. Rising up before them was Mount Gerizim, to which in turn each pointed in their allusions to the noble sanctuary crowning its summit. Looking with compassion upon the Samaritans, anticipating the great work to be wrought among them, and impressed with the necessity of immediately laboring in their behalf, he pointed to the ripe Plains of Mukhnah, warning his disciples not to say, "There are yet four months and then cometh harvest; behold, I say unto you, Lift up your eyes and look on the fields, for they are white already to harvest."[1]

While Jews and Samaritans, Christians and Moslems, agree that this is the Well of Sychar, the ever-restless skepticism of modern times has called in question its otherwise undisputed identity. Because it is two miles from the city of Shechem, it is judged too far away for the woman to have come for water. Nothing, however, is said in the text to cause us to suppose she came from the city; and if she had come from what is now known as Nablous, there are reasons for supposing that the ancient city extended farther east than the present one.

[1] John, iv., 1-42.

Like the village of Belât, her native town might have been adjacent to the spot; or at the noon hour she might have come from an adjoining field, where, with other peasant women, she had spent the morning in the toils of husbandry.

But, in the unmistakable fulfillment of our Lord's prophecy, time has furnished even a stronger proof of Bible inspiration than the exact correspondence between the narration of the event and the description of the scene. The woman of Samaria is dead; the disciples, one by one, have all passed to their reward; the Redeemer has ascended to glory; Gerizim is a desolation; Moriah is the shrine of Mohammed; and the prophetic words of Jesus, that first fell from his lips on the soft air of the Vale of Shechem, and were whispered back by the winds from Ebal and Gerizim, are now heard in all the valleys and on all the mountain summits in two hemispheres.

The tomb of Joseph is in sight of his father's well, around which he was wont to play when young. When dying in the palace of Pharaoh, he had taken an oath of the children of Israel that they should "carry up his bones from hence;"[1] and, true to their solemn vow, "the bones of Joseph, which the children of Israel brought up out of the land of Egypt, buried they in Shechem, in a parcel of ground which Jacob bought of the sons of Hamor, the father of Shechem."[2] Crossing a stream on which stands an old mill belonging to the village of Belât, we descended into the plain, and, passing through rich corn-fields half a mile to the north, we came to a small square area inclosed by a white plastered wall, marking the spot where sleeps in peace he who was the darling son, the wandering shepherd, the captive youth, Potiphar's slave, Asenath's betrothed, Pharaoh's prime minister, the preserver of his country, the joy of a dying father, the exemplary saint, and the model man. How strangely the lines of human actions cross each other in the orderings of Providence! What beautiful coincidences transpire beneath his benign sway! The parcel of land his father purchased of Hamor is now the place of Joseph's sepulchre, and in the very field where he was lost he now rests in death. And though the spot is unmarked by stately granite or marble shaft, Ebal, the mountain of his boyhood, is his imposing tomb-stone, and over the whitened wall a vine is now creeping, the symbol chosen by his dying father

[1] Gen., l., 25.   [2] Josh., xxiv., 32.

to preintimate the prosperity of a beloved son: "Joseph is a fruitful bough, even a fruitful bough by a wall, whose branches run over the wall."[1]

It was five o'clock on a bright spring morning when, attended by a solitary guide, I descended the Vale of Nablous to where the valley widens, and began to ascend the Mount of Cursing. The sun was just peering over the hills of Ephraim, transforming the dew-drops into sparkling jewels, and awakening the matin notes of unnumbered songsters. In an hour we gained the summit; and though the horizon was misty, limiting the view, the familiar peaks of Moab rose above the fog-clouds like islands in the ocean. The sides of Ebal are rough, and its summit broad and stony. A solitary goat-path leads over the mountain to the valleys beyond. Shepherds were roving with their flocks in quest of pasture, and peasants were hastening to their daily toil. The attritions of time and the sacrilegious hand of plunder have destroyed the altar Joshua reared to Jehovah. From its highest peak a noble view is obtained of the fertile hills and valleys to the east, and of the lofty Tellûzeh, the renowned Tirzah, whose beauties Solomon has embalmed in immortal song,[2] and which was once the rival of Shechem as the seat of royalty.[3]

Returning to Nablous, we passed out of the western gate to ascend the Mount of Blessings. At the portal stood a group of lepers, perhaps the descendants of Gehazi, who was cursed with the leprosy of Naaman.[4] Poor creatures, how sad they looked! Their ulcered faces, dull, restless eyes, languid, husky voices, and tattered garments presented a mournful spectacle of fallen humanity. Excluded from society like those of Jerusalem, they live distinct, to grieve, rot, and die in their wretched hovels. Standing afar off and arranging themselves in a semicircle, twenty men and women, in tones of pity, asked our charities. No sight among living things that meets the traveler's eye recalls the days of the benevolent Savior so vividly as the appearance of lepers. Perhaps it was in this same city that "there met him ten men that were lepers, which stood afar off. And they lifted up their voices and said, Jesus, Master, have mercy on us."[5] Distributing bread among the poor creatures, we turned to the left and began the ascent. Our

[1] Gen., xlix., 22.   [2] Cant., vi., 4.   [3] 1 Kings, xvi., 8.
[4] 2 Kings, v., 20-27.   [5] Luke, xvii., 11-13.

path led up a glen of rare beauty, and from a ridge to the south of the town we looked down upon the noble site of the city stretching nearly across the valley, and from amid palms and trees of exquisite foliage rose domes and minarets. Just above the ridge, in a sequestered spot, is the large fountain of 'Asal. Its clear waters, being first gathered into immense troughs, are then conducted by an aqueduct to a mill, from which they flow down the hill-side into a quiet dell rich with shrubs and flowers. Crossing the stream, we followed the path trodden by many ancient pilgrims, and passed through groves of figs and almonds, in the branches of which birds were singing merrily. Here the hill-sides were terraced, supporting groves of fruit-trees and also vineyards. Beyond the orchards the path was steep and stony, and turning abruptly to the left, after half an hour's hard climbing we reached the summit of Gerizim. The top is a broad, irregular plateau, covered with heaps of stones and the remains of vast structures. Crowning a rocky knoll is the white wely seen from the Heights of Ephraim. From the roof a view is obtained rivaling that from Neby Samwil in the extent and variety of the prospect. Far to the east, like a massive wall, stand the trans-Jordanic mountains; on the south a succession of green hills appear as far as the eye can reach; on the west are seen patches of the Plain of Sharon, and through openings in the hills are caught glimpses of the Mediterranean; while dimly in the hazy northern sky Hermon rises, covered with snow and tinged with a purple hue. In all its wealth and beauty, at the mountain base lies the Plain of Mukhnah, stretching eastward a broad green arm amid the dark hills of Ephraim. Indistinctly the modern town of Sâlim appears on its western border, supposed to mark the site of Shalem, where Jacob pitched his tent. Seen in the rays of the setting sun, the plain resembles a magnificent carpet of vast dimensions, of curious figures, and of variant hues, the chocolate-color of the soil, the light green of the corn, the sombre hue of the olive, the dull gray of the protruding rocks, and the purple and azure tints of the hills harmoniously blending.

Of the nature and origin of the immense ruins covering the summit of Gerizim but little is known. There is one vast structure, now in ruins, consisting of two adjacent parts, measuring 400 feet in length and 250 in breadth, with the remains of square towers at each corner. Consisting of blocks of limestone with beveled edges and rough centres, they are regarded by some as the remains of the once grand temple of the Samaritans, and by others as portions of the great fortress here erected by the Emperor Justinian. Though the Samaritans reject these ruins as part of their temple, yet they point to many of their sacred places. Beneath the western wall of what is now called the castle are twelve flat stones, and under them are said to be the veritable twelve stones that Joshua brought up out of the Jordan as memorials of the miraculous dividing of the water. A few yards to the south is their "Holy of Holies." Irregular in form, it is a smooth-faced natural rock, measuring 45 feet in diameter, and gently declining toward a deep-hewn pit called their *sanctum sanctorum*. Regarding it as holy ground, they always remove their shoes before stepping upon it; and as truly as the Moslem turns toward Mecca in the moment of prayer, and the Jew toward Jerusalem, so truly do the Samaritans turn toward this rock-hewn cavern in the time of devotion. Contrary to all history and to all tradition, they claim it as the scene of the offering of Isaac, of Jacob's vision, as the place where the Tabernacle was first set up, and where the Ark rested. Sacred and profane history is too explicit to countenance either of these assumptions; and, besides the unanimous voice of history, the distance from Beersheba to Gerizim is too great to have been accomplished in three days by Abraham and his son. Even had the Father of the Faithful followed the Plain of Philistia, and on the morning of the third day from the Plain of Sharon seen Gerizim, the difficulty of distance would not have been obviated by such a route, as it would have required him to travel thirty miles a day for the first two days and twenty miles of heavy mountain-climbing for the third; and as he and Isaac returned to the young men the same day, the distance would have been much greater. Not far from these ruins is a rectangular area, surrounded with a low stone fence, called the Temple of the Samaritans. Here they annually assemble, pitch their tents, and eat the Passover. Near the inclosure is a circular pit, three feet in diameter and ten deep, in which the paschal lambs are roasted. I was fortunate enough to be present on the 23d of April to witness the celebration of the feast of the Samaritan Passover. According to their custom, their whole community, to the number of 130 souls, consisting of men, women, and children, had ascended the mount and pitched their tents, some of which were white and others of variegated colors, upon its broad summit. The day being regarded by them as a gala-day, all were attired in their gayest costumes, and all rejoiced in the historic significance of the occasion. Occupying an elevated position, the ceremonies were conducted by the venerable high-priest, assisted by his two sons. The male portion of the congregation stood in a group on a small mound, chanting psalms and reciting portions of the Pentateuch, while the females remained in and around the tents. In a group stood seven Levites clad in white garments, each holding by the head a lamb without spot or blemish; near them were large caldrons of boiling water, to scald the sheep like swine, instead of flaying them, as in the ordinary way; and beyond was the circular furnace, already heated, to roast the offering. The going down of the sun was the appointed time to slay the paschal lambs. As the day declined, each face was turned toward the west, eagerly watching the last ray of the setting sun. At length the solemn moment came; the high-priest waved his hand as the signal for the slaughter; in an instant each lamb was slain and lay bleeding at the Levite's feet. Not a sound was heard. Each worshiper bowed his face to the earth, his forehead touching the ground. After an interval of silent prayer, all arose, greeted each other with a holy kiss, and parents sprinkled the blood of the victims upon the forehead of their first-born. The scalding of the sheep followed, and after the fleece had been removed, the seven lambs were suspended on heavy oaken spits, and with much ceremony placed in the heated furnace. It was night before the feast was ready. The paschal moon had risen in unclouded beauty upon the rugged summit of Gerizim, and many a one had fallen asleep, like the three disciples in Tabor. At length a shout is heard—the feast is ready! The lambs being removed from the furnace, the priest's portion was first presented to him, and then the whole company, except those women ceremonially unclean, ate the flesh with bitter herbs and with unleavened bread, in haste, with their loins girded, their shoes on their feet, and their staffs in their hand.[1]

[1] Ex., xii., 11.

CHAPTER XI.

A Price for Politeness. — Escort. — Picturesque Scenery. — Samaria. — Its Founder. — Its Vicissitudes. — Residence of Elisha. — Famine. — City beautified by Herod. — Its Location. — Hill of Omri. — Grand Ruins. — Tomb of John the Baptist. — Temple of Augustus. — Prediction fulfilled. — Departure for Cæsarea. — Night on the Plain of Sharon. — The Sick brought out. — Plain of Sharon. — The Lost Lake. — Cæsarea uninhabited — Dangers. — History. — Imperial City under Herod the Great. — Grand Ruins. — St. Paul a Prisoner. — Death of Herod Agrippa. — Athlit. — Mount Carmel. — Scene of the Sacrifice. — Great Event. — Abode of Elisha.

SAMARIA, the ancient capital of Israel, is seven and a half miles to the northwest from Nablous, and 25 miles beyond, in the same direction, is Cæsarea, on the Mediterranean coast. Intending to encamp that night amid the ruins of the latter city, we ordered our horses at nine A.M. At the appointed time their solid iron shoes were heard on the pavement below, and the impatient Arab servant was crying, "Horses ready, sir." But we had met with an unexpected delay. Judging from the magnanimous manner in which the schoolmaster of Nablous had received us at our arrival, and his affable deportment during our stay, he seemed above the tricks and meanness of other Orientals; but an Arab is an Arab the world over — selfish, money-loving, and untrue, whether Christian, Jew, or Moslem. Eastern hospitality always means an equivalent to be returned for whatever has been received. Gifts are presented with the tacit understanding that presents are to be given in return. Even the merchant assures the buyer that all he has is his, well knowing that in this unbounded generosity he is protected by the customs of the East, which are invested with all the sanctity and authority of law. More than once our host had said, "All I have is yours—my house, my food, my service." To the uninitiated this is equal to his ideal of Oriental hospitality; but when the day of departure comes, the deceptive curtain is lifted, and his Arab host stands before him a persistent creditor. Having paid our host for his apartments and for the entertainment he had furnished, I saw that he wore an expression of disappointment. "What is the matter, my friend? Why is thy countenance sad, seeing thou art not sick? It is nothing else but sorrow of heart." "Ah! my dear sir, you have paid me for my room, for my food, and for my service, but you have not paid me for my politeness." "How much do you charge for your politeness?" A thoughtful moment followed, and he replied, "Two dollars and a half."[1]

Waving him an adieu, we sprang into our saddles, and in a few moments issued out of the western portal of the city. Intending to visit Cæsarea, which is now a desolation and a den of thieves, we had taken the precaution to engage two Turkish soldiers as a guard, for whose service the governor had demanded an exorbitant sum. They were to have met us at the gate of the town, but, true to their traditional indolence, they did not arrive till long after the appointed hour. The sun was high, a long journey was before us, many places of deep interest were to be visited, and we felt impatient at the delay. To wait was the only remedy. At length one came, informing us that his companion had lost his horse. Refusing to linger longer, we ordered him to advance, leaving word with the guard at the gate to hasten the tardy soldier, who overtook us after half an hour's ride.

Our cavalcade now presented a picturesque appearance as we wound round the southwestern spur of Gerizim and descended into the upper end of the Vale of Shechem. Leading the way, our guard were mounted on spirited horses fantastically caparisoned, while they themselves were attired in costumes of the gayest colors. Each was armed with a long gun thrown across the shoulders, a Turkish sword dangling by his side, and a brace of old-fashioned cavalry pistols sticking in his girdle. As we advanced the scenery became surpassingly lovely. Terraced hills rose on either side, casting a grateful shade in the vale below; groves of figs and olives, apples and pomegranates, apricots and almonds, covered the plain and mountain sides. As we rode on, our ears were saluted with the sound of running waters and the song of birds. In less than thirty minutes we passed on our right a noble fountain, covered with a Roman arch, around which were groups of peasants and droves of

[1] Sixty piastres.

asses. An hour beyond we came to an arched mill-race, not unlike a Roman aqueduct, consisting of twelve pointed arches, gray with age and festooned with graceful ferns. It is used for carrying the water to the south side of the valley, where it falls headlong into the heart of an old mill, amid the whirr of wheels, mingling an air of civilization with the crude mechanics of the East. Leaving this terrestrial elysium, our path diverged northward over bleak hills whose limestone ribs had burst through the scanty soil, intensely reflecting the light and heat of a Syrian sun. The path is cut into the solid rock, in some places resembling steps, but now worn smooth by the tread of man and beast. Near the summit of the ridge is the "Shepherds' Spring," where maidens were drawing water for their flocks. Now the royal city of Samaria rose to view. Its unique hill, like a truncated cone, adorned with circular terraces; its marble porticoes, now in ruins; and its hut-like dwellings, rising from amid the remains of more pretentious edifices, formed a picture of singular beauty. Descending through magnificent groves, the path followed the valley, and, after passing beneath an old arched gateway, it abruptly turned to the west up the hill of the Samaria of Omri, the Sebaste of Herod, and the Sebustieh of modern times.

The history of Samaria is among the most thrilling and romantic portions of the Sacred Volume. It dates back to 900 years B.C. "In the thirty and first year of Asa, king of Judah, began Omri to reign over Israel, twelve years; six years reigned he in Tirzah. And he bought the Hill of Samaria of Shemer for two talents of silver, and built on the hill, and called the name of the city which he built after the name of Shemer, owner of the Hill Samaria."[1] Up to this time the revolted ten tribes had no capital city as the object of their pride and the centre of their affections. Originating in rebellion, the kingdom of Israel had been governed by adventurers, who had reared sumptuous palaces as fancy or luxury inclined. From Shechem, the original seat of empire, Jeroboam removed to the enchanting Heights of Tirzah, a magnificent mountain six miles north from Nablous, projecting from the table-land of Ebal. Solomon had praised its beauty in his immortal song: "Thou art beautiful, O my love, as Tirzah;"[2] and for forty years it was the seat of royalty. Ambitious for an imperial

---

[1] 1 Kings, xvi., 23, 24.   [2] Cant., vi., 4.

city near Jerusalem, Baasha, the successor of Jeroboam, abandoned Tirzah for Ramah; but, overtaken by misfortune, he was compelled to return to the mountains of Ephraim. More successful, however, than his predecessor, after a reign of six years Omri finally exchanged Tirzah for the strength, wealth, and glory of Samaria. Succeeding his father Omri to the throne of Israel, and marrying the Sidonian Jezebel, Ahab removed his court to Jezreel, on the slopes of Gilboa. To him belongs the shame of having first erected an idol temple to Baal on the summit of Samaria, which secured for him the divine verdict that "Ahab did more to provoke the Lord God of Israel to anger than all the kings of Israel that were before him."[1] The city was a tempting prize to the military plunderers of that distant day. In the reign of Ahab, Benhadad, king of Damascus, besieged it with a strong and boastful army, but, through the courage and celerity of the young men of the provinces, he was repulsed with terrible slaughter.[2] Long the residence of the Prophet Elisha, Samaria was the scene of many of the most interesting events in his marvelous career. Benhadad, regarding him the cause of the discomfiture of his army, dispatched a detachment of troops to Dothan, six miles to the north, to capture the man of God. Conscious of his danger, Elisha invoked the divine aid, and the Lord smote the men with blindness, and the prophet, whom they had been sent to capture, led them as captives back to Samaria. Forgetting that mercy is due to the vanquished, the king of Israel, in a paroxysm of revenge, cried out, "My father, shall I smite them? shall I smite them?" More humane than his royal master, the kind-hearted Elisha replied, "Thou shalt not smite them: wouldst thou smite them whom thou hast taken captive with thy sword and with thy bow? Set bread and water before them, that they may eat and drink, and go to their master."[3] Benhadad, enraged at his failure to capture the man whom he supposed was the cause of his ill success, sought to accomplish by famine what he had failed to do by the sword. Investing the city on every side, he reduced the citizens to the greatest necessity. It was during the horrors of the long and fearful famine which followed that, as the King of Israel passed along the wall, "there cried a woman unto him, saying, Help, my lord, O king. And he said unto her, What aileth thee? And

[1] 1 Kings, xvi., 33.   [2] Ib., xx.   [3] 2 Kings, vi., 12-22.

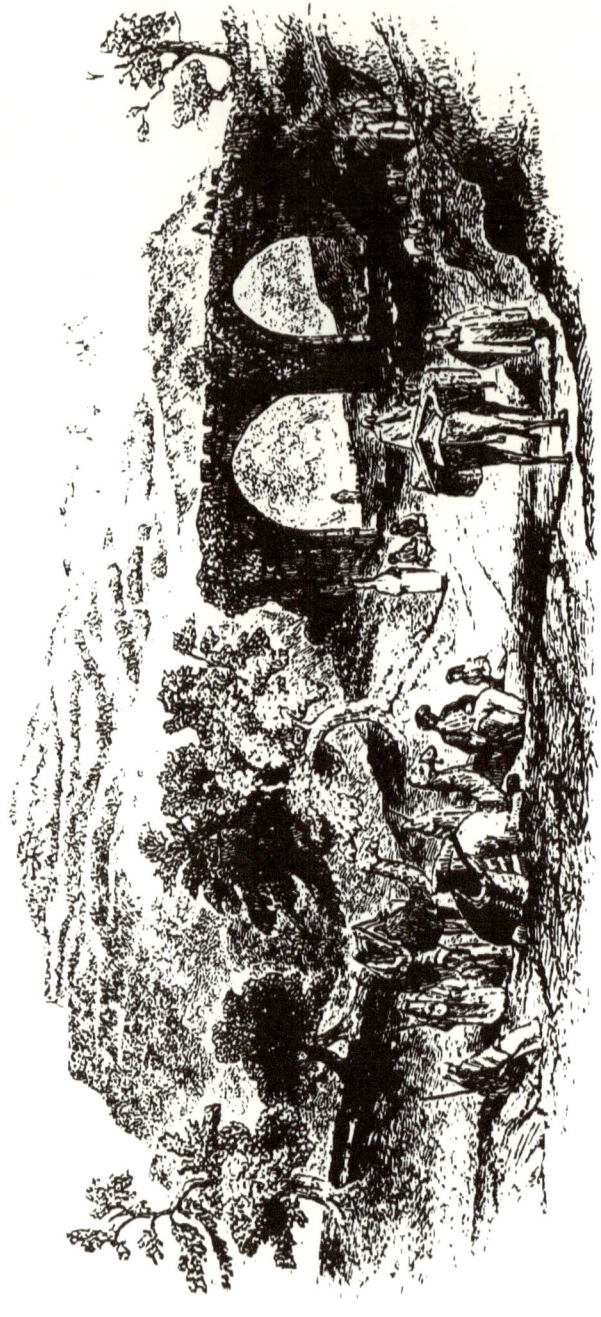

SAMARIA.

she answered, This woman said unto me, Give thy son, that we may eat him to-day, and we will eat my son to-morrow. So we boiled my son and did eat him; and I said unto her on the next day, Give thy son that we may eat him; and she hath hid her son." Rending his clothes at a spectacle so mournful, and erroneously attributing the famine to Elisha, the king swore, "God do so, and more also to me, if the head of Elisha, the son of Shaphat, shall stand on him this day." Conscious of his innocence and undaunted at the threat, the prophet sat calmly in his house; and, contrary to all human probability, but knowing what would befall the enemy that night, he said to the executioner, "To-morrow about this time shall a measure of fine flour be sold for a shekel, and two measures of barley for a shekel, in the gate of Samaria." Terrified by a supernatural noise, that night the Syrians abandoned their well-provisioned camp and fled for safety. Four lepers, who had lingered outside of the city, dying of hunger, in the desperation of despair resolved to enter the enemy's camp and ask for bread; but, to their surprise, the camp was empty of men, but full of the spoils of war. Lepers though they were, they hastened back to the city with the glad tidings of plenty, and that day were fulfilled the prophetic words of Elisha.[1]

No important event occurred in connection with Samaria for 700 years, till the reign of the Emperor Augustus, who bestowed it as a gift upon Herod the Great, by whom it was enlarged and beautified, rivaling Baalbec and Palmyra in the magnificence of its architecture. Herod reared a temple on the summit of the hill in honor of his patron, and inclosed its base with a colonnade, consisting of two ranges of columns 50 feet apart, and extending 3000 feet in length. Such was the splendor of Samaria in the apostolic age, when Philip, together with Peter and John, preached the kingdom of heaven to the Samaritans, and encountered Simon Magus, the sorcerer of Sebaste.[2]

The ancient city was located on one of the most imposing and picturesque hills in Palestine. Situated in a basin-like plain six miles in diameter, it rises in an oval shape to the height of 300 feet. Connected with the mountains on the east by a gentle swell of land, it has the appearance of a noble promontory. Midway its sides is a broad, irregular terrace,

[1] 2 Kings, vi., 24-33; Ib., vii., 1-20.   [2] Acts. viii.

the site of the modern town, while its summit is a long, level plateau. On the north and south are valleys, converging on the west into the Valley of Nablous and running to the sea, bounded on either side by higher mountains, dotted with villages, and fertile in groves of fruit-trees and fields of grain. Nothing evinces the refinement and elegance of Omri's taste more than the selection of this hill to be the site of his imperial city; but, under the degenerating influences of Mohammedanism, the beautiful in nature and the grand in art sink into insignificance. The footfalls of the Prophet are the pitfalls of civilization. Here, as every where else in the East where he sways his sceptre and lifts his sword, shame succeeds glory. Filth and rags, indolence and turbulence, crime and misery, are the chief features of the 400 inhabitants of the modern town. Their sixty wretched huts are constructed of mud, in which are imbedded the polished but now broken columns of costlier edifices. In a region where plenty waits on ordinary industry, they are but little above the condition of common beggars. In such a land indolence is a crime and poverty a dishonor.

Grand amid its ruins and conspicuous in its desolation is the Church of John the Baptist, reared to the memory of that great man some time during the reign of the Crusaders. Standing on the very brow of the broad terrace on the east, its broken arches and crumbling walls recall the beautiful ruins of Melrose and Dryburg Abbeys. In form it resembles a Greek cross. The finish of the interior is of the Corinthian order, and exceedingly beautiful. Measuring 153 feet in length and 75 in width, the interior consists of a nave and two grand aisles, formed by rows of clustered columns ornamented with Corinthian capitals. In the eastern end is the chancel, with pointed arches elegantly adorned, resembling the segment of a circle. But the Gothic roof is gone, and in the aisles grass grows where once cowled monks and mail-clad knights knelt in prayer. On white marble tablets set in the wall are sculptured crosses of the Order of the Knights of St. John, now mutilated by the hand of Moslem ignorance.

The southern half of the interior has been inclosed for a mosque, and under a wely in this inclosure is the reputed tomb of St. John, called by the Arabs "Neby Yahya." It is a small chamber excavated in the solid rock, reached by the descent of 21 steps. Here pious tradition points to the final resting-place of his headless body, brought hither by his friends from the castle of Machaerus, on the east of the Jordan, where it was originally interred. When the brave Crusaders took possession of the Holy Land, they guarded with affection and veneration the sepulchre of their patron saint, and reared over his ashes this church as his funeral pile. Though impossible to determine the correctness of the tradition that here urns the dust of the greatest of prophets, it is no less a tribute to his memory, and a dishonor to the memory of his royal murderer, that the name of John and that of Herod are the only two conspicuous names perpetuated by the ruins of Samaria.

Plucking a memorial leaf from the tomb, we followed the broad, level belt of land to the southwest side of the hill, where are the remains of Herod's colonnade. It is impossible to speak with accuracy of its vastness and magnificence. According to Josephus, Herod enlarged the city, surrounded it with a wall 20 furlongs in circumference, in the midst of which he left an open area a furlong and a half in circumference, where he erected a temple to Augustus, remarkable alike for the vastness of its dimensions and the exquisite beauty of its finish.[1] To rival the renowned city of Palmyra, he constructed a colonnade 50 feet wide and 3000 long, consisting of two rows of polished limestone columns 16 feet high and two feet in diameter, ornamented with Corinthian capitals. Through this imposing colonnade the royalty, the beauty, and military of Sebaste passed up to the temple of Augustus, which crowned the hill of Omri; but, like the grim skeleton of departed beauty, it is now a ruin. For more than 200 feet this avenue is marked by prostrate columns and broken bases. A hundred shafts still stand erect as when reared eighteen centuries ago, but now marred by the rude plowshare of the equally rude Arab. Ascending to the site of the temple, 200 feet above the colonnade, we found 17 columns without capitals, two of which were lying prostrate, overgrown with the ripening grain. Half a mile distant to the right were 15 columns, which are all that remain of that famous quadrangle composed of 170 columns. Where marble walks once ran and exquisite statuary stood, venerable Nature, outliving the monuments of human greatness, has resumed her ancient sway, bearing on her

[1] Book xvi., p. 316.

fertile bosom clustering vines and ripening grains. From the summit the prospect is no less extensive than captivating. Unrivaled by any other hill as a site for a capital, the position of Samaria is strong and central, its environs are fertile, and its summit is fanned with breezes from the distant sea. The vineyards, the cotton-fields, the circlet of mountains green with corn, and the rich Plain of Sharon beyond, bounded by the blue waters of the Mediterranean, form a picture of more than ordinary beauty, and one which Elisha and Herod, Philip, and Peter, and John must have contemplated with delight.

As we descended from the ruins of Sebaste, whose citizens were great in crime as they were great in wealth and power, the prophetic denunciations against the city and their fulfillment were recalled to mind: "I will make Samaria as an heap of the field and as plantings of a vineyard; and I will pour down the stones thereof into the valley, and I will discover the foundations thereof."[1] "Samaria shall become desolate, for she hath rebelled against her God."[2]

It was two P.M. when we mounted our horses for Cæsarea. Reapers were thrusting the sickle into the ripe barley, and maidens were gleaning after them, as we rode over the Plain of Sebaste. Soon we turned westward and again entered the Valley of Nablous, here known as Wady Sh'air, "The Valley of Barley." Through its centre flows a brook, which increases in width and rapidity as it approaches the sea. Following the northern bank of the stream, we passed, at intervals of several hundred yards, Roman aqueducts, near which are mills driven by water power. Reaching the small hamlet of 'Anebta, the road to Cæsarea branches, one continuing down the valley to the Plain of Sharon, while the other, striking across the barren ridges of Wady Mussin, enters the plain by the village of Bâkah. Choosing the latter, we traversed a barren and cheerless region. Night came on apace as we neared the large and flourishing town of Shuweikeh, situated on a lofty hill. Passing the village of Kakón, we mistook Zeita for the town of Bâkah. Riding through its silent streets, we learned from a peasant that the place of our night's encampment was still to the westward. Regaining the road, we lingered for a moment to examine the remarkable Hill of Zit, marking the eastern border of the Plain of Sharon. Its sides are scarped and regular, and

[1] Micah, i., 6.   [2] Hosea, xiii., 16.

its summit is level; around its base are hewn stones and fragments of columns belonging to some unknown city. It was here we had a despicable instance of the military tyranny of the Turks. One of our soldiers rode into a field and cut down grain enough to feed his horse that night, while the owner, who was a poor man, besought him, in the most respectful manner, to spare his grain, as it was all his property. But neither age, prayers, nor poverty touched the heart of that military ruffian.

Anxious, hungry, and weary, we pitched our tents, at eight P.M., in the environs of Bâkah, a small straggling town on one of the richest plains in the world. The mules unloaded, the horses tethered, supper over, prayers offered, my companions asleep, I walked out upon the magnificent Plain of Sharon. A dreamy haze, like gossamer gauze, veiled the skies of night, through which moon and stars softly peered. A scene so lovely recalled the tender strain of one of our finest poets:

> "Oh! sweet and beautiful night,
> When the silver moon is high,
> And countless stars, like clustering gems,
> Hang sparkling in the sky:
> While the breath of the summer breeze
> Comes whispering down the glen,
> And one fond voice alone is heard—
> Oh, night is lovely then."

The horse and his rider lay side by side, and the watch-fires, burning dimly, shed a livid glare upon the sleepers. The moon, growing brighter as she ascended, silvered each spear of grass and blade of corn, while far away to the east, amid the mountain glens of Samaria,

> "Shadows wandered free,
> But spoke not o'er the idle ground."

It was now midnight, and I was alone, a stranger in a strange land, without one near me whose face I had seen beyond the ocean. The heavens only were familiar; the moon and stars of my childhood were as old companions; but, rising above the one and the other, I sought communion with Him who is enthroned on high.

The morning dawned inauspiciously; the gossamer veil of the previous night had been folded into thick clouds, which obscured the summits of the distant hills. While we were waiting for our muleteer to load his beast, there occurred a scene illustrating the tenacity of Eastern customs. In our party was Dr. Barclay, the eminent American physician of Joppa. His fame had preceded him, and, learning of his arrival, the villagers brought out their sick of all ages, and for a time our encampment became a hospital. Among the number was a young girl, who with faltering step came leaning upon the arm of her mother. She was pale and emaciated, and apparently in the last stages of consumption. The doctor examined her symptoms, questioned her mother, and prescribed for the patient, who long since, I fear, has passed to another world. Such was a faint illustration of the days of the Savior, when "they brought unto him those having all manner of diseases, and he cured them." In a country where science is neglected, *materia medica* is unknown, the barber is the physician, bloodletting is the panacea for all diseases, and the "medicine-man" of more enlightened lands is revered next to God.

The sick had scarcely found shelter within their hovels when the storm broke upon us in all its fury. Protected by a thick burnous and a Mackintosh coat, we waited patiently the return of fair weather. The rain ceasing, we advanced, but had not reached the southern limits of the town when the storm was renewed with tenfold violence. Deeming it prudent to halt, we remained upon the plain for an hour, amid a drenching rain and exposed to a raging wind; but when the rain ceased a rainbow spanned the heavens such as seldom appears in Western skies.

Hoping to reach Cæsarea by noon, we dashed over the plain, and in less than two hours came to the Nahr Abu Zabûra, which was so swollen as to render fording dangerous. Exploring the banks for a ford, but failing to find one, we plunged in with a shout, and with difficulty gained the opposite bank. Safely "beyond the floods," the Plain of Sharon lay before us in all its wealth and beauty. It extends like a vast prairie from the base of Carmel on the north to the sea-girt cliffs of Joppa on the south. Eastward the Hills of Samaria look down upon it, with Ebal and Gerizim rising above their fellows. Westward is the sea, whose waters roll their ceaseless waves against its "empire shores." It has a shore line of 50 miles in length, and varies from one to 15 miles in breadth. Undulating in long and graceful swells, it is at intervals dotted with low hills crowned with the ruins of unknown towns. Retaining its ancient character, it is the best pasture-land west of the Jordan valley. Three thousand years ago here Shitrai the Sharonite kept the flocks of David,[1] and over its ample fields the shepherd of to-day might wander with his herds. Of the "rose of Sharon" neither peasants nor scholars have any knowledge at present; if it exists, it is not recognized by its inspired name. There grows upon the plain the "imperial thorn," by some regarded as the thorn of which the Savior's crown was made. Growing to the height of four feet, it has a gorgeous purple blossom, with a long, lancet-like brier, and would well compose a mock imperial crown.

There are no paths over this great plain, which is seldom trodden except by those who till the soil, and the compass or a peasant is the traveler's only guide. Though ordinarily this is a disadvantage, yet to us it proved advantageous, as in our wanderings we discovered a lake that had been lost since the days of the Crusaders. Though it is not large, its waters are pure, of a bluish tint, and abound in fish. Flocks of wild ducks were floating on its placid bosom. Its waters never fail, though they are sensibly increased by the rains in the wet seasons. Its shores are clean and sandy. On the north it is bounded by a high sand-bank of many miles in extent. The sand is of an orange color, like that found on the Debbet er-Ramleh in Arabia. On the south and west there is a meadow rich in rank weeds, and covered with acres of white and yellow daisies. On the north and east there is an oaken grove, lovely as an English park.

Crossing the large sand-hill, we soon entered a tract of country remarkable only for the quantity of thorns and brambles, which scratch both man and beast in the most painful manner. An hour's ride from the lake brought us to the outer walls of Cæsarea, and at one P.M. we encamped within its massive ruins. Fearing an attack, our soldiers immediately left us to return to Nablous, assigning as the cause the worst of military reasons—that they were afraid to remain. An Arab soldier is rarely to be trusted in danger. His convictions of right and wrong, his sense of obligation, his want of personal courage, his habitual meanness of soul, and his traditional hatred of the Christian, disqualify him to be a trusty guard. He is of ad-

[1] 1 Chron., xxvii., 29.

vantage to the traveler in saving him from the petty annoyances of the common people, by whom he is dreaded because he is tyrannical and brutal, but it is his nature to cower in the presence of a superior and courageous foe. There is nothing so mean as an Arab soldier.

It was a dangerous experiment to visit Cæsarea, and especially to remain there during the night without a guard. For many years there has been a standing feud between the Fellahin who dwell in the villages on the plain and the Hawâra Arabs who hover along the coast. It was a novel sight, as we crossed the fields, to see farmers engaged in the peaceful pursuits of husbandry armed to the teeth. Men were threshing with guns slung upon their backs; women were gleaning with heavy clubs dangling at their side; and patrol-men, with sword and pistols, gun and lance, were on the alert to give the alarm at the first appearance of the foe. With brief intervals, such has been the condition of Sharon since the earliest ages, and Isaiah gives it as a sign of the restoration of the Jews, that "Sharon shall be a fold of flocks, and the Valley of Achor a place for the herds to lie down in, for my people that have sought me."[1] Discouraged by such dangers, but few travelers attempt this interesting tour; but there is so much of religious and political importance connected with this renowned city, that we felt justified in making the journey and remaining during the night, after we had been abandoned by our military escort.

The authentic history of Cæsarea commences with Strabo, in the reign of Augustus, who describes it as an insignificant landing-place, marked by "Strato's Tower." From this solitary tower Cæsarea became the most magnificent city in Palestine, under the auspices of Herod the Great. The subject and friend of Augustus, he sought to perpetuate the favor of his royal master by founding an imperial city and giving to it the family name of Cæsar; and, impelled by an unbounded ambition, he aimed, if possible, to make it rival Rome in the elegance of its architecture and in the extent of its commerce. Abandoning the traditions of his fathers, he transferred the capital of his empire from its mountain fastnesses to this inhospitable coast, which exposed it alike to the corruption of Western nations and to the attack of their naval galleys. But

[1] Isa., lxv., 10.

in removing the sceptre of empire from Judah he unconsciously became the accomplisher of prophecy, and in inviting the civilization of the West to his shores he unintentionally opened a highway for the nations to hear from apostolic lips the sublime lessons of Christianity. Sparing neither art nor treasure in founding his new city, he surrounded it with a wall of many miles in circumference, and within the inclosure erected on a commanding hill, which he encompassed by a second wall, a splendid temple of white marble, and dedicated it to Cæsar. According to Josephus, he adorned it with two statues, one representing Rome, and the other his patron Augustus. To attract the commerce of the West, he constructed in front of the acropolis a harbor equaling the Athenian Piræus both in elegance and extent. Sinking huge stones to the depth of 20 fathoms, he constructed an immense and gently-curving breakwater to protect vessels in port from the southern and western gales, but left an open channel on the north for the entrance and departure of ships. To strengthen and beautify the mole, he reared large towers, containing vaulted chambers adorned with arched ceilings, mosaic pavements, polished columns, and sculptured capitals, for the accommodation of naval officers, and connected the towers and the shore by a long quay, designed for the landing of merchandise and the pleasures of a promenade. To tempt the wealth and fashion of Greece and Rome, he erected on the east and south a vast theatre and circus; and to secure the health and comfort of the citizens, he built aqueducts extending miles in length, and large enough to admit a mounted cavalier.[1] But the history of Cæsarea was as brief as it was splendid; its decline was as rapid as its rise was sudden. Forsaken by men, it is now an uninhabited desolation. An unbroken silence reigns within its palaces, the wild Arab refuses to pitch his tent within the crumbling walls, and the shepherd declines to lead his flock amid its wild flowers and rich grasses. Rank weeds grow where royal feet trod, the shy fox barks and the hungry jackal wails where kings reigned, and sobbing winds sigh responsive to moaning waves where the voice of revelry was heard. As the ancient population of the city, consisting of 200,000 souls, could not have resided within the walls of the acropolis, our first attempt was to ascertain the location and direction of the outer wall.

[1] Josephus, A. J., b. xv.

Riding to the east of the town, we could trace a regular mound sweeping from shore to shore in the form of a semicircle, now covered with rubbish, and overgrown with high weeds. Returning, we ascended the second or inner wall, which is well preserved, and is exceedingly strong. On the south, east, and north it is surrounded by a deep moat, and is flanked on three sides by bastions surmounted with towers 120 and 150 feet apart. Commencing on the shore, the north wall runs inland a distance of 900 feet; forming an angle at this point with the eastern wall, the latter extends southward 1728 feet, where it joins the south wall, which runs to the sea, a distance of 657 feet. Having an altitude of more than 70 feet, this wall is supported by 17 bastions. To increase its defensive power, the eastern wall is double, one portion being perpendicular and the other oblique. Near the northeast angle is a large gateway, the chief entrance to the town on the east; and in the southern wall, near the shore, there is another gate, surmounted by one of the watch-towers of the olden city.

Measuring half a mile in length and a quarter in breadth, the whole area within this inclosure is covered with heaps of rubbish, with deep intervening pits; and on the one and in the other grow marigolds, white daisies, chess, thistles, and brambles. Not a fragment of Cæsarea's temple remains to be identified, and on its site are the ruins of the Cathedral of Cæsarea, in which the learned Eusebius officiated as bishop of the diocese for more than a quarter of a century. Of this noble edifice four large buttresses are standing, which, from their height, are seen from afar, presenting an imposing appearance to the traveler, whether his approach is from the plain on the east or from the sea on the west. Though a complete ruin, the outline of this early Christian church can be traced without difficulty. Constructed of beveled stones, the interior consisted of a nave and two lateral aisles. Originally extending 143 feet in length, 121 feet of the south wall continue *in situ*, 13 feet in thickness. In the eastern end is the chancel, which, consisting of three semicircular apses measuring 60 feet in all, is the breadth of the cathedral. Standing from 16 to 20 feet apart, and being from five to seven feet thick, the four remaining buttresses formed the grand portico to this Christian temple. Judging from the projection of the arch, the doorway was 12 feet high, as it is nine wide. Beneath the church is a dark and

ANCIENT CAESAREA.

loathsome vault 77 feet long, gradually declining toward the east. It is now the den of jackals and hyenas.

If any work of art is worthy to be called grand, it is the Herodian harbor of Cæsarea. The breakwater described by Josephus is a continuation of the southern wall of the acropolis, more than 300 feet of which are still visible above the sea. Some of the stones in the lower courses are 20 feet long, six wide, and as many thick. In the southeast corner of the mole are the remains of a tower, reached by 20 stone steps, and commanding a view of the entire port. The ceiling was formerly arched, and a portion of an old arch projects from the side, resting on the figure of a human head. Connected with this tower, and on a level with the shore, were the apartments for the officers of custom, the mosaic floors of which remain in excellent condition. On the very extremity of the mole is another tower, containing a square room 20 feet high, 30 wide, and 35 long, but the waves are fast wearing it away. On the northern side of the harbor, flanked by stones 15 feet long, seven wide, and six thick, are three immense gateways for the entrance of vessels. Following the shell-strewn shore of a small bay, we reached the end of the northern wall of the acropolis. The noble marble pier, once extending into the sea 170 feet, is now a ruin. Its hundred prostrate columns lie as they fell, most of them parallel to each other, with now and then one lifting its head in silence above its fellows, worn by the tireless surges which roll over it, careless of its former grandeur. To me, sitting on one of those columns far out into the sea, time passed unconsciously. The day had declined, the golden sun was sinking into the distant ocean, and, as if an angel had led me back into the past, I thought of the fall of empires and the vanity of human glory.

Hailing the first blush of returning day, I sat on the desolate shore and read the inspired history of Cæsarea. Excepting Jerusalem, no city in Palestine is more intimately connected with the early Christian Church. Coming from the interior, the apostles sought the great centres of commerce, where they preached to men of all nations their catholic faith. Having baptized the Ethiopian eunuch, Philip the Evangelist followed the coast, and, preaching Jesus to the inhabitants of all the maritime cities thereon, he came to Cæsarea.[1] Thirty

---

[1] Acts, viii.

years thereafter, here, with his four daughters, he resided as one of the seven deacons of the infant church, when St. Paul and St. Luke were his guests. It was in his house that Agabus took Paul's girdle, and, binding his own hands and feet, foretold the arrest and imprisonment of the apostle to the Gentiles.[1] Arrested in the Holy City, here Paul was brought a prisoner by order of Claudius Lysias, and somewhere amid these ruins was the dungeon in which he was confined two years. In obedience to Roman law, hither came Ananias the high-priest, with the orator Tertullus, to accuse him before the governor. Here stood the palace of the sordid Felix and his adulterous Drusilla, where he "reasoned of righteousness, temperance, and judgment to come;" and where he made that marvelous defense before Agrippa and Festus, provoking the taunt from the latter, "Paul, thou art beside thyself; much learning hath made thee mad;" and extorting the concession from the former, "Almost thou persuadest me to be a Christian." And from this harbor, now the wreck of earlier grandeur, that apostle entered the ship Adramyttium, under Julius, a centurion of Augustus's band, to prosecute his appeal before Cæsar, and at last to die a martyr at Ire Fontana, beneath the walls of Rome.[2] Here was the home of the devout Cornelius, to whom Peter came from Joppa on the coast, 33 miles to the south, with the keys of the kingdom of heaven, to open its gates to the Gentiles and baptize the first heathen convert. Here, in the year 270 A.D., Eusebius Pamphili was born, and subsequently this was the birthplace of Procopius the historian.

Sending the baggage to Athlit, our party separated to explore the different parts of the city, agreeing to rendezvous at night at the above-named place. Riding down the coast with a single companion, we first examined Herod's amphitheatre. Located a little south of the acropolis wall, it occupies a commanding position. Judging from the shape of the ground, it was originally semicircular in form. Much of the masonry has survived the waste of time, and among the broken granite columns is one nine feet in circumference. The arena has an eastern and western diameter of 69 feet, and a northern and southern diameter of 78 feet. The seats are of stone, arranged in tiers, and recede as they ascend, giving a slope

[1] Acts, xxi.   [2] Ib., xxiii., xxiv., xxv., and xxvii.

from the bottom of the arena to the outside of the uppermost seat of 90 feet. The width of the eastern wall, from the highest tier of seats to its outer edge, is 75 feet, forming a grand promenade. It was not possible to determine whether this is an embankment of earth faced with masonry or a solid wall. It is penetrated with arched passage-ways, like those in the amphitheatres of Capua and Pompeii, which lead to the dens and stalls of the animals designed for the entertainment of the spectators. On the south side is one of the principal vomitories leading to the arena; it is 11 feet wide, 48 long, and is the only one now open. High up in the southeast part of the building is a solitary seat, just as it was left by the last spectator by whom it was occupied. The shape of the mounds on the south indicates that the southern wall of the theatre served as part of the city wall, as on its extreme western end are the remains of an old watch-tower containing a circular chamber, and not far to the north are the ruins of another, occupying a narrow neck of land commanding the approaches to the coast. It is evident, from the present appearance of the mounds, that originally the walls extended to the shore, agreeing with the description of Josephus that "it was conveniently situated for a prospect to the sea."[1]

With this theatre stands connected one of the most mournful tragedies of Bible times. Having murdered the Apostle James and attempted the life of Peter, Herod Agrippa came from Jerusalem to Cæsarea to call to account the citizens of Tyre and Sidon, who had incurred his royal displeasure. Arrayed in robes of gold and silver texture, Herod entered the theatre on a festive day to deliver an oration to his subjects. According to an ancient custom, it was early in the morning, and the sun's rays, falling upon his resplendent garments, dazzled the eyes of the beholders, who, in a delirium of joy at the brilliant spectacle, and at the same time affected by the eloquent tones of his voice, rose *en masse* and cried out, "It is the voice of a god and not of a man. Be thou merciful to us; for, although we have hitherto reverenced thee only as a man, yet shall we henceforth own thee as superior to mortal nature." In this moment of divine homage he looked up and saw above him, on a rope, an owl, a bird of ill omen. It was the messenger of his departure. Refusing to rebuke this impious flattery,

[1] A. B., b. xv.

"the angel of the Lord smote him, because he gave not God the glory, and he was eaten up of worms, and gave up the ghost."[1] Looking upon his flatterers as he expired, the dying king exclaimed, "I, whom ye call a god, am commanded presently to depart this life, while Providence thus reproves the lying words you have just said to me; and I, who was by you called immortal, am immediately to be hurried away by death."[2] The construction of the theatre is in harmony with these serious facts. The imperial throne being on the west side of the edifice, toward the shore; the auditors sitting with their backs toward the east; and the building, like all structures of the kind in Eastern countries, having no roof, the rising sun shone with dazzling brightness upon the monarch's robes, transforming him into an object of indescribable magnificence, and awakening the acclamations of the people.

Riding eastward through lacerating thorns and briers, we saw a red granite block, 35 feet long, five wide, and four thick, lying upon its broad surface, and near it another of less dimensions. Beyond them, to the north, is Herod's circus for chariot racing. It consists of an oblong basin with embanked sides. The three conical shafts of red granite, averaging from eight to ten feet in length, which marked the goal of the ancient course, are still standing; and in the midst of a field not far to the northwest is a deep well, 20 feet in diameter, with circular mouthpiece and arched roof.

The ride from Caesarea to Mount Carmel is less remarkable for its Biblical antiquities than for the pleasures of the tour. It was 11 A.M. when we regained the shore, and I rejoiced in the mysterious companionship of the sea. The aqueducts of Herod extended for miles on our right, and, though dry, are in a good condition. The coast is here lined with low black rocks, against which the waves dash wildly, the spray reflecting the rainbow. At midday we came to the Nahr Zurka, or the Crocodile River of Strabo and Pliny, which is a clear and fordable stream. Having its source among the hills on the east, it flows down a pretty glen, amid wild flowers and dense shrubbery. To the left is a low promontory, jutting into the sea, and covered with the shapeless remains of some unknown light-house. To the right the Samarian Hills creep down to the shore. The beach soon widened, and was strewn for miles

[1] Acts, xii.   [2] Josephus, A. J., b. xix.

with white and purple shells to the depth of several feet. In two hours we passed Tantûra, the Dor of the Scriptures, whose king was the ally of Jabin of Hazor.[1] It is a small village of 30 houses; and on an islet to the west is an old tower, which, like an ancient landmark, is seen from Cæsarea to Carmel. Passing the small towns of Kefr Naum and Surafend on the right, we reached Athlit at six P.M. on Saturday, and pitched our tents on a beautiful lawn, beneath the walls of the *Castellum Peregrinorum*. This is the second most interesting city of Phœnicia, but the date of its origin and the name of its founder are unknown. With ruins as vast and grand as those of Cæsarea, the style of the architecture is superior to that of the city of Herod. Unnoticed by sacred and profane historians, its name remained in obscurity till the twelfth century, when the Crusaders selected it as the chief landing-place for pious pilgrims *en route* for the Holy City, calling it the "Pilgrims' Castle." It occupies a rocky promontory, and is bounded on the west by the ever-majestic sea, and on the east by green hills and fertile plains. Crossing the headland from bay to bay are the remains of an outer wall, which once inclosed a quadrangular area a mile in extent. Within this inclosure stood the citadel, inclosed by a wall 15 feet thick and 30 high. It was constructed of pure Phœnician stones, and was penetrated by three gates, two on the east and one on the south, which were reached by stone steps. Opposite the southern gate is a massive pier 12 feet wide and 150 long, most of which is still above the water. Here the shore is covered with prostrate columns, fallen pendentives, broken entablatures, and marred cornices. Rising out of the sea are sections of the western wall, the southern end of which is formed of circular stones 12 feet in circumference. Originally there sprang from this wall a lofty arcade 35 feet wide, and beneath it ran an arched passage-way across the entire promontory. In the northwest corner is a large room, to the very door of which vessels came to land their passengers and discharge their cargoes. To the northeast of this arcade is a plain Gothic church 20 feet wide and 133 long. The ceiling is supported by 12 arches, springing from as many plain brackets, each arch culminating in an elegant embossed flower. The interior is reached by a single door, and its one square and two pointed windows look upon the sea.

[1] Josh., xi.

Consisting of a few huts, occupied by inhabitants as filthy as they are wretched, the modern town of Athlît is piled upon the ruins of the ancient acropolis. Beneath the citadel are immense vaults, supporting the formidable fortress above. In the midst of these huts stands the once magnificent Gothic church of the Crusaders. The remaining wall is 80 feet high, and is divided into sections by ribs, which rest upon the heads of human figures. These arches, no doubt, spanned the eastern aisle of the church in the days of its glory. Such are the splendid ruins of Athlît. Impressed with its greatness, I experienced the novel emotions of gazing upon a decayed city whose powerful citizens are without a record in history. Enumerating Dor and its towns, Joshua may have included Athlît; or, if it existed at that time, it may not have been possessed by Issachar.

Two roads lead from the "Pilgrims' Castle" to Mount Carmel, one along the coast to Haifa, the other through the Vale of Dor. We took the latter: the path leads over rich plains, where reapers and gleaners were gathering the ripened grain. To the east the trees and blades of corn seemed to rise out of water, but we soon discovered that it was a mirage. In an hour we reached the mouth of a narrow mountain defile. To the south of the entrance are two remarkable caves, which some time have been human habitations. The larger of the two is 300 feet long and 50 wide. The sides and top are formed into sections by 13 natural arches, resembling the ribbed ceiling of a Gothic church. The bottom of the cave declines inward, and near its termination the percolated water drops from the fretted roof. Entering the mountain gorge, the lofty hills on either side are covered with oaks, hawthorn, myrtle, and acacias, and flowers bloomed along the grassy vale. The Sabbath silence that reigned within was unbroken save by the cooing of the dove in its mountain home, and the scream of the eagle as he flew from his inaccessible eyry. The hills soon receded, and the broad valley was dotted with oaken groves and fields of pasture, where herds of cattle and flocks of sheep and goats were browsing. Passing through the village of Asifriah, we descended a steep path leading into a ravine of extraordinary grandeur. Descending the glen, between mountains which arose thousands of feet above us, we turned to the north and began the ascent of Carmel. For two hours we ascended a mountain path steep and rugged, lined with oaks, acacias, and flowers, when we gained the summit of the sacred mount, and stood with Elijah of Tishbe, and Elisha, the son of Shaphat.

Branching off from the northern portion of the mountains of Samaria, Carmel is a bold and grand promontory projecting into the sea. Running in a northwesterly direction, it is the boundary-line between the Plain of Sharon on the south and that of Phœnicia on the north. Rising 2000 feet above the sea, it is 18 miles long and five wide. Covered with evergreen oaks, it is appropriately called "The Fruitful Field." As the type of natural beauty, Isaiah compares the returning glory of his nation to the "excellency of Carmel,"[1] while Amos predicts that "the top of Carmel shall wither,"[2] as descriptive of the utter ruin of his country. From the summit the eye rests upon one of the noblest landscapes in the world. To the west is that "great sea" seen by the prophet's servant; to the south are the Mountains of Samaria; to the north the Hills of Nazareth; while to the east is the Plain of Esdraelon, stretching far away to the Jordan in vast undulations, and dotted with Gilboa, Little Hermon, and Mount Tabor.

But the glory of Carmel is its sacred associations. In the darkest hour in Jewish history, when Jehovah's altars were thrown down and his prophets slain, hither Elijah invited the priests of Baal to test by fire the superiority of their respective gods. The priests conceding the existence of Elijah's God, the contest was to decide whether Jehovah or Baal should be the supreme divinity of the land. Chastened by the evils of a long drouth, the people were prepared for a procedure so extraordinary. Ahab, over whom the infamous Jezebel had gained the ascendency, was upon the throne of Israel; and, while lost to all the better feelings of woman's nature, and irreclaimably abandoned to the worst forms of idolatry, there remained no hope in the case of the queen, yet such a divine interposition might act for good on the mind of the king.

Midway the mountain there is an upland plateau, commanding a view of the entire plain. In this recess there is a noble fountain, three feet square, shaded by oaks, and rising above it is that bold and rocky peak which the prophet's servant ascended to watch the rising cloud. Here, in full view of Ahab's

[1] Isa., xxxv., 2. [2] Amos, i., 2.

palace, the sacrifices were offered. From the loose rocks that here abound were taken the stones to build the altars. From these forests was hewn the wood on which the offerings were placed. From this mountain spring, either miraculously preserved from becoming dry during the long drouth, or created by a divine power for the occasion, were drawn the twelve barrels of water to fill the trench around the altar of Elijah. From the pasture-fields below, up these slopes, came the bullocks to be sacrificed; while, covering the gentle declivities, and extending in vast concentric circles to the plain beneath, and clinging to every crag and tree above, the people were gathered to witness the most interesting of all sacrificial scenes. Around their altar stood the king and priests of Baal, while, wrapped in his mantle, Elijah stood alone. From morning till noon, and thence till evening, the prophets of idolatry implored their god in vain. With an irony that was biting as it was confusing, the prophet of Tishbe urged them to cry aloud. It was the dawn of his triumph. Sublime in his simplicity and strong in his isolation, Elijah invited the people near. Repairing the Lord's altar, he prepared the sacrifice, and, in answer to a prayer no less brief than fervent, the fire descended and the sacrifice was consumed, amid the acclamations of the people, "The Lord, he is the God!" As the defamers of religion and the enemies of God and man, the priests of Baal were led down to the banks of the Kishon, from which they had so recently come in such pomp, and were slain. Ahab and Elijah reascended the Mount, the former to eat and drink, the latter to pray. Hearing, in his prophetic ear, the sound of abundance of rain, Elijah sent his servant up to the loftiest of the mountain peaks to watch the rising cloud from the bosom of the sea. The heavens grew dark, the rain began to fall; and in fear lest the Kishon might not be fordable, Ahab was commanded to hasten to his palace; while, careless of his age, and in the spirit of a loyal subject to a king whom he had humbled in the presence of his people, Elijah girded up his loins, and ran before the chariot of Ahab to the entrance of Jezreel.[1]

Consecrated by an event so remarkable, Carmel subsequently became the abode of Elisha. It was while looking down, one afternoon, upon this same great plain he saw the "woman of Shunem" coming in behalf of her only son. He sent Gehazi

[1] 1 Kings, xviii.

to inquire the object of her visit; but she passed him by, and, pressing up this hill, laid her complaint before him. Descending from his mountain retreat, he hastened to her home of sorrow and restored her child to life.[1]

In after years Carmel was regarded with a superstitious veneration even by the learned heathen. Here Pythagoras passed some time in solitary meditations, and hither Vespasian came to consult the oracle which became so famous.

[1] 2 Kings, iv.

CHAPTER XII.

Plains of Palestine.—No Farm houses.—Great Plain of Esdraelon.—Its Fertility.—Topography. — River Kishon.—World's Battle-field.—Waters of Megiddo.—Deborah and her Victory.—Jeneen.—Bethshean.—Encampment.—Modern Sheikhs and ancient Patriarchs.—City of Ruins.—Jabesh Gilead.—Pella.—Gideon's Fountain.—Mount Gilboa.—Battles.—Jezreel. —Napoleon and the Turks.—Shunem.—Nain.—Endor.—Witch's Cave.— Saul and Samuel. — Witches. — Mount Tabor. — Its Form. — Woods. — View —Misnomer.—Transfiguration.—It occurred at Night.—Argument. —Benighted Party.

There are two classes of plains in Palestine—those upon the sea-board, as the Plains of Philistia, Sharon, and Phœnicia, and those of the interior, as the Plains of Rephaim, Jericho, El-Mukhna, the Bukâ'a, and Esdraelon. They differ from each other chiefly in location, the former being maritime, and consequently more or less affected by the action of the sea; the latter being inland, and subject to the influences of the lofty mountains by which they are encompassed. Though equally beautiful, fertile, and historically important, yet at present those upon the coast are less cultivated and less inhabited than the others, as the wild Bedouins, dreading the sea, prefer to pitch their tents in the interior. Nothing evinces the degeneracy of the Syrian Arabs more than the neglect of these vast garden-plains. Perhaps it is not so much a proof of their degeneracy, as the Turk in Syria has never been otherwise than what he now is—indolent as he is overbearing, the enemy of all improvements, and the destroyer of whatever is elegant in architecture or beneficial in good government. The proverbial richness of the soil of Palestine is evinced by the abundance of grain annually raised at the expense of the least possible labor. Without ever receiving, the land is ever giving. The superficial process of plowing resembles our mode of dragging, and the application of mineral and other kinds of manure is a thing unknown. One often and heartily desires to see an American farmer occupying these noble plains, with his enlightened views of agriculture and his improved implements of husbandry. What golden harvests, in more senses than one, would repay his toil! He would realize the prophetic blessings pronounced on Asher, "His bread shall be fat, and he shall yield royal dainties."

The custom of dwelling in villages, and not upon the land cultivated, is fatal to the thorough development of the natural resources of any country. You may travel for miles through the richest portions of Palestine without seeing a human habitation. In going from Etham to Hebron, a distance of 15 miles, and through a fertile region, we failed to see a single dwelling, though occasionally we observed a small village perched on a mountain top. The traveler never meets with the clean, comfortable farm-house so common in the agricultural districts of America. Here the people dwell in towns, and there is a matter-of fact meaning in the Savior's words, "A sower went forth to sow." If we except its eastern branches, there is not a single inhabited dwelling on the whole Plain of Esdraelon, and not more than one sixth of its soil is cultivated. Occasionally are seen the black tents of the nomadic Bedouin, who, despoiler-like, feeds his flocks till the crop is exhausted, and then removes to another section of rich pasturage, or, mounted on his fleet steed, scours the plain in search of plunder.

Whether considered as to the extent of its area, the fertility of its soil, the beauty of its scenery, or the political and religious importance of its history, the Plain of Esdraelon is the first of inland plains. The southern frontier of Zebulon, it fell to the lot of Issachar, "who saw that rest was good, and the land that it was pleasant;" and, rather than abandon his possession, "he bowed his shoulder to bear, and became a servant unto tribute."[1] Extending from the Mediterranean to the Jordan Valley, it is not unlike a vast rent in the heart of the land. Resembling in form an irregular triangle, its base extends a distance of 15 miles from Jenin to the mountains below Nazareth; and with one side measuring 12 miles long, formed by the Hills of Galilee, the other runs along the Samarian range a distance of 18 miles. Serving as the channel-bed of the ancient Kishon, its apex is a narrow pass half a mile wide, opening into the Plain of 'Akka. From its base three

[1] Gen., xlix., 15.

arms branch out toward the east, divided by Gilboa and Little
Hermon. With Tabor on one side and Little Hermon on the
other, the northern branch has Nain and Endor on its southern border, and was the path taken by the troops of Deborah
and Barak when on their way to the battle of Megiddo. Lying
between Gilboa and Jenin, the southern branch terminates
among the hills to the eastward. But, excelling the others in
extent and richness, the great central branch descends in green
and gentle slopes to the banks of the Jordan, having Jezreel
on the south and Shunem on the north, and is known in Scripture as the "Valley of Jezreel," where Gideon triumphed, and
Saul and his sons were slain. Having its most distant perennial source in the great fountain of Jenin, the famous river
Kishon flows through this plain in a northwesterly direction,
and pours its brackish waters into the sea. Called by the
Arabs Nakr el-Mukuttah, it is ordinarily a clear and rapid
stream, lined on either side with flowers and dense shrubbery.
Increased in the rainy season by numberless mountain torrents,
and by springs from the base of Carmel and from the bases of
the Hills of Nazareth, it varies in depth from four to eight feet,
and from 10 to 40 in width. It is evident that it must have
been swollen by some extraordinary means to have swept
away the fugitive army of Jabin. "The stars in their courses
fought against Sisera" may indicate a tremendous storm that
swept over mountain and plain, sending down torrents of water from the mountain streams, overflowing the steep banks
of the Kishon, and sweeping on to the sea with irresistible
force, bearing on its rapid current the routed foe, who, in the
confusion of defeat and flight, had become entangled in the
dense thickets that line its banks.

But the significance of Esdraelon is its marked history. It
is the battle-field of nations. The hosts of Israel and the wild
tribes of the ancient Canaanites have met in death-grapple
upon its soil, and in later times the powerful armies of Europe
contended on the fields of El-Fûleh with the barbarous hordes
of the Orient. Here Deborah and Barak marshaled their hosts
against Sisera; here Gideon encountered the Midianites; here
the Philistines fought against Saul and Jonathan; here Benhadad put the battle in array against Ahab; here Jehu slew
Ahaziah and Joram; here the knights of mediaeval times grap-
pled with the soldiers of the Crescent, and Napoleon and Klé-

ber led their splendid columns against the relentless Turks. It was a memorable day when we traversed this plain, recalling the clamor of war, and in fancy beholding the onset, the retreat, and fierce pursuit of mighty armies. And equally gratified were we that those scenes of death are past, and that flowers now bloom and harvests ripen where belligerent hosts once fought.

Descending from the heights of Carmel, we followed a winding path through wooded dells to the southwest corner of Esdraelon, and in half an hour reached Wady el-Melhor, "The Salt Valley," which forms the boundary-line between Carmel and the Mountains of Samaria. Up this ravine the French marched in 1799 to attack Ramleh. Fording the Kishon, our path lay along the base of the Samarian Hills, which are furrowed by deep gorges, eleven of which are the channels of as many streamlets flowing into the sacred river. Seven miles beyond is the battle-field of Megiddo. Here, sweeping along the base of a high mound, are the " waters of Megiddo," running northward into the Kishon. On the banks of this stream is the scene of that great battle between Barak and Sisera. Roused by the call of a woman, the former had assembled the northern tribes of Israel on the summit of Tabor, where he was joined by Deborah, who led to the fight the tribes of Central Palestine. Choosing Taanach as his rallying-point, the latter had concentrated his host with 900 iron chariots. Approaching from different points of the plain, the contending foes met hard by the "waters of Megiddo." Then it was that "the stars in their courses fought against Sisera," as at that moment a storm of sleet and hail gathered from the east, and, bursting over the plain in the face of the advancing Canaanites, threw them into confusion, and "the torrent swept them away."[1] Springing from his chariot, Sisera fled on foot into the neighboring mountains, where the nail of Jael awaited him who had escaped the sword of Barak. Then, in the moment of triumph, Deborah sang her wondrous song.[2]

Six centuries later, here Josiah, king of Judah, fought against Pharaoh-necho of Egypt, who was advancing to attack the King of Assyria, and here, in the "Valley of Megiddo, the archers shot at King Josiah, and he said, Have me away, for I am sore wounded."[3]

[1] Josephus, A. J., b. v.   [2] Judges, iv.   [3] 2 Chron., xxxv.

Following the southern border of Esdraelon, we reached Jeneen at sundown, where we encamped for the night upon its beautiful lawn. Taking an Arab guide, we started the next morning for the Beisân of the Arabs, the Scythopolis of the Romans, and the Bethshean of the Bible, on whose ancient walls the dead bodies of Saul and Jonathan were fastened after the fatal battle of Gilboa. Our path lay up a low ridge of limestone hills which overhung the valley of the Jordan on the west, and, crossing the summit, we descended to a noble plain, well watered, overgrown with rank weeds and briers, and dotted with the black tents of wandering Bedouins. Pausing for a moment, we examined, as far as modesty and safety would allow, the encampment of these nomads. Around their tents flocks and herds were grazing, watched by the faithful dog and guarded by mounted patrolmen, who scoured

WOMEN GRINDING AT A MILL.

the plain for a mile in circumference, to discover, if possible, the lurking-place of some neighboring plunderer. In an open

ABAU ENCAMPMENT.

tent "two women were grinding at a mill," while others were kneading bread and spinning flax. Every thing about the encampment wore the aspect of a semi-barbarous state, and the question rose in our minds more than once as to the tent-life of Abraham and his sons. In many points there is an evident similarity. Like the nomads of the present day, the patriarchs wandered from place to place; their property consisted of herds of cattle, and flocks of sheep and goats; their women, to whose lot it fell to grind, spin, and cook, occupied separate tents, as in modern times; and, like them, they were constantly liable to be surprised and plundered; hence then as now, all the males went armed for the protection of their property. But here the parallel ends. There is no comparison as to personal excellence, domestic refinement, and social dignity. If the words and acts of a man reveal his heart and manifest his condition, then the history of those venerable patriarchs bespeaks a purity of character, a refinement of social life, and a dignity of private and public behavior not unworthy the best state of society in this Christian age.

Reaching Bethshean at noon, we found a wretched modern village of 500 Egyptians, whom Ibrahim Pasha had colonized there to protect his frontier, but who are now cruelly oppressed by the wild nomads of the Ghôr. The ancient city was one of the strong-holds of Palestine, which the Israelites were never able to take. It lies in the line of the great caravan route from Damascus to Egypt, and is the same traveled by the Ishmaelites who bought Joseph. Like most of the cities of that distant age, it was built upon a hill, with a walled acropolis crowning the summit. Increasing in wealth and population, the limits of the town were extended to the plain below. Covering a space of more than three miles in circumference, the piles of massive ruins which remain no less indicate the strength of the position than the elegance and affluence of the city. The religious temples of Bethshean were the boast of its citizens, and, judging from the number and finish of the remaining marble columns, they must have equaled in magnificence those of more renowned places. But time has wrought what the marshaled hosts of Israel could not accomplish. Bethshean is a desolation; its site and environs are covered with acres of thorns and brambles; the famous Roman arch, that spanned the streamlet on the east, is broken;

the impregnable wall, upon which the lifeless bodies of Saul and his sons were suspended in derision, has fallen; the proud temples of Ashtaroth, that resounded with songs of triumph over the slain, are no more, and solitary columns rise up amid weeds and thistles, like spectres in the silent vales. The only remaining building is the amphitheatre, having a diameter of 180 feet. Though comparatively well preserved, with all the interior passages and doors nearly perfect, it is so overgrown with weeds and lacerating briers that we examined it with the greatest difficulty.

From the summit of the acropolis we obtained a view which was as interesting as it was commanding. Four hundred feet below us lay the Valley of the Jordan. Measuring more than three miles in width, it is every where well watered, green, and fertile, and dotted with thickets of tamarisk. Directly opposite rose the Mountains of Gilead, in the side of which stood the town of Jabesh Gilead, whose valiant men, under cover of the night, rescued the remains of Saul and his sons, and, recrossing the Jordan, interred them in their own town, beneath a venerable oak.[1] And in the same direction is the site of ancient Pella, the first city of refuge under the Christian dispensation. Called by the natives Tŭbŭkat Fahil, it is a plateau in the mountain's side 1000 feet above the Jordan. More than a mile in length, it is half a mile in width. The soil is a bright red, and the terrace is bordered with verdure, and so singularly formed that the mountains seemed to have receded to give place to the persecuted sons of God.

On leaving this city of ruins we crossed a stone bridge 35 feet wide and 75 long, and entered the "Valley of Jezreel." It is the central branch of the great plain of Esdraelon, and is bounded on the north by Little Hermon and on the south by Mount Gilboa, both of which ridges run eastward and overhang the Jordan valley. This vale is three miles wide, and through its centre flows the Jalûd to the Jordan, which is a clear and noble stream. Extending from its banks to the base of the hills on either side are fertile fields, on which, at intervals of two miles, were Arab encampments. To distinguish it from Mount Hermon proper, the ridge on the northern border of this vale is called Little Hermon, having received this appellation from the ecclesiastics of the fourth century, who er-

[1] Sam., xxxi.

roneously supposed, from its contiguity to Mount Tabor, that the Psalmist referred to it in that sublime passage: "The north and the south, thou hast created them; Tabor and Hermon shall rejoice in thy name."[1] Shapeless and barren, it has neither natural beauty nor historical interest. It has its greatest height toward the west, and its eastern end gradually slopes down into a broad plateau of table-land. But its companion ridge, known as Mount Gilboa, is at once remarkable for its appearance and its historical associations. It is neither high nor rugged, but low and rolling. At a distance it appears smooth and shadowy, but a nearer view reveals the slight gullies that furrow its sides and the bolder ledges projecting from its summit. In its northern base, less than two miles from Zer'in, is the large and famous fountain of 'Ain Jalûd, where Gideon's men evinced their courage by lapping water. Without exception, it is the most beautiful fountain in Palestine. Issuing from two deep caves at the base of Gilboa, the limpid water spreads out into a basin of solid rock 50 feet in diameter. The water is clear and delicious. From the sides and tops of the caverns depend trails of fern, maiden's hair, and other water-plants. Around the border of this basin, and on the banks of the stream that flows from it, is ample room where Gideon's men might have tested and proved their courage. Called by the inspired writer "the Well of Harod," or the "Spring of Trembling," it evidently derives its name from those decisive words of Jehovah : " Whosoever is fearful and afraid, let him return and depart early from Mount Gilboa."[2] For centuries this was the rendezvous of many a hostile army. From its pure waters Gideon crossed the plain at dead of night, and with his pitchers, and lights, and trumpets, surprised the Midianites;[3] and, years after, Saul encamped at the "Fountain of Jezreel."[4] Clad in disguise, he descended the southern border of the plain, and, crossing Little Hermon below Shunem, he went to consult the Witch of Endor as to the fortunes of the coming day. A little to the northwest from the spring the mighty army of the Philistines lay encamped before Shunem, and when the morning came they descended the gently-sloping plain and began the onset; and the fierce Amalekites drove the army of Saul up the rocky aclivi-

[1] Ps. lxxxix., 12.   [2] Judges, vii., 3.   [3] Ib., vii.
[4] 1 Sam., xxviii. and xxxi.

ties of Gilboa, where, on the favorite battle-field of the king and his sons, "The shield of the mighty was vilely cast away, even the shield of Saul, as though he had not been anointed with oil."[1]

In less than half an hour's ride from 'Ain Jalûd we stood amid the desolations of Jezreel, the empire city of Ahab, and the residence of his cruel and impious queen. Situated on the crest of a low spur projecting into the plain from Gilboa, it is but little higher than the plain itself, except on the north side, where there is a descent of 100 feet. Twenty miserable huts compose the modern town of Zer'in, together with a square antique tower called an "inn." Excepting a few sarcophagi, with sculptured ornaments and heaps of rubbish, there is nothing to remind the traveler of the royal city of Jezreel. Here the infatuated Jezebel planned the destruction of the Lord's prophet; and here, having first accomplished his death, she confiscated the property of Naboth, reserving for her weak-minded husband the long-coveted vineyard. Though no sign for its identification remains, it must have been to the east of her palace, as the two kings met the relentless Jehu coming from Ramoth Gilead, which is on the east, "in the portion of Naboth." Here, in the conflict that ensued, Joram was slain on the spot; the queen was trampled under the hoofs of Jehu's horses, while King Ahab, hoping to escape by flight over the plain to En-gannim, was overtaken by his pursuers, and died of his wounds at Megiddo.[2] Here all the sad details of the fearful judgments pronounced against the house of Ahab have been fulfilled, and, were it not for the imperishable places around, it would be impossible to identify the site of Jezreel, where Jezebel held her murderous orgies.

Three miles to the northwest, on the direct road to Nazareth, stands the tower of El-Fûleh, where Napoleon, with 3000 Frenchmen, successfully resisted the attack of 30,000 Turks during a period of six hours, and finally routed his powerful foe. But we had lingered too long on the heights of Zer'in, as night had set in, and we were an hour hunting for our encampment. Riding through fields of wheat and barley, we crossed the Valley of Jezreel, and, after a journey of three miles, arrived at the small village of Shunem, called by the inhabitants Sôlem. Though destitute of architectural elegance,

[1] 1 Sam., xxviii. and xxxi. [2] 1 Kings, xix. and xxii.

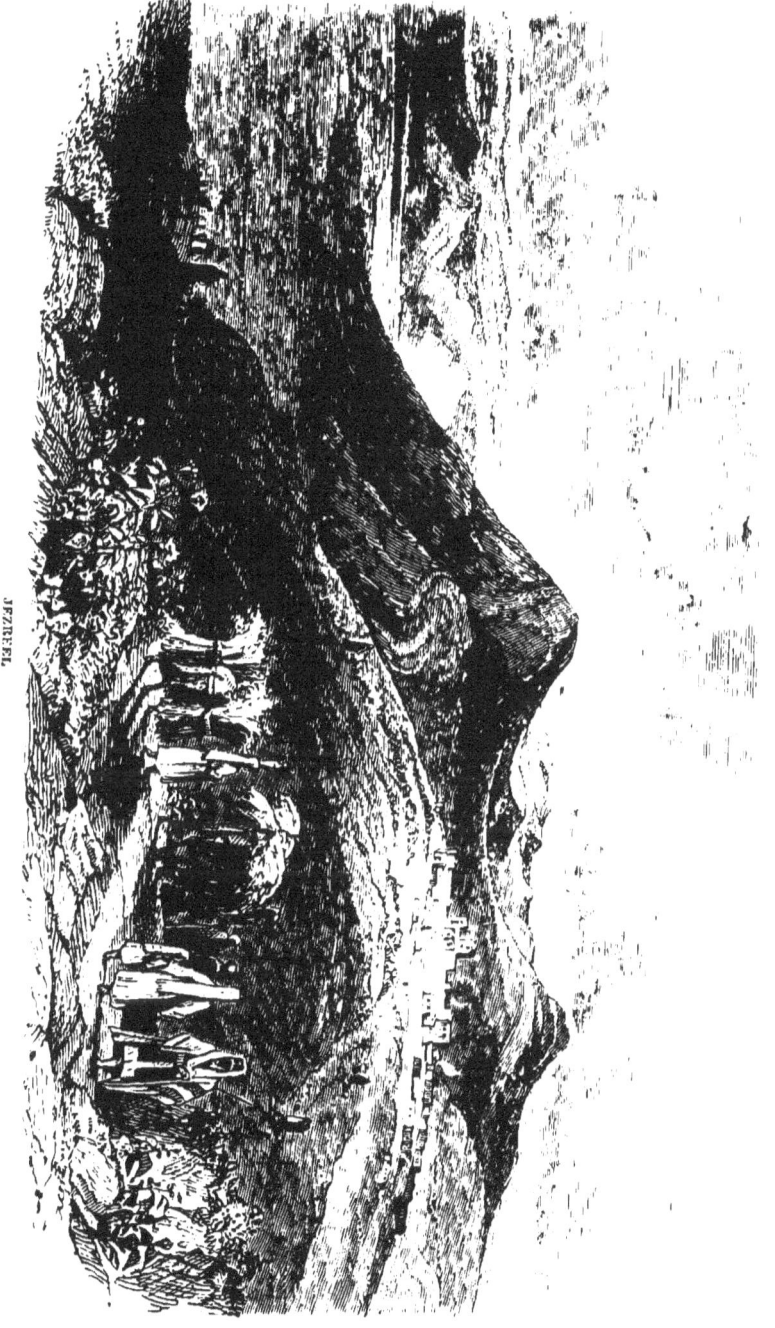

JEZREEL.

its environs are beautified with large and fruitful gardens. Occupying the lower slope of Little Hermon, it consists of a few Arab huts, without a single vestige of antiquity. Belonging to the tribe of Issachar, it was the home of that "great woman" who built a "little chamber on the wall" for the Prophet Elisha, and here she "embraced a son" as a reward for her hospitality, and received that son from the dead as a farther expression of the divine regard. Her house, with the "little chamber on the wall," is gone, but yonder is the field whither the child of promise "went to his father to the reapers," where he received the fatal *coup de soliel*, and from which he was carried back to his mother. Fifteen miles to the southwest, but in full view, is the blue ridge of Carmel, where the prophet and his servant Gehazi lived in solitude, and over this intervening plain the disconsolate mother rode to lay her complaint before the "man of God," who, yielding to entreaties, returned with her to Shunem, and called back the spirit of her departed son.[1] Behind the town is the "Hill of Moreh," along the base of which the Midianites lay when surprised by Gideon, and where the Philistines were encamped the night preceding the battle of Gilboa.

Winding round the western base of Little Hermon, in less than an hour we came to Nain, whose name is suggestive of the most tender associations. Situated on a low mountain spur, its dwellings are small and its inhabitants are few. Directly opposite, standing forth in all its beauty, is Mount Tabor, and rising up beyond, far away on the horizon, is the white cone of Hermon. Though fortune has lavished no favor on this quiet hamlet, yet Christ has linked its memory with one of his most touching miracles. To the east of the village are tombs in the hill-side, where the people now, as of old, bury their dead. It was probably to one of these ancient sepulchres that his neighbors were bearing the "young man" to his burial when Jesus, coming from the north, met the funeral procession, and in tones of divine compassion sweetly whispered to the disconsolate mother, "Weep not," while, with an authority that knew no barrier, he touched the bier and commanded, "Young man, I say unto thee, Arise."[2] Three miles to the northeast, located on a rocky acclivity, is the small village of Endor. The path thither crosses the northern shoul-

[1] 2 Kings, iv.   [2] Luke, vii.

der of Jebel ed-Duhy, and, entering the Plain of Esdraelon, diverges to the right up the hill on which the town stands. The transition between Nain and Endor is too sudden to be pleasant. Tender-hearted mothers and beguiling old witches are too unlike to be grouped together in the same picture or visited the same day. Endor is a wretched place of 30 huts, and the noble view afforded from its rocks is the only natural charm of the village. The sides of the hills that rise above it contain many large and curious caves, some of which are used for human habitations. Tradition has designated the most remarkable one of the number as the sibylline home of the famous witch of Endor. It is a deep and solemn cave. The entrance is guarded by two massive rocks, between which there is a large fig-tree, imparting an air of secrecy to the spot. Within the cavern is a spring of crystal water, and from the rocks above and on either side trails of maiden's hair depend like curtains of Mechlin lace. From its inner chambers come deep and mournful echoes, and the alternate light and darkness within gives to the cave an air of witchery. Placed under the ban of the kingdom, with a price set upon her head, it is not unreasonable that the Pythoness of Endor should have sought a retreat so difficult of access in which to perform her necromantic feats. Celebrated for her skill, it was to her the troubled Saul repaired, in the darkness of an ever-memorable night and in the disguise of a peasant, to revive, if possible, his broken spirit by hopeful disclosures of the coming day. With a duplicity only equaled by her depravity, she evoked the venerable Samuel. Not in obedience to her call, but to forewarn the heart-broken king, the venerable prophet, "covered with a mantle," appeared, and announced with more than Delphic authority, "To-morrow shalt thou and thy sons be with me."[1]

The witch of Endor has left to her female descendants the impress of her brazen-facedness. There is an archness in their countenances and a boldness in their behavior not characteristic of woman in any other part of Palestine. Mounting a horse like a man, they ride with a swiftness and daring hardly excelled even by the plundering Bedouin. Destitute of all those finer virtues which belong to Christian womanhood, they are as vicious as they are uncouth. Not suspecting their honesty,

[1] 1 Sam., xxviii.

NAIN

I had left a leather pouch upon the ground which contained many valuables while I pressed a few ferns from the sibyl's cave. Returning to the spot, it was gone. All swore by the beard of the Prophet they had not seen it. Threats made no impression upon their fears, and they smiled in scorn at being reported to the Pasha. In a moment the town was aroused, and our threats were returned with a shower of stones; but, revolver in hand, we commenced the search of every hovel. Descending a narrow pass in the rocks, I saw a woman standing in the mouth of a cave whose countenance excited my suspicion, and, offering her a *baksheesh*, she drew from the ample folds of her bosom the stolen pouch, with a shamelessness not unworthy Endor's elder witch.

Three miles to the north, diagonally across the northern branch of Esdraelon, stands the Mount of Transfiguration. Whether considered for its natural beauty or as the scene of many thrilling historic events, Tabor is second only to Olivet in religious interest among all the sacred mountains. Separated from the surrounding hills except on the northwest, it stands out alone, having its base swept by the magnificent Plain of Esdraelon. Its shape changing with the stand-point of the beholder, it is not easy to define its graceful form. Having seen it from every point of the compass, its variant forms added not a little to my impressions of its extraordinary beauty. Viewed from the Heights of Carmel, it resembled a truncated cone; seen from the northern Hills of Galilee, it reminded me of the Pyramids of Egypt; from the Mountains of Samaria it appeared like the segment of a great circle; while from the summit of Jebel ed-Duhy and from the plain below it was not unlike a terraced mound or woodland park. More than two thirds of its sides on the east and north, up to its very summit, are covered with noble oaks and beautiful terebinths, not densely like a forest, but with open glades between oaken groves, adorned with grass, and strewn with pheasant-eyes, anemones, and amaranths. Its summit is an oblong area half a mile long and a quarter wide, broken into charming vales and hillocks, enhancing the delights of the spot. In ascending to the top the path resembled the threads of a screw, winding in gentle acclivities up to the highest peak. Now it led through groves of terebinths, now over flowery beds, now verging on the edge of a bold precipice, now entering dells sombre with the thick foliage of stately oaks, and anon opening into glades where the grass was green and the flowers fragrant. Though the heat was intense without, the path was so smooth and shady that we gained the loftiest point in less than an hour, where we were refreshed alike by the unbroken silence of the scene and the unrivaled glory of the view.

Tabor rises 2000 feet above the level of the sea, and the prospect from its summit is one of extraordinary grandeur. The eye sweeps over the Mountains of Samaria, the long ridge of Carmel, the Bay of Haifa, the Plain of 'Akka, the Hills of Galilee, the lofty peak of Safed, the "Horns of Hattin," the majestic form of Hermon, the gray walls of Moab, the dark

MOUNT TABOR.

line of verdure defining the banks of the Jordan, while nearer are the slopes of Gilboa, the rocks of Duhy, and the glorious Plain of Esdraelon, like one unbroken sea of verdure, with its borders dotted with the hamlets of Jezreel, El-Fuleh, Shunem,

Nain, and Endor. And no less significant is the thrilling history of Tabor. Tabor was the northern boundary-line of the tribe of Issachar;[1] here the heroic Deborah and Barak assembled the children of Zebulon and Naphtali to fight against Sisera;[2] years later it was the rendezvous of the brothers of Gideon—"each one resembled the children of a king"—whom Zebah and Zalmunna slew;[3] and at a later period it became the scene of Israel's idolatry, whose priests Hosea denounces for having "been a snare on Mizpah and a net spread on Tabor."[4] Bold in its outline and firm upon its everlasting base, the inspired writers chose it as a symbol of glory—"Tabor and Hermon shall rejoice in thy name,"[5] and as typical of the Lord's unchangeable word, "Surely as Tabor is among the mountains, and as Carmel is by the sea, so shall Pharaoh come."[6] Naturally one of the strong-holds of the land and the key of the plain, it became in our own era the head-quarters of Josephus, as it had been in the year 218 B.C. the strong-hold of Antiochus the Great. But there is one historic honor which does not belong to Tabor, and, if it did, would not enhance the glory of its associations. Proverbial for the application of real or fancied names to the scenes of the great events in their martial annals, and ever fond of a high-sounding name, the French have designated the conflict which occurred on the Plains of El-Fuleh as the "Battle of Mount Tabor." But as the village of El-Fuleh, where Kleber met the advanced guard of the Turks, and which afterward became the central point of attack, is ten miles to the southeast from Tabor, with equal propriety it might have been called the battle of Mount Carmel, and with greater consistency the battle of Mount Gilboa. The simple fact of Napoleon's army coming from Nazareth and sweeping round the northeastern base of Tabor is not sufficient to justify the misnomer, nor warrant the application of the name of this most sacred of "mountains" to a battle fought by a chieftain who had invaded the Holy Land on an ambitious crusade.

But the glory of Tabor is the transfiguration of our Lord. Anxiously I sought to identify the spot of that wondrous scene, that I might look up into the same serene heavens from which came the voice of approval, and in which appeared Moses and

---

[1] Josh., xix.   [2] Judges, iv.   [3] Ib., viii.
[4] Hosea, v.   [5] Ps. lxxxix.   [6] Jer., xlvi., 18.

Elias. High up on the northern slopes, far away from the ruins of the ancient village, is a lovely glade, inclosed with oaks and adorned with flowers. Shut in from the world, all nature breathes a sense of repose, and a holy quiet reigns within undisturbed. The view of the blue skies is unobstructed, and here in the "stilly night," watched only by the stars, the Son of God held converse with Moses and Elias touching "his decease which he should accomplish at Jerusalem;" and, as a pre-intimation of his glorified body after his ascension, "the fashion of his body was altered, and his raiment was white and glistening."

For nearly sixteen centuries Tabor has been regarded as the veritable scene of this great event, and not till within a few years has its claim been called in question. The chief argument against this venerable tradition is drawn from the itinerary of the Evangelists, in which Cæsarea Philippi is mentioned as the last place where Christ had taught previous to his transfiguration. It has been suggested that the probable scene of the event is somewhere on the southern ridge of Hermon. More than once, while on its noble summit, I had occasion to regret that the doubt of its identity had been suggested to my mind, and the more so as the author of the suggestion had nothing better to offer; but the examination which I felt compelled to make not only removed all reasonable doubts, but, proving entirely satisfactory, confirmed the impression of earlier years, and added to the joy of the moment. If our Lord had been transfigured immediately or on the next day after the conversation with his disciples touching men's opinions as to himself, there would be some force in the objection; but two of the evangelists inform us that the event occurred six days[1] after this conversation, and St. Luke assures us it took place "about eight days after these sayings."[2] The distance between Cæsarea Philippi and the summit of Tabor is less than 18 hours, or less than 54 miles, which, on foot or otherwise, can be accomplished in less than three days, thus giving sufficient time for the journey between the two places. And it is a fact equally significant, that immediately after our Lord had been transfigured we find him in the vicinity of Tabor at Capernaum, which is but 21 miles over an excellent road to the northeast; thence crossing the Jordan at the head of the lake,

[1] Matt., xvii., 1; Mark, ix., 2.   [2] Luke, ix., 28.

"he departed from Galilee, and came into the coasts of Judea beyond Jordan;"[1] all of which is consistent with the location of the several places in leaving Mount Tabor for the north, but which would not be true if our Lord came southward from the slopes of Hermon. It has also been objected that, from the days of Joshua to the time of Antiochus the Great, Tabor has been an inhabited mountain, and, as such, would have been inappropriate for the retirement of Christ and his three disciples; but history simply intimates that during fifteen centuries the mount had been the rendezvous of belligerent armies, and that, in process of time, its summit was fortified; but in the times of Josephus the defenses had fallen into decay, and he caused them to be rebuilt about thirty years subsequent to our Lord's ascension. If inhabited at all when Christ ascended its verdant slopes, it was only by a few wretched villagers, such as may be seen in their mud huts, or clinging to ancient ruins in other parts of Palestine; and, though its summit were inhabited, yet, owing to the peculiar configuration of the mount, its high northern acclivities are singularly retired. It is a remarkable fact, that, though accustomed to withdraw from the world for meditation and prayer, Christ never chose a "howling wilderness" as the place of his devotion, but always an inhabited mountain. Even the Mount of Olives, rendered doubly sacred by the frequency of his presence, was in his day, as now, a populous mountain, but in some of its wooded dells was his bower of prayer. Jesus sought the haunts of men, and, like a great warrior sleeping in the midst of his camp, he was ever with his people. St. Luke more than intimates that the transfiguration occurred during the darkness and silence of the night. Referring to the miracle wrought immediately after the descent, he states, "And it came to pass, that on the next day, when they were come down from the hill, much people met him."[2] Such an hour for the display of the divine majesty was singularly appropriate. During the day he would have been subject to intrusion from wandering shepherds and strolling hunters on any mountain in Palestine; but under the cover of the night he would have been unmolested by either, as the former are stationary in the midst of their flocks at that time, and the latter are unable to pursue their vocation. If the vision transpired in the daytime, why were the disciples overcome with

[1] Matt., xvii., 24, and xix., 1.   [2] Luke, ix., 37.

sleep? The suggestion of Peter to build three tabernacles or booths, or provide some temporary shelter made of branches of trees, according to a custom still prevalent in the East, is more than an intimation that night had overtaken them, and, supposing their heavenly guests would tarry with them, they desired to shelter them from the dews of the night.

It was two o'clock on Saturday afternoon when we left the small village of Debûrieh, at the base of Mount Tabor, for the Sea of Galilee. Riding up a fruitful valley, in an hour we came to a branching road—one branch leading directly to Tiberias, and the other to the mouth of the Jordan. Either from ignorance or villainy, an Arab directed us to follow the latter path, which caused us to be benighted, and greatly endangered our safety. The mistake, however, was to our advantage in the end, as we passed through a tract of country rarely visited by travelers, owing to the turbulent and thievish character of the population. Turning eastward, the path lay along the crest of a mountain ridge, where the peasantry of both sexes were engaged in husbandry. Occasionally we passed the extensive ruins of unknown towns, and now and then entered villages remarkable only for their wretchedness and filth. Whether to display their horsemanship or test our courage, three mounted Arabs, armed with Bedouin swords, pistols, and lances 20 feet long, issued from one of those miserable hamlets, and, singing a war-song, dashed by us at a furious speed, when, suddenly wheeling, with their lances leveled at our breasts, they rushed toward us as if to plunge us through. Finding their equestrian feats neither awakened our fears nor inspired our admiration, they returned to their village and allowed us to pursue our unfrequented path. From the summit of the mountain we were crossing we gained a noble view of the Vale of Tiberias and its circlet of green hills. Cheered by the prospect of reaching our destination at an early hour, we rapidly descended 1000 feet into the wild gorge of Fejas, flanked by lofty mountains, and followed the banks of a beautiful stream lined with shrubbery and gorgeous oleanders. Charmed with the surrounding scenery, and confiding in our Arab guide, we passed the hours happily, nor were our suspicions aroused that we had been misdirected till it was too late to retrace our steps. Referring to our maps, we found ourselves in the wild and uninhabited Vale of Fejas, which terminates in the valley of the Jordan, 10 miles to the south from Tiberias. Straining our eyes, as we wound round each jutting cliff, to catch a glimpse through the opening hills of the vale we had seen from the heights above, at length, in the dusk of the evening, we reached the upper terraces of the Jordan. Under other circumstances we would have surveyed the new landscape with delight; but we were now benighted, miles from a human habitation, in a country notorious for its robberies, and with skies already black with the coming storm. Closing up together so as to form a circle with our horses, we held a council, and discussed the question of advancing or encamping for the night. Far to the east, beyond the rushing river, we could discover, by its faint lights, the solitary village of Kanâtir, but were not near enough to reach it before we should be overtaken by the darkness and the storm. Tiberias was 10 miles to the north; night was now upon us; the skies were cloudy; the rain began to fall; the path to the ancient capital of Galilee was unknown, and we were without a guide. Against remaining where we were were the serious facts that our cuisine was empty, and we were without provender for our mules and horses. Deciding to proceed, we forded several torrents, and, on ascending a broad upland plateau, in the darkness of the hour plunged into a marsh, into which our horses sank to their haunches. Crossing a barley-field which had been reaped, we met two mounted Arabs, whom we understood to say that Tiberias was but half an hour to the north. Cheered by the good news, we urged on our jaded beasts to their utmost speed, now stumbling over rocks, now floundering in the soft, marshy soil. But, as we advanced, the darkness increased; each friendly star had withdrawn its guiding ray, and the rain fell in torrents. Part of the company made directly for the shore, while two of us continued on the upland to report the first glimmer of the distant lights of Tiberias. Onward we rode; the hours dragged heavily by. Near midnight the clouds dispersed, and familiar stars came out one by one, and looked softly down upon the lost and weary travelers. The beautiful lake lay quietly in its mountain bed, and the repose of night rested on all nature, undisturbed save by the rippling wave breaking faintly on the pebbled shore, or the sudden leap of the jackal or flight of the stork, startled by the sound of our coming. Beguiling the weary hours by the recollections of the past, hunger and fatigue were forgotten as the visions of other years rose up before my mind, and, by the realization of a sublime faith, I beheld the Redeemer treading the troubled bosom of Gennesaret in the darkness and storm of night, as in the days of old. It was now past midnight; we had failed to reach Tiberias; we knew not the distance to be traveled; and, determining to encamp, we pitched our tents upon the sandy beach, tethered our hungry horses, and, contenting ourselves with a little rice and mish-mish, we laid down to fitful slumber.

The peaceful Sabbath dawned without a cloud. While yet the night struggled with the morn, I ascended a bold bluff, commanding a glorious view. The skies were soft and warm; the mellow light of day lined the east; the sea was placid as an embowered lake, and the surrounding hills were yet dreamy with the haze of night. The impressions of that hour were as hallowed as their memory is imperishable. It was the first time, by the light of day, that I looked upon that most sacred of lakes. Returning to the tent, we learned, to our happy surprise, from a passing Arab, that we were within half an hour's ride of Tiberias. Compelled by the necessities of the case, we passed quietly up the coast and encamped within the walls of the ancient city just as the Jewish population, attired in their most costly robes, were hastening to their devotions around the sepulchres of their fathers.

CHAPTER XIII.

Jerusalem and Capernaum the great Centres of our Lord's Ministry.—Christ a limited Traveler.—Judea and Galilee contrasted.—Provinces of Galilee.—The Herods.—Meaning of Galilee.—Sea of Galilee.—Its Characteristics.—Hallowed Associations.—Imperial City of Tiberias.—Founded by Herod Antipas.—His Crimes.—John the Baptist.—It became a Jewish City and the Metropolis of the Race.—Home of eminent Scholars.—Now an Arab Town.—Citizens.—Miraculous Draught of Fishes.—Jesus never visited it —Warm Baths of Tiberias.—Site of Tarichea.—Naval Engagement —Bridge of Semakh.--River Jarmuk.—City of Gadara.—Ruins.—Tombs.—Not the Scene of the Destruction of the Swine.—Argument.—Ruins of Gamala —Near here was the Scene of the Miracle.—Mouth of the Jordan.—Bethsaida Julias.—Feeding of the Five Thousand.—Our Lord Walking on the Sea.—Home of Mary Magdalene. —Rich Plain of Gennesaret —Parables.—Site of Capernaum.—Fountain of the Fig.—Thrilling History of the City as connected with Christ.—The Woe.—Desolation.—Bethsaida.—Birthplace of Peter, James, and John. —Not Bethsaida Julias.—Influence of natural Scenery upon the Formation of Character —Chorazin.—Sudden Gale upon the Sea.—Extensive Remains of the City.—Without an Inhabitant.—Upper Jordan.—Waters of Merom.—Tell el-Kâdy --- City of Dan.—Its Fountain.—Cæsarea Philippi.—Town of Hasbeiya.—Fountain.—Highest perennial Source of the Jordan.—Mount Hermon.—Vast and grand Prospect from its lofty Summit.—Scriptural Allusions.—"Valley of the Pigeons."—Sublime Ravine.—Mount of Beatitudes.—Battle of Hattin.—Defeat of the Crusaders. —Triumph of Saladin.—Route to Nazareth.—Its authentic History is not older than the Christian Era.—Its Valley and Mountains.—Population —Schools.—Legendary Sites.—Scene of the Annunciation.—House and Shop of Joseph.—Pictures.—Fountain.—Beautiful Girls of Nazareth. —Mount of Precipitation.—True Mount.—View.—Scene of our Lord's Childhood and Manhood.

GALILEE and Judea share the mutual honor of having been the principal spheres of our Lord's public life. Indeed, those spheres may be reduced to two central points, Jerusalem and Capernaum. Occasionally we trace his footsteps to the Mediterranean—"to the coasts of Tyre and Sidon" in the west, and among the mountains of Gilead, beyond the Jordan, on the east; but it is an extraordinary fact that he never went south of Jerusalem, not even to the city that gave him birth, and only as far north as Cæsarea Philippi. Though a limited and infrequent traveler, he chose the great centres of life in which to unfold the doctrines he came to announce, and to perform the miracles he offered to mankind in attestation of his divine mission. As the scene of his death, resurrection, and ascension, Jerusalem will ever stand pre-eminent in Christian affection; but Capernaum will ever be memorable as the city of his adoption after his rejection by the ungrateful Nazarenes. Spending most of his public life on the shores of the Galilean Sea, he called his apostles from the fisheries of Gennesaret; from its teeming population he founded his infant Church; among its inhabitants he performed his grandest miracles; to them he delivered his most impressive parables; and overhanging the sea is the "Mount of Beatitudes," the pulpit from which he preached his incomparable "sermon on the mount." In contrast to the cruel treatment he received in Judea, the Galileans ever welcomed him to their cities, and "great multitudes followed him whithersoever he went." And after the lapse of so many centuries, it is while passing through a region of associations and memories so hallowed that the traveler of to-day realizes the presence of the Lord more than in other parts of the Holy Land.

At the death of Herod the Great his kingdom was divided into three parts, over which his sons reigned. With his accustomed precision and accuracy, St. Luke not only recognizes this historic fact, but defines the territory of each division.[1] To Archelaus was assigned Idumea, Judea, and Samaria, which embraced all that portion of Palestine from the Jordan to the Mediterranean, and from Beersheba to the northern border of Esdraelon. Ancient Idumea included that district of country lying south of Judea, and extending from the southern end of the Dead Sea to the Gulf of Akabah; but the Idumea of the Herodian era embraced only the northern section of the Desert of Tih, together with several towns of Southern Palestine, with Hebron as the capital city. Though subdued by the warlike Maccabees, and by them subjected to the rule of Jewish prefects, the Idumæans of this latter period rose to favor under Cæsar, who appointed Antipater procurator of all Judea, and subsequently his son, Herod the Great, became "King of the Jews."

[1] Luke, iii., 1.

To Herod Antipas was allotted all Galilee, together with the district of Perea, which includes that part of Palestine east of the Jordan to Arabia, and south of Pella to Machaerus, and which in the New Testament is called the "coasts of Judea beyond Jordan."[1]

To Herod Philip were given Iturea and Trachonitis. The former extends from the northern border of Jaulân[2] to the banks of the Jennâny, and from the eastern base of Hermon to the great caravan road to Mecca; and the latter, adjoining Iturea on the east, includes the lesser provinces of Batanea,[3] Gaulonitis,[4] and Auranitis, or the modern Hauran.

St. Luke also mentions the province of Abilene, which is north of Iturea, and extends within 12 miles of Damascus. "It originally included Heliopolis and Iturea, with the mountain region lying between,"[5] and had Chalcis as the capital city, the ruins of which remain. According to Strabo, Ptolemy, the son of Menneaus, was ruler of the province, who, after the annexation of Syria by the Romans, continued to hold his possessions till succeeded to the throne by his son Lysanias. Transferring the seat of his government to Abila, on the banks of the ancient Abana, he reigned till murdered through the artifices of Cleopatra, to whom the kingdom was given by Mark Antony. Subsequently passing into the hands of the tyrant Zenodorus, the province ultimately reverted to a descendant of Lysanias, bearing the same name, and who was "tetrarch of Abilene."[6]

The term Galilee is as old as Joshua.[7] Signifying a "circle" or "circuit," it was originally applied to the region about Kadesh, "a city of refuge."[8] In the reign of Solomon it designated the area containing the twenty cities he gave to Hiram of Tyre, which were afterward known as the "coasts of Tyre and Sidon," and which, in the lapse of time, having become colonized by strangers, received the name of "Galilee of the Gentiles," or of the "nations."[9] Under the jurisdiction of the Romans, Galilee was the designation of all that magnificent region embracing the ancient tribeships of Issachar, Zebulun, Asher, and Naphtali, which extended from the Plain of Esdraelon to Mount Hermon, and from the Jordan to the Mediterranean.

[1] Matt., xix., 1.   [2] Bashan.   [3] Bathanyeh.   [4] Jaulân.
[5] Porter.   [6] Josephus, Antiq., b. xix., c. v., s. 1.
[7] Josh., xx., 7.   [8] Ib.   [9] Isa., ix., 1; Matt., iv., 15.

According to Josephus, this vast section of Palestine was divided into two parts, "called the Upper Galilee and the Lower."[1] The latter was bounded on the south by a line drawn from Carmel to Scythopolis, and on the north by a line extending from the Bay of Akka to Tiberias, and the former extended from this latter line on the south to Hermon on the north, and from this point westward to the sea.

Whether considered geographically or historically, the Sea of Tiberias is the most remarkable feature in the physical geography of Galilee. Either from a town upon its ancient shore or from its harp-like shape, it was early called "the Sea of Chinnereth."[2] At later periods it was successively called the "Sea of Tiberias,"[3] from the imperial city of that name standing on its western coast; the "Sea of Galilee,"[4] because it belonged to the province of Galilee; and, finally, the "Lake of Gennesaret," corrupted from Cinnereth, the title of a noble plain on its northwestern shore.[5] With a depression of 650 feet below the level of the Mediterranean, it is 13 miles long, six wide, and 165 feet deep. Lying in a volcanic basin, its form is oval and its sides are shelving. Unlike the lofty and rugged mountains which encompass the Scotch and Italian lakes, the surrounding hills are neither high nor uniform. On the eastern coast they are steep and barren, and rise to the height of 2000 feet; on the west they are not so lofty, but smooth, more sloping, and are dotted with trees and tufts of grass, and are furrowed by gentle ravines. At either end the western hills retire, permitting the Jordan to enter the sea on the north and to find an exit on the south. The shores are alternately smooth and rocky. The smoother portions are strewn with beautiful shells, while at intervals the everlasting hills plant their dark feet upon the whitened beach. Through an open cliff and between grassy slopes numberless streamlets pour their crystal waters into the sea, and on their green banks gorgeous oleanders bloom and tropical flowers fill the air with their perfume. The water is clear, cool, and sweet, and abounds with fish, as in the days of Bethsaida's fishermen. Though it is almost uniformly calm, there are times when the winds rush down the mountain gorges and up the Jordan valley, lashing

[1] Wars of the Jews, b. iii., c. iii., s. 1.
[2] Num., xxxiv., 11: Josh., xix., 35.
[3] John, xxi., 1.
[4] Ib., vi., 1.
[5] Matt., xiv., 34.

TIBERIAS AND THE SEA OF GALILEE.

the placid waters into foam, and causing the waves to roll high and furiously. Its beauty is most apparent in the freshness of the morning, or amid the golden tints and purple shadows of evening; or in the sweet repose of a summer's moonlight night, when the serene skies, with moon and stars, are mirrored on its quiet bosom; or during the solemn grandeur of a thunderstorm, when the heavens scowl, the wild winds rage, the lightning darts through the gloom in bars of fire or in sheets of light, and along the trembling mountains the thunder rolls responsive to the waves that madly break upon the rock-bound shore.

Other lakes are more exquisitely beautiful; others present to the eye loftier forms of grandeur; but as it is impossible for the mind to dissociate the historical from a scene like this, so the presence of that Divine One has imparted to the "Sea of Galilee" an unparalleled beauty, and his divine works have rendered it the most sacred of earthly lakes. On its northwestern shore stood the city of his adoption; from the deck of one of its fishing-boats he taught the multitude; over its calm waters he often sailed on a voyage of mercy, or to a "desert place" for prayer; on its troubled bosom, as on a pavement of adamant, he walked in the "fourth watch of the night;" twice he rose in majesty, "rebuked the winds," and said to the waves, "Peace, be still;" and on its shores he met his disciples after his passion and resurrection.

Four miles from the southern end of the lake, and occupying a plain two miles long and less than half a mile wide, stands the once imperial city of Tiberias. Though only mentioned by the sacred writers in connection with the sea, it fills no inconsiderable portion of the political history of Galilee. Whether built upon the site of the ancient city of Chinnereth or not, it evidently covers, in part, the site of some old town, as sepulchres of great antiquity are on the sloping plain. Coming in possession of Galilee, Herod Antipas founded the new city, made it the capital of his kingdom, and named it after his friend and patron, the Emperor Tiberius. Inviting citizens from all parts to take up their residence within its walls, he granted them extraordinary privileges, and spared neither art nor treasure to render it worthy of his throne and palace. Here, in the day of his pride and luxury, he so far forgot the respect due the marriage covenant and the obligations of consanguinity as to marry Herodias, his brother Philip's wife. For an offense so grave and notorious the faithful and courageous John the Baptist reproved the king, who, under the pretense of fearing lest John might take advantage of his own popularity and instigate a rebellion, ordered his arrest, and imprisoned him in the tower of Machaerus. It was here in his royal palace, while holding a feast in honor of his birthday, that Salome, the daughter of his incestuous wife, danced before him, and pleased him to such a degree that he swore to give her whatever she should ask, "to the half of his kingdom." Influenced by her infamous mother, Salome asked for "John's head in a charger." Bound by his promise, the king reluctantly yielded, and dispatching one of his guards, the noblest and purest of prophets fell a victim to the revenge of a woman smarting under rebuke, and to the cowardice of a prince whose mortified pride was only excelled by the fears that tormented the dreams of his nights and the vision of his days. Whether intentionally or otherwise, Josephus has given us the pretense of John's death rather than the true cause, in asserting that Antipas feared lest he might cause a revolt; but, as if half conscious of the injustice he had done the character of so eminent a prophet, the Jewish historian tells us that the Jews attributed the subsequent misfortunes of Herod to the death of John the Baptist. Retributive justice was speedily visited upon the son of Herod the Great. Having divorced his first wife, who was the daughter of a celebrated Arabian prince, that he might marry Herodias, Aretas, the father of the divorced wife, resolved to avenge the affront offered to his daughter, and declared war against Herod, and in a single battle vanquished his ungrateful son-in-law, and literally destroyed his army.

Jealous of the prosperity of her brother Agrippa, who from a private citizen had become king of Judea, Herodias persuaded Antipas to visit Rome and request the same dignity from the Emperor Caius. Learning of the conspiracy, Agrippa anticipated the arrival of his uncle, and accused Antipas of conspiracy against Tiberius, and asserted that he was then carrying on a correspondence with Artabanus, king of Parthia, against the Romans. Convinced of the justness of the accusation, the emperor banished him to Lyons, and afterward to Spain, where he and his wife Herodias died in exile.[1]

[1] Matt., xiv. Josephus, Antiq., b. lxxviii., c. v.

Tiberias subsequently bore a conspicuous part in the wars which terminated in the destruction of Jerusalem, and especially during the command of Josephus in Galilee, who fortified the city; but it afterward capitulated to the victorious Vespasian. By this act of voluntary submission Tiberias escaped destruction, and remained undisturbed during those commotions ending in the overthrow of the Jewish commonwealth. Regarding it, with Hebron, Jerusalem, and Safed, as one of their four holiest cities, it became the chief city of the Jews after the destruction of their renowned capital; and, subsequently to their expulsion from Judea, they removed the Sanhedrim first to Jamnia, on the Plain of Philistia, then to Sefforis, and finally, in the middle of the second century, to Tiberias, which for three centuries continued the metropolis of the race. Here, amid those centuries of comparative repose, the most eminent of rabbins of the nation taught in the synagogues, and founded a school for the study of their law and language. As the head of this academy, Rabbi Judah collected and committed to writing the great mass of Jewish traditional law now known as the Mishnah, which was completed about the year 200 A.D. A century later, Rabbi Jochanan here compiled the Gemara as a supplement and commentary to the former work, and which is now usually called the Jerusalem Talmud. And from the same school, at a later period, emanated that critical work called the Masorah, at once designed to preserve the purity of the Hebrew text of the Old Testament and of the language in which it was written.[1]

Sharing the fortunes of other Syrian cities, Tiberias is now an Arab town. Occupying a plain on the shore, formed by the mountains receding, it is encompassed by a wall 20 feet high, 100 rods long, and 40 wide. Describing an irregular parallelogram, the wall is supported by 10 round towers on the west, five on the north, eight on the south, and three on the east. Only one half of the space within the inclosure is occupied by the present population. Most of the buildings are small and filthy, and the streets are neither clean nor straight. The pasha's house and a Mohammedan mosque are the only edifices worthy of attention. The Moslems, who are in the ascendant, number about 1200. The Jews, who are estimated at 800, have a distinct quarter, which is in the centre

[1] Robinson, B. R., vol. ii.

of the town. Like those in Jerusalem, they are divided into two sects—the Sephardim, who are chiefly from Northern Africa and Spain, and the Askenazim, who are fugitives from Russia. As a class they are intelligent, well dressed, and of more comely appearance than those found in other portions of Palestine. The young men are athletic and manly in their bearing, and many of the younger Jewesses are more than ordinarily beautiful. As we entered the gates of the city at an early hour on a charming Sabbath morning, crowds of white-veiled Jewesses and of venerable Jews, with long gray beards, were slowly winding their way up the mountains that rise steeply behind the city, to offer their prayers at the sepulchres of Rabbis Jochanan, Akabi, Maimonides, and others of their ancestors. Still looking for the Messiah, they entertain a prevalent tradition that he will rise from the sea, land first in the city of Tiberias, and thence proceed to establish his throne on the summit of Safed, a lofty and imposing mountain situated 15 miles to the northwest. Christianity in Tiberias is represented by a solitary Latin monk. On the shore, to the north of the Jews' Quarter, is a small convent, traditionally marking the spot where the Savior met the disciples after his resurrection, and where was landed the miraculous draught of fishes.[1] But, judging from the silence of all the evangelists, it is probable our Lord never visited this renowned city. The population was composed of strangers and slaves, unto whom he was not sent, and the city was built in part upon a cemetery, which, according to a Jewish law, rendered whoever entered therein ceremonially unclean; therefore the chief object of his mission and the law of Moses justified him in not entering its gates. It is, however, as remarkable as it is inexplicable that Christ should have spent so much of his public life in the vicinity of this lake, where he was universally known, and never have been seen by Herod Antipas till they met in Jerusalem. St. Luke informs us that "Herod the tetrarch heard of all that was done by him, and he was perplexed, because that it was said of some that John was risen from the dead, and of some that Elias had appeared, and of others that one of the old prophets was risen again. And Herod said, John have I beheaded; but who is this, of whom I hear such things? And he desired to see him."[2] Our Lord having been reared in

[1] John. xxi.   [2] Luke, ix., 7-9.

Nazareth, "he belonged unto Herod's jurisdiction;" and having resided at Capernaum, which is less than eight miles to the north from Tiberias, he was a "political subject" in the tetrarchate of Antipas. Why did not Herod send for him? But, knowing the unscrupulous character of the tetrarch and his wife, together with the reasons assigned above, the Savior wisely avoided his presence; not from fear, for the pure and exalted nature of the Redeemer never knew such a base emotion, but rather to teach his messengers to yield to the storm rather than expose themselves to destruction, when, from known circumstances, the case was evidently hopeless. But the king and the Savior met at last. The former was a guest, and the latter a prisoner in Jerusalem. Finding no fault in Jesus, but willing to subject him to a more searching trial, Pilate "sent him to Herod." "And when he saw Jesus he was exceeding glad, for he was desirous to see him of a long season, because he had heard many things of him, and he had hoped to have seen some miracle done by him." Too wise and holy to display his power to gratify the curiosity of an unprincipled king, our Lord neither performed a miracle nor answered the senseless questions propounded to him by a vain and trifling judge. Offended at his silence and majestic bearing, "Herod and his men of war set him at naught, and mocked him, and arrayed him in a gorgeous robe, and sent him again to Pilate; and the same day Pilate and Herod were made friends."[1]

A mile to the south from Tiberias, and situated on the shore, are the "Warm Baths of Emmaus," consisting of four springs. The water has a temperature of 144° Fahrenheit. It emits a sulphurous smell, and is exceedingly salt and bitter to the taste. It is considered by the natives efficacious in rheumatic complaints and in cases of debility, and the baths are visited by invalids from all parts of the country. Over one of the springs is a bath-house, and near the shore is another, both of which are rapidly going to decay. As we passed, persons of all ages and of both sexes were applying the medicinal waters, and some were bathing in water at over 140° Fahrenheit.

Three miles to the south of these thermal springs is the site of ancient Tarichea. Here, on a narrow peninsula formed by the River Jordan as it leaves the lake, are venerable ruins,

[1] Luke, xxiii., 6-12.

around which are the few huts of the modern town of Kerak. Being a town of considerable importance in the Jewish wars, Tarichea was fortified by Josephus, but stormed and taken, with great slaughter, by Titus. Having the only large and safe harbor on the whole lake, the Jewish chieftain made it his great naval station. With a foresight worthy of better fortunes, Josephus here collected 230 ships, in which to escape if beaten on land, or in which to engage the Romans in naval combat. Yielding to the powerful arms of Titus, Tarichea fell, and the inhabitants took refuge in their ships, and anchored in the middle of the lake. Resolved on the utter destruction of the Jewish army, Vespasian, who was present, immediately ordered the construction of a sufficient number of vessels to attack the enemy, and, having completed his navy, he launched his ships and engaged the foe. The engagement was long and sanguinary. The sea was turned into blood, and on its discolored waters floated the bodies of the dead. Not a Jewish vessel escaped; and for many days succeeding the fight the shores were strewn with shipwrecks, and with the swollen forms of the slain.[1] Thus ended the first and last sea-fight between the Jews and Romans. Like their mighty empires, their navies are also destroyed, and instead of that vast fleet which floated on its bosom, there is but one boat now upon the Sea of Galilee; and, excepting a long causeway resting on arches, through which the water flows into the Jordan when the lake is high, there is nothing entire remaining to mark the site of Tarichea and perpetuate its naval glory.

A mile to the southeast from Jericho is the mouth of the Jordan, which is ninety feet wide, with high rounded banks. Less than a mile to the south is the old bridge of Semakh, which once spanned the sacred river, but is now a ruin. Near it is the modern ford, the present highway between the east and west. Through shrubberies of hawthorns, tamarisks, and oleanders, the path runs to the small village from which the bridge derives its name. Six miles to the south is the Jarmuk of the Hebrews and the Hieromax of the Greeks, called by the Arabs Mandhûr: it drains the whole plain of the Haurân and Jaulân, with a large section of the mountain range eastward. Flowing through a wild ravine, the sides of which are rugged cliffs of basalt 100 feet high, it enters the Jordan

[1] W. J., b. iii., c. x.

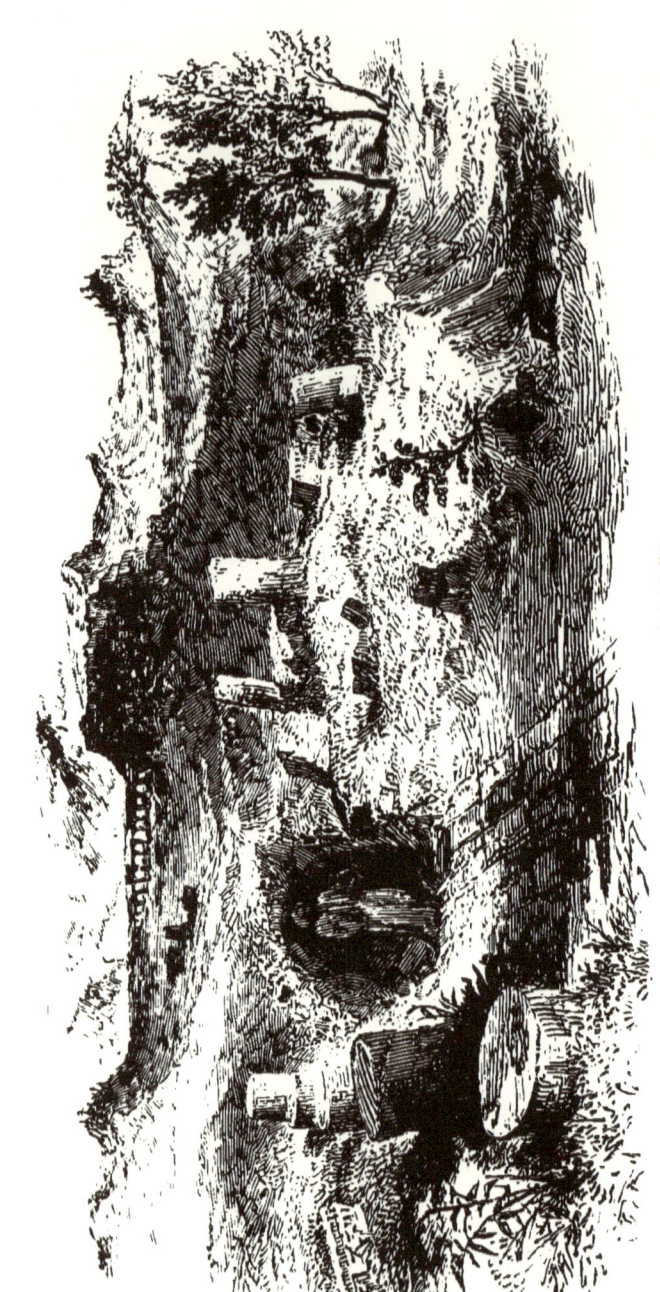

RUINS AND TOMBS OF GADARA.

four miles below the lake, and at the point of junction is more than 130 feet wide. During the Jewish commonwealth it was the boundary between Bashan and Gilead, and during the dominion of the Romans it defined the limits of the provinces of Perea and Gaulonitis. In the gloomy valley through which it flows, bearing the Arabic name of Sheri'at el-Mandhûr, are the famous "Baths of Amatha." Consisting of eight warm springs, they were esteemed by the Romans as second only to those of the Italian Baiæ. Around them are clumps of dwarf palms and the remains of arched buildings. The largest of the eight bubbles up into a basin 40 feet in circumference, and five deep, which is inclosed by dilapidated walls. The boiling water deposits on the stones a yellow sulphurous crust, regarded by the natives a sovereign remedy in certain disorders to which their camels are subject.

Three miles to the south from the banks of the Jarmuk is the celebrated city of Gadara. With an authentic history not older than the third century B.C., it was captured in the year 218 B.C. by Antiochus the Great. Regaining possession of it twenty years later, the Jews held it till destroyed during their civil wars. To gratify one of his freedmen, who was a Gadarene, it was rebuilt by order of Pompey, and during the proconsulate of Gabinius it was the capital of one of the five districts into which he had divided Judea. Considered one of the most impotrant cities east of the Jordan, it was captured by Vespasian in the first outbreak of the war with the Jews: all of its inhabitants were massacred, and the town itself was reduced to ashes.

The ruins of a city more significantly reflect its grandeur than the records of the historian or the descriptions of the traveler. Gadara is in ruins. Occupying a projecting spur at the northwestern extremity of the mountains of Gilead, it is bounded on the north by the Jarmuk, on the south by the valley of El-Arab, and on the west by the Jordan. On the crest of the ridge, covering a space two miles in circumference, are the remains of the fallen city. On the northern side of the hill there is a theatre, the seats of which remain entire. Near it originally stood one of the great gates of the city, from which commenced a noble avenue extending through the town, and flanked on either side by a splendid colonnade. On the western side of the ridge there is another theatre, the walls, seats, and vaulted chambers of which are in good condition. Between these two theatres lay the principal part of the city, on an even piece of ground. But the desolation of Gadara is complete. Neither dwelling, palace, nor column remains standing, and the only work of art, besides the theatres, which has come down to our own age well preserved, is the pavement of the main street, which is as perfect as when laid down, and bears distinctly the traces of the chariot wheels which once proudly rolled along this magnificent thoroughfare.

Whether regarded as works of art or as associated with the history of the Gospel, the tombs of Gadara are replete with interest. Excavated in the limestone rock on the east and northeast sides of the hill, they consist of chambers, some of which are more than 20 feet square. Consisting of massive stone slabs, ornamented with panels, many of the doors remain in their places, and swing upon their hinges with ease, notwithstanding their great weight. Along the hill-side are ancient sarcophagi, ornamented with sculptured garlands and wreaths, gods and genii. As in the days of our Lord, these tombs are inhabited, and though not by maniacs, yet by Troglodytes, who at times are no less dangerous to the traveler. When it is remembered that Gadara is nine miles from the extreme southeastern shore of the Sea of Tiberias, its claim of having been the scene of the Savior's miracle in curing the maniacs who "dwelt in the tombs" may be called in question. The miracle is recorded by three of the evangelists. They all agree as to where the Savior landed, viz., "to the other side;" "over unto the other side of the sea," "which is over against Galilee;" that, on landing, he was immediately met by the demoniacs; and that the place was in the *country or region of a certain people*; but Matthew calls this people Gergesenes, while Mark and Luke call them Gadarenes. The reconciliation, however, is not difficult. Either Gergesa was located near the lake shore, and under the jurisdiction of the larger city, Gadara, and therefore could be properly described as in the "country of the Gadarenes," or, as is more probable, St. Matthew, being a resident of this region, wrote the name correctly, and wrote it primarily to those who were familiar with all the smaller places of the country, while St. Mark and St. Luke, who were strangers here, and who wrote for the benefit of distant Greek and Roman readers, who were only familiar with the well-known district and city of Gadara, simply point out the vicinity of the place where the miracle occurred. Some eminent critics suppose that, as the name of the place given by St. Matthew is variously pronounced Gergesa, or Gerasa, or Cchersa, the close resemblance between Gergesa and Gadara led to the substitution of the latter for the former in transcribing the manuscript.[1] But, whatever may have been the cause of the discrepancy, topographical facts are against Gadara, or any of its dependencies, as having been the scene of the miracle. In addition to the fact that Gadara is nine miles to the southeast from the sea, there is no mountain at this point of the shore adapted to the conditions of the miracle. The intervening space between these two points, even if the last-mentioned difficulty did not exist, would present an insuperable objection. It would have been a miracle in itself if 2000 swine had run down the mountain-side for an hour and a half, then forded the deep Jarmuk, and, having gained the northern bank, crossed a plain five miles wide before they reached the nearest margin of the sea. And as the scene of the miracle could not have been in the immediate neighborhood of Gadara, neither could it have been north of the Jarmuk, as the "country of the Gadarenes" lay south of that great river.

Somewhere midway the lake we must look for the scene of this interesting event. Not two miles to the north from the small village of Semakh is the site of ancient Hippas, which was an important place in the days of Josephus, and four miles farther on are the ruins of the renowned city of Gamala. The ridge on which the city stood is not unlike a camel's back, from which geological formation the town derived its name. So strongly was Gamala built, that the younger Agrippa besieged it seven months in vain, and it only yielded to the assailants when assaulted by a more powerful army under Vespasian. Four thousand perished by the sword, and, rather than surrender themselves captives to the victor, five thousand other citizens threw themselves from the walls of their city and were dashed to pieces in the deep ravines below. Whether this was the city of the Gergesenes it is impossible to determine with accuracy, but the topography of the shore, from

[1] Thomson and Clarke.

Hippas to Wady Semakh, is in harmony with all the facts of the miracle. Here, in the face of the bold cliffs, are many ancient tombs, out of one of which the demoniacs rushed to meet Jesus the moment the boat touched the shore, and on the mountain summit, "a good way off from them, an herd of swine was feeding." Seized with a sudden panic, the maddened herd rushed headlong down the steep mountain side, and as there was neither time nor space to arrest their descent on the narrow shelving shore between the base of the cliff and the sea, they were borne by the velocity of their own motion into the waters and perished. Thus, by a miracle as humane as it was godlike, our Lord condemned the vocation of the swineherds of Gergesa, and restored to reason and happiness two unfortunate men.[1]

Ten miles north from Gamala is the mouth of the Upper Jordan. The path first runs along a rich plateau, separating the shell-strewn beach from the base of the hills, and then passes over a triangular plain of surpassing richness. Three miles beyond this rich field the Jordan enters the Lake of Gennesaret. Southerly winds have driven up an immense bank of sand before the mouth of the river, causing the water to flow through a channel some distance from the eastern shore. Being 70 feet wide, the Jordan is here a lazy, turbid stream, flowing between low alluvial banks. Droves of buffaloes and herds of cattle were standing in the shallow water, while along the banks were flocks of sheep and goats.

Two miles from the mouth of the Jordan, and covering a conspicuous hill, are the remains of Bethsaida Julias. Originally a small village inhabited by fishermen, it was enlarged and beautified by "Philip, tetrarch of Iturea and of the region of Trachonitis,"[2] who made it the imperial city of his kingdom, and called it Julias in honor of Julia, the daughter of the Emperor Augustus;[3] and here, after he had reigned 37 years, he died and was interred with great pomp in a magnificent mausoleum which he had previously prepared for himself.[4] But this eastern Bethsaida is chiefly interesting to the Christian traveler as associated with the life of our divine Lord. Sailing from Capernaum, hither he retired with his disciples "into a desert place apart."[5] This "desert place" was proba-

[1] Matt., viii.; Mark, v.; Luke, viii.   [2] Luke, iii.
[3] Antiq., b. xviii., c. ii.   [4] Ib., c. iv.   [5] Matt., xiv., 13.

bly one of those uninhabited mountains which overhang the lake on the south, and which, owing to the scarcity of springs and the nearer approach to the Bedouin tribes, were not dotted with towns as were the opposite hills, and which naturally became a refuge from the active life of the western shores. Attracted by his miracles and charmed by his presence, "when the people heard thereof they followed him on foot out of the cities,"[1] and sweeping round the head of the lake, while he himself sailed across it, they reached the place where he had landed. Having "healed their sick" and taught them lessons of divine wisdom, the compassionate Savior finished the labors of the day by feeding that multitude of over 5000 souls with five loaves and two fishes.[2] The scene of this extraordinary miracle is the noble plain at the mouth of the Jordan, which during most of the year is now, as then, covered with "green grass."[3] Dismissing the multitude with his blessing, and "constraining his disciples to get into a ship" and return to Capernaum, "he went up into a mountain apart to pray." The imagination dwells with delight upon this parting scene—the thousands of people scattered along the beach absorbed in deepest thought, and moving homeward with lingering step, turning ever and anon to gain another glance at the blessed Savior; the ship upon the sea, containing the twelve disciples, returning to Gennesaret; while, slowly moving up the mountain side, the Master is retiring into solitude for meditation and prayer.

The multitude had reached their homes and were wrapped in slumber; the Savior had finished his devotions and had descended to the shore, but the disciples were in the "midst of the sea, tossed with waves, for the wind was contrary." "In the fourth watch of the night," leaving this beautiful plain, "Jesus went unto them, walking on the sea." Calming their fears by that sublime salutation, "Be of good cheer; it is I, be not afraid," he allowed the impulsive Peter to "walk on the water," which no less evinced the weakness of the apostle's faith than it displayed the compassion and power of his Lord.[4]

Having described a part of the western and the whole of the eastern shore of the Sea of Galilee, it only remains to follow the shore northward from Tiberias to Capernaum, and thence eastward to Chorazin. It was seven A.M. when we left the

[1] Matt., xiv., 13.   [2] Ib., xiii., 21.   [3] Mark, vi., 39.   [4] Matt., xiv.

ancient capital of Antipas to visit the cities upbraided by our Lord. The morning sun had risen upon the Hills of Galilee in cloudless beauty, the surface of the lake was rippled by a soft breeze from the south, and far to the north rose the sublime form of Hermon, its snowy summits reflecting the early light. Two paths were before us, one mounting the uplands on the left, the other following the coast. Choosing the latter, our course was to the northwest. The beach gently declined toward the clear blue waters, and was strewn with shells, and with white and black pebbles of basalt and limestone. In half an hour we passed the wild ravine of Arbela, opening into the interior, and flanked by bold, precipitous cliffs. Travelers were approaching from the north, mounted on fine Arabian horses, and seated on chair-back saddles. As we advanced the banks became steep and rocky, and the mountains above us rose in jutting peaks. In less than an hour we came to Magdala, the birthplace of Mary Magdalene. Standing on the shore, it bears the modern name of Mejdel. Eighteen centuries ago it was a large and thriving town, but at present it contains only 20 huts, on the flat roofs of which children had built booths of reeds. Around the hovels are old foundations and heaps of rubbish, and near a half-ruined tower stands a solitary palm. Attracted by our presence, the women rushed from their wretched homes and gazed at us wildly, and, judging from their frightful appearance, they might be dispossessed of as many demons as was their ancient sister. At Mejdel begins the celebrated Plain of Gennesaret. Formed by the mountains suddenly receding inland, it is an open and level plain two and a half miles wide and five long. Having the form of a crescent, it is encompassed on the west by rugged mountains, and on the east it is washed by the sea. Equaling in fertility the Plains of Jericho, it is well watered, and its soil is in part a rich black mould. No less than four streams flow through it to the lake, and, wherever cultivated, it yields abundantly. Portions of its shore-line consist of a thick jungle of oleander, in whose branches birds of variant forms and of brilliant colors carol the melody of their song. In his description of this plain Josephus is as correct as he is eloquent. Referring to the various kinds of trees which grew thereon, "he calls the place the ambition of nature, where it forces those plants that are naturally enemies to one another to agree togeth-

PLAIN OF GENNESARET AND HOME OF MARY MAGDALENE.

er."[1] Were it cultivated with intelligence and taste, it would be the Paradise of Northern Palestine, producing the choicest fruits luxuriantly, and possessing an eternal spring. Even now, notwithstanding its neglected state, it is dotted with magnificent corn-fields and with groves of dwarf palms; and while from our feet quails sprang up at almost every step, the voice of the turtle-dove was heard on every side. In the days of our Lord it was the most densely populated part of the Holy Land, and through its beautiful gardens he was wont to pass, and in its thriving towns to teach his wondrous truths. Somewhere on its whitened beach he and his disciples landed after he had walked upon the water;[2] and from that beach he stepped into one of the "two boats" standing on its gradual slope, and, praying Peter "that he would thrust out a little from the land, he sat down and taught the people out of the ship."[3] Taking advantage of the promiscuous audience which hung with rapt attention upon his words, he here delivered the remarkable parables of the "Sower and the Seed," of the "Wheat and Tares," of the "Mustard-seed," and of the "Leaven which a woman took and hid in three measures of meal."[4] It is highly probable that the first three of these parables were suggested to his mind by the fields of vegetation which dotted this plain. As in his day, so now, the wheat and tares grow together, and all the facts of the parable are illustrated to the modern traveler. Tares abound throughout the country, and in many respects they resemble the American *cheat*. The stalk stands perfectly erect, and the small grains are arranged compactly one above the other. Having a bitter taste, they produce dizziness when eaten, whether by man or beast, and are regarded as a strong soporific poison. If the Savior designed to represent the existence of the *good* and *bad* in his Church, no illustration could have been selected more appropriate and impressive. The "wheat and tares" derive nourishment from the same soil; they are so much alike before the grain is *headed out* that it is quite impossible to distinguish the stalk of the one from that of the other, even to those accustomed to weed their fields; and so intertwined are the roots of both, "that they must grow together until the harvest" before the wheat can be gathered into the garner and the tares collected to be

[1] W. J., b. iii., c. x.
[2] Matt., xiv., 34.
[3] Luke, v., 1-3; Mark, iv.
[4] Matt., xiii.

burnt. And here, no doubt, was growing then, as it grows now, the mustard-plant, which formed the basis of a second parable. Attaining the height of ten feet, its trunk is slender, the leaves are broad, and the blossoms yellow. Though this *wild* and perennial shrub may aid our conceptions of the tree which our Lord describes, yet it is probable that the variety to which he alludes was *cultivated*, and was the "*least of all seeds*" *sown by the husbandman, and when grown was "the greatest among herbs" in all his garden.*

On the northern horn of this crescent plain is the site of the renowned city of Capernaum. Plucking an anemone in memory of the devoted Mary, we passed up the coast, and found the distance to be scarcely four miles. In attempting to ford one of the mountain streams which pour their turbid waters into the lake, our horses sank into the soft clay bottom, leaving us no alternative but to dismount and wade ashore. Accustomed to such incidents in Oriental traveling, we remounted, and, hastening over the plain, reached Capernaum at ten A.M.

Though its early history is involved in much obscurity, and though it is not mentioned in the Old Testament, it was probably built by the Jews after their return from Babylon. At the commencement of the Christian era it was a large and prosperous town, but it is indebted to the presence and works of Jesus for its present renown. As the history of its origin is obscure, so the time of its destruction is unknown. But whether the evidence of the identity of the site is drawn from the incidental allusions of the evangelists,[1] or from the history of Josephus,[2] or from the writings of the fathers, or from eminent travelers down to the 17th century,[3] or from the topography of the spot, the argument is no less clear than satisfactory. Judging from the heaps of ruins covering portions of the plain, the city stood near the base of a bold bluff, which rises in the form of a truncated cone 300 feet high, and which dips its eastern end into the sea, while its western extremity is bounded by a green meadow stretching along the shore. At the foot of the cliff is the large "Fountain of the Fig," so called from a noble fig-tree that shades the cave from which the stream issues. The water is clear, cool, and sweet, and

---

[1] Matt., xiv., 34; John, vi., 24. [2] B. J., b. iii., ch. x., s. 8.
[3] Robinson's B. R., vol. iii , p. 348.

flows over a broad pebbled bed into the lake. Near the fountain are the remains of a tower, to which is attached a portion of an arched gateway, and south of it is a low mound of shapeless ruins, overgrown with thorns and thistles. Nearly 1000 feet to the northwest from 'Ain et-Tin is the old Khan Minyeh, lying under the western brow of the hill, which, standing on the great caravan route between Egypt and Damascus, is designed for the accommodation of pilgrims.

Ascending the bold cliff behind the city, we found the sides terraced, and the flattened summit covered with wheat and barley, ripe for the harvest. From this lofty position we obtained a delightful view. At our feet lay the lake, smooth and bright, like polished silver, and beyond the broad valley of the Jordan opened before us. On the east the eye glanced over the Plains of Bashan and the Mountains of Gilead; on the north, Safed rose in solitary grandeur; while on the west were the Land of Gennesaret, and, over lower hills, the "Mount of Beatitudes." Charmed with the view and overwhelmed with the recollections of the past, I sat down and read the eventful history of Capernaum. Rivaling Jerusalem in the number and sacredness of its hallowed associations, it is to the north what the former is to the south. Not excepting Olivet, it stands pre-eminent in evangelical history as the scene of our Lord's most instructive discourses and most astonishing miracles. Driven from Nazareth by his ungrateful townsmen, "he came and dwelt in Capernaum,"[1] which from that time forward became "his own city."[2] Returning hither from journeys to other parts, here he was received with affection and revered as divine. Here, in the synagogue, on the Sabbath day, having astonished the people by the authority with which he had enforced his doctrines, he healed the demoniac.[3] Passing from the synagogue, "he entered the house of Simon and Andrew," and finding the mother of Peter's wife "sick of a fever," he immediately restored her to health,[3] and that night the people thronged the door of the dwelling, "and he healed many that were sick of divers diseases."[3] Returning from the "country of the Gergesenes," he cured the paralytic;[4] and passing by the receipt of custom, he called Matthew to the apostleship.[4] Descending from the "Mount of Beatitudes," he

[1] Matt., iv., 13.
[2] Ib., ix., 1.
[3] Mark, i., 21-34.
[4] Matt., ix., 2-9.

here restored the servant of the devout centurion.¹ Yielding to the paternal entreaties of Jairus, he entered the ruler's house, and, taking the dead damsel by the hand, uttered those life-giving words, "Talitha-cumi," and "she arose and walked." It was while going on this errand of mercy that, as he passed through the thronged streets of Capernaum, a daughter of Israel "came in the press behind and touched his garment," and was made whole.² Coming from the visions and glory of Tabor, he was here met by those who "received tribute-money," and sent forth Peter, who miraculously obtained from the mouth of a fish a coin bearing the image and superscription of Cæsar.³ It was here, in a house no longer standing, that, after delivering from the deck of a fish-boat the memorable parables of the "Sower," the "Tares," the "Mustard-seed," and the "Leaven," he gave forth the parables of the "Hidden Treasure," the "Merchant seeking goodly Pearls," and of the "Net cast into the Sea."⁴

Here, in the home of St. Matthew, and around his well-spread board, our Lord discoursed on "fasting."⁵ At a subsequent period he reproved the Scribes and Pharisees for their "formality;"⁶ and on the morning after he had calmed the storm he taught the people the nature of "faith;"⁷ and here, either in the house of Simon or Levi, in the privacies of social life, and surrounded only by his disciples, he chided their ambition, rebuked their sectarianism, and unfolded to them the beauty and power of humility, forbearance, and brotherly love.⁸

Who can wonder at the judgments pronounced upon a city so highly favored, whose citizens refused to be enlightened by such words of wisdom, and convinced by such acts of mercy? Rejecting him, he in turn has rejected them. The "woe" has fallen heavily upon the ungrateful city, and time has proven the fulfillment of prophecy. "And thou, Capernaum, which art exalted to heaven, shalt be brought down to hell; for if the mighty works which have been done in thee had been done in Sodom, it would have remained until this day. But I say unto thee, it shall be more tolerable for the land of Sodom in the day of judgment than for thee."⁹ Whether this exaltation denoted the lofty site of the city, or its pride and

¹ Luke, vii., 1 10. ² Mark, v., 22-43. ³ Matt., xvii., 24-27.
⁴ Ib., xiii. Ib., ix. ⁶ Ib., xv.
⁷ John, vi., 24. ⁸ Mark, ix., 33-50. ⁹ Matt., xi., 23, 24.

prosperity, the abasement is equally true. The desolation is universal; the ruin is complete. There is a dispute among the learned whether the town stood upon the high hill above the fountain, or on the plain below. In all probability the hill served as the acropolis, commanding the entire plain, on the northeast end of which the larger portion of the city was built. As there is no path along the northern shore, we wound up the sides of a precipitous promontory dipping into the sea, and found a path excavated in the rock 20 feet above the water-line, and measuring three feet deep and as many wide. Descending to the shore of a beautiful bay, and riding northeastward, in 20 minutes from Capernaum we came to Bethsaida, the home of Peter and his brethren. Bearing the Arabic name of Et-Tâbighah, this city of the holy apostles stands in a charming little nook in the mountain side. The hills rise around it in graceful gradations, and on the west is a small but lonely bay, encircled by a beach of fine sand, and just such a place as fishermen love to ground their boats and spread their nets upon. Unoccupied except by a few *millers*, the chief attraction of the place is its pools, fountains, and aqueducts. No city of its size in Palestine has so many and valuable water facilities as Bethsaida. The larger fountains burst out from the base of the mountain 300 yards to the north, and around the principal one is a large octagonal reservoir, with two circular holes designed as drains. A flight of steps in the southwest corner leads down to the water, which is warm and sulphurous, and about eight feet deep. From the bottom of the reservoir there were canes growing to the height of 20 feet. Nearer the shore is a circular well, called 'Ain Eyûb, or "Job's Fountain." This reservoir, together with several mills, were constructed by Dhâher el-Omer, and now belong to the government, by whom they are farmed out to villagers from the neighboring towns.

Originally called the "House of Fish," as significant of the vocation of its ancient inhabitants, Bethsaida will ever live in the recollection of the pious as the birthplace of five apostles, who have stamped the world with their influence, and affected the opinions and destiny of mankind in all countries. Here Peter, and Andrew, and James, and John, and Philip spent their childhood, and here they engaged in the humble but honest calling of fishermen. It was probably on the shore of the small bay previously described that Jesus, walking by the Sea of Galilee, saw two brethren, Simon called Peter, and Andrew his brother, casting a net into the sea, and said unto them, "Follow me, and I will make you fishers of men." And going on from thence, he saw other two brethren, James the son of Zebedee, and John his brother, and he called them, and they followed him."¹ And here, no doubt, is the scene of that miraculous draught of fishes, which astonished the disciples, and convinced them of the divine character of our Lord.² But this Bethsaida must not be confounded with the one east of the Jordan, and which has already been noticed as having been enlarged and beautified by Philip the tetrarch. The latter being in Gaulonitis and not in Galilee, it could not have been the native city of the apostles, who were *Galileans;* and though it may appear unusual to find two cities of the same name in such close proximity, yet the singularity disappears when it is remembered that they belonged to separate provinces, and that Bethsaida Julias is not on the lake shore, but on the eastern bank of the Jordan, two miles from the mouth of the river. This distinction sheds much light upon a somewhat obscure passage by St. Mark. After our Lord had learned of the execution of John the Baptist, he left Capernaum, and, with his disciples, "departed into a desert place by ships privately."³ St. John, with greater exactitude, says that "Jesus went over the Sea of Galilee."⁴ The "desert place" is on the northeastern shore of the lake, where he fed the 5000, and is "over the sea." Having dismissed the multitude, "he constrained his disciples to get into a ship, and to go to the other side before unto Bethsaida," which is on "the other side;" and as it is only a mile from Capernaum, agrees with St. John, who records that "they went over the sea toward Capernaum."⁵ They embarked for Bethsaida, but the "wind was contrary," and they were driven from their course to the southward. "About the fourth watch of the night" Jesus came "walking on the sea," and, entering the ship, "the wind ceased." With a minuteness that leaves us without a doubt, St. Matthew and St. Mark say, "They came into the land of Gennesaret;"⁶ and St. John designates which portion of Gennesaret they came to in saying that "when the peo-

¹ Matt., iv., 18-22. ² Luke, v. ³ Mark, vi., 32.
⁴ John, vi., 1. ⁵ Ib., vi., 17. ⁶ Matt., xiv., 34, and Mark, vi., 53.

ple saw that Jesus was on the other side, they took shipping and came to Capernaum seeking for Jesus, and that they found him there."[1] Had the disciples sailed for Bethsaida Julias, it would have been impossible for them to have sailed "*over the sea toward Capernaum*," as the former is not "over the sea," and is not in the same direction with the latter, Capernaum being southwest and Julias northeast. Nor is the difficulty relieved by supposing that Tell Hum is the true site of Capernaum, as the argument drawn from the direction of the place remains in full force.

Having satisfied his mind touching the identity of a place, the traveler lingers about the spot with no ordinary delight. Such were the pleasing emotions I experienced as I stood amid the ruins of the home of Peter, James, and John, and watched the crystal waters flowing into the sea through banks lined with oleanders in full bloom. And the impression was overwhelming as the great fact rose up before my mind that in this retired quarter of the globe — in this Galilean village of humble pretensions, five inspired apostles were born, who from their fish-boats went forth commissioned to evangelize the world, and to be the biographers of the Son of God. It is an ancient suggestion, that the scenery of childhood gives tone to the character of a man and direction to his coming years. Few men whose acts fill so large a portion of the world's history have evinced traits of character so opposite, and transitions in their emotional natures so remarkable as the "fishermen of Bethsaida." Pure as they were simple, benevolent as they were sincere, they loved and hated, hoped and despaired; they were bold and fearful, joyful and sorrowful, firm and inconstant, as the surrounding circumstances were favorable to the development of their better natures, or to disclose the weaknesses of our common humanity. Looking out upon the scene before me, I fancied that their finer feelings and gentler traits were evoked by the deep blue skies, the transparent atmosphere, the mellow dawn, the golden sunset, the placid lake, the flowing fountains, the blooming flowers and shell-strewn shores, while the rugged mountains and boisterous storms at sea aroused their fiery and impetuous spirits. When composed they resembled their embowered lake, whose placid waters mirror the overhanging foliage along its banks;

[1] John, vi., 24.

but when agitated, they were like their native sea during a storm, when the deep was troubled, when thunder answered thunder, and the roar of the waters responded to the howl of the winds.

Three miles to the northeast are the remains of the city of Chorazin. In the intervening space the hills approach the shore, exposing at intervals a rough bank, lined with a tangled thicket of a thorny shrub. In the spring-time the black tents of the predatory farmers dot the table-land, only one of which now remained, and around it a solitary shepherd was keeping his flock. It was while riding over this broad plateau that we were startled by one of those squalls peculiar to this inland sea. The air had been quiet, the lake calm, and the heavens were cloudless, but within five minutes the wind blew a gale, the sea became troubled, the waves rolled high and dashed wildly on the shore. It was a repetition of that scene when the disciples were sailing over the sea; when "Jesus was in the hinder part of the ship, asleep on a pillow;" when " there arose a great storm of wind, and the waves beat into the ship, so that it was now full;" and when, in the moment of danger, they awoke the Divine Sleeper, "who arose and rebuked the wind, and said unto the sea, Peace, be still."[1] The natural causes operating and producing such effects in that distant age are still in force. The sea is 600 feet lower than the ocean; the mountains on the east and north rise to a great height, and their sides are furrowed with deep and wild ravines; and the temperature of this volcanic basin differing from that on the mountains above, these profound gorges serve as vast conductors, through which, at certain periods, the cold winds from above rush suddenly down, causing a tempest in an unexpected moment.

The ruins of Chorazin lie upon the shore, covering a level tract half a mile long and a quarter of a mile wide. Consisting chiefly of the foundations and prostrate walls of dwellings, they are overgrown with a thicket of thistles eight feet high, and so dense that it is almost impossible to penetrate and examine the remains. The walls of a square tower 10 feet high are standing, and are composed of fragments of columns, capitals, and friezes, mingled with hewn stone of different dimensions. To the east of the tower we entered a structure, the

[1] Mark, iv., 37-39.

object of which can not now be determined. Portions of the northern and western walls remain, the former measuring 105 feet long, and the latter about 80. Within this inclosure are strewn, in utter confusion, limestone columns, Corinthian capitals, sculptured entablatures, ornamental friezes, double columns, and immense blocks of stone nine feet long and five wide, with panels sculptured in their sides. This may have been a magnificent Jewish synagogue, a substitute in part for the noble Temple of Jerusalem. In the days of our Savior and five centuries after, Chorazin was a populous and wealthy city. Driven from their ancient capital, the Jews settled on the shores of this lake. Their Sanhedrim found a resting-place at Tiberias, and Magdala, Capernaum, Bethsaida, and Chorazin became their chief towns. In the wealth of her citizens, the grandeur of her architecture, and the influence of her religious institutions, the latter appears to have been as influential as magnificent. But the "woe" has fallen on Chorazin. What the "mighty works which were done" in her were we are not informed, but evidently they were of such a character as to give light to her people, in the rejection of which was involved her ruin. Rejecting that light, she has fallen with her sister towns; and without a single habitation, the most beautiful site for a city on all these shores is now a thorn-bed, where adders crawl and jackals hide. "Woe unto thee, Chorazin! woe unto thee, Bethsaida! for if the mighty works which were done in thee had been done in Tyre and Sidon, they would have repented long ago in sackcloth and ashes." And if the present small but thriving towns of Tyre and Sidon be compared to this "howling wilderness," this "perfection of desolation," the contrast can not fail to suggest to every impartial mind the marvelous and strangely exact fulfillment of our Lord's solemn predictions.[1] Indeed, the Lake of Gennesaret is a beautiful desolation. Her villas are in ruins, her fisheries have failed, her ship-yards are silent, her commerce is destroyed, her manufactories are abandoned, and her waters, which were the rich possession of Naphthali, are without a keel to divide them, or a sail to fly before their mountain gusts.

Turning inland and following a path along the base of the mountain, an hour's ride brought us to the mouth of the Jor-

[1] Matt., xi., 21, 22.

dan. Forty miles to the northeast, up the broad ravine through which the most illustrious of earthly rivers flows, appeared Mount Hermon, with his icy crown brilliant in the midday sun. For nine miles the path follows the river bank to 'Jisr Benât Yakûb, the "Bridge of Jacob's Daughters." It is the only bridge which at present spans the Jordan, and its three arches, with its well-paved roadway, are in good condition. Though traditionally marking the site where Jacob, staff in hand, crossed the stream, yet it is not easy to determine why the word "daughters" should be added. The Jordan is here a rapid stream, 25 yards wide and 10 feet deep, flowing between alluvial banks fringed with thickets of reeds and rank grass. From the bridge on the eastern bank of the river, a beautiful level tract of land extends northward for three miles to the foot of Lake Hûleh. Four and a half miles in length and three and a half in breadth, this charming lake is the first gathering together of the waters of the Upper Jordan as they descend from their perennial springs. Known in the Bible as the "Waters of Merom," and called by Josephus Samochonitis,[1] it was on the shore of this lake that Joshua "smote Jabin, king of Hazor."[2] Passing the probable site of Hazor, two miles to the west from the fountain of Mellâhah, and crossing the deep glen through which the Hasbâny flows to the Jordan, the path runs over undulating ground to Tell el-Kâdy, "The Hill of the Judge," or the Dan of Scripture, situated 12 miles from the northern end of Lake Hûleh. Rising from the midst of a level plain, the hill on which the ancient city stood is 80 feet high and three quarters of a mile in circumference. It is covered with trees and bushes, which conceal the ruins of the old town. Placed by Josephus at the fountain of the Jordan, and located by Eusebius a quarter of a mile from Paneas, on the way to Tyre, there can be no question as to the identity of the place. Its history is as sanguinary as it is romantic. Captured by the princes of Mesopotamia, hither Lot was brought after the pillage of Sodom; and, inspired by a courage that was never blanched with fear, here Abraham overtook the captors of his nephew, and dividing his 318 "trained servants born in his own house," he fell upon the foe by night, "and smote them and pursued them unto Hobah, which is on the left hand of Damascus; and he brought back all his goods, and also brought

[1] B. J., b. iv., ch. i.   [2] Josh., xi., 6-10.

again his brother Lot,[1] and his goods, and the women also, and the people."[2] Called in the days of the Judges Laish, its capture by the Danites forms one of the most romantic stories in the Old Testament. Unable to expel the more powerful Philistines who occupied a large part of their tribeship, 600 armed men from the cities of Zorah and Eshtool went up and smote the rich and careless Sidonians who inhabited the town, and, taking possession of the city, they called it "Dan, after their father." On their way northward they had stopped at Mount Ephraim, where they pillaged the house of Micah of the holy symbols of his religion, and compelled a young Levite to accompany them, "to be to them a father and a priest."[3] Though a trifling conquest when compared to the grand achievements of Joshua and David, the capture of Laish and its occupation by the Danites was the fulfillment of an ancient prophecy: "Dan is a lion's whelp; he shall leap from Bashan;"[4] and from that time the city was regarded as the northern border of the Promised Land, and gave rise to that household expression, "From Dan to Beersheba."[5]

But the city of Dan is no less celebrated for its waters than for its interesting history. At the western base of the hill there is the largest fountain in Syria, and among the largest in the world. Bursting forth from the rocks, the water first forms a small lake, from which it rushes southward a rapid river, called the Leddân. Four miles below it forms a junction with a large stream from Baniâs, and a mile beyond the confluence it is joined by the River Hasbâny, which gives its name to the stream down to the Lake Hûleh. Thus gradually the Jordan is formed.

Winding through oaken groves, and lined with myrtle and oleanders, the road diverges to the northeast, and four miles from Dan is Cæsarea Philippi. Occupying a broad terrace in the mountain side, it is bounded by two sublime ravines, one on the north and the other on the south, between which, and in the rear of the site, rise the castellated heights of Subeibeh 1000 feet high. The terrace is adorned with groves of oaks and olives, and carpeted with the richest verdure. A site so remarkable for its Alpine scenery did not fail to attract the earlier Phœnicians, and, at a later period, the Greeks and Ro-

---

[1] Nephew. [2] Gen., xiv., 14–16. [3] Judges, xviii.
[4] Deut., xxxiii., 22. [5] Judges, xx., 1.

mans. Supposed to be the "Baal Gad" of Scripture, it was early consecrated by the Canaanites to the idolatrous worship of one of their Baals.¹ Chosen by the Greeks to be the shrine of Pan, it retains the name of Bāniās, the Arabic form of Paneas. Coming into the possession of "Philip, tetrarch of Iturea and Trachonitis," it was rebuilt and enlarged by the son of Herod the Great, who named it Cæsarea, in honor of Tiberius Cæsar; and to distinguish it from Cæsarea on the Mediterranean coast, and to perpetuate his own name, he called it Cæsarea Philippi. Among its mighty ruins is a citadel of quadrangular form covering four acres, and surrounded by a massive wall with heavy towers at the angles and sides. Guarded on the east by a deep moat, it is washed on the north and west by a large stream, and on the south it is protected by a profound chasm, which is spanned by a bridge, from which a noble gateway opens into the citadel. Within this inclosure, and surrounded by granite columns and limestone shafts, are the 40 dwellings of the modern town. To the north of the ruins, and at the base of a cliff of ruddy limestone 100 feet high, is a cave of vast dimensions, and as dark as vast. Within are the fragments of noble edifices, and around its mouth are heaps of broken rocks and portions of ancient buildings. In harmony with Grecian mythology, this deep cavern was selected as the temple of the sylvan Pan, and on the face of the cliff a Greek inscription records the sacred history of the cave. The Romans succeeding the Greeks, Herod the Great erected a splendid temple of white marble to Augustus near the place called *Panium*.² Destroyed by some unknown power, the ruins of this temple are entombed in the cave, excepting a fragment clinging to the rocks above, and now dedicated to a Moslem saint. Near this spot is the great fountain of Bāniās, which is one of the principal sources of the Jordan. Bursting forth from beneath heaps of rubbish, the water flows in a rapid, foaming torrent over a rocky bed, and, plunging over a precipice, falls into a dark ravine, through which it runs southward and joins the Hasbāny.

As the northern limit of our Savior's wanderings, Cæsarea Philippi was the scene of one of the most interesting incidents in our Lord's life. Having restored a blind man at Bethsaida Julias, he and his disciples passed up this same route, and,

¹ Robinson.   ² Josephus, Antiq., b. xv., ch. x., s. 3.

SOURCE OF THE UPPER JORDAN.

BITUMEN WELLS.

UPPER JORDAN.

coming into the towns of Cæsarea Philippi, he asked his disciples, "Whom do men say that I am?" Receiving their reply, he tested their faith by the more personal question, "But whom say ye that I am?" Ever ready with an answer, and acting as the mouth-piece of his brethren, St. Peter uttered that extraordinary confession, "Thou art the Christ, the son of the living God." Satisfied with an answer no less satisfactory than true, he returned southward, and "after six days" he was transfigured on the summit of Tabor, commanding a view of his native hills.[1]

Passing on the east the castle of Subeibeh, the road to Hasbeiya is through a region as wild as it is picturesque. Eighteen miles from Cæsarea Philippi is the fountain of Hasbâny, the principal source of the Upper Jordan. At the foot of a volcanic bluff the waters burst forth, and by means of a strong and permanent dam are collected into a pond, from which they are turned into a wide mill-race. Escaping therefrom, they commence their long descent, and, augmented by vast tributaries, they flow on through two successive lakes, to be received into a third, where they are evaporated by the intense heat of the Vale of Siddim. Thus formed, the River Jordan is at once remarkable for its length and descent. Though, as the crow flies, it is not more than 120 miles long from its highest source at Hasbeiya to the point where it enters into the Dead Sea, yet, owing to its tortuous channel, it can not be less than 300 miles in length; and it is an equally extraordinary fact that in its descent from Lake Huleh to its southern termination, which in a straight line is but 80 miles, it has a fall of more than 1300 feet.

The village of Hasbeiya is situated on both sides of a deep glen, which descends from a side ridge of Hermon westward into Wady et-Teim. The head of the ravine being but a little east of the town, the latter is inclosed on three sides by high hills, which are regularly terraced and planted with vineyards, olive-groves, and fig-orchards. Of its 5000 inhabitants, 4000 are Christians, and the remainder Druzes. Aside from its great fountain, the only object of interest is a group of Druze chapels, the most celebrated of all the sanctuaries belonging to that sect. Crowning some of the lofty summits, they are strongly built, and the only architectural peculiarity they pos-

[1] Matt., xvi. and xvii.; Mark, viii. and ix.

sess is the smallness of the windows. Constituting a secret society, the Druzes select the most solitary places for their temples, to which no stranger may intrude.

But the commanding feature in the natural scenery of this region is Mount Hermon. From Hasbeiya it requires six hours of hard climbing to reach its lofty summit. The path first ascends a high wooded ridge; then, crossing a deep ravine, it winds upward over loose stones and amid tufts of coarse grass. A part of the anti-Lebanon range, Hermon is a vast limestone mountain, consisting of three principal summits. The northern one is the highest, and has the appearance of an obtuse truncated cone; the ascent is but 900 feet south from the parent range, and directly beneath its summit, some 5000 feet, in a basin-like glen, are the sources of the River Pharpar, near a small village called 'Arny. The third peak is a quarter of a mile to the west from the latter, and is the lowest of the three.

The second highest mountain in Syria, Hermon is 10,000 feet high. From its loftiest summit the eye sweeps over a landscape of extraordinary grandeur. The two parallel ranges of Lebanon and anti-Lebanon stretch far away to the "entering of Hamath" in the north, with the great valley of the Bukâ'a between them. Turning southward, the eye follows the sacred river, now resting in the basin of Hûleh, now expanding into the Sea of Tiberias, and beyond pursuing its infinite windings through the Jordan valley to the shining waters of the Dead Sea. Along its eastern banks appear in regular succession the rich pastures and "oaks of Bashan, the Mountains of Gilead, and those of Ammon and Moab, and opposite, the Hills of Samaria, of Benjamin, and Judah. Turning westward, there is Carmel and Tabor, and the Hills of Galilee; and on the white coast-line, 'Akka, Tyre, and Sidon; and far out into the "great sea," its waters mingling with the western horizon, is the Isle of Cyprus—the Chittim of the Phœnicians, and the scene of the ministry of Paul and Barnabas. Turning eastward, there is the Hauran, with its unvisited cities; and beyond, the Arabian Desert, from whose burning sands the sun comes forth, to descend at night into the cooling waters of the Mediterranean.

The southern peak of Hermon is crowned with curious ruins. Around the rocky crest is a circular wall, some of the large stones of which are beveled, while others have a plain moulding around the edge. Here are the remains of some grand but unknown temple, one of the columns of which stands upon the brow of a steep declivity. It is supposed that the ancient inhabitants of the land, being worshipers of the sun, here built their altar to that shining orb who is seen running his course in the heavens from the desert to the sea.

Around the base of this noble mountain vegetation is luxuriant, and on the lower ridges radiating from it are forests of oaks, interspersed with mountain shrubs; but the peaks are naked, and are covered with small limestones, rendering them smooth and bleak. Perpetual winter reigns upon their summits. The snow never disappears. All through the springtime to early summer, they resemble white domes standing out against the purple skies. In midsummer and in autumn the intense heat melts the snow from the tops of the ridges, but, owing to its greater depth, does not affect that portion which fills the ravines. And thus Hermon appears, alternately streaked with light and dark lines, till hoary winter comes again to weave his mantle of white, and cover therewith those majestic summits, the symbols of a purer world.

In every age it has had a name significant of some physical peculiarities. Its "lofty conical peak" suggested the name of Hermon; its rounded top, covered with snow and ice, and glittering in the sunlight, appeared to the Sidonians and Amorites like a massive "breast-plate," and by the former it was called "Sirion," and by the latter "Shenir."[1] Towering above its fellows, it is named by Moses "Sion—the Elevated;"[2] and, impressed with its majesty, the Arabs call it "Jebel esh Sheikh—the Chief Mountain."

In the poetry and geography of the Bible it is the image of grandeur and the landmark of national domain. Joshua conquered all the land east of the Jordan, "from the River Arnon unto Mount Hermon."[3] Visible from almost every tribe's possession, Hermon was not only the terminating point of view northward, but to the inspired writer, whether prophet or poet, it was "the image of unearthly grandeur, which nothing else but perpetual snow can give, especially as seen in the summer, when the firmament around it seems to be on fire."[4] In his exaltation of the Creator the Psalmist exclaims, "The

[1] Deut., iii., 9. [2] Ib., iv., 48. [3] Ib., iii., 8. [4] Stanley's S. and P., 396.

north and the south, thou hast created them; Tabor and Hermon shall rejoice in thy name."¹ The summit snows, condensing the vapors which, during summer, float around it in the higher regions of the atmosphere, produce abundant dew, which is a source of unfailing moisture to the adjacent country, while other portions of the land remained dry and parched. As the source of perpetual verdure and refreshing coolness, it was the image to the Hebrew poet of the enduring blessings of unity among brethren to the whole community. "As the dew of Hermon, and as the dew that descended upon the mountains of Zion;² for there the Lord commanded his blessing, even life for evermore."³

Returning to Magdala *en route* for Nazareth, we entered "The Valley of the Pigeons," one of the wildest glens in Northern Palestine. Bearing the Arabic name of Wady el-Hamân, it leads up from the Plain of Gennesaret to the Mount of Beatitudes. Its mouth is a mile to the west from the home of Mary of Magdala. At its entrance the ravine is broad, but contracts to a narrow mountain defile. The cliffs on either side are naked and broken, and rise to the height of a thousand feet. The one on the north is not as high as it is massive; the one on the south is bolder and more precipitous. Far up the gorge, and directly in front of the path, is a perpendicular bluff, terminating in a triangular point, and not unlike in appearance a venerable castle. Near its ancient base is a small but pretty spring, sending forth a soft murmur on the quiet air of Hamân. In the face of the rocks are immense natural and artificial caverns, the resort of pigeons, from which the vale takes its name. During the reign of Herod the Great these caves were filled with robbers, who were the scourges of the whole surrounding country. After the battle of Sepphoris Herod besieged this strong-hold. Failing in his attempt to scale the cliffs, he let boxes filled with soldiers down the face of the precipice, and landed them at the entrance of the caverns. Attacking the bandits with fire and sword, he succeeded in dislodging them, killing some, and dragging others out with long hooks, and then dashing them down on the rocks below.⁴

At the western end of this wild glen is the green plateau of Hattîn. Of irregular form, it is a mile in its greatest breadth.

¹ Ps. lxxxix., 12. ² Sion.
³ Ps. cxxxiii., 3. ⁴ Josephus, B. J., b. i., ch. xvi.

"VALLEY OF THE PIGEONS."

Every where well cultivated, it is bounded on the east, north, and south by low hills, and on the west by the Mount of Beatitudes. Ascending the "Mount," I found it to consist of two low summits, which suggested its present name, Kurûn Hattîn, "The Horns of Hattîn," from a fancied resemblance to the two horns of a camel's saddle. Being a quarter of a mile long, the adjacent ground rises gradually to its base, and the hill forms a crest less than 100 feet high. Relying upon an earlier tradition, the Crusaders revered Kurûn Hattîn as one of the sacred mountains, and, so far as they furnish any proof on the subject, the evangelists confirm the earlier and later traditions. Their simple story is that "Jesus went about all Galilee, preaching the gospel of the kingdom, and healing all manner of sickness and all manner of disease among the people. And there followed him great multitudes of people from Galilee, and from Decapolis, and from Jerusalem, and from Judea, and from beyond Jordan. And seeing the multitudes, he went up into a mountain; and when he was set, his disciples came unto him; and he opened his mouth and taught them."[1] The region of country, the distance from the sea, the magnificence of the surrounding scenery, the city of Safed "set upon a hill," the sloping sides of the mountain, and the lovely Plain of Hattîn at its base, combine to render this a befitting place for the delivery of our Lord's "Sermon on the Mount." Around it are the Hills of Galilee, to the east is seen the sea, and beyond it are Bashan and Bozrah; while to the north, surmounting one of the highest and grandest of the Galilean mountains, is the old Jewish city of Safed, to which, no doubt, the Savior pointed when he compared his Church on earth to "a city that is set upon a hill, that can not be hid." Only those who have seen Safed can appreciate the beauty and appropriateness of our Lord's allusion. From its moss-grown castle is not only obtained a view of the most glorious panorama in Palestine, stretching from the "Mountains of Samaria" to the Arabian Desert, but the allusion amounts to almost absolute truth that the "city can not be hid." Through all my journeyings for a week it followed me, and the "city set upon a hill" was ever suggesting the sublime lessons of the "Beatitudes." Whether on the shores of Tiberias, or on the Plains of Hattîn, or on the Hills of Nazareth, or by the Fountain of Seffûrieh, or on the

[1] Matt., iv. and v.

green fields of El-Buttauf, the city of Safed was before me, rising up from earth like a beacon-light, at once the confirmation of the Savior's words, and the impressive symbol of a living Church.

But Kurûn Hattin has a history other than that of having been the scene of the mild and life-giving teachings of Christ. It has a record of blood. On its heights and around its base was fought one of the saddest and most bloody battles in mediæval times, and the one which sealed the fate of the Crusaders in Palestine, and opened the gates of the Holy City to the profane and tyrannical rule of the Turks. Here, on the fifth of July, 1187, the flower of the Christian army, under Guy of Lusignan, met the barbarous hordes of Mohammedans, led on by Saladin, the mighty prince.

The Christians had succeeded to the full occupation of the Holy Land from ancient Gaza to the venerable city of Antioch. The weak-minded Guy of Lusignan had been elevated to the throne of Jerusalem as the successor of Baldwin V.; and as the powerful vassals of the king, Raynald of Chatillon was Lord of Kerak, and Count Raymond was Lord of Tiberias and Galilee. The Christians were enjoying a period of repose, under a truce which had been concluded with Saladin, the nephew of Nourreddin, and the new Sultan of Egypt. But Raynald of Chatillon, proving faithless to the compact, had plundered a caravan of merchants passing from Damascus to Arabia, and had even threatened the distant cities of Mecca and Medina. Saladin condescended to remonstrate, and demanded the release of the prisoners whom the Lord of Kerak held in chains. His demand rejected, the sultan swore to dispatch the perfidious Raynald with his own hand should he ever fall into his power. To revenge this breach of faith, Saladin lost no time in marshaling a mighty army. Damascus was the appointed rendezvous, and the warriors of the Crescent assembled in thousands, not only from the Assyrian provinces, but also from Egypt, Arabia, and Mesopotamia.

Alarmed by such stupendous preparations, the Crusaders in turn prepared to resist the foe and defend the sacred soil. Five miles to the southwest from Hattin is the large fountain of Seffurieh, which was the gathering-place of the Christian army. As if impressed with the finality of the struggle, the defenders of the Cross came from their mountain castles and their most distant fortresses to conquer or to die. From the banks of the Kadisha and of the Orontes, and from the shores of Tiberias, Raymond came with his faithful followers; from the fortresses of Kerak and Shobêk, Raynald led his well-trained knights; lesser barons advanced from Ascalon, Cæsarea, and Sidon, while the King of Jerusalem led in person a numerous army of Templars and hired troops. To add significance to the hour, the venerable bishops of Ptolemais and Lydda brought the Holy Cross which St. Helena had recovered, and elevated it amid the embattled host as the symbol of their faith and the inspiration of their courage.

More than a month had elapsed before the Moslems appeared. At length Saladin, with 80,000 horse and foot, swept around the head of the Lake of Tiberias, and took possession of the heights above the town. Encamped upon the Plains of Hattîn, and hoping to bring on a speedy and general engagement on his well-chosen field, the sultan sent out light detachments to lay waste the country from Jezreel to Tabor, and thence to Nazareth, within four miles of the enemy's camp. Unsuccessful in this attempt, he then seized Tiberias, and compelled the wife of Count Raymond to retire with her children to the castle of the city.

The intelligence of the capture of the capital of Galilee, and of the imminent danger of the wife and children of the Count of Tripolis, reached the camp of the Christians on the 3d of July. That night a council of war was held to decide upon the action of the coming day. Inspired by the misfortunes of a woman and confident of success, the king and his barons resolved to march in close array for the deliverance of Tiberias. Though unquestionably the most interested party, yet, from motives which have never been explained, Count Raymond opposed the decision of the council, and, having shown the folly of offensive movements in the heat of midsummer, in a region destitute of water and far from the base of their supplies, his policy was unanimously approved of by the king and the other members of the council. But, regarding the decision as unworthy the army of the Cross, the Grand Master of the Templars repaired to the royal tent, and overwhelmed the king with reproaches for having listened to the advice of a traitor, and conjured him not to suffer such a stain of cowardice to rest upon the Christian name. Overpersuaded, the king gave orders to arm, and at midnight the trumpet sounded, while heralds flew throughout the startled camp proclaiming the royal decree.

At dawn on the 4th of July the Christian army was in motion. His scouts had brought Saladin intelligence of the movement, and immediately he dispatched his light troops to harass the Crusaders on their march, while with consummate skill he posted his main army on the plain and along the crest of Hattin. His ardent wishes were about to be gratified, and his long-maturing plans were on the point of consummation. Late in the afternoon of the same day the King of Jerusalem reached the field of El-Lubieh, two miles to the southwest from the "Horns of Hattin," where a desperate battle occurred. Night closed around the belligerent armies without decisive result. That was a dreadful night. The wisdom of Raymond's advice now became apparent. The heat was intense; and, besides being harassed by the fierce Arabs, the Christians were dying for the want of water. Too weak-minded to take advantage of the darkness and order a midnight attack, and at least gain the shores of the lake, the feeble Guy determined to defer the conflict till the morrow. Whether to revenge the insult offered to his prudent counsels, or conscious of the impossibility of success in attempting to force the ranks of the foe, Raymond of Tripolis advised the course pursued. But it was the fatal step.

At length the morning came. It was the 5th day of July, 1187 A.D. The sky was cloudless, and the sun rose amid a fiery haze—the presage of consuming heat. It was a Syrian midsummer day, and the heavens were on fire. Led by their mighty prince, the followers of the Prophet were no less hopeful than brave. But, posted on a rocky plain without water, and with their tormenting thirst increased by the smoke and heat arising from the shrubs and trees which the enemy had set on fire, the Christians received the first shock of battle with a despondency preintimating the defeat that terminated that dreadful struggle. Yet on no previous field had they displayed a truer devotion, nor evinced a loftier courage. With varied fortunes, the battle raged from early dawn till late in the day. Now the Holy Cross was raised in momentary triumph, now the banner of the Crescent waved in transient victory. But in vain did the Knights of St. John launch their burnished spears at a foe they justly hate, and with equal courage receive in return the arrows and javelins of the Saracens. At length, driven to the highest summit of Hattîn, the king and a handful of Templars gathered around the Holy Cross. Again and again they drove back the enemy, and as often repulsed the terrible attacks of Saladin's cavalry. Manfully the bravest of the knights fell wounded around the symbol of their faith, and the Bishop of Ptolemais, who bore the Cross, was pierced with an arrow, and, falling bleeding to the ground, for a moment the sacred ensign disappeared, but, springing forward, the Bishop of Lydda grasped the Cross and bore it on high. But the battle was lost. The Crescent of Mecca shone triumphant. Saladin was the victor. The fields of Lubieh and the hill-sides of Hattîn were covered with the dying and the dead; Count Raymond, with the remnant of his followers, had fled, and safely reached 'Akka; while the defeated king, the Grand Master of the Templars, Raynald of Chatillon, and the Bishop of Lydda, with the Holy Cross, fell into the hands of the Moslems.

Conducted to the pavilion of Saladin, the distinguished prisoners were received with the respect due their rank, and with a kindness of demeanor worthy a great warrior. Glancing at each as the group stood before him, he seemed to pity their misfortunes, till his eye fell on Raynald, on whom he bent a look of mingled rage and scorn. Having ordered sherbet, cooled with ice, to be presented to the king, and the latter having passed it to Raynald, Saladin said, "Thou givest him to drink, not I;" which proverbial saying was equivalent to a sentence of death. Fixing his eye on the doomed count, and reminding him of his perfidy, he offered him pardon if he would embrace the doctrines of the Prophet; but, on Raynald refusing to renounce his Christian faith, the sultan drew his cimeter, and, piercing him through, the guards rushed upon him and dragged him lifeless from the imperial tent. Guy, with the captive princes, was sent to Damascus for imprisonment, and 230 knights, both of the Hospital and the Temple, were beheaded in cold blood and without mercy. Taking advantage of the destruction of the Christian army and of the capture of the king, Saladin advanced, and, after capturing the larger sea-port towns from Ascalon to Beirut, excepting Tyre, in less than three months from the battle of Hattîn he was master of all Palestine, and on the 3d of October, 1187, he entered the Holy City in triumph.[1]

From a scene so ghastly, yet so lovely, we journeyed from the Mount of Beatitudes to Nazareth. The path mounts the northwestern shoulder of Hattin, and descends to the Plain of Lubieh, where, on the summit of a low hill, is a village of the same name. Passing to the southwest, we entered a larger and richer plain, opening into El-Buttauf, and forming one of those fine plateaus which distinguish the mountain scenery of Galilee. A mile in width, it is a vast field of wheat and corn, and through its centre runs a noble road, which was thronged with pilgrims. From its western edge a path leads up to Kefr Kenna, the monkish "Cave of Galilee." Reaching the summit of the ridge at sunset, the Carmel range was overspread with a pink haze, while the castellated heights of Seffurieh reflected the last rays of the setting sun. Nazareth lay at our feet, surrounded with its ancient hills, and, descending the steep declivity, we entered the town amid the deepening shadows of evening, and were kindly received by the monks of the Latin convent.

It is a fact no less true than remarkable, that Nazareth is without an authentic history older than the Christian era; and though, at the time of the occurrence of the great event which has given immortality to its name, it was a considerable village, it is neither mentioned by Josephus nor the writers of the Old Testament. That it was known and generally held in contempt by the people prior to the Annunciation is evident from the significant question of Nathaniel, "Can there any good thing come out of Nazareth?"[2] Encompassed by 15 naked hill-tops, it occupies the western side of an oblong basin, which is a mile long and a quarter of a mile wide. Here, filling portions of the three ravines which penetrate the highest of the hills, the town is built. Constructed of limestone, the buildings are cleaner and neater than those of any other Syrian village. Out of a population of 4000 souls, more than three fourths are Christians. Under their enlightened influence Nazareth is increasing in wealth and numbers, and is now the capital of the district. As if conscious of their superior numbers, intelligence, wealth, and piety, the Christians assert and

[1] Gibbon's Rome, vol. vi., c. lix.; Tytler's U. H., vol. iv., c. ix.; Robinson's B. R., vol. ii., s. xv., p. 372-377.   [2] John, i., 46.

NAZARETH.

defend their rights. In nearly all other parts of Palestine the Christians are cringing and fearful, but the Nazarenes are not afraid either to measure swords or creeds with the followers of the Prophet. The whole town wears an aspect of genuine thrift and business prosperity, and the number of thriving schools, filled with pupils, is the best evidence of a free and enlightened Christianity. Supported by the Protestant Mission of Jerusalem, these schools are furnished with all the appliances requisite to success; and the hundreds of children annually educated can not fail to change the sentiments of the public, and heighten the tone of morals and piety in the city of our Lord's childhood.

The chief objects of interest in Nazareth are the legendary sites connected with the history of the holy family. Strangely enough, the Greeks and Latins contend for separate and rival localities as the scene of the Annunciation. In the southeastern portion of the town is the Latin convent, covering the traditional grotto where Mary stood when she received the salutation of the angel. The monastery is a square, heavy building, encompassed by a high stone wall, and is entered through a massive gate. Along the sides of an interior court are the school-rooms, the pharmacy, and the apartments of the superior. The interior of the church is a square of 70 feet, and consists of a nave and aisles formed by four large piers, on which rests the vaulted roof. The columns and walls are covered with canvas, painted in imitation of tapestry, and illustrative of Scripture scenes. Among the pictures is one representing the marriage of Joseph and Mary, and another portraying the appearing of the angel to the husband of the Virgin. A flight of 15 steps leads down to the sacred grotto, which is 20 feet long, as many wide, and 10 deep. The sides are incased with marble, and on the altar, which is of the same material, are seven vases of flowers, and over it are nine silver lamps, which are kept perpetually burning. Behind the altar is a large and excellent picture of the Annunciation, a gift of the Emperor of Austria. To the right of the altar a small door opens into the remaining portion of the grotto, which has been left in its natural state, and from this apartment a staircase leads up into a low rude cave, called the "Virgin Mary's Kitchen." This grotto is said to have been beneath the house and home of Mary.

Not content with the possession of a site so precious, the Franciscan monks pretend to have rescued from oblivion the "Workshop of Joseph." It is a small arched chapel, plain and neat, and, though a modern structure, is sanctified by a fragment of an old wall, a portion of the veritable "shop." Above the altar is a good painting representing Joseph at work. He is represented as leaning upon the handle of his axe; the youthful Savior is sitting near him reading from the Prophets, while Mary occupies a less conspicuous place. Still another picture adorns the walls of this humble chapel. Joseph is at work at his bench; Jesus is assisting his father by holding one end of the chalk-line while the latter is snapping it; and Mary is sitting opposite them, industriously at work with her needle.

As the rivals of the Latins, the Greeks have identified the site of the angelic salutation on the eastern side of the town, and over the "Fountain of the Virgin" have erected their "Church of the Annunciation." Without exterior elegance, it is a low structure, with arched ceiling supported by small square piers. In the east end is an altar-screen of wood, elaborately carved, on the panels of which are painted Bible scenes. In the opposite end is a large latticed screen, separating that portion of the church which is allotted to women from the main part of the edifice. In the north end is a recess occupied by the nuns, and over the entrance is a splendid picture of the Annunciation. Mary is represented as standing by a fountain, modest and attentive, and of a lovely form; near her is the Angel Gabriel, in the act of salutation; while above them is the august form of the Divine Father, with outspread hands, bestowing his gracious benediction.

Near this church, and at the base of a hill, is the outlet of the sacred fountain, which the Greeks claim to be the veritable spring to which Mary was accustomed to come for water, and where she was saluted by the angel. Having its source beneath the church, the water is conducted to this spot through a stone aqueduct, where, from under a rude arch, it flows into a marble trough. Though not perennial, yet, as this is the chief fountain of the city, and as it probably existed during the residence of the holy family, it was, no doubt, often visited by the mother of our Lord. The legend that the salutation was given at a spring is derived from the apocryphal Gospels, especially the one bearing the name of St. James.

Following the example of Mary, the beautiful maidens of Nazareth resort to this famous fountain not only for water, but for the more agreeable objects of conversation and courtship.

Coming from the "Church of the Annunciation" at the hour of vespers, I witnessed a scene here as novel as it was interesting. From twenty to thirty maidens were waiting to fill their long earthen pitchers from the crystal spring. Attired in a style as neat as it was elegant, they wore close-fitting jackets of different colors, long pointed veils of perfect whiteness, and head-dresses of silver coins. Their forms were straight and symmetrical, their features regular and handsome, their hair full and black, their eyes dark and lustrous, and their complexion of a soft brunette. Waiting their turn to the fountain, they laughed and chatted merrily together, and, gracefully poising the pitcher on head or shoulder, they seemed to regard the labor a delight rather than a task. Celebrated for their beauty, an old writer ascribes it to the special favor of Mary.

The only other great event connected with our Lord's life in Nazareth, and which could have had "a local habitation and a name," is his sermon in the synagogue, and the subsequent attempt of his townsmen to thrust him from the brow of the hill. Unwilling that any site should perish, the Latins pretend to have identified the one and the other. That which is shown as the site of the former may possibly be correct, but the "inventors of sacred places" have displayed less discrimination in the selection of the latter than in their choice of other localities. Selecting it for its precipitous appearance, as it overhangs the Plain of Esdraelon, the monks have designated a rugged mountain two miles to the southeast from Nazareth as the "Mount of Precipitation." But while the height and steepness of this mountain might have answered the murderous purpose of the Nazarenes, yet it is too distant to be in keeping with the letter of the text. With his accustomed minuteness, St. Luke gives a simple narration of the facts of that premeditated tragedy: "And all they in the synagogue, when they heard these things, were filled with wrath, and rose up and thrust him out of the city, and led him unto the brow of the hill whereupon their city was built, that they might cast him down headlong."[1] The lofty hill to the west of the town corresponds, in its relative location, to that of the city, and is more in harmony with

[1] Luke, iv., 28, 29.

the inspired narrative. With Nazareth at its base, covering its lower spurs and creeping up its ravines, it rises to the height of 500 feet. Its sides are steep and covered with white limestone rocks, and, though not smooth, it is not sufficiently uneven to arrest one's fall. Once started downward by a violent push, no human power could resist the force or avert the catastrophe. Desiring to test the difficulty of the descent, I found it impossible to descend with safety except by placing my feet in the fissures of the rocks. With a meekness which was the more remarkable because of its exalted purpose, the Master suffered the infuriated mob to hurry him through the crowded streets, and up through one of the ravines, to the brow of the hill, where, by a display of his wondrous power, he released himself from their grasp, and, "passing through the midst of them, went his way."

From the summit of this hill not only is one of the noblest views in Palestine obtained, but it is the best place for pious reflection. Reaching the highest point in half an hour, we found thereon the ruined wely of Neby Isma'il, and around it were growing the beautiful amaranth and other kinds of Syrian flowers. The wind blew strongly from the sea, which, together with a hazy sky, lessened the enjoyment of the hour; but the wide and glorious prospect was before us. There was Tabor, with its oaken groves; the "Mountains of Gilead," with the brown plateau of Pella; the Plain of Esdraelon, with its graceful undulations and memorable cities; the Hills of Samaria, green and rolling; the long range of Carmel, crowned with its wealthy convent, and casting its deep shadow into the Bay of Haifa, where the navies of Europe were riding at anchor; the Plain of 'Akka, where "Asher dipped his foot in oil, and yielded royal dainties;" the wide sea, "dotted with many a sail;" the intervening hills, all wooded and sinking down in gentle slopes into winding valleys of the richest verdure; the Plain of El-Buttauf, and the Crusaders' Castle of Seffurieh; the long ridges of the Galilean Hills running up toward Safed, "the city set upon a hill;" and rising above them all in grandeur was Hermon, with its mighty dome of snowy whiteness sparkling in the sun like a crown of glory.

Contracting the scope of the vision, the wandering eye returned and rested on the immortal village, quietly nestling at the mountain's base. It is Nazareth! How the sacred associations throng the mind! How the imagination is tempted to picture scenes which must have occurred, but which are not recorded! The theme is too divine for fancy. The same infinite wisdom is displayed in what is not written as is manifested in what is recorded. Lift not the veil that the Father has drawn over the thirty years of seclusion of his Son, nor attempt to be wise above that which is written. It is enough that in this mountain village lived Mary and Joseph; that here they loved and were betrothed; that by its spring, or in its fields, or in her quiet home, ere came the marriage-day, "Gabriel was sent from God unto a city of Galilee, named Nazareth, to a virgin espoused to a man whose name was Joseph, of the house of David; and the virgin's name was Mary. And the angel came in unto her and said Hail! thou art highly favored; the Lord is with thee; blessed art thou among women;" that twice after the annunciation Mary ascended from her native vale, and, crossing these same hills, she journeyed southward into Judea—once to visit her cousin Elizabeth, and again to give a Savior to the world; and that, after the presentation in the Temple, hither the holy family returned to the duties and enjoyments of private life.[1] With one solitary allusion, the silence of thirty years remains unbroken as to the life of Jesus prior to his public ministry. Subject to his parents, here he resided, treading these streets, wandering over these hills, and from this commanding summit beholding the same panorama which now is before us. The imagination pictures his childhood as lovely, his youth retiring and meditative, his manhood studious, youthful, and devout. Here were spent the years of preparation, and from a city without a history he went forth on the most benevolent mission that ever fell to the lot of man— to teach the sublimest truths, to illustrate the purest character, to die as no other man could die, and to establish a kingdom of righteousness, truth, and peace. Only twice is he known to have returned to the "city where he had been brought up;" once when rejected by his townsmen,[2] and again when he was met with the taunt, "Is not this the carpenter, the son of Mary, the brother of James, and Joses, and of Simon, and Judas? and are not his sisters with us?"[3] Unable to do many "mighty works there because of their unbelief," he abandoned Nazareth forever, and, choosing Capernaum as his "adopted city," he was received with joy by the delighted people.[4]

[1] Luke, i. and ii. [2] Ib., iv., 16. [3] Matt., xiii., 55, 56. [4] Luke, iv., 31.

CHAPTER XIV.

Phœnicia.—Its Extent and Fertility.—Origin of the Phœnicians.—Their Commerce.—Their Learning —Departure from Nazareth.—Cana of Galilee.—First Christian Wedding.—Beautiful Vale of Abilin.—Plain of Accho.—City of 'Akka.—Names.—Metropolis of the Crusaders.—Their Destruction.—Gibbon.—The Moslem Nero.—Napoleon's Defeat.—Road to Tyre.—Summer Palace.—Excavations.—Wild and dangerous Pass.—Antiquity of Tyre.—Three Tyres.—Stupendous Water-works.—Continental Tyre.—Sins and Judgments.—Glory departed.—How Prophecy was fulfilled.—Insular Tyre.—Tyre of the Crusaders.—Cathedral.—Tomb of Hiram.—Wonderful Temple.—Sarepta.—Zidon.—Gardens.—Ancient Glory.—Wars.—Harbor.—Citadel.—Tombs.—Interesting Discoveries.—Ornaments.

HISTORICALLY, the Holy Land is divided into three great sections—Palestine, Philistia, and Phœnicia. The latter is that long maritime plain stretching for 120 miles from the Promontory of Carmel on the south to the River Eleutherus on the north. Not exceeding 12 miles in its greatest width, it is washed by the Mediterranean on the west, and is bounded on the east by a mountain barrier, through which there is but one practicable pass from the "Ladder of Tyre" to the island of Aradus.[1] In addition to numberless streams, it is watered with the Rivers Kishon, Leontes, Aulay, Tamyras, Lycus, Adonis, Hadisha, and Eleutherus. Deriving its Greek name from "a palm," as significant of its richness, it is still fruitful where cultivated; and though only occasionally that celebrated tree is seen, yet groves of oranges and lemons environ its modern towns. While in its gardens are produced apricots, peaches, almonds, figs, dates, the sugar-cane, and grapes, which furnish excellent wine, its mountain slopes are covered with oaks, pines, acacias, tamarisks, and the majestic cedar. Divided into sections by bold promontories projecting far into the sea, its general surface is undulating, and its shore-line is indented with small bays, near which stood those renowned cities which have given celebrity to the whole plain.

Originally settled by the descendants of Sidon, the son of

[1] Porter.

Canaan, Phœnicia was included in the promise to Abraham; but, either from inability or unwillingness to expel its powerful and wealthy traders, it was only nominally possessed by his posterity. The grandeur of that promise, the sublime purpose of Jehovah as to the material greatness of his chosen people, together with the religious mission of the Jews, demanded such a maritime possession. Had they had the advantages of a powerful navy and of a vast commerce, Palestine would have been the leading power on earth, and would have held the first rank among the mighty nations of antiquity. It is one of those stupendous facts which illustrate the infinite wisdom of Providence, and the relations of the Promised Land to all the world, that, as Palestine has given to mankind a religion, Phœnicia is the primeval seat of commerce and letters. From their splendid cities of Tyre and Sidon the Phœnicians launched out upon the hitherto unknown Mediterranean, and, having planted colonies on the islands of Cyprus and Rhodes, they sailed into Greece. Emboldened by success, and charmed with the excitement of a new life, they turned to the northwest, and, having visited Sicily, Sardinia, and the northern coast of Spain, they passed through the Straits of Gibraltar, occupied the Isle of Gades, penetrated as far northward as Britain, and returning, they stretched southward from the Straits and founded Carthage, the formidable rival of Rome, and the only one that threatened her destruction.[2] It is a thought as beautiful as it is true, that, while holding commercial relations with all the nations on the shores of their native sea, and on the western coasts of Europe and Africa, and trafficking, by their caravans, with Persia, Arabia, and Asia, their intercourse with those distant nations was marked by the blessings of the arts of peace rather than by the calamities of war. Attaining the summit of their power and glory in the reign of Solomon, how changed would have been the moral aspects of the earth had those early mariners been Jews, disseminating a knowledge of the true God wherever they planted a colony, and illustrating a pure worship wherever they sold their "Tyrian purple." Celebrated for their knowledge of architecture and of various mechanic arts, and also for their learning, it was from one of these Phœnician cities that Cadmus went forth, about 15 centuries B.C., and laid the founda-

[1] Gen., x., 15. [2] Tytler's U. H., vol. i., p. 86; Hibbard's Palestine.

tion of Grecian literature, the pride of succeeding ages, and the glory of modern scholarship. Nowhere upon the globe can be found a tract of land so small as this, where have originated three such powerful agents for "weal or woe" to mankind, and which, still operating, are affecting the opinions and moulding the characters of men in all lands.

So intimately blended are the events of sacred and profane history connected with all that region extending from the Hills of Nazareth to the Mediterranean, and from the Promontory of Carmel to the mulberry groves of Sidon, that the traveler scarcely realizes the transition from Palestine to Phœnicia. Reluctantly leaving those scenes sacred to the life and deeds of our Lord, we found ourselves, at the close of the day, in the midst of new associations, dating back to the earliest authentic records. Stopping for a moment at the Fountain of Seffurieh, around which Guy de Lusignan gathered the heroic Crusaders on the night previous to the fatal battle of Hattin, we ascended the hill of ancient Sepphoris, and, crossing the beautiful plain of El-Buttauf, came to the ruins of Cana of Galilee. Situated seven miles to the north from Nazareth, it occupies a tongue of land extending into the plain, bounded on either side by a small ravine, and behind the town rises a rocky, barren hill. The home of Nathaniel the apostle,[1] and the residence of the bride of St. John, here was celebrated the first Christian wedding on record; and, being present as a guest, here the Savior performed his first miracle,[2] when

"The modest water, awed by power divine,
Confessed its God, and, blushing, turned to wine."

Here, at a subsequent visit, the Master was met by the "nobleman of Capernaum whose son was sick," and, though 20 miles distant, he healed the youth, and commanded the father, "Go thy way; thy son liveth."[3]

In the southern valley is a noble circular well, four feet in diameter, and probably the same from which the water was drawn for the miracle. An Arab, his son, and two daughters were resting there with their flocks, and from them we obtained a drink of the delicious water. But Cana is now a ruin, and is deserted. Not a house remains standing. Heaps of fallen buildings are overgrown with grass; and where the nuptials of the beloved John were celebrated the silence of death

[1] John, xxi., 2.   [2] Ib., ii., 1-11.   [3] Ib., iv., 46-54.

reigns unbroken, and rank weeds grow luxuriantly where Jewish maidens were wont to gather flowers to form the bridal wreath.

Turning westward, we entered the glorious Valley of Abilin. It is not wide, nor are the hills that inclose it high; but it is a scene of surpassing loveliness. Here are rolling hills covered with the richest verdure; wooded glens filled with oaks and acacias; soft lawns bright with flowers; running brooks falling over rocks into sparkling cascades, and birds of rare plumage singing their sweetest songs. Soon the sea, reflecting the sunlight from a smooth surface, burst like enchantment upon our view. Now the valley widens, the hills recede — they die away, and we are on the plain of ancient Accho. Carmel is seen to the south, the *Scala Tyriorum* to the north, while the Hills of Galilee are on the east, giving to the plain the form of a semicircle, with the sea-coast for a diameter. Eight miles wide and 20 long, most of it is a marsh in winter, but a fruitful garden in spring and summer. Falling to the lot of Asher, here " he dipped his foot in oil; his bread was fat, and he yielded royal dainties;"[1] and " here he continued on the sea-shore, and abode in his creeks,"[2] when Deborah called the nations to arms against Sisera.

Occupying a triangular neck of land, with a large bay on the south and the sea on the west, the town of 'Akka is large and well fortified. Having a population of 5000 souls, four fifths of whom are Moslems, it is the residence of the Pasha, whose jurisdiction embraces Nazareth, Safed, Tiberias, and Haifa. Regarded as of the first importance as a military position, it is garrisoned by a strong force. Though its massive fortifications, which were shattered in former wars, have never been repaired, its sea-wall, which is nine feet thick, is in a good condition, and is surmounted by several large guns. The buildings of the town are of stone, built square and high; the streets are narrow and shaded with matting, and the only structures of note within the city are the Mosque of Jezzär and the Temple of the Knights Hospitallers. The mosque is high and square, and is surmounted with a balustrade; the façade is adorned with a fine portico; the open area within is paved with Syrian marble, and is surrounded with an arcade on which are small domes. Beneath the palm and fig trees

[1] Gen., xlix., 20; Deut., xxxiii., 24. [2] Judges, v., 17.

old soldiers and venerable Turks were reclining in silence. Not far from the mosque is the city prison, consisting of an immense cellar, dark and loathsome, in which were 180 culprits of different ages, incarcerated for small and great offenses.

Called by Samuel Accho, by the Greeks Ptolemais, after Ptolemy, king of Egypt, and by the Arabs 'Akka, the Arabic of the scriptural name, the city is mentioned but twice by the sacred writers — once in connection with the tribe of Asher,[1] and again as the landing-place of St. Paul on his way to Jerusalem.[2] But it derives its chief importance from its relation to modern European history. Napoleon called it the "key of Palestine;" and, during the last 700 years, from Baldwin to Napier, it has been grasped by many a rude hand. As it bears three names, so it is remarkable for three historical events—the destruction of the Crusaders, the reign of Jezzàr, and the defeat of Napoleon I.

"After the loss of Jerusalem, Acre[3] became the metropolis of the Latin Christians, and was adorned with strong and stately buildings, with aqueducts, an artificial port, and a double wall. The population was increased by the incessant streams of pilgrims and fugitives; in the pauses of hostility the trade of the East and West was attracted to this convenient station, and the market could offer the produce of every clime and the interpreters of every tongue. But in this conflux of nations, every vice was propagated and practiced. . . . . The city had many sovereigns and no government. The Kings of Jerusalem and Cyprus, of the house of Lusignan, the Princes of Antioch, the Counts of Tripoli and Sidon, the Great Masters of the Hospital, the Temple, and the Teutonic order, the republics of Venice, Genoa, and Pisa, the Pope's legate, the Kings of France and England, assumed an independent command; seventeen tribunals exercised the power of life and death; every criminal was protected in the adjacent quarter; and the perpetual jealousy of the nations often burst forth in acts of violence and blood. Some adventurers, who disgraced the ensign of the Cross, compensated their want of pay by the plunder of the Mohammedan villages: nineteen Syrian merchants, who traded under the public faith, were despoiled and hanged by the Christians, and the denial of satisfaction justi-

[1] Judges, i., 31.   [2] Acts, xxi., 7.   [3] French of 'Akka.

ACRE FROM THE EAST.

fied the arms of the Sultan Khalil. He marched against Acre at the head of 60,000 horse and 140,000 foot; his train of artillery (if I may use the expression) was numerous and weighty; the separate timbers of a single engine were transported in 100 wagons; and the royal historian Abulfeda, who served with the troops of Hamah, was himself a spectator of the holy war. Whatever might be the vices of the Franks, their courage was rekindled by enthusiasm and despair; but they were torn by the discord of seventeen chiefs, and overwhelmed on all sides by the powers of the sultan. After a siege of 33 days the double wall was forced by the Moslems, the principal tower yielded to their engines, the Mamelukes made a general assault, the city was stormed, and death or slavery was the lot of 60,000 Christians. The convent, or rather fortress, of the Templars resisted three days longer; but the great master was pierced with an arrow, and of 500 knights only 10 were left alive, less happy than the victims of the sword if they lived to suffer on the scaffold in the unjust and cruel proscription of the whole order. The King of Jerusalem, the Patriarch, and the Great Master of the Hospital effected their retreat to the shore; but the sea was rough, the vessels were insufficient, and great numbers of the fugitives were drowned before they could reach the Isle of Cyprus, which might comfort Lusignan for the loss of Palestine. By the command of the sultan, the churches and fortifications of the Latin cities were demolished: a motive of avarice or fear still opened the holy sepulchre to some devout, defenceless pilgrims; and a mournful and solitary silence prevailed along the coast which had so long resounded with the world's debate."[1]

Five centuries later 'Akka became the royal city of one of the most infamous characters in history, whose name is to be mentioned only with that of Herod, and whose cruelties constitute him the Nero of modern times. Rising by theft and perjury from the servitude of a common slave to the dignity of a pasha, Jezzâr—"the Butcher," dishonored his pashalic with the most inhuman deeds, perpetrated without cause upon eminent citizens and upon the beautiful slave-girls of his harem.

But the city was destined to witness the exploits of the greatest warrior of our age. To the east of the town is a low mound,

[1] Gibbon's Rome, vol. vi., p. 46, 47.

where, in 1799, the great Napoleon planted his batteries, and from the summit of which, after eight successive assaults, he witnessed the defeat of his army, and with that defeat disappeared forever all his bright visions of an Eastern empire.

The distance from Acre to ancient Tyre is 25 miles, and the journey is replete with interest. Mounting our horses at 11 A.M., our path lay along the western border of the Plain of Phœnicia. In less than half an hour we passed beneath the Aqueduct of Jezzâr, supported by 100 arches. Through the neglect of a people who are indifferent to works of art, it is now a ruin, and in part overgrown with weeds. Two miles beyond is the summer palace of the late Abdallah Pasha. Sixty cypresses line the road-side, and within an inclosed garden, in the midst of orange and lemon trees, is the charming residence. Passing the site of Achzib, a town allotted to Asher,[1] we reached, in an hour, the *Scala Tyriorum*, or "Tyrian Ladder," forming the boundary-line between Phœnicia and the Holy Land. A bold promontory, with a white base dipping into the sea, it is the most southern root of Lebanon, and is the counterpart of Carmel. Sprinkled with shrubs and dotted with tufts of grass, its sides are broken and stony. The path over it is zigzag, and not unlike a flight of winding steps. The descent down the opposite side is exceedingly rough, now over low mountain spurs, and again through a narrow defile leading to a plain below. Passing over sections of an old Roman road, we came to the village of Nâkûrah, and to the east of it, high up in the mountain ravines, was a company of French soldiers excavating a buried city which has neither name nor story. They had succeeded in uncovering one temple and a number of elegant sarcophagi, but no inscriptions had been discovered by which to ascertain the origin of the unknown town. Two miles to the north we came to the white cliffs of Ras el-Abyad, or the *Promontorium Album* of the ancients. This is one of the wildest, and, at times, the most dangerous passes on the Phœnician coast. The sides of the bluff are perpendicular, and the waves dash wildly against its base. The path is cut in the white limestone rocks 500 feet above the level of the sea, and in places it skirts the very verge of the precipice. Huge boulders have fallen from the cliffs above, and others seem ready to follow. Excited by the grandeur of the scene and the dan-

[1] Josh., xix., 29.

LADDER OF TYRE.

TYRE.

ger of the moment, we successfully cleared the pass in half an hour, when we gained our first view of the plain and peninsula of Tyre. Descending rapidly to the plain below, the dreariness of the journey was relieved by the glorious appearance of Hermon, whose snow-capped summits were bright in the evening light, while the plain over which we rode was darkened by the shadows of the adjacent mountains. Traveling on for hours over the deep sandy beach, we reached Ras el-'Ain in the dusk of the evening, and an hour after entered the solitary gate of the renowned city of the ancient Tyrians.

Few cities can boast of a higher antiquity, of grander edifices, and of greater renown than Tyre. Founded by the Phœnicians, rebuilt by the Romans, and again restored by the Christians, there have been three Tyres, the history of each of which would fill a volume. Called by Isaiah the "daughter of Sidon,"[1] it was a "strong city" in the days of Joshua;[2] it was the ally of Solomon;[3] and it was a prize coveted by Shalmanezer, Nebuchadnezzar, and Alexander the Great. The cradle of commerce, Tyre became the mistress of the seas; her merchantmen traded in every port in the known world, and from her thriving shores she sent forth her sons, dotting the coasts of Europe and Africa with flourishing colonies. Nothing can excel the accuracy of detail and the elegance of graphic description contained in the 27th chapter of Ezekiel on the wealth and glory of Tyre; and now, after the lapse of twenty-five centuries, her scattered ruins attest the truth of prophecy. Her walls are destroyed, her towers broken down, her stones and timber are in the midst of the water, her ancient site is "a place for the spreading of nets in the midst of the sea," and the remains of her marble castles, gorgeous palaces, triple gateways, lofty towers, and spacious harbors are now seen half buried beneath the drifting sand or washed by the restless waves. Entering a small boat, and passing out of the inner basin into the larger harbor, we saw immense columns of red granite lying prostrate beneath the surface of the clear water, and others imbedded in the solid rock, or cemented together by some powerful agent.

The Sidonian colonists who founded Phœnician or Continental Tyre evidently settled on the main land, three miles to the south from the modern city, and a quarter of a mile from the

[1] Isa., xxiii.   [2] Josh., xix.   [3] 1 Kings, v.

shore. Here, at Ras el-'Ain, "the Fountain-head," are the most stupendous water-works of ancient times. They consist of four immense fountains, the water of which descends through the mountains on the east, and, rising to the surface here, is collected into separate reservoirs, from which it was originally distributed to irrigate the plain. The most southern of these fountains is the largest. Octagonal in form, it is 66 feet in diameter and 25 high. The lateral walls are eight feet thick, and gently slope to their base. Three hundred feet to the eastward are the other cisterns, one 36 and two 60 feet square, constructed of well-dressed stones, joined by a fine cement, and built directly over the places where the water gushes up from the earth. Formerly the stream was carried from the lower to the upper pools by an aqueduct which is now a ruin; and from the upper reservoirs there can now be traced an old Roman aqueduct, resting on arches, to a mound two miles distant, crowned with the remains of a massive building, from which point it turns westward toward the city. Amid a thicket of willows and groves of mulberry-trees are a few wretched huts, and the only use to which this great water-power is now applied is to drive a single mill and slake the thirst of the transient traveler.

Though they are unquestionably of a high antiquity, the author and finisher of these great works are unknown. There is an Arab legend that Alexander the Great constructed a subterranean canal through which he brought the water from Bagdad! but a more pious tradition ascribes them to Solomon. Quoting Menander the Ephesian, Josephus informs us that they existed in the days of Shalmanezer, who, in his siege of Tyre, placed guards at the rivers and aqueducts to hinder the Tyrians from drawing water."[1]

Around these fountains, and stretching northward over this fertile plain, stood the old city of Tyre. Though neither temple nor column remains to mark the site, yet beneath the drifted sands of many centuries lie entombed those magnificent ruins which have escaped the hand of the spoiler, and which, of late, have been uncovered in part near the hill called Tell Habeish. During the reign of Hiram, Palai-Tyrus consisted of two parts, the larger and grander standing near the fountains on the main land, and the smaller on an island three miles

[1] Anti B., b. ix., c. xiv.

RAS EL-'AIN.

to the north and not far from the shore.¹ It was by retiring to this island that the inhabitants were enabled to maintain the defense of their insular city against the attack by Shalmanezer during a period of five years.² Though subsequently besieged by Nebuchadnezzar for 13 years, yet it was reserved for the son of Philip to be the scourge of Providence, the destroyer of the city, and the accomplisher of prophecy. The continental city falling an easy prey to the victorious arms of Alexander the Great, he laid siege to the insular town for seven months. To capture this strong-hold, he removed a large portion of the materials of the former place, and with them built a causeway connecting the island with the continent. Advancing on this new military road, he took the city by storm; and, having slain 8000 of the citizens in the attack, he crucified 2000 others, and sold 30,000 more into slavery. Thus terminated the wonderful history of Phœnician Tyre, whose wealth was equaled only by her luxury, and whose power was excelled only by her pride. Abandoned to the worst forms of idolatry, she incurred the displeasure of an offended God; intoxicated with prosperity, she broke her "covenant" with the Hebrews, and confederated with other nations against them;³ haughty as she was impious, she scrupled not to demand the wealth and sacred ornaments of the Temple at Jerusalem, which the enemies of the Jews had sacrilegiously pillaged;⁴ forgetting the covenant with David and Solomon, she purchased the Jewish captives from their conquerors, and, loading her vessels with the human cargo, sold them into slavery in distant countries;⁵ and when Nebuchadnezzar had utterly destroyed the Holy City, and had subdued and wasted all the lands of the Jews, she exulted over their downfall, and insultingly exclaimed, "Aha! she is broken that was the gates of the people; she is turned unto me; I shall be replenished now that she is laid waste."⁶

For these sins God denounced against Tyre the severest judgments, and to-day she is a mournful proof of the accuracy and fulfillment of prophecy. Her royal palaces have given place to the abodes of poverty; her magnificent navy, with sails of embroidered linen from Egypt and ivory benches from the Isle of Chittim, has been exchanged for a few crazy fishing-

¹ Anti B., b. vii., c. ii. Hiram's Letter to Solomon.   ² Ib., b. ix., c. xiv.
³ Amos, i., 9.   ⁴ Joel, iii., 4, 5.   ⁵ Ib., iii., 6.   ⁶ Ezek., xxvi., 2.

boats; her famous mariners from Sidon and Arvad are superseded by boatmen whose nautical knowledge is not equal to a cruise on the Mediterranean five miles from land; and her vast commerce in the precious metals of Tarshish, the slaves of Javan, the horses of Togarmah, the coral and agate of Syria, the wheat of Minnith, the wine of Helbon, the spices of Sheba, the cassia and calamus of Dan, the precious clothes for chariots of Dedan, and the fine fleeces of Arabia, has dwindled down to an occasional cargo of millstones and juniper charcoal. Even her hill-sides, once rich in olive-groves, are now forsaken; and such have been the incursions of the sea, that the once fertile plain of Tyre has been transformed into a sandy waste, and she who was the "perfection of beauty is now smitten with baldness;" in her unrelieved desolation, her harps of gold and enchanting minstrelsy are forever silent, and winds and waves alone lament her departed glory. So complete is the ruin of the primal city, and so difficult to determine with exactitude the site of the Phœnician Tyre, that it is still true, "Thou shalt be no more; though thou be sought for, yet shalt thou never be found again, saith the Lord God."[1] In removing the materials of the old town to fill up the arm of the sea between the island and main land, Alexander the Great fulfilled these astonishing words: "They shall break down thy walls and destroy thy pleasant houses; and they shall lay thy stones, and thy timber, and thy dust in the midst of the water."[2] And, as significant of the utterness of her ruin, the traveler of to-day beholds what the prophet saw in the heavenly vision: "I will make thee like the top of a rock; thou shalt be a place to spread nets upon; thou shalt be built no more."[3]

While the words, "Thou shalt be built no more," are singularly and literally true when applied to Continental Tyre, yet the island city, which was not included in the prophetic denunciation, rose to great elegance under the Romans. Attaining to somewhat of the pristine splendor of the parent city in the first century, it resumed in part its ancient sway over the sea. Receiving Christianity at an early period, it was visited by St. Paul when on his way to Jerusalem, "who, finding disciples, we tarried there seven days."[4] Seized by the Arabs in 638 A.D., it remained in their possession till June 27, 1124, when

[1] Ezek., xxvi., 21.
[2] Ib., xxvi., 12.
[3] Ib., xxvi., 14.
[4] Acts, xxi., 4.

it was captured by the Crusaders, who held it for 150 years, when it fell again into the hands of the Moslems on the evening of the day on which 'Akka was captured. Declining under their withering sceptre, at the close of the 17th century it was without a house, and its vaults were occupied by a few fishermen.[1] Under the fanatical Metawileh, in 1766 it was partially restored. Modern Tyre is a village of 4000 inhabitants, equally divided in their religious faith between Christ and Mohammed. What was once Alexander's causeway is now a sandy isthmus, and what was once an island is now a peninsula. Originally extremely narrow, but increased by the action of the winds and waves upheaving the loose sands, the isthmus is half a mile wide, and that which was formerly the island is a ridge of rocks parallel to the shore, nearly a mile long, three quarters of a mile broad, and half a mile distant from the coast-line. The general surface is uneven, in part strewn by rocks, and in part encumbered by the accumulation of rubbish. The present town occupies the northwestern portion of the peninsula, and is near the ancient harbor. A single gate admits the traveler to the city. Around it are the remains of old towers, and near it are two deep wells, from which the inhabitants obtain their principal supply of water. With few exceptions the buildings are mere hovels, the streets narrow and crooked, and the citizens filthy and ignorant. As if to hide the fallen glory of Tyre, there are a few palms and pride of India trees growing in the gardens. Within the shattered walls and along the shore fishermen were mending their nets, and in the gloomy bazars were a few bales of cotton and tobacco, several tiers of millstones, and heaps of charcoal. The Moslems have a mosque crowned with two domes, and from beside it rises a tapering minaret; the Christians have two small churches, which are remarkable neither for their size nor elegance. In the southeast corner of the town are the remains of the famous Cathedral of Tyre, erected in the fourth century by Bishop Paulinus, and consecrated by Eusebius, and by the latter described as the most splendid of all the temples of Phœnicia. It was 216 feet long by 136 broad, and its ruins indicate its great magnificence. The south wall, the east and west ends, together with the chancel, remain standing; but the arched roof, the massive columns which sup-

[1] Robinson, vol. ii., p. 470.

ported the triforium, and the lofty tower, with its spiral staircase, have fallen into a thousand fragments. Somewhere within these broken walls reposes the dust of Origen and of the Emperor Frederick Barbarossa.

TOMB OF HIRAM.

Five miles to the east of the town is the Tomb of Hiram, king of Tyre. It is an imposing mausoleum, and one of the most interesting monuments in the Holy Land. It is less remarkable for its beauty and ornaments than for its grandeur and durability. Crowning a graceful hill, it consists of a pedestal and a sarcophagus. The former is composed of four layers of immense blocks of limestone, about ten feet high; the latter is hewn out of a solid block, and is twelve feet long, eight wide, and six high, and is surmounted with a pyramidal lid five feet thick. The ends of the lid are beveled, the top rounded, and it is fitted on with such care that it is difficult to remove it. On the north side of the monument is an arched vault 20 feet square and 12 deep, which no doubt served as the place for the final repose of the royal family. Commanding a view of the City of the Great King, and of the sea beyond, the country around the tomb is strangely solitary; neither ancient ruin nor human habitation is near, but, standing alone, it is at once a venerable relic of the past and an impressive monument of the loneliness of death.

On the same road, but some distance to the west, the French have excavated one of the most splendid temples yet discovered in the environs of Phœnicia. Consisting of a nave, two side aisles, a chancel, and an altar-piece, it is 75 feet long by 36 wide. The roof and portions of the walls are gone. Of the 14 columns which formed the aisles only the bases of 11 of them remain, on each of which is sculptured the Maltese cross. But its great beauty consists in its magnificent mosaic pavement, covering more than two thirds of the entire area. Formed of small square blocks of white and black marble, it is arranged in the most curious manner. In the aisles are circles 30 inches in diameter, containing figures of sheep, fish, fowls, fruits, tigers, elephants, buffaloes, dogs, horses, rabbits, deer, lions, antelopes, and leopards, together with ten mythological busts, representing the gods and goddesses of Greece and Rome. Before the high altar is a lengthy inscription in Greek characters; but, owing to their curious forms and the numerous contractions, it was impossible to decipher it without reference to learned works. From all that we could learn from those having the work in charge, it was originally a heathen temple, was converted into a Christian church by the Crusaders, and, abandoned during the mediæval wars, it has since remained buried beneath the accumulated sand and rubbish of centuries.

A single historic site breaks the monotony of the journey from Tyre to Sidon, a distance of 25 miles. The path follows the coast along the Plain of Phœnicia, over which "a mournful and solitary silence now prevails."[1] While the hills which bound it on the east are carefully cultivated, and the summits thereof are adorned with villages, this vast and rich plain is deserted. Less than two miles from the gate of Tyre we passed a large fountain, believed by the Arabs to possess medicinal

[1] Gibbon.

virtues, and four miles beyond we came to the banks of the Leontes of the old geographers, and the Nahr el-Kâsimíyeh of the natives. The third largest river in Syria, its highest source is not far from the ruins of Ba'albek; and draining the southern section of the Bukâ'a, with the adjoining sides of the Lebanon and anti-Lebanon, it bursts the everlasting gates of the former, and, descending through a wild ravine, crosses the plain to the sea. It is twenty-five feet wide; its clear waters flow rapidly through a deep gorge, which is now spanned by a modern bridge, having a single arch. Nine miles to the north is Khan el-Khudr, the Zarephath of the Old Testament and the Sarepta of the New. On a fine hill overhanging the plain is the large town of Sŭrafend, the Arabic of the Scriptural name. The original city stood near the shore; its site is now marked by a Mohammedan tomb and a noble fig-tree. Driven by famine from his retreat by the "brook Cherith that is before Jordan," hither Elijah came, and was received into the house of that poor widow whose "barrel of meal wasted not, neither did the cruise of oil fail," and whose son, as a reward of faith and charity, the prophet raised to life.[1] And here an early tradition has preserved the site of that touching scene of the meeting of Christ and the woman of Syro-Phœnicia, whose daughter he healed during his first and only visit "to the coasts of Tyre and Sidon."[2]

Ten miles to the north appeared the towers and minarets of Zidon, surrounded with the most luxuriant gardens in the world. In the intervening distance sections of the old Roman road can still be traced, and along the highway are several milestones. On one are inscribed the names of Septimius Severus and his son, M. Aurelius Antoninus, better known in history as Caracalla. The inscription bears the date of 198 A.D. Entering the famous gardens of the modern Saida, we rode for an hour through lengthened avenues of acacias and tamarisks, and amid mulberry groves, and vast orchards of peaches, pears, apricots, plums, quinces, oranges, lemons, bananas, and citrons, which filled the air with a delightful fragrance, and presented to the eye a variety of finely-tinted and exquisite foliage. Interspersed through these beautiful groves are country seats possessing all the charms of an earthly paradise. Our rural path terminated at the very gate of the city, which was care-

[1] 1 Kings, xvii.   [2] Mark, vii., 24-30.

SIDRA.

fully guarded by Turkish soldiers. Entering the town, we found it situated on a small promontory projecting obliquely into the sea. Thoroughly Oriental in character and appearance, its narrow, shaded streets and groups of trees give it an air of repose. While many of its buildings are small, like those in most Syrian towns, there are several large and costly. The population is not less than 10,000, and is composed of Moslems, Maronites, Greeks, and Jews. The chief vocations of the citizens are the cultivation of fruits and the manufacture of oil and silk, which are exported into Egypt and to ports along the Mediterranean.

With an antiquity anterior to authentic history, Sidon is among the oldest of known cities. Mentioned by the inspired historian in connection with Sodom and Gaza,[1] it is supposed it was founded by Sidon, the grandson of Noah.[2] Increasing in wealth and power, the city had achieved such fame at the time the Hebrews entered Canaan that it is designated by Joshua the "Great Zidon."[3] As early as the Trojan war the Sidonians were celebrated for their skill in the arts, especially for the manufacture of gorgeous robes, to which Homer alludes:

> "The Phrygian queen to her rich wardrobe went,
> Where treasured odors breathed a costly scent;
> There lay the vestures of no vulgar art,
> Sidonian maids embroidered every part,
> Whom from soft Sidon youthful Paris bore,
> With Helen touching on the Tyrian shore.
> Here, as the queen revolved, with careful eyes,
> The various textures and the various dyes,
> She chose a veil that shone superior far,
> And glow'd refulgent as the morning star."[4]

Increasing in population and commerce to such a degree as to demand another city, the Sidonians passed down the coast and founded Tyre, which is called by Isaiah the "daughter of Zidon," and which in after years divided with the parent city the empire of the seas.[5] Excelling all other nations of that period in art and science, her architects were employed by Solomon in building his magnificent temple.[6] According to early historians, the Sidonians were versed in astronomy, ge-

[1] Gen., x., 19.   [2] Ib., x., 15; Josephus, Anti B., b. i., c. vi.
[3] Josh., xix., 28.   [4] Pope's Il., b. vi., 360-370.
[5] Isa., xxiii., 12.   [6] 1 Kings, v.

ometry, and philosophy, and the vastness of their commerce evinces their knowledge of navigation. But with them, as with all the other great nations of antiquity, the usual vices attended their prosperity, and the increase of luxury was counterbalanced by the decline of national virtue. Practicing the worst forms of idolatry, indulging in the grossest immoralities, and violating the most solemn treaties with God's people, they drew down upon themselves the severe denunciations of Jehovah's prophets. Sentenced by the Lord to the calamities of war, the prophetic judgments were executed by Shalmanezer in 720 B.C.; by Artaxerxes Ochus four centuries later; by Alexander the Great, who entered the gates of the city without a struggle; and subsequently it has been pillaged and destroyed as often as rebuilt, by the Ptolemies, the Syrian kings, the Romans, the Moslem invaders, the Crusaders, until at present its port is without a merchantman, and the town of Beirût, to the north, has become the successful rival of the once affluent and powerful Sidon.

The three great objects of interest connected with the modern town are the harbor, the citadel, and the tombs. The harbor is formed by a low ridge of rocks running parallel to the shore and extending out from the northern point of the peninsula. On the rocks stands an old castle, weather-beaten and much dilapidated, connected with the main land by a bridge of nine arches. On a commanding hill to the south of the city is the shattered tower of Louis IX., which is now the citadel of the town. On the plains and in the hill-sides to the east of Sidon is the cemetery of its ancient inhabitants, called Mûgharet Tubloon. The surface of the rock has been cut away to form a perfect level, and here are the mansions of the dead, arranged in the form of catacombs, from 10 to 30 feet below the surface of the ground. From a deep, broad avenue, doors open into lateral halls and rooms, in which are cut the receptacles for the dead. Descending to the depth of 20 feet, we entered a broad avenue 25 feet long, which had just been opened. Running at right angles with the former was a spacious passageway, in the sides of which are six niches, each five and a half feet deep, four wide, and ten long. In these niches are magnificent marble sarcophagi, their sides, ends, and lids being adorned with sculptured lion heads, horns of plenty, and garlands of flowers. On one, which I took to be the sarcophagus of a queen, is carved the bust of a female in relief, surrounded with a wreath of roses. Passing into another chamber, more elegant than the rest, and which is 20 feet deep, I traced the beautiful floral paintings on the sides and ceilings of the vault. Here, in the very centre of the floor, are three entire sarcophagi, of equal grandeur with the others, measuring eight feet long, three wide, and as many deep. The largest of the three, which had that day been uncovered for the first time, *was filled with clear water*, and on the bottom were human bones, and what appeared to be a fine sediment—perhaps the dust of the departed. How the water came there remains a mystery. Some suppose it had percolated through the rocks above; but this will hardly account for the equally remarkable fact that the other sarcophagi are dry. Neither inscription nor symbol had been discovered revealing the name and history of the dead, and I was left to the reflection that I was gazing upon the disorganized forms of those who had lived and died nearly 4000 years ago. Several sarcophagi have been removed to a museum of antiquities within the city. Male and female figures are sculptured on them, the faces of the former resembling the facial features of Nero, and of the latter those of Minerva. Among the relics is a leaden coffin beautifully moulded with beaded work, flowers, and leonine heads; and in the " Cabinet of Ancient Coins and Curiosities" are a Phœnician tear-bottle, gold rings, gold coins of the age of Alexander, a Crusader's silver cross which was worn in battle, and many rare jewels of great intrinsic value.

CHAPTER XV.

Mountains of Lebanon.—Grand Scenery.—Sublime View.—Mountain Traveling.—Scriptural Allusions.—Cedars of Lebanon.—Their Number, Appearance, and symbolic Character.—Population of the Mountains.—Districts and Peculiarities of the Druzes and Maronites.—New Road.—Crossing the Mountains.—Plain of the Buká'a.—Leontes.—A swollen River.—Ancient Cities.—Imposing Cavalcade.—Wives of the Pasha of Damascus.—First View of Damascus.—Splendor and Enjoyments of the Interior of the City.—Great Plain of Damascus.—Abana and Pharpar.—Scene of St. Paul's Conversion.—City without Ruins.—Antiquity and thrilling History of Damascus.—House of Judas.—Home of Ananias.—"Street called Straight."—Naaman's Palace.—Tombs of the Great.—Location of Damascus.—Walls and Gates.—Old Castle.—Great Mosque.—Gardens of Damascus.—Commerce of the City.—Curiosities in the Bazars.—Population.—Christian Citizens.—Origin of the Massacre of 1860.—Its Progress.—Terrible Scenes.—American Vice-Consul.—Ruins.—Sad Results.—Defense of the Christians by Abd-el-Kader.—Visit to the Chieftain of Algiers.—Our Reception.—Testimonials.—His Appearance.—Conclusion.—Political History of Palestine.—Its Condition under the Turks.—It is now in a Transition State.—Possessions of European Nations.—Future of the Holy Land.—Christian Missions.—Decline of Mohammedanism.—Religious Liberty.—Future Glory.

BRANCHES of the ancient Taurus chain, the parallel mountain ranges of Lebanon and anti-Lebanon, extend from north to south through the whole length of the Land of Promise. Geologically they consist of a hard, calcareous, whitish stone, and are disposed in strata variously inclined. Varying in altitude from 3000 to 13,000 feet above the sea, and skirted with plains at different points, they continually change their form and appearance with their levels and situation. Their three highest summits are Hermon, Sunnîn, and Mukhmel. The first is 10,000 feet high, the second 11,000, the third 13,000. Their surface is generally smooth, bare, and rounded, but in sections it is broken and rugged, resembling huge piles of rocks, not unlike, in form, the ruins of towns and castles. They abound in springs, which, together with the melting snows covering their higher portions, form torrents, that descend to the plains on either side, refreshing the parched fields, and imparting an air of liveliness to the scene. Both their sides and summits are dotted with forests and groves of oak, fir, larch, box, laurel, myrtle, and cedar-trees; and, though the soil is scanty, the industrious peasants have planted vineyards on artificial terraces which yield the most delicious wines. In the region about the great Valley of Kadisha are vast mulberry groves, the leaves of which serve as food for the silk-worm, and the villagers in that section are chiefly employed in the production of silk in its raw state.

In crossing the Lebanons the traveler meets with scenes in which Nature displays beauty or grandeur, sometimes romantic wildness, but always variety. The sublime elevation and steep ascent of this magnificent rampart, which seems to inclose the country, and the gigantic masses which shoot into the clouds, inspire him with astonishment and reverence. At times he seems to be traveling in the middle regions of the atmosphere; above him the sky is clear and serene, below him the thick clouds are dissolving into rain and watering the plains. On gaining the loftier peaks, he is filled with delight by the immensity of space which expands around him, and which becomes a fresh subject of admiration. On every side he beholds a horizon without bounds, while in clear weather the sight is lost over the desert, extending to the Persian Gulf, and over the Mediterranean, the waters of which wash the shores of Europe. Apparently his view commands the world; and the wandering eye, surveying the successive chains of mountains, transports the mind in an instant from Antioch to Jerusalem. Approaching nearer objects, he observes the white coast of the "Great Sea" on the west, with a boundless expanse of water beyond, and examines with greater minuteness the rocks, the woods, the torrents, the sloping sides of the hills, the villages and towns around him, and exults at the diminution of objects which formerly appeared so great. He sees the valleys obscured by storm-clouds with fresh delight, and smiles at hearing the thunder muttering beneath his feet. The once threatening summits now appear like the furrows of a plowed field or the steps of an amphitheatre, and he feels himself gratified by an elevation above so many lofty objects, on which he now looks down with inward satisfaction.

On penetrating into the interior districts of these mountains, the roughness of the roads, the steep descents and precipices, strike him at first with terror; but the sagacity of the horse he rides, which can traverse them with safety, soon relieves him, and he calmly surveys those picturesque scenes that entertain him in quick succession. He travels whole days together to reach a place which was in sight at his departure; he winds, descends, skirts hills, and climbs their precipitous sides, and in this perpetual change it seems as if Nature herself varied for him at every step the decorations of the scenery. Sometimes he beholds villages clinging to the steep declivities on which they are built, and so arranged that the terraces of one row of houses serve as streets to those above them. Sometimes he espies the habitation of a recluse standing on a solitary height, or a gray convent, whose bell awakens the echoes of the Lebanons. At times he sees a rock perforated by a torrent, and which has become a natural arch, and another worn perpendicular, resembling a high wall. On the hill-sides he passes beds of stones, uncovered and detached by the waters, rising up like artificial ruins; and in many places, where the waters meet with inclined beds, the intermediate earth has been washed away, leaving immense caverns, or subterranean channels have been formed, through which rivulets flow the year round.[1]

In traversing the Lebanons, the traveler is impressed with the accuracy of the allusions of the inspired writers to these wonderful mountains. Such was their fame in the days of Moses that he earnestly prayed, "Let me go over and see the good land that is beyond Jordan, that goodly mountain, and Lebanon."[2] Considered wild and dreary, the seat of storm and tempest, Lebanon was the type of national desolation in the mind of the prophet; and regarding its restoration to fertility as the symbol of returning national prosperity, he asks the significant question, "Is it not a very little while, and Lebanon shall be turned into a fruitful field, and the fruitful field shall be esteemed as a forest?"[3] Always regarded a strong barrier to the Land of Promise, and opposing an almost insuperable obstacle to the movements of chariots of war, it was the arrogant boast of Sennacherib, "By the multitude of my chariots am I come up to the height of the mountains, to the sides of

---

[1] Volney's Trav., vol. i.; Paxton's Illustrations, vol. i.
[2] Deut., iii., 25.   [3] Isa., xxix., 17.

Lebanon; and I will cut down the tall cedars thereof, and the choice fir-trees thereof; and I will enter into the height of his border, and the forest of his Carmel."[1] As of old, so now, the less inhabited portions of the range are the chosen haunts of beasts of prey, to which the prophet thus alludes: "The violence of Lebanon shall cover thee, and the spoil of beasts, which made them afraid, because of men's blood, and for the violence of the land, of the city, and of all that dwell therein;"[2] and to such ferocious animals that roam on its summits and lodge in its thickets, and occasionally descend to the plain in quest of prey, Solomon refers, in that animated invitation to his spouse, "Come with me from Lebanon, my spouse, with me from Lebanon; look from the top of Amana, from the top of Shenir and Hermon, from the lions' dens, from the mountains of the leopards."[3] In allusion to the fragrant odors wafted from the aromatic plants growing upon its sides, the poet apostrophizes the same imaginary being in these elegant words: "And the smell of thy garments is like the smell of Lebanon."[4] The large vineyards which adorn the terraced sides of the mountains produce wines of great richness and choice flavor; they are of a beautiful color, and so oily that they adhere to the glass. It was to their reviving effect and odor that Hosea refers: "They that dwell under his shadow shall return; they shall revive as the corn, and grow as the vine; the scent thereof shall be as the wine of Lebanon."[5] The rapid growth of the Christian Church, her great extent, and the countless number of her converts, was announced in the no less sublime than truthful figure, "There shall be a handful of corn in the earth upon the tops of the mountains; the fruit thereof shall shake like Lebanon."[6] The stupendous size, the extensive range, and great elevation of Lebanon; its towering summits capped with perpetual snow or crowned with fragrant cedars; its olive plantations; its vineyards, producing the most delicious wines; its clear fountains and cold-flowing brooks; its fertile vales and odoriferous shrubberies, combine to form, in Scripture language, "the glory of Lebanon." In preintimating the conversion of the Gentiles from their idolatry and corruption to the purity and blessings of Christianity, Isaiah employs the majestic figure, "The wilderness and the solitary place shall be glad for

---

[1] Isa., xxxvii., 24.   [2] Hab., ii., 17.   [3] Song, iv., 8.
[4] Ib., iv., 11.   [5] Hosea, xiv., 7.   [6] Ps. lxxii., 16.

them; and the desert shall rejoice, and blossom as the rose. It shall blossom abundantly, and rejoice, even with joy and singing; the glory of Lebanon shall be given unto it, the excellency of Carmel and Sharon, they shall see the glory of the Lord, and the excellency of our God."[1]

In all ages the cedar of Lebanon has been regarded as an object of unrivaled grandeur and beauty in the vegetable kingdom. It is, accordingly, one of the natural images which occur in the poetical style of the Hebrew prophets, and is appropriated to denote kings, princes, and potentates of the highest rank. In the days of Solomon the cedar forests of Lebanon were extensive, but at present there is but one known group on all the range. At the head of Wady Kadisha, in a vast but secluded recess formed by the loftiest of the Lebanon summits, and encircled by a region of perpetual snow, is the small remaining forest of 400 trees of all sizes and ages. The axe of the builder and the ruthless hands of peasants have done much to reduce the once grand forests to this small clump of trees, to preserve which the mountains seem to have gathered round, covering them from the gaze of the destroyer. Their solitude strangely affected me; they stand alone, without another tree in sight or a patch of verdure on the surrounding acclivities. They cover the sides and summits of a pretty knoll, which is at the northeastern end of a recess eight miles in diameter, in the central ridge of Lebanon. The encircling summits are the highest in Syria, and streaked with perpetual snow. They are white and rounded, and their sides descend in naked, uniform slopes in the form of a semicircle. Some of the trees are in the vigor of their growth, others are gnarled and venerable. In form they are perfect images of grace and majesty. They are tall and straight, with fanlike branches, contracting like a cone toward the top. The shag-bark is coarse and heavy; the leaves are small, narrow, rough, exceedingly green, of a sombre hue, and arranged in tufts along the branches; they shoot in spring, and fail in early winter; the cones resemble those of the pine. From the full-grown trees a fluid trickles naturally and without incision; it is clear, transparent, whitish, and, after a time, dries and hardens. In most cases the branches shoot out horizontally from the parent trunk, forming beautiful pyramidal circles. On the summit of the knoll are

[1] Isa., xxxv., 1, 2.

CEDARS OF LEBANON.

several aged trees 40 feet in girth, and on the northern side is one the very image of strength and grandeur; its branches are larger than the trunks of ordinary trees, and its majestic limbs, stretching out over a vast area, afford a grateful shade. In the centre of the group is the patriarch of the grove. Measuring 48 feet in circumference, the trunk is gnarled, the stronger branches have fallen off, and its once majestic form bends toward the earth under the weight of many years. Standing beneath its patriarchal shade, I could but ask, "How old art thou?" for it seemed to have come down from the days of the ancient seers.

Pre-eminently the cedars are "sacred" trees. The inspired narrator has linked them inseparably to many of the grandest events of Bible history. These are the "trees of the Lord," the "cedars of Lebanon which he hath planted;"[1] here is the remnant of that forest from which the timber was taken for God's Temple in Jerusalem;[2] these are the inspired similitudes of grandeur, strength, power, and glory. In denouncing the judgments of the Lord upon the proud and arrogant, the prophet declares: "For the day of the Lord of hosts shall be upon every one that is proud and lofty, and upon every one that is lifted up, and he shall be brought low; and upon all the cedars of Lebanon that are high and lifted up, and upon all the oaks of Bashan."[3] To awaken grateful emotions in the hearts of the degenerate Jews, Amos reminds them, "Yet destroyed I the Amorite before them, whose height was like the height of the cedars;"[4] and, as an illustration of Jehovah's displeasure with royal pride, Ezekiel exclaims, "Behold, the Assyrian was a cedar in Lebanon with fair branches, and with a shadowing shroud, and of a high stature; and his top was among the thick boughs."[5] To break the cedars, and shake the enormous mass on which they grow, are figures selected by the Psalmist to express the awful majesty and infinite power of God. "The voice of the Lord is powerful; the voice of the Lord is full of majesty. The voice of the Lord breaketh the cedars; yea, the Lord breaketh the cedars of Lebanon."[6] The forests of the East, always near the point of ignition under the intense beams of a vertical sun, are frequently set on fire by the carelessness of those who have taken shelter in their recesses, and the de-

---

[1] Ps. civ., 16.   [2] 1 Kings, v. and vi.; Ezra, iii., 7.   [3] Isa., ii., 12, 13.
[4] Amos, ii., 9.   [5] Ezek., xxxi., 3–10.   [6] Ps. xxix., 4, 5.

vouring element continues its ravages till extensive plantations are consumed. To such a conflagration the prophet compares the destructive operations of the Roman armies under Vespasian and Titus against the Jews, when the nobles and rulers were slaughtered, the city and temple reduced to ashes, the people either put to the sword or sold into slavery, and the whole country laid waste. "Open thy doors, O Lebanon, that the fire may devour thy cedars. Howl, fir-tree, for the cedar is fallen; because the mighty are spoiled: howl, O ye oaks of Bashan, for the forest of the vintage is come down."[1] And as the noblest of trees, and the most perfect symbol of prosperity when in their prime, they contain the significance of the precious promise, "The righteous shall flourish like the palm-tree; he shall grow like a cedar in Lebanon."[2]

The population of Lebanon is generally estimated at 400,000 souls, residing in more than 600 towns, villages, and hamlets. The inhabitants are designated according to their religious faith, and are known as Moslems, Jews, Greeks, Latins, Armenians, Maronites, and Druzes. Though the Mohammedans are in power, they are not the ruling class in these mountain regions. The Maronites and Druzes form the chief part of the population, and are the hereditary and inveterate foes of each other. The former occupy chiefly Lebanon, and number about 200,000. They derive their sectarian name from John Maron, a monk, who was the great apostle of the Monothelitic heresy in the seventh century, and who died in 701 A.D. Renouncing their Monothelitism in 1180, they submitted to the Pope, and are now devoted to the See of Rome. Though residing in villages from Nazareth to Aleppo, their strong-hold is in the district of Kesrawân; and their patriarch, who receives his robe of investiture from Rome, resides in the convent of Kanobin, in the romantic glen of Kadisha, near the cedars. They have 82 convents, in which are 2000 monks and nuns, who have a revenue of $350,000 per annum. Though brave, independent, and industrious, the Maronites are illiterate and superstitious, and are subject to the dictation of their clergy in all matters of religion and politics.

The Druzes occupy the southern half of Lebanon, extending over to Mount Hermon, and out into the Hauran. They are the descendants of Arabs who came from the eastern confines

[1] Zech., xi., 1-2.   [2] Ps., xcii., 12.

of Syria about 900 years ago, and now number 100,000. They believe in the unity of God; the transmigration of souls; in the ministry of Hâkim; in the mutual obligation of veracity and protection; and in the renunciation of all other religions, and their separation from those in error. Their peculiar doctrines were first propagated in Egypt by the notorious Hâkim, third of the Fatimite dynasty, who asserted that the Deity resided in Aly. In 1017 A.D. the error of the Fatimite was embraced by a Persian by the name of Mohammed Ben-Ismail ed-Derazy, who settled in Egypt, but who, having excited the displeasure of the Egyptians by his fanaticism, was compelled to fly to the base of Mount Hermon, where he became the founder of the Druzes. At a later period, Hamza, a Persian, asserted that Hâkim was the expected Messiah, who is to reign triumphant over all the earth. Secret and exclusive in their worship, the sect is divided into two classes, the "initiated" and the "ignorant." Absolute privacy being their object, their temples of devotion are in remote but conspicuous places—most of them on the summits of hills. Professedly religious, they are, nevertheless, a political body, and aim at the conquest of Syria. They are thoroughly organized. Their whole country is divided into districts. In each district a weekly council is held, and, by means of delegates, constant communication is maintained between the different branches of their community. In peace the Druzes are industrious and hospitable; in war, daring and ferocious. In their mountain homes they are readily distinguished from all other sects by their trim beards, and their neatly-folded turbans of spotless white.[1]

Thanks to the civilization of the West, and especially to French enterprise, a Macadamized road has been constructed from Beirût to Damascus. It is a noble highway, 16 feet wide, with deep water-drains on each side, and with drains, bridges, and buttresses of substantial mason-work. Regarding bad roads as barriers to the advance of an invading army, but forgetting that such also impede the retreat of their own forces, the Turks are the enemies of good roads. And although the antiquary, with the Turk, may deprecate the destruction of the camel-route which had been the great highway from Damascus to the sea since the days of Abraham, yet the

[1] Porter's Palestine; Thomson's Land and the Book, vol. i., p. 248.

interests of commerce and religion will be promoted by this new and grand turnpike.

Following the Mediterranean coast from Sidon to Beirût, which is the commercial emporium of Syria and Palestine, we passed through the busy streets of the latter town, and, leaving the pine forests and mulberry groves which environ the city to the west, we began the ascent of Lebanon. Riding rapidly over the newly-made road, we soon mounted the western spurs of Lebanon, and at midday reached the summit. The skies were lowery, and a dense fog hung upon the mountains. At times the fog was impenetrable, and the muleteers were compelled to call to each other frequently, and ring the warning bell of their approach. Turning to the southeast of Wady Hummâna, we began to descend amid wild and varied scenery. The clouds now were lifted up; the sun shone with unwonted splendor; and at our feet lay the glorious Plain of the Bukâ'a. The descent was along the southern side of this magnificent glen, the upper part of which is nine miles across; the bottom is dotted with villages, and the rocky sides are sprinkled with pines. The banks are shelving, and the new road not having been completed to this point, our horses cautiously picked their way among the rocks. To the north of the ravine, and on the summit of a lofty spur of the mountain, stand the ruins of a Druze castle, and to the south of it are a few excavated tombs.

Misdirected by a muleteer, our dragoman attempted to cross the Bukâ'a in a straight line, avoiding a long sweep over the ordinary path; but the recent rains had flooded the plains to the depth of three feet, and the Leontes swept by with increased velocity. Fording one branch of the river in safety, we were compelled to ride for several miles in water up to our horses' haunches, and, on reaching the main channel of the Leontes, we found the banks too steep and the stream too deep and rapid to ford. Night was upon us, and, as our only alternative, we rode northward eight miles, and, after crossing four or five bridges, pursued our journey in the darkness of the hour to the small village of Mejdel, where, after having been in the saddle fourteen consecutive hours, we obtained lodgings in the humble cottage of a Maronite Christian.

Not far from the town is a hill crowned with the ruins of some extraordinary but unknown temple, and from its broken walls we obtained a view of the great Plain of Bukâ'a. The eye followed the mountains on each side to the northward till lost to view, and southward to where the chains converge and form the gorge of the Leontes. "The plain is smooth as a lake, and the artificial mounds which here and there dot its surface might well pass for islands." Three miles to the northeast are the remains of the ancient city of Chalcis, and 25 miles beyond are the stupendous and splendid ruins of Ba'albek, the Heliopolis of Antoninus Pius, and the rival of Athens in the grandeur and proportions of its temples and palaces.

Mounting our horses, in half an hour we entered the defiles of anti-Lebanon. Ascending the long but picturesque glen of Wady Harîr, we met a pompous cavalcade, escorting the wives and female slaves of the Pasha of Damascus to Beirût. The ladies rode in sedans, the sides of which were of glass, and which were borne on poles by two mules, one in front and the other behind. The chief ladies were in the maturity of womanhood, and their countenances were exceedingly fair. They were attired in the most costly manner, and over their faces were drawn thin white veils. In the sedans which followed were beautiful Circassian girls, and behind them came Nubian girls, remarkable only for their blackness. All seemed happy, and each returned our salutation with exquisite grace. The eunuchs were mounted on magnificent Arabian horses, elegantly caparisoned, and the Turkish cavalry, well mounted, and each bearing a long lance, appeared proud and vigilant.

On leaving Wady Harîr we ascended a ridge of gray hills, and were soon on the desert plateau of Sahl Judeideh. In all my wanderings in Arabia and Palestine, I had seen nothing to exceed the sterility and forbidding aspect of this upland plain. But, as Nature loves contrasts, the bleak hills and plains of Judeideh only enhance, by way of contrast, the glorious Plain of El-Merj, on which Damascus stands. Reaching the summit of the ridge, the city of Eliezer and Naaman lay before me, embowered in gardens of vast extent and of the most enchanting beauty. Beholding it for myself, I could no longer wonder at the sublime encomiums which Arabian writers and modern travelers have pronounced upon this entrancing prospect. On a magnificent plain, bounded by lofty mountains, are gardens of olive, apricot, pomegranate, cypress, poplar, willow, walnut, lemon, and orange trees, covering an area of 30 miles in circuit, from the midst of which rise tapering minarets, swelling domes, castellated towers, and white-roofed palaces, the abodes of merchant princes. It is this half-opened and half-secluded view of the city that gives power and charm to the vision. Now you see a golden crescent peering above the bright green foliage, sparkling in the sunlight like a diamond in a circlet of emeralds; now appears a half-ruined castle through an opening glade of cypresses and walnuts; and again is seen the white dome of an ancient mosque, embowered with stately palms and gracefully drooping willows.

Unlike other Oriental cities, Damascus retains the charm of her beauty even when seen from within. There is a fascination in her sparkling fountains and golden-flowing Abana, meandering amid bright oleanders and tall poplars, and breaking ever and anon into dashing cascades; in her marble palaces, with mosaic walls and arabesque ceilings, and splendid mosques, where the khalifs of a thousand years have worshipped; and in her long, rich bazars, where are seen the shawls of Cashmere, the carpets of Persia, the silks of the East, and her own Damascus blades, jeweled daggers, and gold-embroidered robes.

The great plain on which Damascus stands is 21 miles wide, and has an elevation of 2200 feet above the sea. Triangular in shape, it is bounded on the northwest by the anti-Lebanon range, which varies in height from 500 to 1500 feet; along its southwestern border flows the River Pharpar, beyond which are the Mountains of Haurán, which are dimly seen upon the horizon; on the east are three lakes, surrounded by a dense thicket, and bounding the horizon beyond is a range of conical hills. On this rich plain, covered with vegetation, are over 100 villages, containing a population of 40,000 souls. The eastern portion is called El-Merj, while that lying around the city bears the name of Ghútah. Its perennial fertility is due to the Abana and Pharpar, " rivers of Damascus." The highest sources of the latter are near the village 'Arny, in a large basin-like glen in Mount Hermon. Enlarged by several smaller streams near Sa'sa', its clear waters sweep along in a deep, narrow bed, confined on one side by a rugged wall of volcanic rock, and on the other by cliffs of limestone. At first a small, lively stream, it increases in volume as it flows eastward, and, after meandering through rich meadows, it enters the southern of the three lakes, not far from the town of Heijány. The Abana rises in a high plain south of Zebedány, on anti-Lebanon. The head of the stream is called Fijeh, and is one of the largest and most beautiful fountains in Syria. Bursting forth from a narrow cave, it leaps, foams, and roars as it descends to a confluence with other streams, when at once it becomes a rapid torrent 30 feet wide and four deep. Cutting its way through the mountain, its channel widens and deepens, and from its bed rise cliffs 1000 feet high, and white almost as the snow of Hermon. Rushing in a southeasterly direction down the mountain, and issuing upon the plain through a wild chasm, it turns eastward, and, flowing along the north wall of Damascus, takes its way across the plain to the two northern lakes. Whether we consider the beautiful blue tinge of its waters, or their deliciousness, or their fertilizing power, or the sylvan lakes and pretty cascades they form, the Abana is deservedly the most celebrated of Syrian rivers. To secure the advantages to be derived from such a deep, broad stream, its waters are diverted from its channel through not less than nine canals for the supply of the city and the irrigation of the plain.

Somewhere on this plain, to the southeast of the city, occurred two great events—the meeting of Hazael and the Prophet Elisha,[1] and the conversion of St. Paul.[2] Elisha came from Palestine, and, when near Damascus, Hazael met him with a present from Benhadad, the then reigning king, who was lying dangerously ill. Ambitious and unscrupulous, Hazael returned to his royal master with the prophetic promise of recovery; but, taking advantage of the king's debility, Hazael murdered Benhadad and mounted the throne of Syria.

Nearly a thousand years later, and perhaps upon the same spot, occurred the other and grander event. On leaving Jerusalem, Saul of Tarsus pursued the ancient caravan track to the capital of Syria. Having passed in his journey the most renowned cities in Palestine, and the scenes of the most important events in the history of Christ, he at length drew near to Damascus. It was while his heart swelled with pride and hope at the prospect of the speedy consummation of his terrible mission that "suddenly there shined round about him a light from heaven, above the brightness of the sun," and he "heard a voice saying unto him, Saul, Saul, why persecutest

[1] 1 Kings, xix., 15; 2 Kings, viii., 7-15.   [2] Acts, ix., 1-22.

thou me?" Though it is not possible to identify the exact spot where he fell to the ground, the features of the landscape remain unchanged. There now, as then, the white dome of Hermon is on the south; the bare ridge of anti-Lebanon is on the north; while to the east are the gardens, the domes, and towers of Damascus. Now, as then, the sky is cloudless, and a Syrian sun shines in his strength; and now, as then, the peasant in the same field drives his oxen with sharp goads, which illustrate, if they did not suggest, the words of Jesus, "It is hard for thee to kick against the pricks."

Damascus is too old to have ruins. She has outlived Nineveh, and Babylon, and Thebes, and Palmyra, and Ba'albek, and Greece, and Rome, and, retaining the freshness of her youth, seems destined to live throughout all time. Though successively the prize of the Persian, the Greek, the Roman, the Saracen, the Christian, and now of the Turk, yet by some mysterious law she has resisted the changes of fortune incident to the change of rulers, and, prospering under each dynasty, she is still the greatest commercial city of Asiatic Turkey, carrying on, as in olden times, an extensive trade with Egypt, Persia, Bagdad, and the Bedouins of the Eastern desert.

But her high antiquity and thrilling religious history possess a peculiar interest. Coming from Southern Mesopotamia, the cradle of our race, across the Syrian desert, the great grandchildren of Noah settled on the banks of the Abana. Here, in after years, Abraham found Eliezer, the faithful steward of his household;[1] and in the little town of Burzeh, near by, the patriarch lived. Here flow the Abana and Pharpar, which Naaman thought "better than all the waters of Israel;" and here was the captive home of the little maid, whose simple story about the Lord's prophet of Samaria induced the proud Syrian to visit Gilgal to be "recovered of his leprosy."[2] Hither came Elijah and Elisha to reprove kings and anoint their successors;[3] and hither, but paramount in the grandeur of its results to all other events, came St. Paul, to receive his sight and obtain the peace of heaven.[4] Christian affection has preserved the memory of the sites of many of these events. The house of Judas, where Paul lodged, and the home of Ananias, who baptized the great apostle of the Gentiles, are still

[1] Gen., xv., 2
[3] Ib., viii.
[2] 2 Kings, v., 1–14.
[4] Acts, ix.

pointed out with affectionate remembrance. The "street which is called Straight," into which the repentant persecutor was led, is correctly named, being a mile long, and running east and west through the centre of the town. In the Roman age it was 100 feet wide, and divided into three avenues by rows of Corinthian columns, with corresponding portals; but at present neither the gates nor the colonnades remain. To the south of the city is the gate Kisàn, which has been closed for 700 years. Near this portal is located the scene of St. Paul's escape, where, in his own words, "Through a window in a basket was I let down by the wall and escaped."[1] In the lapse of time and through the devastations of war the window is gone, but on the east wall of the city are several buildings, with projecting windows, from which many persons were let down during the recent massacre; and to the east of the wall is the traditional site of Naaman's palace, on which has been erected a leper's hospital, probably for his descendants.

Though Damascus has survived the mightiest cities of the past, the vast cemeteries in the environs of the town, crowded with the dead, are a mournful proof that the countless generations, which from the most remote ages have dwelt within her gates and reclined in her fragrant gardens, have gone down to their graves. Wandering among the monuments of those venerable grave-yards, I saw the tombs of three of Mohammed's wives; of Fatima, his granddaughter, the unfortunate child of Aly; of Moawyeh, the founder of the dynasty of the Ommiades; and of Saladin, the victor of Hattin.

Damascus is built on both banks of the Abana, a mile and a half from the base of the lowest ridge of anti-Lebanon. It is encompassed with a wall, exhibiting specimens of the masonry of every age from the Roman to the present time, and which is penetrated by seven gates occupying their ancient sites. Of an irregular oval shape, the old city, the nucleus of the present town, is on the south bank of the river. Here stands the massive castle, a large quadrangular building 840 feet long by 600 broad, the foundations of which were laid by the Romans and the superstructure reared by the Saracens. Through this portion of the city runs the "street called Straight," and on its northern side are the principal buildings—the churches of the Christians, the Khan As'ad Pasha, and the Great Mosque.

[1] 2 Cor., xi., 33.

The latter structure is the most imposing and magnificent edifice in Damascus. Built in the form of a quadrangle, it is 489 feet long by 324 wide. On its northern side is a spacious court 431 feet long and 125 broad, surrounded by cloisters, with arches springing from granite and marble columns. The interior is divided into a nave and aisles, formed by two rows of Corinthian columns. The floor is of tesselated marble, covered with Persian carpets, and the walls are incased with mosaics and various colored marbles. Beneath the transept is a cave, said to contain, in a gold casket, the head of John the Baptist. From the centre of the transept rises a noble dome, 50 feet in diameter and 120 high, resting on four massive piers. The exterior is adorned with three minarets, the loftiest of which is 250 feet high. It is generally supposed that this grand mosque stands on the site of the temple of the god Rimmon, and that here Naaman deposited the "two mules' burden of earth" which he had brought from the Plains of Jericho;[1] and here probably stood that beautiful altar which excited the admiration of King Ahaz, and which served as the model for the altar he caused to be constructed in Jerusalem.[2]

On the opposite bank of the river is a large suburb, the Turkish quarter of the city, containing the residences of the chief officers of the government and of the army. To the west are the barracks, and to the southward is the Meidân, through which runs a broad avenue, the ordinary route taken by the pilgrim caravan on its way to Mecca.

The chief resorts of the Damascenes for pleasure are the numerous and elegant cafés, several of which are on the banks of the Abana. Here platforms are erected over the foaming waters, shaded by willows, poplars, palms, and cypresses. At night a thousand miniature lamps of varied forms and colors glimmer among the branches of the trees and are reflected in the river below, while turbaned Turks while away the hours sipping delicious Mocha coffee from thimble-sized cups, whiffing the best Stamboul tobacco-smoke through ornamented chibouks, humming some monotone chant, or listening to the recital of some Oriental tale of love, prodigality, or war. Damascus is at once a commercial and manufacturing city. The principal articles manufactured are silks, woolen and cotton cloths, gold and silver ornaments, confections, nargilies, boots,

[1] 2 Kings, v., 18.   [2] Ib., xvi., 10-16; Porter's Five Years in Damascus.

shoes, slippers, and pattens worn by the belles of the town. The bazars are usually filled with articles of home manufacture, and those imported from Manchester, Birmingham, Lyons, Paris, Constantinople, Cashmere, and Bagdad. Arranged in open stalls, the bazars are among the most interesting objects to be seen by the Occidental. Here he witnesses the activity and trade of the city, and beholds scenes unlike any thing of the kind to be seen in the West. He is soothed by the odor of perfumes and spices; his appetite is tempted by preserved fruits and confectioneries; he is delighted or offended by the scent of various kinds of tobacco; he is bewildered by the sound of the hammers of the silversmiths; his curiosity is awakened by the odd-shaped boots and slippers; and his admiration is excited by costly diamonds, emeralds, rubies, robes, antique armors, Damascus blades, and jeweled daggers.

Previous to the fearful massacre of 1860 the population of Damascus numbered 150,000 souls. Of these, 129,000 were Moslems, 6000 Jews, and 15,000 Christians; but the murders, captivities, and dispersions incident to that dreadful tragedy have reduced the Christian population to less than two thirds its original number. The Christians were among the most wealthy and intelligent citizens; their dwellings and churches were of the most splendid order, and by their thrift and industry they had added largely to the revenues of the city. But the fanaticism of the Moslems culminated in a murderous assault, the results of which are too well known to the world. The cause was deep-seated and inveterate, the occasion puerile and trifling. Several Mohammedan and Christian boys were at play in one of the streets, and the former, evincing the spirit of persecution, drew the figure of a cross upon the sand, and then attempted to compel the latter to trample upon it; but, equally and strongly attached to the religion of their fathers, they resisted, and a scuffle followed. Learning the cause of the trouble, the parents of the Christian boys caused the Mohammedan lads to be arrested and brought before the city judge. It was the torch applied to the magazine. Indignant and infuriated, the Moslem parents collected their friends, who proceeded to the Christian Quarter and commenced the terrible assault. The fathers, sons, and husbands of the Christian families were absent from their residences, absorbed in the business of their several callings. The attack was made in mid-afternoon, and

21

in an hour the whole Moslem population was engaged in the work of death and destruction. Their religious hatred had been long suppressed, but their pent-up fury now burst forth like the sudden and violent irruption of a volcano. The tocsin was sounded, and the followers of the Crescent hastened to exterminate the adherents of the Cross. Entering their dwellings, Christian mothers, wives, and daughters were surprised by their ravishers and murderers, while their husbands, fathers, and sons were slain in the streets by hundreds while hastening to rescue their beloved ones. Escaping through windows, and leaping from the roofs of their dwellings, the Christian women sought refuge in their churches and monasteries; but, forgetful of the reverence due the sacred sanctuaries, the Moslems applied the torch, consuming the edifices and the helpless refugees within them. The flames continued to spread till a third of the city, and by far the most elegant portion, had been reduced to ashes. Where the house of a Christian adjoined that of a Mohammedan, it was torn down rather than fired, lest the ungovernable flames might consume what had not been doomed to destruction. In a covered alley not far from "Straight" street, 300 women, the accomplished wives and daughters of merchant princes, took refuge; but their merciless persecutors added death to insult, and sabred them on the spot. The wild Bedouins who chanced to be in the city dispatched couriers to their companions, who, mounted on their fleet horses, came as on the wings of the wind to abuse and murder the helpless.

The third point of attack on that memorably sad day was the residence of the American Vice-Consul, Dr. Mashaka, one of the most eminent of Arabic scholars. His ample fortune allowed him to live in princely style, and his family is the most accomplished I saw in the East. His daughter was wounded, his son was missing for three days, and the person of his beautiful and excellent wife was barely rescued from the licentious and murderous Moslems by the timely interposition of a female friend. He himself was wounded, and only escaped death by the heroic behavior of his Mohammedan cawass, and by flight to the residence of Abd-el-Kader.

Day after day the work of death and conflagration went on. Magnificent cathedrals, stately monasteries, and splendid private residences were reduced to heaps of shapeless ruins.

Every where were to be seen broken fountains, shattered vases, fragments of mosaic pavements, tesselated marble walls, and arabesque ceilings, with costly furniture strewn about in utter confusion. Even the small stone house which tradition had consecrated as the home of the good Ananias suffered from the torch of persecution. The fine residences of the American missionaries were consumed, and their large and valuable libraries scattered among the débris of their homes. In addition to the slain, 500 of the fair sisters and daughters of those who survived the massacre were carried to the mountains by the wild Bedouins of the Hauran. Thousands of Christian families became fugitives, their homes, fortunes, and hopes forever ruined. The Christian Mission was broken up, and their church, in which 400 worshipers assembled on the Sabbath in the enjoyment of a pure faith, was consumed. Bishops, priests, and monks fled, and Damascus was given over to Mohammed and the Devil. The authorities of the city connived with the mob, and the government troops joined in the acts of violence. But there was one humane Mohammedan who attempted to stay the massacre, and whose home afforded shelter to the defenseless. Abd-el-Kader, with 300 Algerian soldiers, who had followed their celebrated chief into exile, stood as a wall of brass against the fanaticism and fury of the murderers. At the head of his little band, he drove the mob from places which they had attacked, he pursued those who were bearing off helpless women, and swore the death of any who should invade his home to dispatch those who had taken refuge beneath his roof. Inflexible in purpose as he was invincible in courage, he himself became the object of their revenge. Undaunted by their threats and repelling their attacks, he became the enemy of the Moslem, but the friend and benefactor of the Christian. Great as he is humane, he will long be remembered with delight by the civilized world.

It was in the afternoon of the last day I spent in Damascus that I enjoyed an interview with this distinguished man. After waiting in the reception-room, which was plainly furnished, while the servant announced our names, the Emir appeared at the fountain in a spacious court-yard, and invited us to seats in an elegant apartment, on divans of embroidered satin. Small cups of Mocha coffee were passed, according to the invariable etiquette of a Mohammedan house. The conversation, which had been general, now turned upon the recent massacre, and the noble part he had acted in the sad drama. His modesty, however, allowed him to say but little, but he kindly showed us the several national presents he had received as testimonials of his generous deeds. Greece had sent him two gold stars, on one of which was a medallion likeness of King Otho, and on the other were the words, "Thy right hand, O Lord, is glorified;" Turkey had presented him with two massive silver stars, bearing the appropriate inscription, "Protection, Zeal, and Fidelity;" France had conferred on him the "Cross of the Legion of Honor," encircled with emeralds and diamonds, and surmounted with a gold crown; the "Free and Accepted Masons" had bestowed upon him the symbols of their Order; Sardinia, and Russia, and Austria, and Prussia had honored him with gold stars set with jewels; and from the United States he had received a magnificent brace of revolvers, of which he seemed justly proud. Though thus honored by all these great powers, he had received no gift of remembrance from England; and when assured by an English gentleman present that much had been said in his country about a gift, the Emir quietly replied, "I prefer works to words." This failure on the part of England to recognize the magnanimity of this extraordinary man is inexplicable. By the Turks it is regarded as an acquiescence in the fearful slaughter. This is unjust; the cause, however, is to be found in her truckling policy toward the Turkish empire, and in her unwillingness to offend the religious sensibilities of the inhuman Moslem. Abd-el-Kader is now in the prime of life, of full habit, above the medium height, with a full face, large head, high, rounded brow, eyes large, black, and lustrous, beard slight and dark, and the expression of his countenance, when in repose, is that of benevolence and kindliness; but the peculiar shape of his mouth, together with his general air, indicate decision, courage, and the capacity of being, when circumstances demand, impetuous and even desperate. He is celebrated for the terrible battles he fought with the French in Algiers, and at present is confined within the limits of Damascus as their prisoner of war. The protection he extended to the Christians has rendered him unpopular with the Moslems of the city of his exile, and he desires another more congenial with his tastes and sentiments. He is a devout Mohammedan, but, were he a Christian, what a splendid leader he would make to unite and lead the Syrian Christians to victory!

CONCLUSION.

Some master-mind is yet to write the political history of the Holy Land from the conquest of Titus to the death of the late Sultan Abd-al-Medjid. Such a history would bring to light crusades the most chivalrous and ruinous, political schemes the most ambitious and degrading, and religious systems the most fanatical and corrupting the world has ever known. Such a work would advance the science of government and the higher purposes of Christianity; it would be the echo of the prophetic voice uttered centuries ago, and furnish an unanswerable argument that the present physical and moral condition of the Land of Promise is the result of misrule, and of a stupendous system of oppression, extortion, and fanaticism. It would especially prove the undeniable fact that the Turk is the enemy of good government, of national greatness, of social and intellectual refinement, of domestic and individual purity, and demonstrate beyond dispute that the reign of the Turk is the reign of ruin. Suited best to the excitement of battle, and to the plunder and murder of the vanquished, in times of peace the unrestrained passions of the Turk drive him to vices no less destructive of himself than they are blighting to civilized society. In the camp and on the field he has always prospered; but when unimpelled by the excitement of war, his vigor has disappeared, and he has been a leech on the body politic, and a drone in community. Whether in Europe, Asia, or Africa, he has run a regular course of rapid attainment of power by bloody and devastating wars, and then as regularly declined from the moment when, as conqueror, he sat down to reap the fruits of victory. The Turk and Islam are identical; the former is the embodiment of the latter, and the latter is exterminating to all who refuse submission to the sway of the False Prophet, and annihilating to every thing which does not subserve the ends of his religion. No country has risen to greatness under his power; and those which were great in national resources, in splendor of architecture, in the wealth of agriculture, and in the superiority of art and science, have dwindled into insignificance, or utterly perished under his deteriorating influence.

Palestine is a deplorable instance of national wretchedness, to which one of the fairest lands upon the face of the globe has been reduced since the reign of the Islamitic Turk. From the Arab invasion in 633 A.D., headed by the famous generals Khâled and Abu Obeidah, to the present time, the cultivation of the soil has been neglected, commerce diminishing, and government perverted to the worst of purposes. Sixteen years subsequent to that invasion the Crescent was the ensign of dominion from the shores of the Atlantic to the confines of India. Of the then nine flourishing cities in Syria, Damascus alone retains its earlier grandeur, and this only in part, as in the conflagration and massacre of 1860 a third of its most magnificent edifices were destroyed, and 15,000 of its noblest citizens slain, captured, or dispersed. Led by the heroic Godfrey, the Crusaders in 1099 A.D. recovered the much-abused land from the neglect and cruelty of the Turk, and for three quarters of a century the Land of Promise was restored to comparative prosperity. Under those Christian rulers the resources of the country were developed to an astonishing degree; the fleets of Pisa, Genoa, and Venice traded along its shores, and populous cities sprung up as if by magic. But in 1187 the battle of Kurûm Hattîn decided the fate of the Crusaders. Jerusalem was retaken by Saladin; the Franks were expelled from Palestine; and four years thereafter the celebrated Melek-ed-Dhâher replaced all Syria under the domination of the Turks, and thenceforward to the present time the Holy Land has been the prey of Mohammedan adventurers, and is now a dependency to the Porte, divided into three pashalics.

Six centuries prove that the Moslem is neither the fosterer of the fine arts nor the promoter of agriculture, commerce, manufactures, or public works of any kind. When, in the 12th century, the Christians were expelled, the large and fertile plains of Sharon, Phœnicia, Esdraelon, and Mukhnah were fruitful fields yielding golden harvests, the reward of honest husbandry; but now those plains are the camping-grounds of the wandering Arab, where he feeds his flocks *ad libitum*, and then, mounting his fleet horse, scours the adjoining country in search of plunder. The Crusaders left to their conquerors large and flourishing maritime cities, with a lucrative commerce with Europe and the Levant; but, under the dominion of the Turks, those commercial towns are poor and filthy, without harbors, without vessels, without mariners, without trade. The Koran, forbidding the "making of any thing like unto that which is in heaven above or in the earth beneath," has not only left Syria without a picture and without a statue, but has also led to the wanton destruction of the splendid edifices of mediæval times. The knights of that period rivaled the Romans, and even Herod the Great, in the erection of costly temples, palaces, and churches. In Jerusalem, Ramleh, Ludd, Beeroth, Bethel, Samaria, 'Akka, Tyre, Sidon, and especially in Athlit—the *Castellum Peregrinorum* of the defenders of the Cross, were structures worthy to adorn any age; but, content with a shade-tree under which to whiff his nargily, and an ill-formed hovel for the accommodation of his many wives, the Moslem has allowed those magnificent buildings to crumble to ruins, or has ruthlessly destroyed them. With one or two exceptions, the celebrated edifices which remain are the work of other hands. The great mosque in Damascus was originally a Christian church, erected by Arcadius, the son of Theodosius, and dedicated to John the Baptist; the Mosque of El-Aksa, in Jerusalem, was once a church, built by order of the Emperor Justinian, and dedicated to "My Lady," the Virgin Mary; and the mosque covering the cave of Machpelah was also a Christian temple. Excepting the Mosque of Omar, the Mohammedans have scarcely a structure of any importance of their own erection in the Holy Land, and, unlike the descendants of the Greeks and Romans, the posterity of the Turks will never sit amid the splendid ruins of ancestral greatness.

Palestine is now in a transition state, and there are indications that great political and moral changes are at hand. Numbering in all more than a million and a half, the present inhabitants are a mixed race, the several portions of which are designated by their religion rather than by their nationality. Their religious appellations are party names, and are the symbols of power, fear, or reproach, according to the comparative strength of the different parties. Three of the most numerous of the sects represent three great powers—France, Russia, and Turkey, and by intrigue, bribery, and fanaticism, will inevitably involve those mighty nations in a bloody strife for the possession of the Holy Land. Palestine seems destined to be again contended for by the nations of Western Europe, and the Plain of Esdraelon may once more become the battle-field of nations. At present most of these powers have landed possessions there, and are annually making new purchases. On Mount Akra, to the southwest of the Holy City, the Russians have inclosed a large area with high, strong walls; within is a monastery, which in time of war will serve all the purposes of a fortress, and to the inclosure they have given the name of "New Jerusalem." Prussia has a large hospice within the city, and also several flourishing religious and literary institutions. The French hold possession of the ancient Church of St. Anne, and have recently purchased the land adjoining it; they own the large green plat of ground opposite the Church of the Holy Sepulchre, which was once occupied by the Knights of St. John; they have bought the old castle in Beirût, and have constructed a noble Macadamized road from that city to Damascus, and have the right of way for 49 years. And on Mount Zion England has a consular building, and a church of which any nation might be justly proud, and by her diplomacy controls the policy of the Sublime Porte more than any other European power.

But, whatever may be the political relations of Palestine in the future, the great and only hope of her regeneration and elevation is to be found in her Christian missions. These are established in Jerusalem, Bethlehem, Joppa, Nablous, Nazareth, Sidon, Beirût, Damascus, and in several of the larger towns in the Lebanon Mountains. In Jerusalem the mission is well and thoroughly organized, and is attended by the happiest results; the numerous schools are in a prosperous condition, and the places of worship filled with sincere and attentive listeners. But the Beirût Mission is really doing the greatest work in evangelizing the land. The Bible has been translated into Arabic, and is now given to the millions who speak that language. At Abuh, in the mountains, there is a seminary for the training of native missionaries, and a college of a high order will soon be opened in Beirût, liberally endowed by American citizens.

Smitten with decay, and retiring before the advance of Western civilization, Mohammedanism is yielding to the superior power of Christianity. The Crescent, which for so many centuries was the ensign of the conquering Turk, no longer excites alarm. It was once the Crescent of the new moon, expanding and brightening till it shone resplendent on the plains of Asia, the shores of Africa, and the hills of Europe; but it is now the Crescent of the old moon, contracting and dim, from the horns of which are slipping the conquering sword of the Prophet and the diadem of Othman. Demanded by the Christian powers of the earth, and protected by their armies and navies, religious liberty in Palestine is offered to the Christian and the Jew. The Land of Promise has a glorious past, and an equally glorious future awaits to dawn upon it. Prophecy is big with an exalted destiny, the unfoldings of which will turn all eyes to the land of sacred song, the cradle of our religion, and the scene of our Lord's incarnation. Thrice happy will be that day when Jerusalem shall be rebuilt and made holy; when the scattered tribes shall be recalled, and go up to worship in a temple more magnificent than that of Solomon; and when, from the Plains of Bethlehem to the snow-capped summits of Mount Hermon, and from the coasts of Tyre and Sidon to the Mountains of Gilead, light shall arise out of darkness, and the voice of Christian praise, mingling with the song of angels, shall be as sincere as it shall be universal.

THE END.

www.ingramcontent.com/pod-product-compliance
Lightning Source LLC
Chambersburg PA
CBHW051201300426
44116CB00006B/396